The Politics of Democratic Inclusion

The Politics of Democratic Inclusion

Edited by

CHRISTINA WOLBRECHT AND
RODNEY E. HERO

with PERI E. ARNOLD AND ALVIN B. TILLERY

TEMPLE UNIVERSITY PRESS
Philadelphia

Temple University Press
1601 North Broad Street
Philadelphia PA 19122
www.temple.edu/tempress

Copyright © 2005 by Temple University
All rights reserved
Published 2005
Printed in the United States of America

⊗ The paper used in this publication meets the requirements of the American
National Standard for Information Sciences—Permanence of Paper for Printed
Library Materials, ANSI Z39.48-1992

Library of Congress Cataloging-in-Publication Data

The politics of democratic inclusion / edited by Christina Wolbrecht and Rodney E. Hero [et al.].
    p.   cm.
    Includes bibliographical references and index.
    ISBN 1-59213-358-4 (cloth : alk. paper)—ISBN 1-59213-359-2 (pbk. : alk. paper)
    1. Political participation—United States.   2. Minorities—United States—Political activity.
    3. Representative government and representation—United States.   I. Wolbrecht, Christina.
    II. Rodney E. Hero.   III. Peri E. Arnold.   IV. Alvin B. Tillery.

    JK1764.P675 2005
    323'.042'0973—dc22

                                                                        2004055381

2 4 6 8 9 7 5 3 1

Contents

1   Introduction

THE POLITICS OF DEMOCRATIC INCLUSION seeks to contribute to our understanding of the processes and mechanisms by which traditionally un-derrepresented groups have and have not achieved political incorporation, representation, and influence—or what we refer to broadly as *democratic inclusion*—in American politics. The issue of democratic inclusion has been central to American politics since the Founding. The challenges are evident in the juxtaposed perceptions of America as a "nation of immigrants" on the one hand, and the historical "dilemma" of race (Myrdal 1944) on the other. The former suggests an open, pluralistic system in which diverse groups, including successive waves of immigrants, are eventually able to achieve status and influence in the political system, while the latter emphasizes that the political position of disadvantaged groups (particularly, but certainly not only, African Americans) remains structurally and centrally problematic and unequal. Using different lenses and considering distinct phenomena, the chapters in this volume seek to determine how various institutions have or, more characteristically, have not served as mechanisms for democratic inclusion in the United States. The analytic approach of this volume gives particular attention to the role of institutions in structuring the potential for political incorporation of traditionally disadvantaged groups. Taken together, the chapters evaluate and advance our understanding of the ways in which the structure, processes, rules, and context of the American political order encourage, mediate, and hamper the representation and incorporation of traditionally disadvantaged groups.

The politics of democratic inclusion are central to an understanding of the quality of American democracy. The standards of political equality and popular sovereignty imply broad and deep representation of the governed. Throughout American history, the degree to which these standards are achieved by traditionally disadvantaged groups, such as women, ethnic and racial minorities, and immigrants has been a persistent question and controversy. The last half-century or so has witnessed significant strides in the incorporation of many such groups into the mainstream of American political life. At the same time, unevenness and limitations in that incorporation continue to characterize American politics. Not coincidently, recent decades also have seen the emergence of a rich body of research examining the political activities and experiences of disadvantaged groups where once attention to such issues was sparse and underdeveloped (important exceptions include Key 1949; Myrdal 1944). There has not yet been, however, an effort to systematically consider and take stock of the recent past, this literature, and its many implications. Now is a propitious time to step back and reflect on the current state of knowledge.

In bringing together work addressing various groups and institutional arenas, this volume provides valuable evaluations of the state of research on democratic inclusion. Unlike typical edited volumes, the chapters do not present a slice of a related research endeavor. Instead, the authors aspire to offer broad, "big picture" assessments of the ways in which particular institutions and behaviors have, or have not, served as mechanisms for the representation of certain disadvantaged interests in American politics. More than simply literature reviews, these papers are critical syntheses of the state of research in specific areas. The chapters consider a number of related questions: What has been the record of democratic inclusion? How have institutions, group characteristics, and historical context (among many other factors) shaped the process of democratic inclusion for different groups? What have changes over time and across groups meant for democratic inclusion? What overarching conclusions about democratic inclusion can be drawn from the literature? What are the questions that should drive our future research, and why? By providing theoretical and empirical synthesis, the chapters in this volume should be of interest to anyone concerned with the incorporation and representation of disadvantaged groups. More broadly, by focusing our attention on the ways in which American political institutions may systematically facilitate or hamper democratic inclusion, this volume requires consideration from any scholar seeking to understand how American politics really functions.

The primary argument of this volume is that an understanding of the politics of democratic inclusion requires close attention to the role of institutions. As we argue below, institutions determine the context (incentives, constraints, opportunities) in which political elites respond to demands for inclusion by disadvantaged groups. If we want to know, for example, why there are so few blacks in Congress, or immigrant political mobilization is low, or education policy fails to serve the needs of the poor, the institutional context should be a central focus of inquiry.

The analytic approach distinguishes this volume from much of the previous research on democratic inclusion, in large part because that literature has been overwhelmingly interested in mass behavior and attitudes. The character, experience, and behavior of the disadvantaged groups themselves are not unimportant. Indeed, we maintain that an understanding of democratic inclusion must be attentive to inter- and intra-group diversity. How institutional structure will affect any specific group's progress toward political incorporation is in part a function of the group's experiences and characteristics. Yet, even in the analysis and examination of group diversity, the chapters in this volume emphasize the role of institutions in structuring and constructing group identity and behavior as well.

The remainder of this introduction proceeds as follows. We begin with some definitions, highlighting the importance of attention to group diversity and the many forms of democratic inclusion. We then proceed to (1) demonstrate that the previous work in this area has generally, though not entirely, underemphasized the role of institutions, (2) argue for the utility of institutional analysis for understanding the politics of disadvantaged groups, and

(3) illustrate how the papers in this volume contribute to our understanding of democratic inclusion through the lens of institutional analysis.

DEFINING TERMS

The very goals and conceptualization of this project immediately present some definitional questions. These are not minor issues: The failure to clearly define terms can hamper the development of knowledge across groups and institutions. In this section, we provide a set of broad guidelines as to how this volume in general approaches various concepts, while simultaneously arguing that these definitions remain contested, as the diversity of work between these covers attests both implicitly and in some cases, explicitly.

What Groups?

When we examine the mechanisms and institutions by which disadvantaged groups seek political inclusion, what sort of groups do we have in mind? Our interest here is in understanding how those social groups traditionally *without power* (or with relatively little power) seek and achieve greater power and influence in the American political system. Thus, within the American context, this definition draws our attention to groups identified by an ascriptive status, such as race, ethnicity, and gender, as well as to particular economic and immigrant groups. As befits the American historical experience, racial and ethnic minorities and immigrants tend to be center stage in this analysis. To a lesser extent, the authors also consider the experience of other disadvantaged groups, such as women and the poor.[1]

To some degree, these and other group identities and categorizations may blur or overlap. Latinos, for example, may be thought of as both an ethnic group and in some cases, an immigrant population. Black women often struggle with the multiplicative effects of their various identities. Indeed, this blurring may be of such a degree that traditional categorizations no longer "work analytically, politically, or normatively as they used to," in the words of Jennifer Hochschild (this volume). While most of the authors work within traditional categories, Hochschild's chapter calls our attention to the ways in which many politically, economically, and socially relevant differences may take place *within* groups and across other sorts of characteristics and experiences other than blunt (but increasingly blurred) racial categories.

Many of the chapters also remind us that important inter- and intra-group diversity shapes our ability to draw broad conclusions and develop an encompassing theory of democratic inclusion. Chong and Rogers, for example, note that the multiple ethnic identities of new minorities complicate our original conceptions of group consciousness developed largely from the black experience. Both the Jones-Correa and the Andersen and Cohen chapters highlight the diversity of immigrant interests vis-à-vis democratic inclusion deriving from varying ties to home countries, English-language skills, and motivations for immigration. Thus, we are interested in this volume, broadly speaking, in disadvantaged groups, particularly racial minorities and immigrants, while seeking to incorporate an understanding of the substantial variation both between and within the groups that fall under our definition.

What Is Democratic Inclusion?

Our goal is to consider how the institutions of American *democracy* bring about or hinder the *inclusion* of disempowered groups into the political system. Broadly speaking, we view democratic inclusion as the incorporation, influence, and representation of various disadvantaged social groups within democratic institutions in the United States. We are specifically interested in the processes, mechanisms, and behaviors by which traditionally disadvantaged groups pursue power and influence in American politics. As the organizers of this project, we purposely invited papers from authors who could address various aspects of and arenas for democratic inclusion. The resulting essays both conceive of the goal of inclusion in various ways (e.g., formal citizenship rights, active political participation, presence in Congress, substantive policy outcomes, social or economic parity) and consider divergent means to inclusion (e.g., through political parties, voting, the courts, and so on).

We might think about various forms of democratic inclusion as benchmarks (see the Andersen and Cohen chapter for a similar argument). For example, Schmidt et al. (2002) suggest that full incorporation into democratic politics involves (1) full access to participation, (2) representation in important decision-making processes and institutions, (3) influence in/power over government decisions, (4) adoption of public policies that address group concerns or interests, and (5) socioeconomic parity. Implicit in these benchmarks is a notion of linearity or cumulativeness; that is, that most of the time, a group must achieve one prior to the other, and that as one is achieved the later stages become more likely.[2]

With the exception of the final benchmark, the Schmidt et al. (2002) conceptual framework tends to focus on democratic inclusion as a characteristic of the political system. As such, this construction is somewhat distinct from the focus of much of the literature on democratic inclusion as a characteristic of the group. For example, the political system might allow full formal access (benchmark 1), but scholars have tended to examine whether and why disadvantaged groups are less likely to participate than other citizens. Presence of group members in decision-making institutions (benchmark 2) is a characteristic of the political system; research has often focused on whether and why a group is less likely to have members who achieve the skills and experiences necessary to emerge as viable candidates. Adoption of public policies that address group interests (benchmark 4) is another political system characteristic; research has tended to examine whether a group can attain the necessary prerequisite of a certain degree of group consciousness of shared concerns and an ability to articulate an agenda. The traditional emphasis of the literature on political attitudes and behaviors thus reflects an interest in democratic inclusion as a characteristic of those seeking incorporation. A unique contribution of this volume is that the papers consider democratic inclusion as a characteristic both of the groups themselves *and* of the political system as a whole, with particular attention given to the typically less-examined latter.

The first of the Schmidt et al. (2002) benchmarks—access to participation—has been the focus of considerable research, as various chapters within testify. Certain aspects of formal access, at least formal access to the electoral process, are now largely assured by constitutional amendment and voting rights legislation. Yet, as the Jones-Correa and the Andersen and Cohen chapters detail, immigrant populations still face substantive formal (not to mention informal) barriers to legal access to political participation. Moreover, in terms of democratic inclusion as a characteristic of the group, what full access to participation may mean and whether it is accomplished in arenas outside the electoral process is much less clear (Verba, Schlozman, and Brady 1995). The chapters in this volume provide ample evidence of the inability of many groups to take full advantage of formal access to political participation (see, e.g., Leighley, this volume, on voter turnout).

The literature on representation, specifically descriptive representation (the second Schmidt et al. [2002] benchmark), is wide-ranging and rich, with most of the evidence finding substantial under-representation. The Canon and the Kittilson and Tate chapters draw our attention to the myriad causes of this under-representation, ranging from the legal and political context of legislative elections (e.g., reapportionment) to the role of party institutions in candidate recruitment. Kittilson and Tate, for example, conclude that a mass-driven (rather than an elite-driven) model of party responsiveness to minorities best characterizes the American experience, emphasizing that the activities of groups themselves can be influential in shaping democratic inclusion. At the same time, they attribute this difference with the United Kingdom, where the process is more elite driven, to institutional differences, particularly federalism and the decentralized party politics that flow from it, in the United States. Thus once again, the processes of democratic inclusion appear to be determined in large part by the institutional structure of the political system as a whole.

Beyond these first two benchmarks, both the amount of research and the evidence of achieved incorporation become thinner. It is thus particularly notable that these aspects of democratic inclusion attract particular attention from our contributors. For example, papers in this volume seek to understand how social movements (Costain) and political parties (Frymer, Kittilson and Tate) may help or hinder access not only to political positions (benchmark 2) but to the policy agenda (benchmark 4) as well. Canon explores how group members in political office have (and have not) been able to achieve substantial influence and power over decision making (benchmark 3). Others (Clarke, Meier, Canon, Lovell and McCann, Conley) ask how and why specific institutions have and have not adopted and implemented policies that address group interests (benchmark 4). Finally, all contributors question the potential for achievement of the final benchmark, socioeconomic parity, providing ample evidence of the failure to achieve this goal thus far (see, e.g., Andersen and Cohen, Jones-Correa, and especially Hochschild).

As this discussion illustrates, democratic inclusion is multifaceted and complex. Asking whether and to what extent a group is incorporated into the American political system directs our attention to phenomenon as diverse as campaign rhetoric, voter turnout, school board policy, and congressional representation. While by no means exhausting the possible indicators, the papers in this volume offer insight into a wide variety of aspects of democratic inclusion, helping paint a broad and nuanced picture of the many possibilities and challenges.

INATTENTION TO INSTITUTIONS

There have been countless studies, including many edited volumes, addressing various aspects of democratic inclusion. Many of the better known and most influential studies in political science focus on attitudes and behavior, typically drawing on survey and experimental research.[3] Virtually all focus on individual beliefs, opinions, and perceptions; occasionally they note *social* contexts, but seldom, if ever, institutional context and impacts. In contrast, this volume is fairly unique in its focus on aspects of democratic inclusion including, but mostly extending beyond, mass behavior.

In addition to the large and important literature on political attitudes and participation of and related to disadvantaged groups, there is an equally large and august research tradition relating to the prospects for democratic inclusion within the American political system more broadly. One way to conceive of this tradition is in terms of three primary analytical approaches to the study of democratic inclusion: pluralist ethnic integration, class stratification, and racial hierarchy (see Schmidt et al. 2002 for a full discussion of this delineation). While this influential literature has been more attentive to institutional factors than the strictly behavioral school, we believe important work remains to be done in thinking through the role of institutions in shaping democratic inclusion within this line of research as well.

The *pluralist ethnic integration model*, exemplified by Robert Dahl's (1961) classic *Who Governs?*, describes "outsider" ethnic and racial groups as able to make their way into positions of influence in political institutions by organizing cohesively, acting strategically, and eventually becoming members of governing coalitions in those policy arenas most relevant to their interests. Depicting a political system relatively open to new groups seeking influence, this model assumes a plurality of political interests and multiple access/decision points such that no single political arena or interest will dominate all aspects of public life in a given polity (e.g., Browning, Marshall, and Tabb 1984; Sonenshein 1993). Much of the participation/behavior research as well as the research on descriptive and substantive representation fall within this genre (for a critique, see Hero 1992).

A second model adds *class stratification* as an essential component for understanding the relationship between social groups and the political system (see, e.g., Stone 1980). A major claim of this approach is that capturing most of the key political offices in a polity does not necessarily make a social group an equal partner in the polity's "governing coalition." Because many important decisions governing key aspects of the polity's allocation of resources and future development may lie outside the confines of the formal governmental institutions, particularly in a polity that combines a market-based economic system with the relatively limited authority granted to local governing institutions, as is typical in the United States, access to formal political roles is not sufficient for attaining actual political power. In short, the class stratification model argues that the political and governmental institutions in a polity are not autonomous but are embedded in a wider network of social, economic, and cultural forces. Political incorporation into a governing coalition must take this broader understanding of political power into account.

The central argument of a third model, the *racial hierarchy* model, is that *racialized* identity operates as an independent force in structuring the relationships between social groups and the political system in the United States (Pinderhughes 1987). A claim of this model is that the U.S. political system was relatively open for white ethnic immigrant groups from Europe, but functions in a decidedly and uniquely exclusive way to diminish the political influence of blacks, as well as other racial minorities. Identifying a substantial contrast between political *ethnicity* among white ethnics and *racial* hierarchy, this model finds white ethnic immigrants able to overcome initial prejudice and political opposition to attain political incorporation, while blacks continue to operate politically under severe constraints more than two hundred years after their arrival in the country. Recent examples of the racial hierarchy model include Hero's (1992, 1998) work on two-tiered pluralism and Kim's (2000) exploration of "racial triangulation" of Asian Americans in relationship to blacks and whites.

However one perceives the accuracy, completeness, and overall utility of the three dominant models, they share an important trait: They tend to pay rather little attention to institutional factors. To be sure, important aspects of these traditions give some attention to institutions. The fragmented American political structure, rooted in federalism and separation of powers, is essential to the "multiple access/decision points" element so central to the pluralist ethnic integration model, for example. Other studies (particularly of urban politics) consider the impact of electoral structure, such as at-large versus district elections, on the election and thus the "descriptive representation" of racial minorities, but the relevance for other dimensions of inclusion is not clear.

Thus, we argue, our central ways of thinking about democratic inclusion have tended to be somewhat inattentive to the role of institutions. This deficiency is somewhat striking given the centrality of institutional analysis to much of the work on American politics. We envision this volume as an attempt to encourage greater attention to the role of institutions in our theorizing about and analysis of democratic inclusion.

INSTITUTIONAL ANALYSIS OF DEMOCRATIC INCLUSION

Students of American politics have been profoundly conscious of the importance of institutions (e.g., March and Olsen 1984). In *The Federalist Papers,*

Madison describes the central goal of the American Constitution as the creation of institutions and structures to curb detrimental behavior, taking the presence and pervasiveness of interests (factions) as a given, while also assuming that certain ideas are legitimate and widely accepted. The rules and practices—be they informal norms, mediating institutions such as parties, or formal governmental institutions—structure interactions, confer power and legitimacy, reward certain skills and resources and devalue others, create incentives, encourage particular behaviors, and otherwise go a long way toward shaping—even determining—the outcome of political conflicts over interests and ideas. Yet even institutions motivated by the most democratic and inclusive of goals may create structures that hamper the cause of equal and broad participation and influence in politics (see Morone 1998). If we want to understand how American politics works, we must be attentive to institutions. It follows, then, that if we want to understand democratic inclusion in American politics, institutions must be center stage in our analysis.

Heclo (1994) has insightfully contended that there are three pillars of politics: ideas, interests, and institutions. In Heclo's framework, *ideas* are "mental constructions"; *interests* refer to "self-interested and purposive pursuit of material goals"; and *institutions* are "enduring rules, procedures, and organizations that tend to structure individual conduct" (1994, 375). Politics occurs in the interaction of the three: "ideas tell interests what to mean," "interests tell institutions what to do," and "institutions tell ideas how to survive" (1994, 383). This framework is useful in thinking about the previous literature on democratic inclusion, including the literature's limited attention to institutions. The pluralist ethnic integration model, which has arguably dominated the literature on democratic inclusion, essentially argues that as weak entities typically lacking organizational resources, minority *interests* are seldom able to "tell institutions what to do," or at least not able to effectively tell them very much for very long (cf. Stone 1980, Hero 1992, Verba, Schlozman, and Brady 1995). But interest-based approaches emphasize the nature (weakness) of interests rather more than specifying how various institutional factors and processes also affect minority influence. The class stratification model suggests that interests may not be able to tell certain important institutions, particularly economic institutions, what to do. However, that model often neglects important *political* or *governmental* institutions as such. The racial hierarchy model recognizes that the prevalent *ideas* in American politics commonly make assumptions about, or assume away, racial, class and other inequalities relevant to inclusion (see, e.g., Smith 1993). Yet while the racial hierarchy model indeed stresses ideas, it has tended to say little about how institutional context may alter or channel those ideas.

The argument of this volume might be conceived of as an amended version of the last of Heclo's points: "Institutions tell ideas, *and interests*, how to survive." Based on their authority, organization, structure, and procedures, institutions have implications for whether interests and ideas will be more or less likely to be partly or fully incorporated, and how sustainable they will be. In short, institutions structure politics (Steinmo, Thelen, and Longstreth 1992). How and the extent to which they structure certain kinds of politics and policies emerging from the interests, needs, concerns, and ideas of particular (types of) disadvantaged groups is at the core of what this volume seeks to illuminate.

CONTRIBUTION OF THIS VOLUME

We have argued that the role of institutions has not been directly and adequately addressed in the analysis of democratic inclusion. The papers in this volume are an effort to *begin* such an analytical undertaking. We do not claim that these chapters provide a complete institutional analysis of democratic inclusion, or that institutions are the sole focus of these authors' evaluations (nor do we believe they should be). What these papers do at minimum is provide a critical synthesis of existing research, highlighting the central role of various democratic institutions. In doing so, they reveal the (mis)match and/ or (in)capacity of various institutions with group interests, beliefs, and goals. They begin to point the way to research strategies that are macro-oriented, to complement the prevailing micro-orientation of the research. Similarly, they emphasize context—institutional context primarily, but also social and other contexts as well.

The volume is organized to reflect our analytical focus. In the first part, *Diversity Within and Across Groups*, the various chapters examine the multiplicity of definitions, experiences, and concerns that characterize some of the different groups for which democratic inclusion is a goal. In the next two parts—*Mediating Institutions* and *Governing Institutions*—authors consider the ways in which institutions ranging from social movements and interest organizations to school boards and federal courts have both facilitated and hindered democratic inclusion. As indicated by our multiple references to the chapters in this volume throughout our discussion above, the authors' arguments overlap and complement each other both within and across the sections. In this section, we provide an overview of each part, while keeping in mind that all of the chapters speak to our overarching argument regarding attentiveness to intra- and inter-group complexity and the central role of institutions.

Diversity within and across Groups

As we have argued above, an important first step to understanding the politics of democratic inclusion is to think theoretically and critically about diversity both within and between excluded groups. The chapters in this section raise crucial questions about group identity, interests, and diversity. Do our traditional ways of thinking about racial groupings no longer help us to understand the politics of democratic inclusion in the twenty-first century? How does variation within one kind of group (e.g., "immigrants" or "Hispanics") affect processes of inclusion and incorporation? How can we best conceive of group consciousness among different disadvantaged populations? Can our models simply be extrapolated from one social group to another? One barrier to the development of a coherent literature on democratic inclusion is the degree to which different disadvantaged groups have been studied in isolation from each other. The papers in the first part of this volume address this problem by confronting questions of group definition directly and indirectly. In doing so, they point to important definitional issues with which any attempt to build a coherent literature must contend.

Each of these chapters confirm (1) the need to be attentive to important inter- and intra-group differences in understanding the processes of democratic inclusion and (2) the central role that institutions play in shaping group definition and delineation. Hochschild argues that the reality that skin tone may explain a great deal more variation in social, political, and economic achievement than do traditional racial or ethnic demarcations has important implications for how we think about who is disempowered and what that might mean for political representation. She claims that the ways in which political institutions, particularly the U.S. Census, solicit and use racial self-identification have clear political consequences in terms of recognition, legitimization, and representation, not to mention access to specific material policy benefits. In Jones-Correa's careful evaluation of immigrant incorporation, he recognizes the considerable variation in immigrant experience and stresses the different processes of inclusion across time, place, and immigrant group. His essay shows how formal rules and practices (e.g., voting rights acts, naturalization laws), together with other factors, contribute to an increasingly complicated set of immigrant identities (see also the Andersen and Cohen chapter). Moreover, the process of incorporation is clearly mediated by political parties and other organizational institutions in ways that are not always conducive to effective democratic inclusion (for a similar conclusion vis-à-vis parties and racial groups, see the Frymer chapter). Chong and Rogers call for an understanding of group consciousness that is attentive to its multiple dimensions, particularly common fate and support for group autonomy, while simultaneously delineating the ways in which an understanding of group consciousness developed from the black experience may require significant and appropriate revision when applied to other racial and social groups. Accurate measurement of consciousness is important as it appears to be a crucial psychological prerequisite for effective participation within political institutions.

Mediating Institutions

Social movements, political parties, and interest groups link citizens to the formal institutions of government. Thus the degree to which these institutions facilitate or hamper the influence and representation of disadvantaged groups is a crucial aspect of democratic inclusion. The papers in this section detail the ways in which such mediating institutions interact with governing institutions and the characteristics of the groups themselves to shape the potential for and reality of democratic inclusion. For example, Costain argues that social movements must be understood primarily in terms of who uses them as vehicles for attaining political influence—the disempowered and excluded—rather than by the tactics they use, as is the case in recent work on contentious politics. Such a reorientation of the literature (in many ways a return to traditional approaches to movements) focuses attention on the ways in which social movements as unique institutions shape and mediate group demands on the political system, and gives greater urgency to questions of how and why movements succeed and fail.

As Frymer points out in his chapter, political science generally has held that political parties, in their pursuit of broad electoral coalitions, socialize and mobilize disadvantaged social groups to the benefit of the cause of democratic inclusion. This view, however, neglects the ways in which institutional structure—majoritarian elections, minority-protecting institutions (e.g., design of the Senate, supermajority requirements in legislatures), and the two-party system—create (in many cases, purposively) disincentives for the representation of the interests of racial minorities. Indeed, several chapters highlight the institutional incentives that lead strategic political parties to fail to (1) include race on the campaign agenda (Frymer), (2) facilitate the election of minority candidates (Kittilson and Tate), and (3) provide voter mobilization for racial minorities, the very groups that most benefit from such efforts (Leighley). Finally, Andersen and Cohen suggest how political institutions (such as federalism) and the structure and nature of civic and interest (mediating) institutions, along with the characteristics of the groups themselves, interact to shape democratic inclusion for immigrant groups. Moving beyond the traditional focus on political parties as the mechanisms for immigrant incorporation, they inquire into the role played by other mediating institutions, such as labor unions, religious organizations, and civic groups (see also Jones-Correa on this same point).

Governing Institutions

How can we understand the ways in which governing institutions in the United States have (or more characteristically, have not) provided for democratic inclusion of disadvantaged groups? Together, the chapters in this section examine an uncommonly broad collection of American governing institutions ranging from school boards to the presidency. While diverse in scope and power, each of these institutions has a potentially central role to play in democratic inclusion. In some cases, this contribution is obvious, such as the capacity of Congress to legislate nationally on issues of great importance to disadvantaged groups. But such underexamined institutions as school boards are also critical; as Meier notes, the education system is the source of the necessary skills for effective political participation by underprivileged groups. As a result, access to educational opportunities has its greatest effect on the prospects for democratic inclusion of the most disadvantaged members of society.

What is clear from each chapter is that democratic inclusion is not simply a function of the goodwill of those individuals who happen to occupy various elected and appointed offices, but is determined in large part by the incentives and opportunities afforded by specific institutional arrangements. At the local level, Clarke claims political institutions are characterized by what she terms *splintering*, an increasing fragmentation and "unbundling" of political authority coupled with a growing separation between residents and local political power as a result of both economic and political change. These developments are so profound that our previous assumptions about democratic inclusion processes at the local level may be inadequate in the present context. Both Meier and Clarke illustrate that local political institutions are clearly central to democratic inclusion but have implications we do not yet fully understand; institutional choices seemingly unrelated to democratic inclusion (federalism, state and local relationships, school district structures and processes) can have significant consequences for the representation of minority interests.

At the national level, the representation of minority interests is similarly mediated by the particular shape and character of those institutions. Canon's thorough survey of the congressional literature highlights the ways in which rules and structures (e.g., reapportionment, voting rights, reelection demands, campaign finance reform, single-member districts) shape the politics of democratic inclusion in American legislatures. Conley similarly notes the institutional constraints on and opportunities for democratic inclusion that presidents face. The president's role as "nation-maintainer," for example, may push presidents toward policies that privilege domestic tranquility over racial justice; whereas "saving the Union" might have led Lincoln to do more for blacks than he would have otherwise, the same unifying impetus might lead other presidents to downplay racial discrimination in the name of national peace and order (e.g., every president from Reconstruction through at least the middle of the twentieth century). By virtue of their much-vaunted independence, we might expect the courts to be the most free to facilitate the inclusion of the disadvantaged groups; the characterization of courts as countermajoritarian mechanisms for progressive change is a dearly held American belief. Lovell and McCann challenge this depiction, focusing on the need to understand the judicial system in terms not of its independence but of its institutionally constructed interdependence within the separation of powers system. As a result, courts have functioned largely to replicate and reinforce the prevailing wisdom, rather than as unique instigators or supporters of disadvantaged populations.

We will let readers draw their own conclusions from the arguments and evidence presented by our contributors. Suffice it to say, as a whole, the chapters in this volume paint a picture of democratic inclusion in the United States as a difficult, complex, and contested process. Opportunities for inclusion exist and real progress can be identified. Yet the barriers and disincentives are also quite real, and many of them stem not from a lack of good will (although certainly that is a factor as well) but from the incentive structures created by the institutions of American government, which often function to exclude more than to include. Understanding these dynamics can help us achieve a more thorough picture of the prospects for a full and equal American democracy.

NOTES

Acknowledgments: The chapters in this volume had their genesis at a lively and productive three-day conference entitled *The Politics of Democratic Inclusion*, held on the campus of the University of Notre Dame, October 17–19, 2002. The conference was the inaugural event of the Program in American Democracy (http://www.nd.edu/~amdemoc/), established by the College of Arts and Letters and faculty of the Department of Political Science to further the understanding of democratic politics and policy making in the United States. We gratefully acknowledge the generous support of Notre Dame's Dean of the College of Arts and Letters, Department of Political Science, Henkels Lecture Series, African and African American Studies Program, Gender Studies Program, Institute for Latino Studies, and John W. Gallivan Program in Journalism, Ethics, and Democracy. The conference was organized by Peri E. Arnold, Rodney E. Hero, Alvin B. Tillery, and Christina Wolbrecht, all of whom also served as editors for this volume. Ericka Benavides provided invaluable editorial assistance. We thank the anonymous reviewers for their careful and excellent feedback, and our editors at Temple, Peter Wissoker and Alex Holzman, for the enthusiasm, attention, and guidance they provided this project.

1. The focus of the papers in this volume on race, ethnicity, and immigrant status should not be taken to suggest that other groups, such as women or the poor, have faced any less of a struggle in their pursuit of democratic inclusion.

2. Some critics (e.g., Linda Chavez or Thomas Sowell) would suggest that this order is incorrect, indeed probably reversed. That is, they would argue that empirically the most "successful" racial/ethnic groups have focused on economic and social achievement first, and that political influence then followed. And these writers often insist that this is how it *should* be. They also argue that once the former is achieved the latter is less pressing. Moreover, such writers often claim that individuals should think of themselves as individuals, and not as members of groups, particularly racial/ethnic groups.

3. Examples include both monographs (Dawson 1994, 2001; Hochschild 1995; Kinder and Sanders 1996; de la Garza et al. 1992; Lien 2001; Tate 1993, 2003) and edited volumes (Peterson 1995; Sears, Sidanius, and Bobo 2000).

REFERENCES

Browning, Rufus P., Dale Rogers Marshall, and David H. Tabb. 1984. *Protest Is Not Enough: The Struggle of Blacks and Hispanics for Equality in Urban Politics*. Berkeley: University of California Press.

Dahl, Robert. 1961. *Who Governs? Democracy and Power in an American City*. New Haven: Yale University Press.

Dawson, Michael C. 1994. *Behind the Mule: Race and Class in African-American Politics*. Princeton: Princeton University Press.

———. 2001. *Black Visions: The Roots of Contemporary African-American Political Ideologies*. Chicago: University of Chicago Press.

de la Garza, Rodolfo, Louis DeSipio, F. Chris Garcia, John Garcia, and Angelo Falcon. 1992. *Latino Voices: Mexican, Puerto Rican, and Cuban Perspectives on American Politics*. Boulder: Westview Press.

Heclo, Hugh. 1994. "Ideas, Interests, and Institutions." In *The Dynamics of American Politics: Approaches and Interpretations*, edited by Lawrence C. Dodd and Calvin Jillson, 366–392. Boulder: Westview Press.

Hero, Rodney E. 1992. *Latinos and the U.S. Political System: Two-Tiered Pluralism*. Philadelphia: Temple University Press.

———. 1998. *Faces of Inequality: Social Diversity in American Politics*. New York: Oxford University Press.

Hochschild, Jennifer L. 1995. *Facing Up to the American Dream: Race, Class, and the Soul of the Nation*. Princeton: Princeton University Press.

Key, V. O. 1949. *Southern Politics in State and Nation*. New York: A.A. Knopf.

Kim, Clair Jean. 2000. "The Racial Triangulation of Asian Americans." *Politics and Society* 27 (March):105–138.

Kinder, Donald R. and Lynn M. Sanders. 1996. *Divided by Color: Racial Politics and Democratic Ideals.* Chicago: University of Chicago Press.

Lien, Pei-te. 2001. *The Making of Asian Americans Through Political Participation.* Philadelphia: Temple University Press.

March, James G. and Johan P. Olsen. 1984. "The New Institutionalism: Organizational Factors in Political Life." *American Political Science Review* 78 (September): 734–749.

Morone, James A. 1998. *The Democratic Wish: Popular Participation and the Limits of American Government,* Revised Edition. New Haven: Yale University Press.

Myrdal, Gunnar. 1944. *An American Dilemma: The Negro Problem and Modern Democracy.* New York: Harper & Brothers.

Peterson, Paul E., ed. 1995. *Classifying by Race.* Princeton: Princeton University Press.

Pinderhughes, Dianne M. 1987. *Race and Ethnicity in Chicago Politics: A Reexamination of Pluralist Theory.* Urbana: University of Illinois Press.

Schmidt, Ronald, Sr., Rodney E. Hero, Andrew Aoki, and Yvette Alex-Assensoh. 2002. "Political Science, The New Immigration and Racial Politics in the United States: What Do We Know? What Do We Need to Know?" Paper presented at the American Political Science Association Annual Meeting, August 29–September 1, Boston.

Sears, David O., Jim Sidanius, and Lawrence Bobo, eds. 2000. *Racialized Politics: The Debate About Racism in America.* Chicago: University of Chicago Press.

Sonenshein, Raphael J. 1993. *Politics in Black and White: Race and Power in Los Angeles.* Princeton: Princeton University Press.

Stone, Clarence N. 1980. "Sytemic Power in Community Decision Making: A Restatement of Stratification Theory." *American Political Science Review* 74 (December): 978–990.

Smith, Rogers M. 1993. "Beyond Tocqueville, Myrdal, and Hartz: The Multiple Traditions in America." *American Political Science Review* 87 (September): 549–566.

Steinmo, Sven, Kathleen Thelen, and Frank Longstreth, eds. 1992. *Structuring Politics: Historical Institutionalism in Comparative Analysis.* New York: Cambridge University Press.

Tate, Katherine. 1993. *From Protest to Politics: The New Black Voters in American Elections.* Cambridge: Harvard University Press.

———. 2003. *Black Faces in the Mirror: African Americans and Their Representatives.* Princeton: Princeton University Press.

Verba, Sidney, Kay Lehman Schlozman, and Henry Brady. 1995. *Voice and Equality: Civic Volunteerism in American Politics.* Cambridge: Harvard University Press.

1. DIVERSITY WITHIN AND ACROSS GROUPS

ALVIN B. TILLERY

HERO AND WOLBRECHT write in the introduction to this volume that "an important first step to understanding the politics of democratic inclusion is to think theoretically and critically about diversity both within and between excluded groups" (9). The chapters in this first section of the volume successfully respond to this call in myriad ways. All three chapters raise important (and long overdue) questions about the constitutive elements of group membership. Indeed, while reaching their conclusions using a variety of approaches, the voices presented in this section speak with unanimity in proclaiming that political scientists must pay closer attention to the relevant differences between groups (e.g., how and when they were constructed) when building theories about the process of democratic inclusion. At the same time, these chapters highlight the importance of grappling with intra-group distinctions when thinking about the pathways that lead to democratic inclusion. In other words, all of the authors share a belief that variation within groups is so significant that scholars must begin to think about the breakdown of the ascriptive hierarchies that signify exclusion as a process that occurs in multiple stages. Finally, in keeping with the overarching theme of this volume, the chapters in this section all identify the central role that both formal and informal institutions play in shaping the relevant distinctions within and across groups. The following passages explore these connections more thoroughly and establish links to other sections of this volume.

Michael Jones-Correa's chapter follows in the tradition of a prominent group of scholars associated with the University of Chicago's sociology department in the 1920s. Like the central figures of this circle, who gave us the first systematic studies of the experiences of new immigrants (Park, Burgess, and McKenzie 1925; Wirth 1928), Jones-Correa is at the forefront of a new movement in political science to identify the factors promoting the incorporation of the twenty-five million immigrants who have arrived in the United States since 1970. At the same time, Jones-Correa's chapter represents a distinct break with the legacy of the Chicago sociologists.

The studies produced by the Chicago scholars uniformly viewed the experience of their subjects through the lens of "Americanization" (Park 1950). In other words, as Mary Waters (1990) writes, "the belief that assimilation should occur as a function of length of residence in the United States [abounds in these studies]" (4). A generation of political scientists (Merton 1957; Dahl 1961; Wolfinger 1972) influenced by the Chicago school argued that the competitive party system was the lynchpin of this Americanization process. While Jones-Correa still sees a role for political parties, he rejects the view that they remain the primary force shaping the experience of new immigrants. He joins Andersen and Cohen (in the section entitled *Mediating Institutions*) in a call for the discipline to pay closer attention to the role other institutions (particularly immigration laws and other rules of the game) play in the incorporation of new immigrants. Moreover, by identifying a "paradox of contemporary immigrant political incorporation" (75), which he defines as a political reality that leaves new immigrants "simultaneously more and less incorporated than perhaps ever before" (75), Jones-Correa echoes the warnings contained in Paul Frymer's chapter about how the normal functioning of the system can sometimes work against democratic inclusion. Finally, Jones-Correa's contention that we must be sensitive to the fact that racial and ethnic diversity (including the existence of multiple identities) within the ranks of the new immigrants generates distinct processes of democratic inclusion connects very well with themes raised by the other two chapters in this section.

The chapter by Dennis Chong and Reuel Rogers, for example, joins Jones-Correa in challenging orthodoxy. A series of important studies (Verba and Nie 1972; Miller et al. 1981; Shingles 1981) in the late 1960s and 1970s found that African Americans who exhibited a strong group consciousness were more likely to participate in politics. This view was the dominant approach to understanding the foundations of African American political behavior in the 1980s. During the last decade, a number of researchers (Bobo and Gilliam 1990; Tate 1993; Verba, Scholzman, and Brady 1995) initiated a paradigm shift by arguing that group consciousness has only a marginal effect (if any) on African American political behavior. Through a reanalysis of data from the 1984 National Black Election Study, Chong and Rogers argue that group consciousness does play a significant role in motivating African Americans to participate in politics. It is important to note, however, that their findings do not simply represent a return to the view of group consciousness articulated in earlier studies. On the contrary, they present a far more nuanced account of group consciousness—one that recognizes its multi-dimensionality and why it matters—than do the classic works in the field.

Another important contribution of Chong and Rogers' chapter is found in their cautionary tale about exporting frameworks used to study the African American experience to Latinos and Asian Americans. Indeed, Chong and Rogers join Paul Frymer (in Part II) and David T. Canon (in Part III) in suggesting that the African American experience is somewhat exceptional. Finally, in calling for more research into the foundations of group consciousness among distinct subgroups within the Latino and Asian American communities, Chong and Rogers echo themes extant in Jones-Correa's chapter.

Like W.E.B. Du Bois (1903), who identified the "color-line" as "the problem of the twentieth century" (3), Jennifer Hochschild is fundamentally concerned with the link between skin color and the production of ascriptive hierarchies. Du Bois would likely take comfort in Hochschild's assertion that "conventional racial and ethnic categories no longer do as much work analytically, politically, or normatively as they used to" (19). However, he would be equally likely to find disheartening Hochschild's claim that a "skin-color hierarchy," with lighter-skinned people at the top and darker-skinned people on the bottom, remains a predictor of life chances for Americans.

In arguing for a unique heuristic for understanding the process of democratic inclusion regardless of differences across group boundaries, Hochschild's chapter is distinct. At the same time, however, her focus on the role of institutions in shaping the universe of choices for persons living the realities of America's "skin-color hierarchy" ties her to the other authors in this volume. Indeed, to some extent her emphasis on the role the U.S. Census plays in generating identity and shaping our understanding of outcomes links her to Andersen and Cohen's chapter in Part II. Moreover, Hochschild's concern for the varied experiences of persons who share ascriptive categories but reside on different locations within the "skin-color hierarchy" echoes themes raised by the other two chapters in this section about the impact of diversity within groups.

REFERENCES

Bobo, Lawrence, and Frank Gilliam, Jr. 1990. "Race, Socio-Political Participation, and Black Empowerment." *American Political Science Review* 84: 377–393.

Dahl, Robert. 1961. *Who Governs?* New Haven: Yale University Press.

Du Bois, W. E. B. [1903] 1996. *The Souls of Black Folk*. New York: Random House.

Merton, Robert K. 1957. *Social Theory and Social Structure*. Glencoe, IL: The Free Press.

Miller, Arthur, Patricia Gurin, Gerald Gurin, and Oksana Malanchuk.1981."Group Consciousness and Political Participation." *American Journal of Political Science* 25: 494–511.

Park, Robert. 1950. *Race and Culture*. New York: The Free Press.

Park, Robert, Ernest Burgess, and Roderick McKenzie. 1925. *The City*. Chicago: University of Chicago Press.

Shingles, Richard D. 1981. "Black Consciousness and Political Participation: The Missing Link." *American Political Science Review* 75: 76–91.

Tate, Katherine. 1993. *From Protest to Politics: The New Black Voters in American Elections*. Cambridge: Harvard University Press.

Verba, Sidney, and Norman Nie. 1972. *Political Participation in America*, 1967. Ann Arbor: ICPSR.

Verba, Sidney, Kay Scholzman, and Henry Brady. 1995. *Voice and Equality: Civic Volunteerism in American Politics*. Cambridge: Harvard University Press.

Waters, Mary. 1990. *Ethnic Options: Choosing Identities in America*. Berkeley: University of California Press.

Wirth, Louis. 1928. *The Ghetto*. Chicago: University of Chicago Press.

Wolfinger, Raymond. 1972. *The Politics of Progress*. Englewood Cliffs, NJ: Prentice Hall.

JENNIFER L. HOCHSCHILD

2

From Nominal to Ordinal

Reconceiving Racial and Ethnic Hierarchy in the United States

> There are many ... variables that are *not* matters of degree. And it is these variables that define what it means to be black in America. ... Police do not stop whites for "driving while black," but police do stop blacks, including wealthy blacks, for this offense. ... Thus it would be wiser to regard "driving while black" and being black not as two variables but, instead, as part of the same condition. It is this second type of variable that forces one to conclude that by definition blacks and whites do not occupy the same social space.
>
> —Samuel Lucas, 2000

> I knew some [other black people] who not only had complexions ten shades lighter than [a] brown paper bag, and hair as straight as any ruler, but also had multiple generations of "good looks," wealth, and accomplishment. ... It was a color thing and a class thing. And for generations of black people, color and class have been inexorably tied together.
>
> —Lawrence Graham, 2000[1]

IN THE VIEW of Samuel Lucas, the nominal category of blackness so outweighs the distinctions anatomized by Lawrence Graham that variation in skin color has no impact on the degree of blacks' exclusion from American society. But Graham and many others have pointed to the profound effect that skin color has had within the black—and by extension, other—communities throughout American history. This chapter argues that the United States is moving away from the situation that Lucas describes toward a more publicly relevant version of the society depicted by Graham. That might imply greater democratic inclusion for some Americans previously excluded from our society and polity—perhaps at the cost of even firmer ostracism of others. How to weigh those equal but opposite trajectories remains a dilemma.

I begin with the observation that our conventional racial and ethnic categories no longer do as much work analytically, politically, or normatively as they used to. Analytically, they are blunt, so that they often run roughshod over subtle but important distinctions or must be strung together in awkward locutions in an effort to signal those distinctions (e.g., non-Asian minority, non-Hispanic white, "mixed race black children" [McBride 1996]). Politically, the category "black," for example, must encompass conservative insiders such as Condoleezza Rice or Clarence Thomas as well as radical outsiders like the followers of Al Sharpton or Sonny Carson, who probably agree with one another on almost nothing of political importance. The category "Hispanic" similarly ranges from Republican Cubans through Democratic Mexican Americans to radical dreamers about Aztlan. (The same, of course, holds for Asians and European Americans.) Normatively, we get tangled in the nuances of different connotations between black or African American or Afrikkan, Latino or Hispanic or Chicano, minorities or people of color, and so on. Economically, a substantial number of blacks or Hispanics are wealthier and have better jobs than a substantial number of whites or Asians. Demographically, an increasing number of Americans simply do not belong in any one of these categories.

I begin this chapter by articulating more fully the arguments behind the assertion that our conventional racial and ethnic categories no longer do enough work. Given that motivation, I then propose an alternative framework for thinking about the complexities of racial and ethnic hierarchy. Assuming the alternative framework is persuasive, I suggest a new way of understanding who is included or excluded from real participation in the American polity and how the new framework might therefore have implications for racial politics and policy. In short, this exercise seeks to capture a moment in which the United States might be moving to a new and possibly more liberating construction of race and ethnicity—or simply reifying in a more complicated way the age-old barriers among us.

CONVENTIONAL RACIAL AND ETHNIC CATEGORIES ARE INCREASINGLY PROBLEMATIC

My argument is predicated on the changing demography of the United States. About 20 percent of Americans are immigrants or children of immigrants—a figure that has not been reached since the early days of the twentieth century. Most are from Latin America and they are spreading across the nation from the original gateway cities and states. A substantial influx of immigrants from various nations in Asia and Africa is also transforming particular cities or regions. By 2020, if current immigration policies persist and if current racial and ethnic lines remain fixed (which they will not), more than one-third of U.S. residents will be Asian, black, Latino, or Native American, up from about 15 percent in 1960. Sometime before 2100, if one continues with this exercise, "whites" will be a minority of Americans.

But those figures are artificial for a variety of reasons.[2] The most relevant one here is what is now virtually an article of faith among most social scientists: Race is a social construction. The meaning of the very term *race*—as distinguished from ethnicity, culture, nationality, and religion—has changed over the past few centuries (Sollors 1989; Fredrickson 2002; Hattam 2004). Sometimes analysts or political actors sharply distinguish race from ethnicity; sometimes the two terms are used synonymously. What groups are perceived to be separate races has similarly varied over the centuries. For example, a Harvard anthropologist's 1939 textbook, *The Races of Europe*, showed eighteen races spread across the continent, including "Partially Mongoloid," "Lappish," "Brunn strain, Tronder etc., unreduced, only partly brachycephalized," "Pleistocene Mediterranean Survivor," "Neo-Danubian," and so on (Coon 1939).[3] That is no longer, to put it mildly, how we conceive of Europeans. Who is defined in and out of a given race varies over time and occurs for different reasons, including deliberate political choice; Matthew Frye Jacobson, for example, argues that the category of "white" expanded, then contracted, then expanded again during the nineteenth and twentieth centuries (Jacobson 1998; see also Gerstle 1993; Omi and Winant 1994; Ignatiev 1996). American courts struggled mightily for decades with the question of defining who is white and eventually threw their hands up in despair (Haney López 1996; Pascoe 1996; Jones 2000; Johnson 2003).

Generally, human races have vastly more shared than distinct genes, and the mixtures of genetic pools over time and across space is extremely complex (Cavalli-Sforza, Menozzi, Piazza 1994). Partly as a consequence, the American Anthropological Association declared the concept of race to be "a worldview, a body of prejudgments that distorts our ideas about human differences and group behavior," and recommended that the term be dropped from the census and scholarly writings (American Anthropological Association 1998). The editorial policy statement of the major medical journals similarly holds that "authors should avoid terms such as 'race,' which lacks precise biological meaning, and use alternative descriptors such as 'ethnicity' or 'ethnic group' instead" (International Committee of Medical Journal Editors 2001).

Many medical professionals and some scientists dissent, arguing that "race" remains a meaningful, even essential, descriptor. Doctors point out that for genetic reasons sickle cell anemia occurs most often among Africans, that northern Europeans are most likely to have lactose intolerance, and that Swedes are most susceptible to the mutation that causes hemochromatosis. In their view, these differences matter for medical diagnoses and treatment; "a 'race-neutral' or 'color-blind' approach to biomedical research is neither equitable nor advantageous, and would not lead to a reduction of disparities in disease risk or treatment efficacy between groups" (Risch et al. 2002; see also Satel 2001–2002). In 2003, medical researchers at Howard University pledged to collect DNA from 25,000 patients seen by the Howard College of Medicine over the next five years; most are expected to be African American. The dean of the medical school "said genetic information would increasingly find the causes of disease, predict susceptibility to an illness, and choose which drugs would work best for a particular patient" (Pollack 2003). But these are almost the only voices in mainstream academic or professional communities claiming that race is "real."

The United States census provides another indicator of the complications of the concept of race. It is hard to see the census as an initiator of postmodern identity fragmentation, but that is what it has become. The instructions in 2000 permitted respondents to "mark one or more" of fifteen "races" (including "some other race"), and provided three lines inviting further differentiation. It also included a separate category asking if the respondent is Hispanic (with further subcategories). By combining some of these choices to generate only (!) six races,[4] and ignoring write-ins, the United States now

officially recognizes sixty-three possible racial categories—126 if one includes Hispanic or Latino as a "race." Kenneth Prewitt, the former director
of the census, points out that there is no reason to assume that we will not add
"partly Hispanic" to the ethnicity question, and perhaps other "races," such
as Middle Eastern or South Asian to the race question in the next census.
Any addition will increase the possibilities to 200, 300, or more—and the
statistical and political mess now evident in the census will become a total
quagmire (Hochschild 2002; Prewitt 2002).

Perhaps the census's embrace of multiple identities will go the way of its
earlier seventy-year-long enumeration of "mulatto" (along with "quadroon"
and "octoroon" in the 1890 census, "Mexican" and "Hindu" in 1930[5] and
an array of Asian nationalities since the late nineteenth century) (Anderson
and Fienberg 1999, 174–184). But that seems unlikely. Census respondents
now choose their own racial identification rather than having it chosen by the
enumerator, which makes a great deal of difference in the connotations of
racial labeling. In 2000, fewer than 3 percent of Americans chose more than
one race (although 823 people chose all six). Another 12.5 percent reported
being Hispanic, along with a racial designation (Bureau of the Census 2001).[6]
Depending on whether one treats being Hispanic and white as analogous to
being black and white, a tiny or small minority of Americans have a mixed
racial identity. There was, however, no advertising or advance information
provided to alert respondents that they would have this new option on the 2000
census; within a few years, forms for all federal agencies will be required to
permit people to "mark one or more," and most universities, corporations,
hospitals, state and local government agencies, and other large organizations
will probably follow suit. Thus the idea is becoming more familiar and may
be commonplace by the next census. Furthermore, the people who did choose
more than one race in 2000 were disproportionately young and well educated.
All of this suggests that the proportions choosing multiple racial identities
will grow; Prewitt (2002) speculates that by 2010, perhaps 10 percent of
the population will mark more than one, and by 2020 perhaps a quarter of
Americans.

The phenomenon of being multiracial is not new to Americans, of course
(Sollers 2000; Hollinger 2003); neither is governmental identification of some
Americans as racially mixed. What is new is that multiracial identity has
become a point of public pride and assertiveness, and a social movement
built around multiracial identity has shown surprising political strength and
social cachet. I will return to the issue of multiracialism and democratic
inclusion; my immediate point is that the political and social legitimization
of multiraciality blurs nominal racial categories in conception as well as in
practice.

If larger proportions of Americans mark more than one race box on the
next few censuses, it will not only be because they increasingly accept the
concept and understand the procedure. There really will be more multiracial
Americans, since intermarriage rates and the number of multiracial children
is rising. About 7 percent of African Americans marry outside their race

(as of 1990), which means that about 13 percent of children with at least one black grandparent have a non-black grandparent as well. To assume that black outmarriage will rise to about 12 percent "is not a radical assumption. Yet if this rise does occur, a fifth to a quarter of children with a black grandparent being born in 2010 would also have a non-black grandparent. And from such levels, . . . the history of outmarriage in other groups suggests it might well soar within a generation after 2010" (Perlmann 2002, 15–16). African Americans have by far the lowest rate of outmarriage of any non-white group; as of 1990, for example, 36 percent of Asian Americans were married to a member of one of the other three major ethnic or racial groups (Qian 1997, table 1).[7] Depending on how multiraciality is defined, analysts estimate that up to 12 percent of youth can now be called multiracial (Goldstein and Morning 2000; Hirschman, Alba, and Farley 2000; Harris and Sim 2002). By 1999, more than 20 percent of births to native-born mothers in California were multiracial or multiethnic (Tafoya 2002, figure 3.2); if California is the harbinger of the United States' racial and ethnic future, as many argue, the number of multiracial Americans will grow rapidly.

Since families do not contain only parents and children, a single intermarriage or interracial child can have an impact well beyond the people most immediately involved. As of 1990, "one in seven whites, one in three blacks, four in five Asians, and more than 19 in 20 American Indians are closely related to someone of a different racial group. Despite an intermarriage rate of about 1 percent, about 20 percent of Americans count someone from a different racial group among their kin" (Goldstein 1999, 399). And those calculations do not include marriages or offspring involving a Latino and a non-Latino.

Individuals and families who are visibly and politically multiracial introduce fluidity into nominal racial categories at the aggregate level; the issue of whether one identifies as a multiracial person introduces another kind of fluidity, at the individual level. The fluid category of multiracial is itself fluid: "When more than 10,000 middle and high school students were asked to report their race on separate school and home surveys, about 12 percent failed to provide consistent responses. Seven percent reported being multiracial on only one of the surveys, and nearly 3 percent of the youth switched between single-race groups. Multiracial reports were almost twice as likely on the school survey . . . as on the home survey" (Harris 2001). Having parents of two different races was neither necessary nor sufficient for a child to call him- or herself biracial on this survey (Harris and Sim 2000; Harris and Sim 2002; Harris 2003).[8]

Fluidity in individual categorization or self-identification is not limited to multiracials. People's self-identified race may differ from that assigned to them by observers (Telles and Lim 1998; Harris and Sim 2000); people are sometimes assigned different races at birth and at death (Hahn et al. 1992); and the race assigned to them by observers may itself differ depending on the race of the observer (Harris 2002). More than half of young adult children of immigrants in San Diego reported having a different ethnicity, and more than a quarter reported a different race, in 2002 than in 1995, barely seven years earlier (Rumbaut 2002, table 6).

If we look at the status of groups across time, we find once again that racial categories are increasingly problematic for understanding the bound-aries around inclusion. One can no longer talk simply about "minority status" in the United States because of the astonishing trajectory of Asian Americans. Seventy-five years ago, they personified literal exclusion; almost all were de-nied the right to immigrate into the United States. Some Asian nationalities were denied the right to own certain types of property. Sixty years ago, most Japanese Americans were interned during World War II, although few German Americans or Italian Americans were. It was barely fifty years ago that members of all Asian nationalities were granted the right to become naturalized citizens. Movies and cartoons about the yellow peril, "Japs," and mysterious Chinese gangsters casually abounded until a few decades ago.

But now Asian Americans are described as the model minority, with very high rates of intermarriage with Anglos and higher average incomes and levels of educational attainment. The most select universities must use informal quotas to keep too many from beating out their non-Asian competitors; a *Newsweek* cover story promotes the strength and attractiveness of Asian men (Pan 2000); whites who live near a lot of Asians are more likely than those who don't to endorse increased immigration (Hood and Morris 1997). All is not perfect for Asian Americans of course, and I discuss problems and persistent racial bias below. But we can no longer assume that the status of not being European American is sufficient for exclusion from American society and politics—an astonishing change.

The category of Hispanic or Latino is also decreasingly useful, for different reasons; the term is a conceptual mess. Is it a race, an ethnicity, or simply a bureaucratic convenience? Hispanics may identify as white, black, Native American, or even Asian; more than 40 percent rejected all of these choices in favor of "other" or a specific nationality on the 2000 census. When Latinos were a tiny fraction of the American population, this anomaly was statistically confusing but politically unimportant in most locations. Now that there are more Hispanics than African Americans, and given that there will most likely be twice as many within our lifetimes, the conceptual confusion is empirically consequential. More generally, the degree to which Latinos are included in American society and politics varies enormously with nationality, location, and immigration status; it is often not helpful to discuss Cubans in Miami and Dominicans in New York with the same terminology.

Even the category of black is becoming less useful as a racial category, given increasing levels of immigration from Africa and the West Indies. Dark-skinned immigrants do not necessarily identify as black (or African American), nor are they always seen as black by other Americans (Kasinitz 1992; Rogers 2001; Waters 2001). The choice of identity (by oneself or others) and the degree of political inclusion are mutually causal; political parties and other groups may be more willing to include dark-skinned immigrants than blacks, and immigrants do or do not identify as black partly as a consequence of how included they perceive themselves to be. Thus even the quintessential racial category in American politics is blurring around the edges.

Finally, who is white? Ironically, the group which until recently received the least attention from social scientists is perhaps the one for which a nominal racial designation is least informative. Some analysts and political activists retain the traditional black–white binary by treating Hispanics like non-Hispanic whites, while others make sharp differentiations between whites and Hispanics. We lack settled conventions about whether non-Jewish immigrants from the Middle East or subcontinental Indians are white. In addition, if only because they are such a large share of the American population, whites are perhaps the most varied group in terms of income, political ideology, social practices, religion, and other measures of ethnicity. In simple comparisons across nominal groups, whites epitomize inclusion, but if other dimensions such as class or religion are permitted to intrude, the boundaries creating inclusion must be renegotiated.

AN ALTERNATIVE CONCEPTUALIZATION: SKIN COLOR HIERARCHY

Arguably, then, our traditional nominal racial categorization of Americans is not much help in analyzing the politics of democratic inclusion. But to conclude from this that the United States is now colorblind or approaching the end of racial exclusion would be as bootless as to insist that races are biologically pure or politically insulated. Is there an alternative?

I propose a thought experiment; even if we reject it as a guide to action, we can learn a great deal about patterns of racial inclusion and exclusion in the United States by identifying why and how it fails empirically, emotionally, and politically. What would we gain and lose by moving from nominal categories of Anglo, African American, Latino, and Asian to ordinal measures of skin color as a way of giving order to our understanding of American racial hierarchy?

The basic and most radical hypothesis is simple: the darker a person's skin color, the lower he or she is likely to be on any scale of whatever is broadly perceived to be desirable in the United States.[9] Thus, the basic racial hierarchy runs from European American to Asian American, to Latino, to African American. More interestingly and controversially, if the hypothesis is correct, light-skinned blacks are likely to be better off than dark-skinned Hispanics, light-skinned Hispanics are likely to be better off than dark-skinned Asians, and light-skinned Asians are likely to be better off than dark- skinned Anglos.

Qualifications and extensions follow immediately. First, the basic hypothesis will be complicated, though probably not deeply undermined, by gender differences. Second, this is a probabilistic, not a deterministic, hypothesis: some dark-skinned people have more of the qualities typically desired in our society than some light-skinned people.[10] Most importantly, a few nationality groups are on average "too high" or "too low" on the status hierarchy given their appearance. Third, neither the content nor the intensity of a person's racial or ethnic identity tracks the skin-color hierarchy very well; the hierarchy mostly refers to socioeconomic status or treatment by others. In the vocabulary of this chapter, there may be a disjunction between individuals' commitment to a nominal category and their own inadvertent role in creating an ordinal continuum.

Finally, the skin color continuum may be more contextual or historically bounded than the basic hypothesis suggests. In some periods of history, political environments, or social settings, darker-skinned people may be perceived as more authentic, closer to "the people," or otherwise of higher status than lighter-skinned people. If there are a large number of such "exceptions" that can be contextually and not just idiosyncratically explained, then the basic hypothesis will need to be raised a level of abstraction, to read: "Skin color matters much more than we have typically taken into account, but whether dark or light skin tone is associated with advantage will depend on the circumstances." That will still be interesting and important; I read the evidence, however, to imply that light tone is almost always advantageous so the abstract hypothesis remains less informative than the concrete one.

A softer version of the basic hypothesis melds the nominal and ordinal. That is, it may be that skin tone has (increasing?) importance in determining patterns of inclusion and exclusion *within* each racial or ethnic category, and that because two of the three non-Anglo groups are gaining in salience in the United States, the whole issue is increasingly important as a public matter—but that the nominal categories persist in creating sharp exclusionary boundaries. The image here is not one continuum arrayed by skin tone, but four separate continua (or five, if we add Native Americans), each in parallel fashion arrayed by skin tone but remaining distinct from one another. To put the point less abstractly, inclusion is still more likely for dark-skinned European Americans than for light-skinned Asians because Asians still seem ineluctably "foreign" to the majority and dominant population. Similarly, one is still better off as a dark-skinned Hispanic than as an African American, because the former lacks the stigma of being black and can substitute the less-stigmatized identity as an ethnic American or immigrant.

The evidence described below lies almost entirely in the realm of the softer hypothesis; with rare exceptions, it compares outcomes by skin tone within a given nominal race or ethnicity. I am compiling evidence about the plausibility of the basic (one-continuum) hypothesis, but in this chapter I largely leave this question open.

A final preliminary point: the use of skin tone to determine who warrants inclusion in a polity is not new. The connection between lightness and virtue is at least as old as Shakespeare;[11] in the United States, one need only point to phrases such as "the black Irish" or "the blue vein test" to identify long-standing color hierarchies within groups (Morgan 1975, Drake and Cayton 1993 [1945]; Lawrence-Lightfoot 1995; Graham 2000). Nor is the focus on skin tone unique to African or European Americans—or to Americans at all. For example, a dark-skinned Dominican reported for a job interview, only to find the interviewer surprised into stammering, "I was looking for someone who looked different, I mean Hispanic, I mean ..." (Foner 2000, 158–59;

more generally, see Menchaca 2001). According to an ancient Japanese proverb, "White skin makes up for seven defects" (quoted in Wagatsuma 1968, 129).

Before evaluating what is in fact new about skin color hierarchy and whether it implies greater or lesser inclusion in a democratic polity, let us look at the evidence of its breadth and depth.

SKIN COLOR HIERARCHY WITHIN RACIAL GROUPS

It is uncontroversial to point out that the level of inclusion within the American polity, society, and economy varies by skin color, with the lightest-skinned nominal racial or ethnic groups most strongly included and the darkest-skinned most firmly excluded. The more interesting question is the degree to which the same skin tone hypothesis obtains within groups. The basic answer is: "A good deal."

African Americans

Differentiation in outcomes is one way to measure degrees of inclusion. Strictly speaking, of course, poor or unemployed people are "included" in the economy as much as affluent and fully employed ones. Similarly, in formal terms people who are disfavored as marital partners or who lose in a campaign for electoral office are also included within the system, just not on very favorable terms. But the connotation of inclusion is that people are "able to seek and achieve status and influence" rather than "remain[ing] structurally ... unequal," in the words of the introduction to this volume. Thus it is a slide, but not too long a leap, to move from the concepts of inclusion and exclusion to the facts of affluence or poverty, popularity or disfavor, electoral victory or defeat.

By that route, we can conclude that dark-skinned African Americans suffer from even more socioeconomic exclusion than light-skinned ones. To begin with, both African and European Americans use skin tone as a cognitive organizing device (Maddox and Gray 2002), and those cognitions have real impact. Boys who were identified as mulatto in the 1920 census grew up to be more likely to attain a white collar job, at a statistically significant level, than similarly situated boys who were labeled black (Hill 2000). The 1968 Kerner Commission survey of 2,800 blacks in fifteen cities showed increasing levels of income, college attendance, and white collar occupations as respondents' categorization moved from dark to medium to light skin tone (Edwards 1972). According to the 1979–1980 National Survey of Black Americans, light-skinned blacks attain more years of education, higher status jobs, higher incomes, and higher family incomes than do dark-skinned blacks. All of these differences are statistically significant, and in each case, the movement in five steps from "very dark" to "very light" exactly tracks the increasing levels of success (Keith and Herring 1991; Allen et al. 2000; Hunter 2002; Allen et al. 2000).

Three other recent surveys yield similar findings. In the 1982 General Social Survey (GSS), light-skinned blacks received more education, had higher occupational prestige, and enjoyed higher family incomes in their teens than did dark-skinned blacks. All of these results are highly significant statistically. This survey showed no difference in current income between dark- and light-skinned African Americans, and minimal to no differences in political ideology, policy views, or levels of alienation (especially when the survey results were controlled for education; Seltzer and Smith 1991). Analyses of the 1994 Los Angeles Study of Urban Inequality show that "being a dark-skinned African American male reduces the odds of working by 52 percent" (Johnson et al. 1998: 32). Highly educated light-skinned black men had an unemployment rate similar to that of comparably educated white men (10.3 percent and 9.5 percent respectively), whereas dark-skinned men with the same level of education were twice as likely to be unemployed (19.4 percent). The same pattern holds among men who have participated in job training programs. Being a high school dropout, having a criminal record, and living in a very poor neighborhood similarly penalized dark-skinned black men in the labor market even more than light-skinned black men (Johnson et al. 1998). Finally, a 1990s survey of young black adults also found that dark-skinned respondents were more likely to be in the working class than to be professionals, had lower family incomes, and were more likely to have dropped out of high school (Krieger et al. 1998).

Several of these studies move beyond bivariate relationships into more sophisticated multivariate analyses. The theoretical question here is whether "colorism" is primarily a direct response to the person standing before the potential employer or teacher, or an indirect effect of being able to take advantage of the higher social origins that have accrued over many generations to light-skinned African Americans. The evidence shows consistently that both phenomena are at work, but some studies suggest that the direct effects of skin tone are more powerful than the indirect effects of being born into a light-skinned black family. As Mark Hill summarizes, "Differences in social origin are responsible for only 10 to 20 percent of the color gap in adult attainment" (Hill 2000, 1454; see also Hughes and Hertel 1990; Keith and Herring 1991).

Other scholars, typically with smaller and more opportunistic samples, have shown how skin color affects interpersonal relations among African Americans. Blacks (especially men) perceive light skin to make people more attractive as a dating or marriage partner (Bond and Cash 1992; Ross 1997; Hill 2002; Hunter 2002) or as an adoptive child (McRoy and Grape 1999; Kennedy 2003). Both blacks and whites attribute more positive psychological traits to light-skinned African Americans (Maddox and Gray 2002).

I know of no systematic research on the relationship of skin color to political participation or electoral success (I am currently conducting such research). Some analysts have suggested that "looking 'more white' in appearance might help Blacks initially as they try to cross the color line in statewide campaigns" by helping them to "blend more easily" (Strickland and Whicker 1992). Governor Douglas Wilder of Virginia is a frequently used example. One laboratory experiment similarly showed that highly prejudiced whites with little tendency to monitor themselves for social desirability are indeed likely to prefer lighter-skinned to darker-skinned hypothetical black candidates, whereas whites with less prejudice or more monitoring expressed little or even the reverse preference (Terkildsen 1993). In some cases, in other words, light skin makes it more likely that black candidates will be included in the group of potential office-holders that white voters deem acceptable.

Occasionally the political dynamic is reversed; dark-skinned black candidates persuade (predominantly black) voters that they will include more members of their own race within the fold. The most spectacular recent use of dark skin color as a political tool came in the 2002 mayoral race in Newark, New Jersey, between two self-identified African Americans. Incumbent Sharpe James reportedly called his opponent, Cory Booker, many things—a tool of the Ku Klux Klan and Jewish interests, a Republican, and a "faggot white boy." For whatever reason, James won the race.

Latinos

Skin color appears to have the same impact among Latinos, although the academic literature is not as extensive or well developed. With a few exceptions, light tones are associated with greater economic success, more social status, and probably more electoral victories—that is, more inclusion of a positive sort in the American polity.

As before, I begin with economic outcomes. The 1979–1980 National Chicano Study showed that dark-skinned Mexican Americans earn less than their light-skinned counterparts, at a statistically significant level in some though not all analyses. They also receive significantly less schooling, are less proficient in English, and are less likely to be unionized workers. The latter results hold even after a long string of controls are added; in some analyses they are stronger for men than for women, and in some the reverse (Telles and Murguia 1990; Murguia and Telles 1996; Allen et al. 2000; Hunter 2002). As with African Americans, skin color appears to directly affect Chicano men's position in the labor market and earnings even more than it indirectly affects their life chances through the human capital acquired through their family of origin (Telles and Murguia 1990; for disagreement based on an alternative methodology, see Bohara and Davila 1992).

Other analyses based on different data find the same patterns. White Hispanic men earn more than black or dark-skinned Hispanic men; white Hispanics with little education or labor market experience succeed more in the job market than similarly situated black Hispanics. These results hold even with standard social and economic controls (Cotton 1997, Gomez 2000).

Spatial location suggests a different dimension of inclusion and exclusion, again to the general disadvantage of Latinos with dark skin. Census data from 1970 and 1980 show that black Hispanics are much more residentially separated from Anglos than are white Hispanics in all of the ten metropolitan areas studied. Black Hispanics are, conversely, much more residentially integrated with African Americans than are white Hispanics. White and black Hispanics are also residentially separated from one another. White Hispanics are just as likely to live near Anglos as near black Hispanics; black Hispanics are more likely to live near non-Hispanic blacks than near white Hispanics. When His-panics are divided into three groups rather than two (with a self-identified "Spanish race" occupying the space between white and black), levels of sep-aration for the newly added group fit in between the other two just as the skin color continuum would predict. Finally, the pattern of skin color hierarchy holds even with controls; as we have seen in the case of African Americans, skin color is not merely a stand-in for social class but rather generates a di-rectly discriminatory response on its own (Denton and Massey 1989; see also Relethford et al. 1983).

Evidence on psychological and interpersonal correlates of skin color among Latinos is sparse and not clearly patterned. "Dark Indian-looking men who were born and raised in the United States had significantly higher depression scores" than other Mexican Americans on the National Chicano Study—but so did lighter European-looking women who had emigrated from Mexico (Montalvo and Codina 2001, 331; see also Codina and Montalvo 1994). Other findings are qualitative or impressionistic or driven by the ana-lyst's own framework for analysis; this is an arena that awaits further serious research.

Asians and Asian Americans

There is even less systematic research on skin color within the Asian American population. Female South Asian–Canadian university students "wished to be significantly lighter in skin color than they perceived them-selves to be, compared with European-Canadian participants" in one study. "The idealization of lighter skin was found to be greater the further the per-son was from the cultural White ideal" (Sahay and Piran 1997, 169). These are not residents of the United States, but arguably students at the Univer-sity of Toronto are not dissimilar to students at universities south of the border.

Skin color gradations certainly occur in the nations from which Asian im-migrants to the United States come. In Japan, members of the upper class have lighter skin tones than do members of the middle or lower classes; the author of one study concludes that "social selection for light skin color has had some genetic effect" in a nation that was genetically isolated for almost 1,500 years (Hulse 1967, quotation in abstract). Japanese and Indonesian university students consistently report that fair skin tones are more beauti-ful and that people with fair skin present a more likeable impression (Saito et al. 2001). In South Asia, "skin coloring tends to be a minutely calibrated index (of beauty, of Aryan ancestry, often of class). ... Lighter skin color-ing is the overwhelmingly preferred shade" (George 1997, 34). Perhaps not surprisingly, therefore, a "preference for light-skinned spouses can be easily verified by the matrimonial columns of some of the Hindu dailies [in India]. Among the most desirable traits a bride can have are virginity and light skin, as evidenced by those placing ads" (Hall 1995, 179).[12] None of this is close to dispositive—but it reinforces rather than contradicts the hypothesis of a skin color continuum within the Asian American population.

European Americans

Even European Americans, the quintessentially "included" group, have experienced the same relationships between inclusion and skin-color gradations, at least in earlier generations. Compared with southern Europeans, northern immigrants and their descendents enjoyed higher status, greater wealth holdings, and more political power in America until well into the twentieth century. As late as 1950, nationalities of the "old" immigration (from England, Wales, Ireland, Norway, Sweden, and Germany) averaged more than eight years of education in the first generation of immigrants, whereas nationalities of the "new" immigration (from Poland, Czechoslovakia, Austria, Italy, and Russia or the USSR) averaged significantly less than eight years. Except for the Irish, northern Europeans in the old wave of immigration were more likely to be in agricultural or professional occupations and less likely to be in domestic or personal service occupations than those in the new (Lieberson and Waters, 1988).

After the first generation, however, white immigrants' trajectories get more complicated. Occupationally, the pattern is one of continuity: "There is almost an exact correlation between the present-day ethnic participation in agriculture and the levels observed for immigrant groups 80 years earlier." A similar, though weaker, relationship holds for domestic and personal service workers (Lieberson and Waters 1988). Social status has also been continuous; light-skinned northern Europeans have always had higher standing in the eyes of fellow (white) Americans than have darker-skinned newer immigrants. On the Bogardus ethnic distance scale, for example, all ten nationalities from northern Europe of the former were preferred to all eight nationalities from southern Europe from the 1920s through the 1970s. The single exception was Italians, who made it into the top five preferred groups by 1977 (Smith and Dempsey 1983, 588). Even so, more than four times as many GSS respondents in 2000 stated that the English had made "one of the most important positive contributions to this country" as said the same thing about Italians (Davis, Smith, and Marsden 2001, 758–761).

Nevertheless, with regard to educational attainment and the likelihood of holding a professional job, the chief pattern has been discontinuity across immigrant generations. Perhaps most importantly, "the old–new distinction does not operate with respect to distinguishing between the incomes earned by the groups. As a matter of fact, ... [average income by 1980] is slightly higher for the six SCE [Southern, Central, and Eastern] European groups than for the ten northwestern European ones" (Lieberson and Waters 1988, 137).

In short, skin color hierarchy no longer operates among European Americans the same way it continues to affect other nominal racial or ethnic groups. After a century of intermarriage among Europeans, and perhaps as a consequence of the "whitening" of all who are not black, Hispanic, or Asian, skin tone is now a poor predictor of many measures of inclusion for whites. Whether this blending within what is now seen as a single racial group and its subsequent blurring of exclusionary boundaries signals the future for the other groups—or whether it is a good predictor for Hispanics and Asians but *not* for blacks, or whether whites will continue to occupy a unique status and pursue a unique dynamic—remains to be seen.

EVIDENCE FOR THE THOUGHT EXPERIMENT: SKIN COLOR HIERARCHY ACROSS RACIAL GROUPS

So far, I have demonstrated the exclusionary impact of dark skin tone *within* nominal racial or ethnic groups; let us turn briefly to the more radical hypothesis of a single skin color continuum *across* groups. If it holds, light-skinned African Americans do now or will soon have more education and income, higher status jobs, and more social standing than dark-skinned Hispanics, and so on up the skin tone chain.

I know of no direct measures of this overlap, beyond the research I and my co-authors are currently conducting,[13] and current sources of data will not permit a full comparison. Nevertheless, evidence suggests that the proposed overlap is plausible. First, one of the best studies of the effects of skin color finds that the income gap between light- and dark-skinned African Americans is almost as wide as the gap between African Americans and whites (Hughes and Hertel 1990). Second, census data clearly show that the bottom tails of the distributions of income and education among Latinos, Anglos, and even Asians fall well below the top tails of the distributions among African Americans, and so on up the nominal skin tone hierarchy (Bureau of the Census, 2003 and 2004).[14] Census data, of course, do not include measures of skin tone, but we have seen over and over that lighter-skinned members of each nominal category are better off than darker-skinned members.

Third, multiracial youth, who on average can be expected to have a skin tone somewhere between their darker and lighter parents, occupy socioeconomic positions between the average positions of their two ancestries. "In terms of annual family income and parents' education and occupation, multiracial blacks are solidly between monoracial whites and monoracial blacks" (Harris 2003, 65; summarizing Kao 1999). Similarly, in suburban Chicago, "monoracial blacks live in neighborhoods with the highest percentage of poor residents (10.4 percent), followed by multiracial blacks (9.1 percent), multiracial whites (7.5 percent), and monoracial whites (5.3 percent)" (Harris 2003, 65; summarizing Corrin and Cook 1999). The families of multiracial children with one Asian and one white parent are on average less wealthy than the families of children with two Asian parents, but not significantly different from the families of children with two white parents. The same pattern holds for parents' educational levels (Kao 1999). An elaborate study compares adolescents who identify themselves as multiracial at school, home, or both, and disaggregates by the particular racial combination reported (it does not consider Hispanics). Its detailed conclusions can be summarized as following the same pattern: multiracial children fit between their two monoracial groups. That finding holds for family income, parents' education, and residential separation. Multiracial children live in census tracts that are more racially diverse than is average for people like their lighter-skinned parent, but less racially diverse than is typical for people like their darker-skinned parent (Harris 2003). These results hold across various multiracial pairings.

The evidence on the simple, radical hypothesis is incomplete. Most strikingly, we lack data on levels of discrimination and social status for light-skinned members of disfavored groups compared with dark-skinned members of more favored groups. So the question of whether patterns of inclusion and exclusion can be boiled down to skin color *tout court* remains open.

EXCEPTIONS TO THE SKIN COLOR HIERARCHY

Individuals can move in either direction along the continuum from where they "belong." Some dark-skinned individuals from disfavored groups are more fully included in the American polity than are almost all light-skinned people of favored groups by virtually any conventional measure; think of Clarence Thomas, Colin Powell,[15] Michael Jordan, Richard Parsons, Oprah Winfrey, Henry Cisneros, Jennifer Lopez, Jackie Chan, and Gary Locke. And certain light-skinned individuals are more excluded than almost all dark-skinned people deeply poor residents of eastern Kentucky, junior members of Asian gangs in Minneapolis, or disfranchised white imprisoned felons are examples.

An accumulation of individual exceptions could at some point overturn the basic rule of skin color hierarchy within or across groups; I cannot say when that point might be reached or how we would recognize it, but our nation is not now close to it. One might also ask whether "excessively" included exceptions are most likely to be economic (wealthy individuals), political (national leaders), or cultural (sports heroes or stars of popular culture). I also set that question aside for another day.

More important here is the fact that entire nationalities can be located at different points from where their racial or ethnic groups "belong" on the skin color continuum. For example, as of 1989 the median U.S. family income was just over $30,000. But Filipino, Japanese, and Indian Americans had median family incomes of $47,000 or more and the latter two groups enjoyed extremely high per capita incomes as well. However, the median family income for Cambodian, Laotian, and Hmong Americans ranged from $14,000 to $23,000 (Lien 2001, 175–76). The same pattern holds for education, poverty status, and proportions holding a professional or managerial job.[16] The best-off Asian nationalities are lighter-skinned than the worst-off, so the skin tone hypothesis continues to hold within the Asian race. But Japanese are not usually considered lighter than European Americans or Hmong darker than African Americans—so the standard skin tone hierarchy is violated when Asian nationality groups are compared with whites or blacks. Subcontinental Indians present another complexity; the skin-tone hierarchy holds within this group, but it is confounded in complicated ways when Indians are lumped together with other Asians.

The question again arises: when will these sorts of nationality-based exceptions accumulate enough to topple the basic rule that levels of inclusion parallel lightness of complexion? But in the case of groups as in the case of individuals, the rule is not yet in danger even from these important anomalies.

DO RACIAL IDENTITY AND COMMITMENT FOLLOW THE SKIN COLOR HIERARCHY?

The main answer to that question is, we do not know. The evidence is sparse, inconsistent, and unsystematic. Some data suggest that dark-skinned people correctly perceive that their complexion is associated with a high degree of exclusion, as the skin color hierarchy would predict. In 1968 and 1980, for example, dark-skinned African Americans reported more discrimination than did their light-skinned counterparts (Edwards 1972; Keith and Herring 1991; see also Ransford 1970). The 1968 survey also showed that dark-skinned blacks perceived whites to be more hostile and untrustworthy than did light-skinned blacks and "suggest[ed] a greater sense of black pride or identification with blackness among the darker population." The differences between dark- and light-skinned African Americans were small but consistent, and they persisted when gender or (to a lesser degree) family income were controlled (Edwards 1972, p. 79). In the 1990s, dark-skinned working class black men perceived more bias from police and courts (Krieger et al. 1998). Among Mexican American students in the 1990s, "dark-skinned subjects, who reported being oriented towards the Mexican culture, identified mostly with the ethnic community and least with the Anglo community" (quotation from Montalvo and Codina 2001, 330, citing Vasquez et al. 1997). Another study similarly found that light-skinned Mexican Americans perceived less discrimination (Arce et al. 1987).

But researchers have also found the reverse, which would work against the skin color hypothesis. In the Coronary Artery Risk Development in Young Adults (CARDIA) survey, light-skinned men of all economic classes perceived more bias at school (Krieger et al. 1998). Similarly, in another study, "the highest levels of interest in the Latino community occurred among those who self-reported having intermediate skin-color and regarded themselves as bicultural" (Montalvo and Codina 2001, 330, citing Vasquez et al. 1997). One analyst "described whiteness as a 'bleaching' agent that could rob her of her culture, language, and Chicana identity if she was not diligent about consistently reasserting it" (Hunter 2002, 179, describing Moraga 1983), and others found that English-speaking Mexican American women were much more likely to call themselves brown and less likely to call themselves white than were their Spanish-speaking counterparts. The color brown "is associated with mestizo heritage. . . . Choosing 'brown' is probably more related to increased awareness of the ethnic group than to racial identification with one's individual appearance" (Montalvo and Codina 2001, 332; see also Mason and Martinez 1998).

Finally, some studies find little or no effect of skin color on racial or ethnic identity or perceptions of exclusion from mainstream society. In the CARDIA survey, skin color was not associated with reports of racial discrimination in five out of seven specified situations (Krieger et al. 1998; see also Hughes and Hertel 1990). Light-skinned African Americans have taken dark-skinned African Americans to court with claims of color discrimination—and the reverse; so far plaintiffs have won none of these cases (Russell, Wilson, and

Hall 1992, chap. 8). The growth of a politically active multiracial movement, and a proliferation of small groups who identify as multiracial, mulatto, mestizo, or hapa further complicates the picture (Williams 2003, DaCosta 2003). It is not clear how widespread this new identity is or how consequential it will be. Nevertheless, defining oneself as a mestizo or hapa or joining a group of like-minded others has a very different connotation from identification as mulatto by a census enumerator a century ago. If these movements grow, they will confound conventional racial or ethnic identifications and might change the perception and practice of racial exclusion.

TOWARD A PARADIGM SHIFT

The evidence for a single continuum of skin color that cuts across nominal racial and ethnic categories, or even for multiple parallel skin color continua within categories, is not tidy. But neither is the world. The politics of democratic inclusion or exclusion are shifting, and we simply cannot predict how far these changes will go and with what political or social consequences. These shifts include: challenges from both within and outside the black community to the one-drop rule for defining African Americans; the growth of multiraciality in fact, political standing, and social and emotional legitimacy; the growth and dissemination of the Latino population, such that most Americans will have to come to grips with the concept and practice of mestizaje; and the changing status of Asian Americans, with the implication that Americans need to reconsider the implications of "minority" status. For these reasons and more, nominal racial and ethnic categories are blurring around the edges and their social meaning is becoming less and less settled. Skin color has always mattered within racial or ethnic groups, but its import for inclusion or exclusion from the polity may be growing as traditional group categorizations are loosening their hold.

"Skin color hierarchy" encapsulates these profound changes. Whether any of this represents an improvement in the sorry story of American racial domination and exclusion or is simply another way to reify old racial or ethnic hierarchies remains to be seen. That will depend on demographic changes, the state of the economy and the practice of important institutions, political leadership, and choices by the citizenry not yet conceived of, never mind made. Instead of predictions, then, I conclude with some judgments about the meaning of this shift—if it persists—for a liberal democratic polity as the United States purports to be.

From the perspective of the individual, moving from a strict and simple racial and ethnic hierarchy of nominal groups to a more fluid continuum within or cutting across groups might be liberating. Children with one black and one Hispanic parent, or one Asian and one Anglo parent, for example, need not feel forced to choose one heritage over the other; light-skinned blacks can elide the painful choice to "pass" or stigma of "passing"; and dark-skinned whites can avoid the appellation of "wigger" if barriers across races become more permeable. Degrees of inclusion would depend less than they now do on physical appearance, which one cannot control. From the vantage point of liberal individualism, this will be an advance.

However, a focus on skin tone rather than race is simultaneously deeply troubling for individuals, especially if it does not generate new identities outside traditional racial or ethnic groups. Attention to phenotype has an intensely personal quality; categorization as "black" or "white" is cruder and therefore less directly relevant to a person's self-image than categorization as "light-skinned black" or "dark-skinned white." A discussion of skin tone always evokes uncomfortable anecdotes about variations within one's family or community and its consequences for differential treatment and self-image,

More theoretically, focusing on skin color risks shifting our analytic and behavioral explanations for inclusion or exclusion from structures and institutions onto relationships among people. Political and economic institutions create and maintain the basic nominal hierarchy, reinforced by and reifying racial sentiments; those institutions clearly have a major impact on which individuals and groups are included in the polity. But variations within that racial and ethnic order, and boundary blurrings across its categories, cannot be blamed in any simple way on institutions or external oppression. The variations grow out of, but move beyond, the institutions that structure inclusion and exclusion, superiority and inferiority. It is intensely infuriating to be an "invisible man" in a white-dominated society, but at least that can be explained in terms of something outside oneself. It may be worse to feel oneself to be the object of "the gaze" or to know oneself to be participating in such a gaze.

In short, from the perspective of the individual, focusing on skin tone, or phenotype more generally, does not make the institutions that foster democratic inclusion or exclusion disappear, but it does make them recede into the background—for better in some cases and for worse in others.

From the perspective of most actors concerned with civil rights and voting rights laws, attention to a skin color continuum is deeply problematic (Williams forthcoming 2005). Representatives of the NAACP, National Council of La Raza, and other racial advocacy groups testified against creating a multiracial option on the 2000 census on the grounds that it would make it very difficult to enforce the Voting Rights Act and similar laws.[17] The former chief of racial statistics at the census bureau concurs, arguing that the new census categorization

> leaves the entire statistical mechanism for monitoring and enforcing civil rights vulnerable to a successful challenge in courts.... The nation should certainly determine ... whether it still wishes to monitor and enforce equal opportunity legislation using the current methods and systems of assessing disparate impact.... However, the system should not crumble because federal statisticians. [did not] understand ... the full ramifications of their revisions.... They are placing that system [of civil rights monitoring and enforcement] in jeopardy. (Harrison 2002, 159)

In this view, in other words, moving from a legal and political focus on nominal racial groups to a focus on racial combinations and permutations will reinforce the old and persistent forms of exclusion.

Some proponents of multiracialism do in fact endorse the blurring of racial categories through the census and other means precisely because they anticipate that it will make it more difficult to pursue race-based policies. Prominent examples include former speaker of the House of Representatives Newt Gingrich and the libertarian Center for Equal Opportunity (Clegg 2002 [general counsel for Center for Equal Opportunity]).[18] In their view, racial and ethnic exclusion has been abolished, legally and behaviorally; it is time to move beyond concerns about group exclusion to a focus on individual self-definition, hopefully with little racial content at all.

Just to confuse matters, other proponents of multiracialism *are* deeply committed to traditional civil rights enforcement, but add that multiracial individuals are themselves excluded from full participation in the American polity and therefore merit attention on their own terms. As Ramona Douglass, former president of the Association of MultiEthnic Americans, put it, the change in the 2000 census "allow[s] for the celebration of diverse heritages, support[s] the continued monitoring of existing civil rights legislation, ... and provide[s] the most information for the accurate collection of racial/ethnic data for medical diagnosis and research" (Douglass 2002, 1–2).

So the debate over "mark one or more" involves almost all possible positions: full inclusion requires continued focus on nominal racial or ethnic groups; full inclusion requires us to stop focusing on nominal groups; full inclusion requires continued focus on nominal groups *and* attention to newly emergent, crosscutting groups. (There is also a small segment of the multiracial community arguing that full inclusion is best attained by focusing *only* on multiracial groups, which in this view are a large segment of the American population.)

Multiracialism is not the same thing as a skin color hierarchy, although its increased visibility will be necessary for the hierarchy to move from parallel continua within each racial or ethnic group to the radical hypothesis of a single continuum across groups. Multiracials represent in my view the positive possibilities of a single continuum—a nation in which racial identity and identification are part of what matters about individuals and groups, but not dispositive and not confining. Just as fluidity in racial lines can be liberating for individuals, it could possibly become liberating for the nation, moving us closer to David Hollinger's postethnic America in which race continues to matter, but only as much as or in ways that people want it to (Hollinger 2000). No one can think that we are there yet, but arguably a move from nominal groups to an ordinal continuum is a step in the right direction, to the degree that it suggests that institutions and hierarchies are permeable rather than solid.[19]

A skin color hierarchy, however, can exclude as much as it can include—or possibly it can only include *because* it simultaneously excludes. One must not forget that a skin color hierarchy is based on, requires, traditional—even atavistic—associations of darkness with low status and lightness with high status. If a skin color hierarchy connotes shades of whiteness rather than multiracial fluidity or cultural mestizaje, then giving flexibility to the racial and ethnic order by allowing people maneuvering room at the top margins of each group simply strengthens that order, just as brittle iron becomes stronger by adding alloys to give it the flexibility of steel. That is, if a continuum (or multiple continua) of skin color simply allows the best-off members of a group to escape any sense of connection with their group or any commitment to abolishing the racial and ethnic hierarchy that permits their inclusion in the higher status group, then individual liberation comes at the considerable cost of group and national reification. In that case, the institutions that have changed enough to make skin color publicly salient will be engaged simultaneously in generating more democratic inclusion (for the lucky) and deeper exclusion (for the unlucky). That is not an appealing image.

NOTES

Acknowledgments. My thanks to participants in the conference and the participants in the Cluster on Immigrant Incorporation at the Radcliffe Institute for Advanced Studies; and Victoria Hattam, Vesla Weaver, Traci Burch, and two anonymous reviewers for very helpful comments and suggestions. Many thanks also to the Radcliffe Institute, the Guggenheim Foundation, the Weatherhead Center for International Affairs at Harvard University, and the Mellon Foundation for support.

1. Lucas 2000, 467; Graham 2000, 4.

2. Other reasons for mistrusting these projections include the fact that they depend on a continuation of current immigration laws, they pay little or no attention to differing and growing levels of intermarriage, and they necessarily make heroic assumptions about birth and death rates.

3. There are no new ideas; in the first paragraph of the introduction, Coon (1939) writes, "If there is one consistent theme in this book, it is that physical anthropology cannot be divorced from cultural and historical associations, and that there is no such thing as 'pure' biology, at least in reference to human beings" (vii).

4. The census bureau grouped seven categories into "Asian," and another four into "Native Hawaiian and Other Pacific Islander."

5. "The Mexican government responded with an official protest to the effect that all Mexicans are white and the category was dropped for the next few censuses" (Perlmann and Waters 2002, 5).

6. Almost half of Hispanics identified as white, more than 40 percent chose a nationality or "some other race," 4 percent chose black or one of the other named races, and about 6 percent reported two or more races.

7. This analysis did not include Native Americans, well over half of whom marry non-Native Americans.

8. These analyses did not treat Hispanics as a distinct category; doing so would presumably raise all of the numbers here.

9. There is a complicated relationship between skin color and broader phenotypic qualities that make a person look more or less European. For much of the following discussion, it would be appropriate to substitute "a more European appearance" for "lighter skin color." That substitution does not hold, however, for Asian Americans, who may be as light as or lighter than Europeans but do not have Anglo features. By focusing on skin color per se, I will ignore this complexity in this chapter.

10. This point raises the question of how to determine when changes stop being exceptions to a rule and become instead an indication that the rule no longer holds. This whole paper is an assertion that the paradigm of nominal racial or ethnic groups is so riddled by exceptions and changes that we should consider substituting a new one, or that a new paradigm is in the making through people's behavior regardless of our constructions. But I

cannot identify in the abstract the point at which the weight of more and more exceptions topples a standing rule.

11. Gold, says poor King Timon of Athens, "will make black white, foul fair, wrong right, base noble, old young, coward valiant" (William Shakespeare, *Timon of Athens*, act IV, scene iii).

12. Asians' preference for light skin may be partly due to the western colonial influence over the past few hundred years, but that is not the entire story. Centuries before westerners were known, Japanese literature depicted white skin as the most beautiful; upon first meeting westerners, in fact, Japanese in the 1960s often denigrated them as insufficiently light (Wagatsuma 1968).

13. Vesla Weaver and Traci Burch, both of Harvard University, and I are examining patterns of skin color overlap among groups, to the degree that it is possible with extant survey data. We will also analyze various characteristics of people who identify with more than one race.

14. For example, 49 percent of non-Hispanic white adults have a high school education or less, as do 41 percent of Asians and 73 percent of Latinos. Yet 40 percent of African American adults have at least some college, and 14 percent have a college degree or more.

15. In recent Gallup polls, Powell was the most popular political figure in the United States (Moore 2002).

16. From 1990 through 2001, roughly 9 percent of Anglos were poor; comparable rates for blacks averaged 28 percent, for Latinos 29 percent, and for Asian Americans, 13 percent (Bureau of the Census 2002, table 2). Fully 30 percent of Samoans and Vietnamese, however, were poor during the 1990s (Frey and Fielding 1995; see also Brackman and Erie 1995; Wyly 1997, table 3). Obviously, these outcomes are totally confounded with home country resources and recency of immigration, so I am not making any causal claims here.

17. See testimony or written statements by Rep. Eleanor Holmes Norton, Harold McDougall (director of the Washington bureau, NAACP), Eric Rodriguez (policy analyst for National Council of La Raza), JoAnn Chase (executive director of National Congress of American Indians), Jacinta Ma (legal fellow of National Asian Pacific American Legal Consortium), in U.S. House of Representatives (1997).

18. Speaker Gingrich testified in the census hearings on the multiracial option that "it is wrong for some Americans to begin creating subgroups to which they have a higher loyalty than to America at large.... America is too big and too diverse to categorize each and every one of us into four [*sic*] rigid racial categories.... Ideally, I believe we should have one box on federal forms that simply reads, 'American.' But if that is not possible at this point, ... allow[ing] them [i.e., Americans] the option of selecting the category 'multiracial', ... will be an important step toward transcending racial division and reflecting the melting pot which is America" (U.S. House of Representatives 1997, 661–662).

19. Thinking in terms of a skin color hierarchy, or even parallel continua within racial and ethnic groups, also has the advantage of allowing us to analyze the trajectories of different racial groups within the same theoretical framework. That might be an advantage that only an academic could love, but it is not one to be thrown away lightly absent a better broad framework.

REFERENCES

Allen, W., E, Telles, and M. Hunter. 2000. "Skin Color, Income and Education: A Comparison of African Americans and Mexican Americans." *National Journal of Sociology* 12(1): 129–180.

American Anthropological Association. 1998. "Statement on 'Race'." *American Anthropologist* 100: 712–713.

Anderson, M., and S. Fienberg. 1999. *Who Counts? The Politics of Census-Taking in Contemporary America.* New York: Russell Sage Foundation Press.

Arce, C., E. Murguia, and W. Frisbie. 1987. "Phenotype and Life Chances among Chicanos." *Hispanic Journal of Behavioral Sciences* 9(1): 19–32.

Bohara, A., and A. Davila. 1992. "A Reassessment of the Phenotypic Discrimination and Income Differences among Mexican Americans." *Social Science Quarterly* 73(1): 114–122.

Bond, S., and T. Cash. 1992. "Black Beauty: Skin Color and Body Images among African American College Women." *Journal of Applied Social Psychology* 22(11): 874–888.

Brackman, H., and S. Erie. 1995. "Beyond 'Politics by Other Means'? Empowerment Strategies for Los Angeles' Asian Pacific Community." In *The Bubbling Cauldron: Race, Ethnicity, and the Urban Crisis,* edited by M. P. Smith and J. Feagin, 282–303. Minneapolis: University of Minnesota Press.

Bureau of the Census. 2001. *The Two or More Races Population: 2000.* Washington, DC: U.S. Department of Commerce,

———. 2002. "Historical Poverty Tables." www.census.gov/hhes/poverty/histpov/hstpov2.html.

———, Current Population Survey. 2003. *Annual Demographic Survey,* Table HINC06. Income Distribution to $250,000 or More for Households: 2003. http://ferret.bls.census.gov/ macro/032004/hhinc/new06_000.htm.

———. 2004. *Educational Attainment in the United States: 2003.* Educational Attainment of the Population 15 Years and Over, by Age, Sex, Race, and Hispanic Origin: 2003. http//www.census.gov/population/www/socdemo/education/cps2003.html.

Cavalli-Sforza, L. L., P. Menozzi, and A. Piazza. 1994. *The History and Geography of Human Genes.* Princeton: Princeton University Press.

Codina, G. E., and F. Montalvo. 1994. "Chicano Phenotype and Depression." *Hispanic Journal of Behavioral Sciences* 6(3): 296–306.

Coon, C. 1939. *The Races of Europe.* New York: MacMillan Co.

Corrin, W., and T. Cook. 1999. *Spanning Racial Boundaries: Multiracial Adolescents and Their Families, Peers, Schools, and Neighborhoods.* Evanston, IL: Northwestern University, Institute for Policy Research, Working Paper 99-20.

Cotton, J. 1997. "Color or Culture? Wage Differences among Non-Hispanic Black Males, Hispanic Black Males, and Hispanic White Males." In *African Americans and Post-Industrial Labor Markets,* edited by J. Stewart, 61–75. New Brunswick, NJ: Transaction.

DaCosta, K. 2003 "Multiracial Identity: From Personal Problem to Public Issue." In *New Faces in a Changing America: Multiracial Identity in the 21st Century,* edited by L.Winters and H. DeBosse, 85–98. Thousand Oaks CA: Sage.

Davis, J., T. Smith, and P. Marsden. 2001 *General Social Surveys, 1972–2000: Cumulative Codebook.* Chicago, IL: National Opinion Research Center.

Denton, N., and D. Massey. 1989. "Racial Identity among Caribbean Hispanics: The Effect of Double Minority Status on Residential Segregation." *American Sociological Review* 54(5): 790–808.

Douglass, R. 2002. "Shaping the Multiracial Experience: AMEA Past, Present, and Future." AMEA's Multiracial Child Conference, Tucson, AZ.

Drake, S. C., and H. Cayton. 1993 [1945]. *Black Metropolis: A Study of Negro Life in a Northern City.* Chicago: University of Chicago Press.

Edwards, O. 1972. "Skin Color as a Variable in Racial Attitudes of Black Urbanites." *Journal of Black Studies* 3(4): 473–483.

Foner, N. 2000. *From Ellis Island to JFK: New York's Two Great Waves of Immigration.* New Haven: Yale University Press; Russell Sage Foundation Press.

Fredrickson, G. 2002. *Racism: A Short History.* Princeton: Princeton University Press.

Frey, W., and E. Fielding. 1995. "Changing Urban Populations: Regional Restructuring, Racial Polarization, and Poverty Concentration." *Cityscape* 1(2): 1–66.

George, R. 1997. "'From Expatriate Aristocrat to Immigrant Nobody': South Asian Racial Strategies in the Southern California Context." *Diaspora* 6(1): 31–60.

Gerstle, G. 1993. "The Working Class Goes to War." *Mid-America* 75(3): 303–322.

Goldstein, J. 1999. "Kinship Networks That Cross Racial Lines: The Exception or the Rule?" *Demography* 36(3): 399–407.

Goldstein, J., and A. Morning. 2000. "The Multiple-Race Population of the United States: Issues and Estimates." *Proceedings of the National Academy of Sciences* 97(11): 6230–6235.

Gomez, C. 2000. "The Continual Significance of Skin Color: An Exploratory Study of Latinos in the Northeast." *Hispanic Journal of Behavioral Sciences* 22(1): 94–103.

Graham, L. 2000. *Our Kind of People: Inside America's Black Upper Class.* New York: Harper.

Hahn, R., J. Mulinare, and S. Tetsch. 1992. "Inconsistencies in Coding of Race and Ethnicity Between Birth and Death in U.S. Infants: A New Look at Infant Mortality, 1983 through 1985." *Journal of the American Medical Association* 267(2): 259–263.

Hall, R. 1995. "The Bleaching Syndrome: African Americans' Response to Cultural Domination Vis-à-Vis Skin Color." *Journal of Black Studies* 26(2): 172–184.

Haney López, I. 1996. *White by Law: The Legal Construction of Race.* New York: New York University Press.

Harris, D. 2001. The Multiracial Count. *Washington Post*, March 24: A21

———. 2002. *In the Eye of the Beholder: Observed Race and Observer Characteristics.* Ann Arbor: University of Michigan, Population Studies Center Research Report 02-522.

———. 2003. "Does It Matter How We Measure? Racial Classification and the Characteristics of Multiracial Youth." In *The New Race Question: How the Census Counts Multiracial Individuals*, edited by J. Perlmann, and M. Waters, 62–101. New York: Russell Sage Foundation Press.

Harris, D., and J. Sim. 2000. *An Empirical Look at the Social Construction of Race: The Case of Mixed-Race Adolescents.* Ann Arbor: University of Michigan, Population Studies Center, Research Report 00–452.

———. 2002. "Who Is Multiracial? Assessing the Complexity of Lived Race." *American Sociological Review* 67(4): 614–27.

Harrison, R. 2002. "Inadequacies of Multiple-Response Race Data in the Federal Statistical System." In *The New Race Question: How the Census Counts Multiracial Individuals*, edited by J. Perlmann, and M. Waters, 137–160. New York: Russell Sage Foundation Press.

Hattam, V. 2004. "Ethnicity: An American Geneology," In *Not Just Black and White*, edited by N. Foner and G. Fredrickson, 42–60. New York: Russell Sage Foundation Press.

Hill, M. 2000. "Color Differences in the Socioeconomic Status of African American Men: Results of a Longitudinal Study." *Social Forces* 78(4): 1437–1460.

———. 2002. "Skin Color and the Perception of Attractiveness among African Americans: Does Gender Make a Difference?" *Social Psychology Quarterly* 65(1): 77–91.

Hirschman, C., R. Alba, and R. Farley. 2000. "The Meaning and Measurement of Race in the U.S. Census: Glimpses into the Future." *Demography* 37(3): 381–393.

Hochschild, J. 2002. "Multiple Racial Identifiers in the 2000 Census, and Then What?" In *The New Race Question: How the Census Counts Multiracial Individuals*, edited by J. Perlmann and M. Waters, 340–353. New York: Russell Sage Foundation Press.

Hollinger, D. 2000. *Postethnic America: Beyond Multiculturalism.* New York: Basic Books.

———. 2003. "Amalgamation and Hypodescent: The Question of Ethnoracial Mixture in the History of the United States." *American Historical Review* 108(5): 1363–1390.

Hood, M. V., III, and I. Morris. 1997. "¿Amigo o Enemigo?: Context, Attitudes, and Anglo Public Opinion toward Immigration." *Social Science Quarterly* 78(2): 309–323.

Hughes, M., and B. Hertel. 1990. "The Significance of Color Remains: A Study of Life Chances, Mate Selection, and Ethnic Consciousness among Black Americans." *Social Forces* 68(4): 1105–1120.

Hulse, F. 1967. "Selection for Skin Color among the Japanese." *American Journal of Physical Anthropology* 27: 143–156.

Hunter, M. 2002. "'If You're Light You're Alright': Light Skin Color as Social Capital for Women of Color." *Gender & Society* 16(2): 175–193.

Ignatiev, N. 1996. *How the Irish Became White*. New York: Routledge.

International Committee of Medical Journal Editors. 2001. "Uniform Requirements for Manuscripts Submitted to Biomedical Journals," *The Lancet*. 2002.

Jacobson, M. 1998. *Whiteness of a Different Color: European Immigrants and the Alchemy of Race*. Cambridge: Harvard University Press.

Johnson, J. J., W. Farrell, and J. Stoloff. 1998. "The Declining Social and Economic Fortunes of African American Males: A Critical Assessment of Four Perspectives." *Review of Black Political Economy* 25(4): 17–40.

Johnson, K., ed. 2003. *Mixed Race America and the Law*. New York: New York University Press.

Jones, T. 2000. "Shades of Brown: The Law of Skin Color." *Duke Law Journal* 49: 1487–1557.

Kao, G. 1999. "Racial Identity and Academic Performance: An Examination of Biracial Asian and African Youth." *Journal of Asian American Studies* 2(3): 223–249.

Kasinitz, P. 1992. *Caribbean New York: Black Immigrants and the Politics of Race*. Ithaca, NY: Cornell University Press.

Keith, V., and C. Herring. 1991. "Skin Tone and Stratification in the Black Community." *American Journal of Sociology* 97(3): 760–778.

Kennedy, R. 2003. *Interracial Intimacies: Sex, Marriage, Identity, and Adoption*. New York: Pantheon Books.

Krieger, N., S. Sidney, and E. Cookley. 1998. "Racial Discrimination and Skin Color in the CARDIA Study: Implications for Public Health Research." *American Journal of Public Health* 88(9): 1308–1313.

Lawrence-Lightfoot, S. 1995. *Balm in Gilead: Journey of a Healer*. New York: Penguin.

Lieberson, S., and M. Waters, 1988. *From Many Strands: Ethnic and Racial Groups in Contemporary American*. New York, Russell Sage Foundation: Press.

Lien, P. 2001. *The Making of Asian America through Political Participation*. Philadelphia: Temple University Press.

Lucas, S. 2000. "Hope, Anguish, and the Problem of Our Time: An Essay on Publication of *The Black-White Test Score Gap*." *Teachers College Record* 102(2): 461–73.

Maddox, K., and S. Gray. 2002. "Cognitive Representations of Black Americans: Reexploring the Role of Skin Tone." *Personality and Social Psychology Bulletin* 28(2): 250–259.

Mason, P., and P. Martinez. 1998. "Is Race Endogenous? Some Preliminary Evidence on Latinos." www.nd.edu/~pmason/paperMasnMart.pdf.

McBride, J. 1996. *The Color of Water: A Black Man's Tribute to His White Mother*. New York: Riverhead Books, Putnam's.

McRoy, R., and H. Grape. 1999. "Skin Color in Transracial and Inracial Adoptive Placements: Implications for Special Needs Adoptions." *Child Welfare* 78(5): 673–692.

Menchaca, M. 2001. *Recovering History, Constructing Race: The Indian, Black, and White Roots of Mexican Americans*. Austin: University of Texas Press.

Montalvo, F., and G. E. Codina. 2001. "Skin Color and Latinos in the United States." *Ethnicities* 1(3): 321–341.

Moore, D., 2002. "Powell Remains Most Popular Political Figure in America," Gallup Poll. June 30. www.gallup.com/poll/releases/pr020930.asp?Version=p

Moraga, C. 1983. "La Guera." In *This Bridge Called My Back: Radical Writings by Women of Color*, edited by G. Anzaldua and C. Moraga. New York: Kitchen Table Press.

Morgan, E. 1975. *American Slavery, American Freedom: The Ordeal of Colonial Virginia.* New York: Norton.

Murguia, E., and E. Telles. 1996. "Phenotype and Schooling among Mexican Americans." *Sociology of Education* 69(4): 276–289.

Omi, M., and H. Winant. 1994. *Racial Formation in the United States.* New York: Routledge.

Pan, E. 2000. "Why Asian Guys Are on a Roll." *Newsweek*: 48–51.

Pascoe, P. 1996. "Miscegenation Law, Court Cases, and Ideologies of 'Race' in Twentieth-Century America." *Journal of American History* 83(1): 44–69.

Perlmann, J. 2002. The Intermingling of Peoples in the United States: Intermarriage and the Population History of Ethnic and Racial Groups since 1880. Levy Economics Institute of Bard College: Proposal to Russell Sage Foundation.

Perlmann, J., and M. Waters. 2002. "Introduction." In *The New Race Question: How the Census Counts Multiracial Individuals,* edited by J. Perlmann and M. Waters, 1–30. New York: Russell Sage Foundation Press.

Pollack, A. 2003. "DNA of Blacks to Be Gathered to Fight Illness." New York Times, May 27:A1.

Prewitt, K. 2002. "Race in the 2000 Census: A Turning Point." In *The New Race Question: How the Census Counts Multiracial Individuals,* edited by J. Perlmann and M. Waters, 352–361. New York: Russell Sage Foundation Press.

Qian, Z. 1997. "Breaking the Racial Barriers: Variations in Interracial Marriage between 1980 and 1990." *Demography* 34(2): 263–276.

Ransford, H. E. 1970. "Skin Color, Life Chances, and Anti-White Attitudes." *Social Problems* 18(2): 164–179.

Relethford, J., M. Stern, S. Gaskill, and H. Hazuda. 1983. "Social Class, Admixture, and Skin Color Variation in Mexican Americans and Anglo-Americans Living in San Antonio, Texas." *American Journal of Physical Anthropology* 6(1): 97–102.

Risch, N., E. Burchard, E. Ziv, and H. Tang. 2002. "Categorization of Humans in Biomedical Research: Genes, Race, and Disease." *Genome Biology* 3(7): 1–12.

Rogers, R. 2001. "Black Like Who? Afro-Caribbean Immigrants, African-Americans, and the Politics of Group Identity." In *Islands in the City: West Indian Migration to New York,* edited by N. Foner, 163–192. Berkeley: University of California Press.

Ross, L. 1997. "Mate Selection Preferences among African American College Students." *Journal of Black Studies* 27(4): 554–569.

Rumbaut, R. 2002. Handout on "Inequality and Achievement Paths among Children of Immigrants in Early Adulthood: A Decade-Long Panel Study." December 2. Cambridge, MA: Harvard University, Kennedy School of Government.

Russell, K., M. Wilson, and R. Hall. 1992. *The Color Complex: The Politics of Skin Color among African Americans.* New York: Harcourt Brace Jovanovich.

Sahay, S., and N. Piran. 1997. "Skin-Color Preferences and Body Satisfaction among South Asian-Canadian and European-Canadian Female University Students." *Journal of Social Psychology* 137(2): 161–71.

Saito, M., J. Matsumoto, A. Date, and J. Li. 2001. "Beyond the Pale." *SPC Asia* 25: 18–22.

Satel, S. 2001–2002. "Medicine's Race Problem." *Policy Review* 110: 49–58.

Seltzer, R., and R. Smith. 1991. "Color Differences in the Afro-American Community and the Differences They Make." *Journal of Black Studies* 21(3): 279–286.

Smith, T., and G. Dempsey. 1983. "Ethnic Social Distance and Prejudice." *Public Opinion Quarterly* 47(4): 584–600.

Sollors, W., ed. 1989. *The Invention of Ethnicity.* New York: Oxford University Press.

————. 2000. *Interracialism: Black-White Intermarriage in American History, Literature, and Law.* New York: Oxford University Press.

Strickland, R. A., and M. L. Whicker. 1992. "Comparing the Wilder and Gantt Campaigns: A Model for Black Candidate Success in Statewide Elections." *PS: Political Science and Politics,* 25(2): 204–212.

Tafoya, S. 2002. "Mixed Race and Ethnicity in California." In *The New Race Question: How the Census Counts Multiracial Individuals,* edited by J. Perlmann and M. Waters, 102–115. New York: Russell Sage Foundation Press.

Telles, E., and N. Lim. 1998. "Does It Matter Who Answers the Race Question? Racial Classification and Income Inequality in Brazil." *Demography* 35(4): 465–474.

Telles, E., and E. Murguia. 1990. "Phenotypic Discrimination and Income Differences among Mexican Americans." *Social Science Quarterly* 71(4): 682–696.

Terkildsen, N. 1993. "When White Voters Evaluate Black Candidates: The Processing Implications of Candidate Skin Color, Prejudice, and Self-Monitoring." *American Journal of Political Science* 37(4): 1032–1053.

U.S. House of Representatives. 1997. Hearings on "Federal Measures of Race and Ethnicity and the Implications for the 2000 Census." Subcommittee on Government Management, Information, and Technology of the Committee on Government Reform and Oversight. April 23, May 22, July 25.

Vasquez, L., E. Garcia-Vázquez, S. Bauman, and A. Sierra. 1997. "Skin Color, Acculturation, and Community Interest in Mexican American Students: A Research Note." *Hispanic Journal of Behavioral Sciences* 19(3): 377–386.

Wagatsuma, H. 1968. "The Social Perception of Skin Color in Japan." In *Color and Race,* edited by J. H. Franklin, 129–165. Boston: Houghton Mifflin.

Waters, M. 2001. *Black Identities: West Indian Immigrant Dreams and American Realities.* Cambridge: Harvard University Press.

Williams, K. 2003. *The Next Step in Civil Rights? The American Multiracial Movement.* Cambridge: Harvard University, John F. Kennedy School of Government.

————. forthcoming 2005. *Race Counts: American Multiracialism & Civil Rights Politics.* Ann Arbor: University of Michigan Press.

Wyly, E. 1997. *Social Trends and the State of the Nation's Cities.* New Brunswick, NJ: Rutgers University, Center for Urban Policy Research.

3 / Reviving Group Consciousness

GROUP CONSCIOUSNESS has been a key concept for understanding how racial minorities and newcomers to the United States have overcome prejudice, discrimination, and socioeconomic barriers to achieve democratic inclusion. The feelings of identification and solidarity that accompany group consciousness have helped motivate these groups to engage in collective action to secure equal rights in American society. The concept thus holds an important place in most accounts of how immigrants, African Americans, and other disadvantaged minorities have struggled to achieve political incorporation in this country.

The impact of group consciousness on political behavior first began to draw serious attention from political scientists in early studies of political participation among blacks and whites. Whites on average proved to be significantly more active in politics than were blacks. This finding was hardly surprising. Whites have a greater share of socioeconomic resources like education and income that are known to facilitate political engagement and activity. More remarkable was the discovery that blacks appeared to participate at *higher* rates than whites after controlling for differences in socioeconomic status (Orum 1966; Verba and Nie 1972).

Researchers hypothesized that a pronounced group consciousness among African Americans gave them an additional or alternative source of motivation to engage in political activity beyond the standard socioeconomic resources (Olsen 1970; Verba and Nie 1972; Shingles 1981). Studies of the civil rights movement, for example, suggested that group consciousness helped galvanize thousands of disadvantaged African Americans to engage in collective action and demand the equal rights that would pave the way for their political incorporation (McAdam 1982; Morris 1984; Chong 1991). The classic literature on early immigrants to the United States also emphasized group identification as a resource for political engagement. Group identification was believed to motivate participation among newcomers who might otherwise find American politics confusing or daunting, owing to their lack of knowledge and resources (Dahl 1961; Wolfinger 1965). Among the triumvirate of factors that promote participation—civic skills and resources, psychological engagement, and political mobilization—group consciousness was another psychological resource that made politics relevant to people's lives and supplied them with reasons to become active.

This hypothesis has been tested over the years with mixed results in a number of studies of African Americans. It also has been reexamined in recent scholarship on the political participation of other racial minority groups in the United States, such as Asians and Latinos. Earlier studies conducted in the 1960s and 1970s generally confirmed that racial consciousness boosted rates of participation. But more recent studies have suggested that the effects of consciousness among both blacks and other minorities have moderated, if not faded entirely, leading some to speculate that it is no longer a critical psychological resource for political participation and democratic inclusion.

In this chapter, we examine this research and explore the reasons behind the inconsistent findings. We offer evidence from a reanalysis of the 1984 National Black Election Study (NBES) that the influence of group consciousness may depend critically on how consciousness is conceptualized and measured and on which types of political participation are studied. In so doing, we elaborate on a theory of group solidarity that might be applied to future research on the political effects of group consciousness among blacks, Latinos, Asians, and other minorities. Finally, we discuss why researchers should exercise caution before transferring to research on new racial minorities the approach to group consciousness already developed in studies of blacks.

GROUP IDENTIFICATION AND GROUP CONSCIOUSNESS AMONG AFRICAN AMERICANS

Group *identification* refers to an individual's sense of belonging or attachment to a social group. Group *consciousness*, in contrast, combines basic in-group identification with a set of ideological beliefs about the group's status and alternative means to improving it.[1] The political science literature has not always differentiated between the components of identification and consciousness. Some researchers have used the terms interchangeably, loosely, or inconsistently, with the result that consciousness sometimes refers to a narrow form of group identification and other times to a more complex belief system. In our review of the literature, we follow the terminology originally employed by individual authors, while also focusing on their operationalization of identification and consciousness to illustrate the different approaches to measuring these concepts.

Most of the early research on the political effects of group consciousness concentrated exclusively on African Americans. Researchers routinely included group consciousness as a key variable in analyses of black participation and policy preferences, but rarely did so in the case of whites (for an exception, see Hagner and Pierce 1984). They assumed that group identification held political significance for whites in their first generation as immigrants but ceased to have any meaningful influence on their attitudes and behavior once they melted into the American mainstream (Dahl 1961). The attention paid to African Americans in the literature, on the other hand, was linked to the concept of relative deprivation emphasized in early psychological models of group consciousness. Researchers cast group consciousness as a concept more useful for understanding participation among blacks because of their long history of disadvantage relative to whites. The literature's concentration on group consciousness among African Americans has thus reinforced the thinking that the concept best applies to subordinate minority groups that have yet to achieve full democratic inclusion, although, in principle, the concept would seem relevant to all social groups.[2]

The earliest quantitative analyses confirmed that racial minority group consciousness could provide a motivation to participate in politics separate from other individual or collective resources. In their analysis of a 1967 national survey, Verba and Nie (1972) found that blacks who evinced racial consciousness in the manner in which they discussed political issues were more likely to participate in politics than non–racially conscious blacks and whites of similar socioeconomic status. Olsen (1970) subsequently corroborated this result in finding that blacks who expressed racial identification participated at higher levels than whites across a variety of political activities after controlling for education and income. Racial identification appeared to be a proxy for membership in a community that exerted normative pressure on individuals to think in group terms and to contribute to collective goals.

But what exactly are the mechanisms that connect racial identification and consciousness to political participation? Several early studies specified models that explain how collective sentiments translate into political actions. Shingles' (1981) reanalysis of the 1967 Verba and Nie participation survey is the most powerful available demonstration of how group consciousness affects attitudes and behavior. Shingles (1981) provided empirical support for several psychological links: consciousness promotes political efficacy, but also reduces political trust, a potent combination that contributes to greater political activism especially among lower-income blacks (77).

The psychological dynamic works as follows: Black consciousness turns the blame for unequal racial outcomes away from the individual toward the system. Attributing responsibility to the system for unequal group outcomes produces stronger feelings of personal efficacy. Efficacy and trust are thus inversely related to each other. High trust and high efficacy lead to allegiant participation while low trust and high efficacy produce protest activity.

Shingles (1981) found that blacks who display group consciousness are substantially more efficacious than either blacks who are less racially conscious or whites of all income levels. Low-income, racially conscious blacks express greater feelings of efficacy than even high-income white respondents.[3] Poor whites participate less than poor blacks because they do not have a comparable ideology that raises their sense of efficacy and places blame for their predicament on the political system.

Miller et al. (1981) similarly argued that there is a multiple-step progression from identification and consciousness to political activity. They presented a general model of group consciousness and political participation that combines group identification with beliefs about the group's status in society. In their model, there is no necessary direct relationship between simple identification and participation; instead, the relationship is mediated by several intervening cognitive factors.

The authors identified four components of group consciousness: (1) identification with the group—that is, a belief that one shares interests with other group members; (2) favoritism toward one's own group; (3) discontent with the relative status of one's own group; and (4) attribution of blame to the injustice of the political system rather than to one's own actions. Using evidence from the 1972–1976 National Election Study, Miller et al. (1981)

demonstrated that it is the conjunction of these factors that produces activism in the political arena. Each of these factors therefore is generally insufficient to propel participation; but when they are present simultaneously, the likelihood of participation increases significantly.[4]

More recent studies, however, have not found the same positive correlation between group consciousness and political participation. Newer models typically have relied on a more limited conceptualization of group identification that combines a feeling of closeness to other group members with a belief that one's own life is affected by the status of the group as a whole—often referred to as acceptance of a "common fate." Tate (1993) found that this measure of group identification is significantly related to voting and campaign activism, but that the effect is modest. She considers identification to be a "soft" resource that is secondary to more substantial organizational resources such as church membership. Tate (1993) also speculated that because levels of group identification are high among blacks and have not fluctuated greatly since the 1960s, they cannot explain much variation in participation (92).

Other studies in the last decade or so (Verba, Schlozman, and Brady 1995; Leighley and Vedlitz 1999; Marschall 2001) have also been unable to reproduce the positive effect of group consciousness on African American participation rates. In their 1989 national study of political participation, for instance, Verba, Schlozman, and Brady tested the effect of group consciousness in a model that included indicators of individual skills and organizational resources and several other measures of psychological engagement, including political interest, awareness, and efficacy (1995, 343–344). They found that of the four psychological elements, political interest is the most powerful determinant of participation followed by political information. Group consciousness has a surprisingly negligible influence.

NEW MINORITY GROUPS: ASIANS AND LATINOS

Although the empirical significance of group consciousness appears to have diminished in most recent studies on African American participation, the concept may very well be resurrected in the emerging research on the political behavior of Asians and Latinos in the United States. Researchers studying these minority populations have taken their cues for understanding group consciousness from the existing scholarship on African Americans. The assumption seems to be that consciousness will play the same mobilizing role in these groups' quest for democratic inclusion as it did in the case of African Americans. Most of the recent work on these other minority groups explores individual attachments to group identity and its impact on political behavior— largely the same line of inquiry researchers have long pursued in the case of African Americans.

It is perhaps still too early in the development of this new literature to draw any definitive conclusions about general patterns in the research findings. Nevertheless, there are some preliminary trends worth noting. Several studies have found that modest proportions of Asians and Latinos subscribe to a panethnic identity; but there is significant variation in the level of attachment to that identity across subgroups (Jones-Correa and Leal 1996; Lien 2001; Lien et al. 2001). Moreover, Asians and Latinos are both more apt to choose their specific ethnicity or nationality, say Korean or Mexican, over a panethnic label as their primary form of self-identification (de la Garza et al. 1992; Jones-Correa and Leal 1996; Lien et al. 2001). In fact, de la Garza et al. (1992) concluded that national-origin identification is the overwhelming preference of most Latinos, with panethnic labels trailing well behind.

There is a hint of one other interesting trend in the research findings on panethnic identification among Asians and Latinos. A few studies suggest that this form of identification may increase with long-term adjustment to life in the United States (Fugita and O'Brien 1985; Jones-Correa and Leal 1996; Lien 2001). Jones-Correa and Leal (1996) found that later-generation better-educated Latinos are more likely to embrace a panethnic identity. Similarly, Lien's study reveals that Asians who are registered voters are more inclined to express panethnic concerns, although her analysis fails to turn up any clear correlation between this form of identity and education or length of residence.

These findings vaguely suggest that panethnic identification among these groups may be a product of American socialization; more to the point, exposure to some of the adaptive norms of the United States may very well increase panethnic identification among Asians and Latinos. That possibility does beg an intriguing question: that is, whether panethnic identification is an indication of straightforward group attachment, or rather, a signal of growing "American-ness" among Asians and Latinos. Whatever the case, these early findings suggest that there is some modest basis for panethnic identification among these minority groups; but individual attachment to this form of identity is highly contingent on a number of factors. The latter observation is, in fact, the emerging consensus in the literature.

There is no such line of agreement, however, in the research on the political effects of group identity among these minority populations. Extant studies have yet to turn up consistent evidence of a relationship between group identity and participation for Asians and Latinos. Indeed, a number of studies—using a range of simple traditional measures of group identification or consciousness—have concluded that there is no reliable positive correlation between these forms of identity and political participation (Uhlaner, Cain, and Kiewiet 1989; Lien 1994; Verba, Schlozman, and Brady 1995; Leighley and Vedlitz 1999).[5] Several authors are puzzled by this result. The assumption is that group consciousness ought to have the same positive impact on political engagement and participation among these minority groups as it had in earlier studies of African Americans.

Nonetheless, these findings are consistent with the more recent research on black political behavior, which likewise has turned up weak or insignificant effects for group consciousness. To be fair, a few studies have found a positive relationship between identification or consciousness and some types of civic engagement. In analyses using different measures of group consciousness and identification, Jones-Correa and Leal (1996) and Marschall (2001) demonstrated that these forms of identity motivate Latinos to attend community meetings and participate in a handful of other nonelectoral activities.

Still, there are some curious inconsistencies even in these findings.[6] All told, there is no reliable pattern of a positive correlation between group identity and political participation in the literature on Asians and Latinos.

THEORETICAL AND CONCEPTUAL ISSUES

These uneven findings might be interpreted as a signal that group consciousness is no longer a powerful predictor of political behavior in the United States. After all, the relevance or currency of the concept among minority groups may be diminishing with the decline in racial inequalities over the last quarter-century. If group consciousness is mostly applicable to disadvantaged minority populations struggling to achieve democratic inclusion, some researchers speculate that it is sure to lose its political significance as these groups improve their lot (Bobo and Gilliam 1990; Verba, Schlozman, and Brady 1995). Others suggest that class has replaced race as a source of group identification, especially among upwardly mobile minorities (Wilson 1978, 1980).

Neither of these conclusions is altogether convincing. First, racism remains a serious problem for the United States. Most surveys find that racial minorities—especially blacks, but Asians and Latinos as well—remain acutely aware of their vulnerability to continuing discrimination. Second, although the middle-class ranks of minority populations have increased considerably in recent decades, there is little evidence that upward mobility or emerging class divisions have vitiated racial group consciousness. Indeed, some studies of African Americans have revealed that middle-class individuals express stronger feelings of racial group consciousness than do their lower status counterparts (e.g., Dawson 1994; Hochschild 1995). Further, racial and class consciousness may reinforce each other instead of being mutually exclusive as they are often represented in the literature.

We offer several alternative hypotheses for the finding of weak or negligible effects of consciousness on participation. One possibility is that some of the disparate results can be explained by variations in the conceptualization and operationalization of group identification and consciousness. A second possibility is that these studies have not taken adequate account of the complexity and heterogeneity of ideological beliefs and identifications in a minority population that might foster psychological engagement with politics. Finally, the connection between consciousness and political activity may not be equally manifest across political activities, but may be stronger for certain forms of participation than for others.

Measures

Group identification and consciousness have been measured in a number of different ways in the research literature. Tate (1993), for example, builds a measure of group identification using only two items from the 1984 NBES, asking respondents whether they are affected by what happens to blacks in this country and the degree to which they think consciously about being black (90). Verba, Schlozman, and Brady employ a more complex measure, combining multiple items that tap into feelings of closeness to the group, perceptions of common problems, experiences with discrimination, and support for government programs to help the group.

Taking her cues from Shingles (1981), Marschall (2001) uses a combined measure of low political trust and high political efficacy as a proxy for group consciousness. Leighley and Vedlitz (1999) construct a model of group consciousness utilizing the closeness item and an intergroup distance scale. Others have used a simple item asking whether a respondent identifies as a member of a particular group (Jones-Correa and Leal 1996). Clearly, there is little consistency in how group consciousness and identification have been measured in the literature.

Degrees of Group Identification and Consciousness

Perhaps, even more critically, most existing models in the literature also do not take full account of the complexity of group consciousness. Group consciousness can be conceptualized either narrowly or broadly, depending on whether we are testing the effect of basic psychological identification with a group or the influence of ideological beliefs and evaluations that comprise a more expansive consciousness. It is likely, as the earliest studies suggested, that the effects of identification and consciousness increase the more we account for the intervening beliefs that connect identification to political action. Consciousness potentially heightens awareness and interest in politics, changes the group bases for social comparisons, bolsters group pride and political efficacy, alters interpretations of group problems, and promotes support for collective action. Acquiring a group identity and a sense of common fate is therefore just the first step toward a fully developed group consciousness.

Many studies on the political effects of group identity among Latinos and Asians focus strictly on group identification rather than on the cognitive elements of consciousness (de la Garza 1992; Jones-Correa and Leal 1996; Lien 2001; Lien et al. 2001). They typically rely on one or more of three items to measure group consciousness: (1) self-identification with one's racial or ethnic group, (2) a feeling of closeness to one's group, and (3) a belief that one's fate is linked to that of the group. All of these replicate or parallel similar items used to study group identity among African Americans. Although these items are reasonable probes of group identification, only the measure of linked fate begins to capture the more complex political or ideological elements of group consciousness. There is no theoretical reason to expect that group identification by itself—without the mobilizing ideology of group consciousness—would increase an individual's propensity to participate in politics.

Multiple Identities

Just as there are different *degrees* of group consciousness, different *kinds* of group consciousness may have varying effects on political participation. The assumption underlying this line of research is that group consciousness leads to higher levels of political participation by individuals on behalf of the group. But not all group ideologies necessarily promote political participation to the same degree; some may even direct individuals away from political activities. Ethnic group identification, for example, can hinder participation rates by slowing rates of acculturation and thereby reducing interest and participation in political affairs (Greeley 1974). Even more intriguing, there may be instances of competing ideologies circulating within a group. When there is no ideological consensus, the various forms of group consciousness may tend to influence individual behavior in different directions.

Among African Americans, for example, there has been a long history of debate over the wisdom of engagement with the mainstream culture versus withdrawal into separatist institutions. These two strains of group consciousness were labeled "militancy" and "black nationalism" in Gary Marx's 1964 study of black attitudes. Militants expressed high levels of black group pride, endorsed equal rights for blacks, were frustrated by the slow speed of integration, blamed the system for racial inequality, and preferred demonstrating to praying as a means to improve group status. Like civil rights militants, black nationalists also emphasized pride in being black and celebrated black culture and history. But they were cynical about the integrationist goals of the movement and skeptical about its accomplishments and prospects for improving the situation of blacks. They argued instead for developing black institutions, supporting black business enterprises, segregating the races, and considering violent tactics to achieve equality.

Most important for our purpose, black nationalists participated in different social and political activities than did militants. Militancy was correlated with membership in civil rights organizations such as the NAACP and CORE, likelihood of voting in the 1960 election, intention to vote in 1964, newspaper reading, knowledge, and support for civil rights demonstrations. In contrast, black nationalists were less likely to read general circulation magazines and newspapers or black publications; but they were significantly more likely to read the newspaper of the Nation of Islam. Nationalists were less likely than militants to participate in organizations or to vote. Nevertheless, nationalists were still *more likely* to participate than blacks who showed neither form of racial consciousness. Like militancy, black nationalism reflected a form of psychological engagement with politics that boosted participation, albeit to a lesser extent.

We believe that different kinds of group consciousness continue to exist among African Americans and that they are likely to have varying effects on political participation.[7] For example, Brown and Shaw (2002) recently identified two distinct forms of black nationalism among African Americans surveyed in the 1993 National Black Politics Study (NBPS). Although the authors do not explore what impact these group-based ideologies have on political participation, we suspect that each may have its own distinct effects, just as "militancy" and "nationalism" did in Marx's classic study.

Conventional and Unconventional Forms of Participation

Finally, group consciousness may not influence all types of political participation to the same extent. Instead, it may have its greatest impact on those kinds of activities that require solidarity over and above political interest and civic skills. It is no coincidence that studies of costly or risky forms of social protest are more likely to reserve a place for the role of group consciousness than studies of conventional political participation. Protest is a difficult activity that requires more sacrifice of individual interests than does voting or contacting a government official about a personal problem. Many conventional political activities do not require group consciousness because they are sufficiently motivated by personal concerns and other normative or social factors.

In sum, we offer the following three conjectures: First, the effects of group consciousness need to be gauged with comprehensive measures of identification and consciousness. Second, complementary or competing ideologies in the black community may offer additional psychological resources that foster participation. Finally, the greatest effects of consciousness may not occur at the polling place but in the street in the form of demonstrations, pickets, and protests. We offer some evidence for these hypotheses in the empirical analysis that follows.

EMPIRICAL TESTS USING THE 1984 NBES

We use the 1984 NBES to test these ideas because this survey contains a rich array of racial identification and consciousness measures, in addition to a full complement of questions about participating in political activities ranging from voting to protest. Perhaps we have placed ourselves in a favorable position by studying black participation in the 1984 presidential election. The effects of group consciousness on black political behavior are likely to be stronger in elections involving black candidates, civil rights initiatives, or other activities that might affect the status of blacks. Jesse Jackson's presidential run created a political context in which the influence of group consciousness on black participation rates was probably enhanced by media and campaign messages and the mobilization of the black community.

The contextual effect of Jackson's campaign, however, does not compromise our comparison of different measures of racial identification and consciousness or of alternative means of participating in politics. Tate's (1993) previous analysis of the 1984 survey has already established that group identification, defined narrowly, only weakly influenced voting turnout. We ask whether a more comprehensive measure of identification and consciousness has any greater impact on voting and whether the effects of identification and consciousness vary systematically according to the type of participation.

Operationalization of Group Identification and Consciousness

Our operationalization of group identification and consciousness borrows from the conceptual distinctions Gurin, Hatchett, and Jackson (1989) established in their original design and analysis of the NBES. The items in this survey allow us to build measures of two broad forms of racial identification: a group identity based on acceptance of a *common fate* with other blacks; and a more exclusive black identity based on a preference for racial *autonomy* rather than integration. Those who endorse the notion of a common fate are conscious of sharing an interest with other blacks and acknowledge that the civil rights movement affected them personally. Support for black autonomy, on the other hand, is reflected in a tendency to think of oneself as being black as opposed to being an American (or to being both black *and* American) and in a preference for separation between blacks and other groups in social and economic relations (e.g., a preference for shopping in stores owned by black entrepreneurs and avoiding contact with whites).

The average inter-item correlation for the common fate identity items is .28; the four black autonomy items have an average inter-item correlation of .13. The feeling of sharing a common fate is empirically distinguishable from support for black autonomy, as the average inter-item correlation across the two sets of items is a meager .06.

Group consciousness augments group identification by articulating collective discontents and strategies for improving the status of blacks. We examine four components of consciousness: (1) discontent with the amount of influence enjoyed by blacks and other disadvantaged groups (women, youth, the poor, and those on welfare); (2) a belief that group disparities are produced by discrimination and are illegitimate; (3) support for collective strategies to correct group inequalities; and (4) belief in the political efficacy of group action. (See the Appendix for scale reliabilities and the full text of the items used to construct the measures of identification and consciousness.)

Of the four components of consciousness, three are measured with multiple-item scales. The five items measuring discontent with group status have an average inter-item correlation of .26. The three items in the group efficacy scale have an average inter-item correlation of .33. The correlation between the two items measuring perception of discrimination is .12. In the following multivariate analysis, we treat the four components of consciousness separately except in one test where we combine the four dimensions of consciousness into a single scale in order to estimate its aggregate effects.[8]

All of the dimensions of consciousness are positively correlated with one another and with the two forms of identity (see Table 3.1). A common fate identity however is significantly associated with higher socioeconomic status while black autonomy is not significantly related to either education or income. We expect this contrast between common fate and black autonomy will be manifest in the kinds of political activity that each is likely to promote. In particular, we anticipate that the more intense beliefs associated with black nationalism will lend themselves more readily to direct action such as protests and demonstrations while the more moderate common fate identity will bear a stronger connection to conventional acts of political participation.

There is generally no relationship between identification and consciousness and age and gender, although older individuals tend to be more supportive of black autonomy and women tend to have a stronger sense than men of sharing a common fate with other blacks. Membership in a black community organization is much more strongly correlated with the elements of identity and consciousness than is church attendance.

TABLE 3.1. Correlates of Group Identity and Consciousness

	Common fate	Black autonomy	Discontent with status	Discrimination	Collective strategies	Group efficacy
Individual Skills and Resources						
Education	.24	(.00)	.12	.14	.10	.11
Income	.18	(−.03)	.12	.13	.11	.08
Age	(−.02)	.08	(.00)	(.00)	(−.06)	(.03)
Gender (Female)	.14	(−.01)	(.05)	(.03)	(.00)	(−.04)
Organizational Resources						
Church attendance	(−.03)	(−.01)	(−.02)	(−.02)	(−.04)	(.03)
Organizational membership	.21	.08	.08	.11	(.04)	.12
Psychological Engagement						
General political interest	.24	(.03)	.16	.09	(.05)	.25
Interest in black politics	.17	.07	.10	.09	.08	.21
Personal political efficacy	.15	−.06	(−.01)	(.02)	(.05)	.08
Trust in government	−.13	−.10	−.24	−.24	(−.06)	−.15
Partisanship	(.03)	(.00)	(.02)	(−.01)	(.04)	.08
Group Identity and Consciousness						
Common fate identity	1.00					
Black autonomy	.14	1.00				
Discontent with group status	.18	.10	1.00			
Perceive discrimination	.27	.10	.24	1.00		
Support collective strategies	.13	.09	.09	.08	1.00	
Believe in group efficacy	.20	.07	.17	(.06)	.07	1.00

Note: Entries are Pearson's *r*. All coefficients except those in parentheses are significant at .05 level. See the Appendix for the items in the group identification and consciousness scales.

EXPLAINING PARTICIPATION

Our strategy in the following tests is to first estimate the aggregate effect of identification and consciousness on different acts of political participation. For shorthand, we will use the term *racial solidarity* when referring to the combined elements of identification and consciousness. Then we focus on the influence of the various components of identification and consciousness. The purpose of this sequence of tests is to offer a synopsis of the overall impact of solidarity on participation, then to identify the specific components of solidarity that are providing the major impetus. In the process, we test the effects of both forms of racial identity to see whether they are mutually reinforcing or whether they produce contrasting effects on participation; plus we examine whether the additional dimensions of consciousness included in the model make a difference. Finally, we test whether group identification and consciousness are more strongly connected to certain acts of participation, such as political protest, that place a premium on cooperation and coordination with other group members.

All of the dependent variables in the analysis are dichotomously coded (yes versus no) participatory acts that can be grouped into four categories:

(i) *voting* in the primaries and presidential election; (ii) *traditional campaign activities* (influencing how others vote, attending political meetings, donating money, campaigning for black candidates, working for a party, and assisting with voter registration); (iii) *petitioning* (signing a petition or contacting a public official); and (iv) *direct action* (attending a protest, picketing, or boycotting).

The explanatory variables in the model are also grouped into four categories: (1) *individual resources and characteristics* (education, income, age, gender); (2) *organizational resources* (church attendance, membership in a black community organization); (3) *psychological engagement* (general political interest, interest in black politics, partisanship, personal political efficacy, and political trust); and (4) *group identity and consciousness*.

The probit model we estimate is similar in structure to the participation model constructed by Verba, Schlozman, and Brady (1995) and others, and is based on the assumption that people are more likely to participate if they have the civic skills to participate, the psychological motivation to participate, or if they are recruited to participate by social and political organizations. However, in contrast to Verba, Schlozman, and Brady's model, we incorporate several dimensions of identity and consciousness, and we examine the racial solidarity–participation connection across a broader range of political activities.

The Added Value of Racial Identification and Consciousness

We first test whether racial solidarity provides additional explanatory power beyond the individual characteristics, organizational resources, and psychological motives included in the standard participation model. To address this question, we use probit regressions to compare the standard "baseline" model against the "augmented" model that combines the base variables and racial solidarity. The appropriate statistical test of the null hypothesis that identity and consciousness are irrelevant is the increment in the log likelihood between the two models that is attributable to the additional explanatory variables. The difference in the log likelihoods (multiplied by two) is distributed according to a chi-square distribution with 3 degrees of freedom. There are only 3 degrees of freedom because we have, for the purpose of this test, aggregated the four components of consciousness into a single measure. This test gives priority to the full set of baseline variables in explaining participation before apportioning credit to the solidarity variables. Therefore, if the components of racial solidarity that influence participation are adequately captured by individual skills, psychological engagement, and organizational membership, we will find that solidarity adds nothing "extra" to the explanation of participation.

We report in Table 3.2 the summaries of the likelihood ratio tests contrasting the baseline and augmented models for each act of participation. The pattern that emerges from this series of tests generally supports our expectations about the conditional effects of solidarity. The addition of racial solidarity does not contribute significantly to the explanation of presidential voting or to several of the traditional campaign activities, such as voter registration, attending political meetings, and campaigning for a black candidate. Identity and consciousness, however, do promote voting in the primary, giving money

TABLE 3.2. Log Likelihood Ratio Test Comparing Baseline and Baseline
and Solidarity Models

	Log likelihood				
	Baseline model + solidarity	Baseline model	Chi square (3 d.f.)	Prob	N
Voting					
Voted in primary	−186.03	−190.39	8.71	.03	355
Voted for president	−226.20	−228.68	4.95	.18	597
Campaign Activities					
Influenced vote choice	−356.36	−363.29	13.87	.00	596
Helped voter registration	−261.46	−263.89	4.86	.18	597
Went to political meeting	−281.33	−282.35	2.03	.57	597
Gave money to candidate	−255.70	−261.79	12.18	.01	595
Campaigned for black candidate	−228.25	−230.83	5.17	.16	595
Worked for a party	−267.08	−270.37	6.59	.09	539
Petitioning					
Contacted a public official	−298.35	−304.31	11.93	.01	595
Signed a petition	−339.46	−347.44	15.97	.00	595
Direct Action					
Attended a demonstration	−235.56	−244.69	18.24	.00	595
Picketed or boycotted	−146.33	−153.9	15.14	.00	595

Note: The baseline model includes: (1) individual skills and resources (education, income, age, gender); (2) organizational resources (church attendance, membership in a black community organization); and (3) psychological engagement (general political interest, interest in black politics, partisanship, personal political efficacy, and political trust). The augmented model includes the baseline variable plus *solidarity* (two forms of group identity—common fate and black autonomy—and an aggregated measure of consciousness).
Source: 1984 NBES.

to candidates, and working for a party ($p < .10$). But the greatest value added by identification and consciousness occurs in conjunction with petitioning and direct action. The likelihood of engaging in both acts of petitioning and both forms of direct action is given a substantial boost by the addition of racial solidarity.

Base Model Factors

A detailed examination of the probit coefficients for the individual elements of racial solidarity provides further insight into their contingent relationship to political activities. Tables 3.3–3.6 summarize the effect of the full set of individual, organizational, and psychological factors on all four classes of political participation: voting, campaign activities, petitioning, and direct action. To help gauge the relative impact of different factors, we also calculate the first differences for each explanatory variable. The first difference represents the change in the probability of engaging in each act of participation that accompanies a movement from the lowest to highest values of each explanatory variable, holding constant all other explanatory variables at their mean values.

Consider first the general influence of the base model factors across the array of participatory acts. Organizational membership and general political

TABLE 3.3. Explaining Voting Participation

	Voted in primary		Voted for president	
	b	Δ	b	Δ
Individual Skills and Resources				
Education	−.07	−.03	.51*	.12
	(.34)		(.30)	
Income	.74***	.27	.04	.00
	(.27)		(.25)	
Age	.02***	.50	.02***	.22
	(.00)		(.00)	
Gender (Female)	.20	.08	.08	.02
	(.17)		(.15)	
Organizational Resources				
Church attendance	.16	.06	.60***	.14
	(.25)		(.22)	
Organizational membership	.58**	.20	.29	.05
	(.23)		(.26)	
Psychological Engagement				
General political interest	1.90***	.63	1.67***	.47
	(.38)		(.28)	
Interest in black politics	.15	.05	.24	.06
	(.37)		(.33)	
Personal political efficacy	−.01	−.00	.19	.04
	(.27)		(.22)	
Trust in government	.40	.14	.25	.05
	(.32)		(.27)	
Partisanship	.61	.24	.80***	.25
	(.41)		(.29)	
Group Identity and Consciousness				
Common fate identity	−.12	−.04	−.03	−.00
	(.32)		.28	
Black autonomy	.59	.20	−.16	−.04
	(.47)		(.40)	
Discontent with group status	.77	.30	.26	.07
	(.48)		(.38)	
Perceive discrimination	.34	.13	.47***	.12
	(.30)		(.25)	
Support collective strategies	−.20	−.07	−.20	−.04
	(.16)		(.14)	
Belief in group efficacy	1.24***	.45	.80**	.23
	(.44)		(.32)	
Likelihood ratio chi^2	117.17***		146.58***	
Pseudo R^2	.24		.25	
N	355		597	

Note: Entries are probit regression coefficients, standard errors in parentheses. Δ represents the first differences for each independent variable, with the values of all other independent variables held at their means.
* $p < .01$
** $p < .05$
*** $p < .01$
Source: 1984 NBES.

TABLE 3.4. Explaining Participation in Campaign Activities

	Influenced how people vote		Helped with voter registration		Went to political meeting		Gave money to candidate		Campaigned for black candidate		Worked for a party	
	b	Δ	b	Δ	b	Δ	b	Δ	b	Δ	b	Δ
Individual Skills and Resources												
Education	.08	.03	-.59**	-.16	.35	.09	.40	.10	.19	.04	.93***	.27
	(.24)		(.29)		(.27)		(.28)		(.30)		(.28)	
Income	.10	.04	.62***	.16	.27	.08	.51**	.14	.38	.09	.42*	.14
	(.20)		(.23)		(.22)		(.22)		(.23)		(.23)	
Age	-.00	-.00	-.02***	-.22	.00	.07	.01**	.22	-.00	-.01	.01	.18
	(.00)		(.00)		(.00)		(.00)		(.00)		(.00)	
Gender (Female)	-.09	-.04	.01	.00	-.02	-.00	.06	.01	.03	.00	.12	.04
	(.12)		(.14)		(.13)		(.14)		(.14)		(.14)	
Organizational Resources												
Church attendance	.04	.02	.37*	.09	.04	.01	-.14	-.04	-.24	-.05	-.38*	-.12
	(.18)		(.21)		(.20)		(.21)		(.22)		(.21)	
Organizational membership	.34*	.13	.60***	.18	.73***	.24	.77***	.24	.91***	.26	.58***	.20
	(.18)		(.19)		(.18)		(.18)		(.19)		(.18)	
Psychological Engagement												
General political interest	1.40***	.46	1.32***	.24	1.00***	.22	.59**	.13	1.42***	.22	.58***	.15
	(.26)		(.33)		(.30)		(.30)		(.38)		(.18)	
Interest in black politics	.16	.06	.64**	.13	-.10	-.03	-.20	-.06	-.06	-.02	-.08	-.03
	(.26)		(.30)		(.30)		(.31)		(.33)		(.30)	
Personal political efficacy	.28	.11	.03	.00	.46**	.13	.38*	.09	.10	.02	.63**	.20
	(.18)		(.21)		(.21)		(.22)		(.22)		(.21)	
Trust in government	-.53**	-.20	.24	.07	.04	.02	-.14	-.03	.32	.07	-.09	-.03
	(.23)		(.26)		(.25)		(.27)		(.28)		(.26)	
Partisanship	-.13	-.05	.32	.06	.17	.04	-.17	-.05	-.13	-.04	.39	.10
	(.26)		(.33)		(.31)		(.29)		(.32)		(.37)	

	Influenced how people vote		Helped with voter registration		Went to political meeting		Gave money to candidate		Campaigned for black candidate		Worked for a party	
	b	Δ	b	Δ	b	Δ	b	Δ	b	Δ	b	Δ
Group Identity and Consciousness												
Common fate identity	.22	.09	.06	.01	.11	.03	.93***	.23	.16	.03	.26	.08
	(.23)		(.27)		(.26)		(.28)		(.29)		(.26)	
Black autonomy	1.03***	.39	.48	.14	.47	.14	.28	.08	.79*	.20	.22	.07
	(.34)		(.39)		(.37)		(.39)		(.41)		(.40)	
Discontent with group status	.12	.04	.21	.04	.20	.05	.14	.03	.28	.05	.69*	.19
	(.32)		(.38)		(.36)		(.39)		(.41)		(.39)	
Perceive discrimination	-.04	-.02	-.47**	-.12	.08	.23	-.19	-.05	-.04	-.02	.04	.01
	(.21)		(.24)		(.23)		(.24)		(.26)		(.24)	
Support collective strategies	.19	.07	-.03	-.01	-.11	-.03	.16	.04	.15	.03	.07	.02
	(.12)		(.13)		(.13)		(.13)		(.14)		(.13)	
Belief in group efficacy	.06	.02	-.86***	-.27	-.16	-.05	-.61*	-.19	-.33	-.09	.16	.04
	(.29)		(.32)		(.32)		(.33)		(.35)		(.36)	
Likelihood ratio chi^2	108.28***		72.35***		93.76***		115.75***		97.27***		115.15***	
Pseudo R^2	.13		.12		.14		.19		.18		.18	
N	596		597		597		595		595		539	

Note: Entries are probit regression coefficients, standard errors in parentheses. Δ represents the first differences for each independent variable, with the values of all over other independent variables held at their means.

* $p < .10$

** $p < .05$

*** $p < .01$

Source: 1984 NBES.

TABLE 3.5 Explaining Petitioning

	Contacted a public official		Signed a petition	
	b	Δ	b	Δ
Individual Skills and Resources				
Education	.62**	.20	.45*	17
	(.26)		(.24)	
Income	.15	.05	.72***	.27
	(.21)		(.21)	
Age	.00	.03	−.01***	−.34
	(.00)		(.00)	
Gender (Female)	.03	.01	.20	.08
	(.13)		(.12)	
Organizational Resources				
Church attendance	−.25	−.08	−.26	−.10
	(.19)		(.18)	
Organizational membership	.74***	.27	.77***	.28
	(.18)		(.20)	
Psychological Engagement				
General political interest	1.00***	.28	.52***	.21
	(.29)		(.25)	
Interest in black politics	−.95***	−.34	−.40	−.16
	(.29)		(.28)	
Personal political efficacy	.57***	.19	.34*	.13
	(.20)		(.19)	
Trust in government	−.36	−.11	−.38	−.15
	(.25)		(.23)	
Partisanship	−.02	−.01	.40	.16
	(.28)		(.26)	
Group Identity and Consciousness				
Common fate identity	.44*	.14	.50**	.19
	(.25)		(.23)	
Black autonomy	.03	.01	−.38	−.15
	(.36)		(.34)	
Discontent with group status	.88*	.25	.71**	.28
	(.36)		(.33)	
Perceive discrimination	−.14	−.05	.16	.06
	(.23)		(.21)	
Support collective strategies	.07	.02	.02	.01
	(.12)		(.11)	
Belief in group efficacy	.50	.14	.31	.12
	(.33)		(.29)	
Likelihood ratio chi^2	142.73***		141.24***	
Pseudo R^2	.19		.17	
N	595		595	

Note: Entries are probit regression coefficients, standard errors in parentheses. Δ represents the first differences for each independent variable, with the values of all other independent variables held at their means.
* $p < .10$
** $p < .05$
*** $p < .01$
Source: 1984 NBES.

TABLE 3.6 Explaining Collective Action

	Attended a demonstration		Picketed or boycotted	
	b	Δ	b	Δ
Individual Skills and Resources				
Education	.61**	.12	.29	.03
	(.29)		(.38)	
Income	−.12	−.02	.58**	.07
	(.24)		(.28)	
Age	.00	.06	−.01*	−.06
	(.00)		(.01)	
Gender (Female)	−.05	−.01	.30	.03
	(.14)		(.18)	
Organizational Resources				
Church attendance	−.05	−.01	−.35	−.04
	(.21)		(.27)	
Organizational membership	.58***	.16	.29	.04
	(.19)		(.24)	
Psychological Engagement				
General political interest	.22	.04	.81*	.06
	(.31)		(.43)	
Interest in black politics	−.12	−.03	−.49	−.07
	(.32)		(.41)	
Personal political efficacy	.50**	.11	.50*	.05
	(.22)		(.28)	
Trust in government	−.22	−.04	−.54	−.05
	(.28)		(.38)	
Partisanship	.25	.04	.04	−.01
	(.33)		(.40)	
Group Identity and Consciousness				
Common fate identity	.55**	.11	.79**	.08
	(.28)		(.38)	
Black autonomy	1.45***	.40	1.00**	.16
	(.40)		(.50)	
Discontent with group status	−.44	−.11	.38	.03
	(.39)		(.54)	
Perceive discrimination	−.18	−.04	.16	.01
	(.25)		(.33)	
Support collective strategies	−.07	−.02	−.06	−.00
	(.14)		(.17)	
Belief in group efficacy	.10	.01	.95*	.06
	(.36)		(.56)	
Likelihood ratio chi^2	71.71***		80.79***	
Pseudo R^2	.13		.22	
N	595		595	

Note: Entries are probit regression coefficients, standard errors in parentheses. Δ represents the first differences for each independent variable, with the values of all other independent variables held at their means.
* $p < .10$
** $p < .05$
*** $p < .01$
Source: 1984 NBES.

interest are the most consistently powerful influences. This reflects the close proximity between being interested in politics, joining an organization, and taking an active political role. Being a member of an organization increases the probability of participation in most campaign and petitioning activities by more than .20, but exerts a weaker influence on direct action. Similarly, general political interest has a whopping effect on primary and presidential voting (the first differences are .63 and .47 respectively), moderate to strong influences on most campaign activities and petitioning, but a weak influence on direct action. As an organizational resource, membership in an organization routinely outweighs the effect of church attendance. Church attendance is the stronger influence on presidential voting, which is consistent with Tate's (1993) analysis, but this is the exception to the rule that church-going is typically weakly related to political participation. In contrast to general political interest, specific interest in black politics is hardly a factor, boosting participation in voter registration efforts but lowering the likelihood of contacting public officials.

The direct effects of education and income are occasionally significant, but in general the effects of socioeconomic status are mediated through the organizational and psychological factors in the model. Age is positively associated with voting, but older individuals are predictably less inclined to engage in direct action. Gender is a consistently insignificant predictor of participation. Strength of partisanship has a strong effect on presidential voting (the first difference is .25), but is an insignificant influence on other forms of participation.

Previous studies (especially Shingles, 1981) have hypothesized that low trust and high efficacy work in concert with group identification to spur political participation. In our analysis, neither trust nor personal efficacy significantly affects the likelihood of voting. Personal efficacy, however, is among the more consistently significant influences on other types of political participation, increasing engagement in several campaign activities, petitioning, and direct action. Trust, on the other hand, is rarely a factor, bearing a significant (inverse) relationship only to the likelihood of influencing how others vote.

The Elements of Identification and Consciousness

Our analysis of the NBES corroborates recent studies that have found a weak connection between racial identification and voting. As reported in Table 3.3, neither belief in a common fate nor support for black autonomy makes a difference in the likelihood of voting in the primary or general election. *Consciousness* however does promote voting. Of the four elements of consciousness, *group* efficacy (in contrast to *personal* political efficacy) has a sizable influence on voting in the primary—trailing in magnitude only the effects of age and political interest—and influences voting in the presidential election roughly on a par with age and partisanship. A second element of consciousness—perception of racial discrimination—is also significantly related to voting in the presidential election.

However, once we move beyond voting to different forms of political participation, we uncover stronger effects for identification and other facets of consciousness. With respect to the campaign activities reported in Table 3.4, advocacy of black autonomy has a powerful influence on the propensity to influence people to vote; the first difference of .39 associated with this dimension of identity is second only to the first difference of .46 for general political interest. Support for black autonomy is also among the strongest predictors of participation in the campaign of a black candidate.

The other form of racial identification—belief in a common fate—is among four primary factors (along with age, organizational membership, and income) that significantly increase the likelihood of contributing money to a candidate. Therefore, the two forms of identity provide independent sources of motivation to participate and tend to encourage different forms of political activity.

Of the four elements of consciousness, those who are dissatisfied with the amount of influence enjoyed by blacks are more likely to have contacted public officials, worked for a political party, and signed a petition. There are also a couple of anomalies in the findings on consciousness: group efficacy and perception of discrimination are negatively related to the likelihood of helping with voter registration; and group efficacy is also inversely related to giving money to candidates.

Most impressive are the powerful influences of racial solidarity on petitioning and direct action. Solidarity, socioeconomic status, general political interest, and organization membership are the four dominant influences on petitioning public officials (see Table 3.5). Two of the six components of identification and consciousness exert a significant influence on petitioning. Those who are unhappy with the status of minorities are significantly more likely to have contacted public officials and signed a petition. Belief in sharing a common fate with other blacks registers a statistically significant effect on both forms of petitioning. By contrast, support for black autonomy is related to neither form of petitioning.

As we hypothesized would be the case, the dominant influence of racial identification and consciousness is manifest in participation in protests, demonstrations, and boycotts (see Table 3.6). Support for black autonomy dwarfs all other influences on participation in a demonstration. The first difference for black autonomy is .40; organizational membership, education, and belief in a common fate are the next most influential factors and have first differences of .16, .12, and .11 respectively. Likewise, support for black autonomy exerts the single largest influence on the likelihood of joining pickets and boycotts, increasing the probability of participation by .16. These results give further evidence of the different effects of the two forms of racial identification. Whereas belief in a common fate was the only form of identity significantly related to petitioning, support for black autonomy wields much greater influence over participation in political activities that bypass conventional channels.

Belief in a common fate and group efficacy have modest but still statistically significant first differences of .08 and .06, respectively, on participating in pickets and boycotts, which makes their influence roughly comparable in magnitude to general political interest and income. In a departure from the pattern associated with conventional political activities, younger respondents are more likely to join pickets and boycotts than older respondents. Personal political efficacy is the only other psychological resource that significantly increases involvement in demonstrations and boycotts and pickets.

These tests reveal that the effects of identification and consciousness fluctuate across the range of participatory acts, but show evidence of the patterns we hypothesized. Our analysis, like Tate's (1993) earlier study, confirms that the effect of group identification on voting is modest after controlling for other individual and organizational factors. However we offer several significant amendments and elaborations to this result. First, group consciousness further elevates the propensity to vote. Moreover, racial solidarity (i.e., identification and consciousness combined) has stronger effects on other, generally more demanding, forms of political participation.

Second, the influence of racial solidarity varies with the type of political activity. Racial solidarity is most effective, relative to other explanatory factors, in generating participation in group activities that call for teamwork, cooperation, and coordination with others such as joining petitions or engaging in boycotts and political protests. The influence of racial solidarity on protest behavior outweighs all other factors.

Third, there are different forms of racial identity, each of which may constitute an added psychological resource for blacks. The results reaffirm the distinction between a black nationalist orientation and a non–separatist group identity. The two forms of identification appeal to different segments of the black community and exert significant independent influences on participation. Although both forms of racial identity are conducive to direct action, the more radical separatist identity is a much stronger predictor of participation in boycotts and demonstrations and support for black political candidates, whereas the common fate identification is more likely to promote conventional political activities such as contacting government officials, signing petitions, and contributing money to political candidates.

Among the cluster of elements that comprise group consciousness, the two components that make the greatest difference are a conviction that the group can make a difference if it acts together—in short, group efficacy— and dissatisfaction with the status of the group. It is perhaps no coincidence that the group efficacy and group status measures were also the two most reliable consciousness scales. Support for collective strategies is the dimension of consciousness that is the most weakly related to participation. This item, however, may have been compromised because respondents were asked to choose between either blacks' joining organizations *or* working hard as individuals as the best way to improve group status. Many respondents may not have viewed these alternatives as mutually exclusive and may have been reluctant to renounce personal diligence in favor of collective strategies.

Given the low reliability of the items measuring perceptions of discrimination and support for collective strategies, we suspect that improved measures would provide stronger evidence of the relationship between these facets of racial consciousness and political participation. As we discuss below, the task of developing better measures of identification and consciousness that are specific to the groups under consideration should be a priority of future studies of racial and ethnic solidarity.

Approaches to Studying Group Consciousness among Asians and Latinos

Our analysis of the NBES confirms the need for a comprehensive measure of group identification and consciousness. When measured appropriately, group consciousness displays far-reaching and often substantial influence (relative to other conventional factors) on both electoral and nonelectoral acts of political participation. At the same time, this analysis suggests reasons to be cautious in applying the same measures of group solidarity used in studies of African Americans to the study of Latinos, Asians, and other minority groups.

Common fate among Asians and Latinos may not reflect the same strong correlation with group consciousness or the same mobilizing potential as occurs with African Americans. First, these other minority groups do not boast the same long, extensive history of collective action in the United States as African Americans. To be sure, some Asians and Latinos historically have engaged in movements for group rights. But that history is neither as widespread nor as well known as it is for African Americans. What is more, the Latino and Asian populations include large numbers of newcomers to the United States, who have had little or no exposure to that history.

Even more important than those historical differences, however, is the political context at any given moment. We expect the sense of common fate to take on political meaning for Asians and Latinos in instances where the political context transforms what it means to be Asian or Latino into a salient issue for group members. For example, such a transformation might happen in an election where an Asian or Latino is making a first-ever bid for office or an issue relevant to the group is at the fore of political debate. Instances such as these have been far fewer for Asians and Latinos than for their black counterparts.

But that may change if the numbers of Latinos and Asians in the country continue to increase at the current rate, if they are geographically concentrated enough to allow for effective bloc voting or other forms of collective political action, and if elites seize opportunities to raise group consciousness and infuse the sense of common fate among individual Asians and Latinos with political meaning. Those conditions are certainly emerging for Latinos. Some research already indicates that Latinos turn out to vote when they are mobilized by Latino organizational elites (Wrinkle et al. 1996; Shaw, de la Garza, and Lee 2000). Mobilizing Latinos as a group likely entails some degree of consciousness raising or stirring feelings of common fate.[9]

Still, we should not expect group consciousness to assume the same forms among Asians and Latinos as it has among African Americans. Likewise we cannot expect to measure group identity in the same fashion across all minority groups. Most of the existing studies on Latinos and Asians have relied on fully replicated or slightly modified measures of group identity borrowed from previous research on African Americans. Although some of these items may be good starting points, others may not be appropriate for measuring group identification among these minority groups.

If consciousness varies over time and from individual to individual, as we and others have argued, it surely must also vary from group to group. There is no reason then to expect that items used to capture group consciousness among African Americans will necessarily apply to Asians and Latinos. Earlier we suggested that group ideologies among blacks have likely changed over time in response to changes in the political environment. Those shifts require that we make corresponding adjustments in how we measure the concept among African Americans.[10] It follows that we should also tailor items specifically to measure group consciousness among Asians and Latinos. If the ideological content of consciousness varies across groups, researchers must devise measures that can accurately capture these differences.

Consider for instance two of the items that have been used to measure group consciousness among blacks. One item asks whether respondents have been affected by the civil rights movement (Gurin, Hatchett, and Jackson 1989). Though this may still be a valid measure of consciousness among African Americans, it may not be relevant to Latinos and Asians, especially those who are relative newcomers to the United States. Another item asks whether government should address the problems blacks face or whether the group should rely on its own efforts (Gurin, Hatchett, and Jackson 1989; Dawson 1993; Verba, Schlozman, and Brady 1995). This may no longer be a good measure of group consciousness even among blacks, due to changes in ideology within the population over the last quarter-century. The conventional wisdom used to be that highly race-conscious blacks were more likely than their less race-conscious counterparts to call for government solutions to group problems. Today it is less clear that race conscious blacks would necessarily look to government to redress group grievances. For example, black leaders like Louis Farrakhan and others routinely call for blacks to rely on their own resources to solve group problems rather than turn to government, all in the name of race consciousness.

Following that same logic, prescribing government solutions or even certain kinds of collective action to address group problems may not be associated with the forms of consciousness that exist among Asian and Latino populations. Conventional measures that correlate consciousness with those kinds of attitudes thus may have very little applicability to these groups. To devise measures that capture the forms of group consciousness that prevail among Asians and Latinos, researchers will first need to undertake studies that explore and describe the kinds of political values, beliefs, and ideologies that circulate within these populations.

Consciousness is the result of a variety of environmental or contextual influences such as elite messages, social interaction, and exposure to a common culture or history (Smith 1991; Dawson 1993; Hardin 1995; Horowitz 1995; Turner 1999). Taken together, these influences constitute a socialization process that produces group consciousness (Herring, Jankowski, and Brown 1999; Rogers 2001). This socializing process is informed by the ideologies that predominate in a population. Researchers therefore need to excavate the range of systematic political beliefs and ideas to which Asian and Latino individuals are exposed during this process. Although some of the questions about political attitudes on existing national surveys are a useful starting point, they do not offer anything like a complete road map to the potentially diverse set of political beliefs that exist within these populations. Similarly, the salience and content of group consciousness will also vary from subgroup to subgroup within the Asian and Latino populations. Recent research findings showing that some Asian and Latino subgroups exhibit higher levels of panethnic identification than others are suggestive of such variation (Jones-Correa and Leal 1996; Lien 2001; Lien et al. 2001).

Scholars like Michael Dawson (1993) have called for more careful studies of the diverse ideological strands that circulate within the African American population. His recent book mapping a variety of significant African American ideologies is an important contribution to that enterprise (Dawson 2001). Scholars studying Asians and Latinos will need to undertake similar inquiries to gain insight into the various forms of group consciousness that circulate among these minority populations.

SUMMARY AND CONCLUSION

Consciousness raising is a term that was popularized during the tumultuous social movements of the 1960s. It refers to the diffusion of an ideology that bolsters group pride and identification, diagnoses group problems, offers prescriptive solutions, and encourages group members to act in solidarity to achieve common ends. The empirical literature on group consciousness and participation lacks both consensus on the conceptualization and measurement of consciousness and specificity about the conditions under which it will influence political behavior. The effect of group consciousness on political participation depends on which components of identification and consciousness are measured and tested, as well as on which acts of participation are examined.

We have argued that a fair test of group consciousness requires using a comprehensive measure that captures its multiple dimensions. Our analysis of the 1984 NBES indicates that the more narrowly circumscribed measures of group identity used in recent studies are likely to have underestimated the influence of identification and consciousness on political participation. We found that two kinds of racial identification have only a modest influence on voting turnout but a significant influence on participation in several traditional campaign activities, petitioning government officials, and especially participation in protests and boycotts.

The two forms of racial identity bolster participation in somewhat different venues. Those who believe in a common fate are more likely to express their demands through conventional political channels while those who endorse the more radical notion of racial autonomy are more inclined to favor protests and other forms of direct action. The independent influence of two forms of racial identification—a sense of common fate and black autonomy—confirms that minority populations can have multiple identities and ideologies, each of which may constitute a source of political engagement for different sectors of the group.

In contrast to racial identification, group consciousness exerted its largest effect on voting. But it also had moderate effects on contacting public officials, working for a party, and signing a petition. Overall, as we hypothesized, the largest effects of identification and consciousness are manifest in the realm of collective political activism.

A new generation of studies have adopted and applied the concept of group consciousness developed in research on African Americans to the study of other racial and ethnic minorities. There are solid intuitive grounds for looking to the research on African Americans for guideposts to studying the political behavior and attitudes of these new groups. Latinos and Asians share some obvious commonalities with African Americans: racial minority status, non-European backgrounds, vulnerability to discrimination, and in some cases, socioeconomic disadvantage. These shared predicaments naturally invite comparisons between these minority groups and their black counterparts.

Nevertheless, researchers should exercise caution before transferring wholesale the measures used in studies of African Americans to the study of new minorities. Studies of group consciousness in Asian Americans and Latinos need to explore the political ideas and values that are prevalent in the Asian American and Latino communities and develop measures specific to these groups. The diversity of ideas and identities in these populations will complicate the development of group consciousness and affect the likelihood that individuals will view their grievances in collective terms. There is every reason to expect that the contrasting historical experiences and contemporary circumstances of Latinos, Asian Americans, and other minorities will cause them to follow a course of political incorporation that is notably different from that traversed by African Americans in the last century.

APPENDIX

Items from the 1984 NBES used to construct the measures of group identification, group consciousness, and political participation:

(1) *Group Identity*

    (i) Common Fate: Cronbach's Alpha = .53

        V1105. Do you think what happens generally to black people in this country will have something to do with what happens in your life? [Yes, No] Will it affect you a lot, some, or not very much?

        V1107. Do you think that the movement for black rights has affected you personally?

        V1108. People differ in whether they think about being black—what they have in common with blacks. What about you—do you think about this a lot, fairly often, once in a while, or hardly ever?

    (ii) Black Autonomy: Cronbach's Alpha = .37

        V2142. Which is more important: being black, being both black and American, or being American?

V2145. Black children should learn an African language.

V2147. Black people should shop in black-owned stores.

V2148. Blacks should not have anything to do with whites.

(2) *Group Consciousness*

   (i) Discontent with Group Status: Cronbach's Alpha = .63

   V1099. Do *blacks* as a group have too much influence, just about the right amount of influence, or too little influence [in American life and politics]?

   V1087. Do *poor people* as a group have too much influence, just about the right amount of influence, or too little influence [in American life and politics]?

   V1091. Do *young people* as a group have too much influence, just about the right amount of influence, or too little influence [in American life and politics]?

   V1093. Do *women* as a group have too much influence, just about the right amount of influence, or too little influence [in American life and politics]?

   V1101. Do *people on welfare* as a group have too much influence, just about the right amount of influence, or too little influence [in American life and politics]?

   (ii) Perception of Discrimination: Pairwise $r = .12$

   V2143. If black people don't do well in life, it is because: they are kept back because of their race; or they don't work hard enough to get ahead.

   V2093. Discrimination against blacks is no longer a problem in this country.

   (iii) Support for Collective Strategies

   V2144. To have power and improve their position in the United States: black people should be more active in black organizations; or each black person should work hard to improve his or her own personal situation.

   (iv) Group Political Efficacy: Cronbach's Alpha = .58

   V1081. If enough blacks vote, they can make a difference in who gets elected President. [Agree strongly, Agree somewhat, Disagree somewhat, Disagree strongly]

   V1082. Black people can make a difference in who gets elected in *local* elections.

   V1084. If blacks, other minorities, the poor, and women pulled together, they could decide how this country is run.

(3) *Political Participation*

   (i) Voting

   V1043. Voted in primary

   V2062. Voted in presidential election

   (ii) Traditional Campaign Activities

   V2086. Influenced people to vote for/against party/candidate

   V2087. Went to political meetings in support of candidate

   V2089. Gave money to candidate

   V2090. Campaigned for a black candidate

   V2088. Helped with voter registration; got people to polls

   V2179. Worked for a party

   (iii) Petitioning

   V2173. Contacted a public official

   V2174. Signed a petition

   (iv) Direct Action

   V2175. Attended a protest meeting or demonstration

   V2176. Picketed or boycotted

NOTES

Acknowledgments. We thank Dukhong Kim, Jean-Francois Godbout, Demelza Baer-Bositis, and Dale Vieregge for their research assistance on this chapter.

1. This chapter does not explicitly consider how group identification and consciousness develop. Scholars across a number of fields have explored this question, offering explanations emphasizing a mix of social and psychological factors (Smith 1991; Hardin 1995; Horowitz 1995; Turner 1999; Laitin 1998; Brady and Kaplan 2001). Some of our discussion in later sections draws on the insights of this literature.

2. For example, Miller et al. (1981) found that group consciousness promoted participation among the poor, blacks, and women, all groups that occupy subordinate positions in American society. But the authors also convincingly showed that group consciousness had similar mobilizing effects on businessmen.

3. These results are not reproduced in the 1995 Verba, Schlozman, and Brady study, (nor, we would guess, in other surveys). In the Verba, Schlozman, and Brady (1995) study, efficacy varies positively with income and education and is greater on average among whites than among blacks. The other major predictor of black participation in the Shingles (1981) analysis was political trust, which also has been found in more recent studies to be insignificantly related to participation.

4. A shortcoming of the Miller et al. (1981) study is that no statistical controls appear to have been applied to the data presented, although the authors note that controls for education and income do not generally alter the main conclusions.

5. In fact, Leighley and Vedlitz (1999) found that one dimension of group consciousness—inter-group distance—actually depresses political participation among Asians and African Americans.

6. Jones-Correa and Leal (1996) found paradoxically that the positive relationship between panethnic identification and participation disappears for individuals who subscribe to this form of identity exclusively; in other words, the correlation holds only for those who choose a panethnic identity in combination with other forms of self-identification. Marschall (2001), on the other hand, found that the mobilizing effect of group consciousness does not extend to activities like voting and contacting community officials.

7. Likewise, we suspect that different forms of group consciousness may exist among Latinos and Asians, a point that awaits study and on which we elaborate later.

8. The aggregated eleven-item consciousness scale has a Cronbach's alpha reliability of .55.

9. The massive voter mobilization in black communities during Jackson's 1984 presidential campaign appears to have had a similar effect on African Americans, heightening feelings of common fate and galvanizing political activism all at once. See Gurin, Hatchett, and Jackson (1989).

10. It might be useful to think about this measurement issue by analogy. Researchers who study racism recognize that items used to measure prejudice in the 1950s are too crude to capture the more subtle forms of racial bias that prevail today. Accordingly, they have updated their items to measure these new forms of racism.

REFERENCES

Aoki, Andrew, and Don T. Nakanishi. "Asian Pacific Americans and the New Minority Politics." *PS: Political Science & Politics* 34:625–630.
Arvizu, J., and F. Chris Garcia. 1996. "Latino Voting Participation: Explaining and Differentiating Latino Voting Turnout." *Hispanic Journal of Behavioral Sciences* 18:104–128.

Brady, Henry, and Cynthia Kaplan. 2001. "Categorically Wrong? Nominal versus Graded Measures of Ethnic Identity." *Studies in Comparative International Development* 35: 56–91.

Bobo, Lawrence, and Frank Gilliam, Jr. 1990. "Race, Socio-Political Participation, and Black Empowerment." *American Political Science Review* 84:377–393.

Brown, Robert A., and Todd C. Shaw. 2002. "Separate Nations: Two Attitudinal Dimensions of Black Nationalism." *Journal of Politics* 64.

Cho, Wendy K Tam. 1999. "Research Notes—Naturalization, Socialization, Participation: Immigrants and (Non)Voting." *The Journal of Politics* 61:1140–1156.

Chong, Dennis. 1991. *Collective Action and the Civil Rights Movement*. Chicago: University of Chicago Press.

Cohen, Cathy J., and Michael C. Dawson. 1993. "Neighborhood Poverty and African-American Politics." *American Political Science Review* 87:286–302.

Conover, Pamela Johnston. 1984. "The Influence of Group Identifications on Political Perceptions and Evaluations." *American Journal of Political Science* 46:760–785.

Dawson, Michael. 1994. *Behind the Mule: Race and Class in African-American Politics*. Princeton: Princeton University Press.

———. 2001. *Black Visions: The Roots of Contemporary African-American Political Ideologies*. Chicago: University of Chicago Press.

Dawson, Michael, Ronald Brown, and Richard Allen. 1989. "A Schema-Based Approach to Modeling an African-American Racial Belief System." *The American Political Science Review* 83:421–441.

Danigelis, Nicholas. 1978. "Black Political Participation in the United States: Some Recent Evidence." *American Sociological Review* 43:756–771.

Diaz, W. A. 1996. "Latino Participation in America: Associational and Political Roles." *Hispanic Journal of Behavioral Sciences* 18:154–174.

Ellison, C. G., and D. A. Gay. 1989. "Black Political Participation Revisited: A Test of Compensatory, Ethnic Community, and Public Arena Models." *Social Science Quarterly* 70:101–119.

Falcon, Angelo, F. Chris Garcia, and Rodolfo de la Garza. 1996. "Ethnicity and Politics: Evidence From the Latino National Political Survey." *Hispanic Journal of Behavioral Sciences* 18:91–103.

Greeley, A. M. 1974. "Political Participation among Ethnic Groups in the United States: A Preliminary Reconnaissance." *American Journal of Sociology* 80:170–204.

Gurin, Patricia, Shirley Hatchett, and James S. Jackson. 1989. *Hope and Independence: Blacks' Response to Electoral and Party Politics*. New York: Russell Sage Foundation.

Guterbock, Thomas, and Bruce London. 1983. "Race, Political Orientation, and Participation: An Empirical Test of Four Competing Theories." *American Sociological Review* 48:439–453.

Hagner, Paul, and John Pierce. 1984. "Racial Differences in Political Conceptualization." *Western Political Quarterly* 37:212–235.

Hardin, Russell. 1995. *One for All: The Logic of Group Conflict*. Princeton: Princeton University Press.

Hardy-Fanta, Carol. 1993. *Latina Politics, Latino Politics: Gender, Culture, and Political Participation in Boston*. Philadelphia: Temple University Press.

Hero, Rodney, and Anne G. Campbell. 1996. "Understanding Latino Political Participation: Understanding the Evidence from the Latino National Political Survey." *Hispanic Journal of Behavioral Sciences* 18:129–141.

Herring, Mary, Thomas B. Jankowski, and Ronald E. Brown. 1999. "Pro-Black Doesn't Mean Anti-White: The Structure of African-American Group Identity." *Journal of Politics* 61:363–381.

Jones-Correa, Michael, and David L. Leal. 1996. "Becoming 'Hispanic': Secondary Panethnic Identification among Latin American–Origin Populations in the United States." *Hispanic Journal of Behavioral Sciences* 18:214–253.

Klobus, Patricia A., and John N. Edwards. 1976. "The Social Participation of Minorities: A Critical Examination of Current Theories." *Phylon* 37:150–158.

Laitin, David. 1998. *Identity Formation: The Russian-Speaking Populations in the Near Abroad.* Ithaca: Cornell University Press.

Leighley, Jan E., and Arnold Vedlitz. 1999. "Race, Ethnicity, and Political Participation: Competing Models and Contrasting Explanations." *Journal of Politics* 61:1092–1114.

Lien, Pei-te. 1994. "Ethnicity and Political Participation: A Comparison between Asian and Mexican Americans." *Political Behavior* 19:237–264.

———. 2001. *The Making of Asian America through Political Participation.* Philadelphia: Temple University Press.

Lien, Pei-te. Christian Collet, Janelle Wong, and S. Karthick Ramakrishnan. 2001a. "Asian Pacific American Public Opinion and Political Participation." *PS: Political Science & Politics* 34:625–631.

Lien, Pei-te, M. Margaret Conway, Taeku Lee, Janelle Wong, and Pitima Boonyarak. 2001b. "The Mosaic of Asian American Politics: Preliminary Results from the Five-City Post-Election Study." Paper presented the Midwest Political Science Association Annual Meeting.

London, Bruce, and Michael W. Giles. 1987. "Black Participation: Compensation or Ethnic Identification." *Journal of Black Studies* 18:20–44.

Marschall, Melissa. 2001. "Does the Shoe Fit? Testing Models of Participation for African-American and Latino Involvement in Local Politics." *Urban Affairs Review* 37:227–248.

Marx, Gary T. 1967. *Protest and Prejudice.* New York: Harper and Row.

Miller, Arthur, Patricia Gurin, Gerald Gurin, and Oksana Malanchuk. 1981. "Group Consciousness and Political Participation." *American Journal of Political Science* 25:494–511.

Morris, Aldon D. 1984. *The Origin of the Civil Rights Movement.* New York: Free Press.

Morris, Aldon D, Shirley J. Hatchett, and Ronald E. Brown. 1989. "The Civil Rights Movement and Black Political Socialization." In *Political Learning in Adulthood: A Sourcebook of Theory and Research*, edited by Roberta S. Sigel. Chicago: University of Chicago Press.

Olsen, Marvin. 1970. "Social and Political Participation of Blacks." *American Sociological Review* 35:682–697.

Orum, Anthony. 1966. "A Reappraisal of the Social and Political Participation of Negroes." *American Journal of Sociology* 72:32–46.

Pinderhughes, Dianne. 1987. *Race and Ethnicity in Chicago Politics: A Reexamination of Pluralist Theory.* Urbana: University of Illinois Press.

Rogers, Reuel. 2001. "Black Like Who? Afro-Caribbean Immigrants, African Americans and the Politics of Group Identity." In *Islands in the City: West Indian Migration to New York*, edited by Nancy Foner. Berkeley: University of California Press.

Shaw, Daron, Rodolfo A. de la Garza, and Jongho Lee. 2000. "Examining Latino Turnout in 1996: A Three-State Validated Survey Approach." *American Journal of Political Science* 44:332–340.

Shingles, Richard D. 1981. "Black Consciousness and Political Participation: The Missing Link." *American Political Science Review* 75:76–91.

Smith, Anthony. 1986. *The Ethnic Origins of Nations.* Cambridge: Blackwell.

Tate, Katherine. 1993. *From Protest to Politics: The New Black Voters in American Elections.* Cambridge: Harvard University Press.

Turner, John. 1999. "Some Current Issues in Research on Social Identity and Self-Categorization Theories." In *Social Identity*, edited by Naomi Elmers, Russell Spears, and Bertjan Doosje. Cambridge: Blackwell.

Uhlaner, Carol, B. Cain, and D Kiewiet. 1989. "Political Participation of Ethnic Minorities in the 1980s." *Political Behavior* 11:195–231.

Verba, Sidney, Kay Schlozman, and Henry Brady. 1993. "Race, Ethnicity, and Political Resources: Participation in the United States." *British Journal of Political Science* 23:453–497.

———. 1995. *Voice and Equality: Civic Voluntarism in American Politics*. Cambridge: Harvard University Press.

Wrinkle, Robert D., Joseph Stewart, J. L. Polinard, Kenneth Meirer, and John Arvizu. 1996. "Ethnicity and Nonelectoral Participation." *Hispanic Journal of Behavioral Sciences* 18 (1996):142–143.

MICHAEL JONES-CORREA

4   Bringing Outsiders In

Questions of Immigrant Incorporation

IN 2000, THE CENSUS BUREAU announced that 10.4 percent of the U.S. population was made up of first-generation immigrants, the highest proportion since the 1940s and more than double the percentage in 1970 (4.7 percent). In the 1990s, 8.6 million immigrants arrived, adding to the 8.3 million who came in the 1980s and the 11.5 million who arrived before 1980. Although the number of immigrants arriving since 1965 has surpassed the level of the last great wave of immigration to this country (1880–1920), few researchers have studied how contemporary immigrants are incorporating into the U.S. political system. As a result, after forty years of renewed large-scale immigration to the United States, we have a sense of its economic, but not its political, consequences, neither for immigrants nor for the American political system. Yet it seems increasingly obvious that an understanding of immigrants and their political incorporation is essential for an understanding of American politics.

This chapter raises questions about the nature of political incorporation, why it matters for democratic inclusion, and who incorporates and is incorporated. It delves deeper into the paradox of contemporary immigrant political incorporation—the fact that immigrants today are simultaneously more and less incorporated than perhaps ever before—and the complexities of immigrant identities. The last portion of the chapter lays out an agenda for the study of immigrant political incorporation, arguing for the need for comparisons across ethnic groups, places, institutional layers, and time.

WHAT IS POLITICAL INCORPORATION?

What do we mean by the "political incorporation" of immigrants? The question is not easy to answer because the answer presupposes that we can agree on the meaning of "politics." *Incorporation* could be taken to mean, at the least, the process of naturalization, the choice to naturalize being a basic political act. Most commonly, political scientists think of political incorporation as defined by participation in formal electoral politics (DeSipio 1996). In this sense, participation would be measured by whether immigrants are registered and voting. However, because many native-born citizens do not vote yet are arguably nonetheless incorporated, perhaps incorporation might be defined minimally as living within the polity as a law-abiding citizen (Plotke 1999). Or if there is more to participation than simply formal politics, then perhaps the definition of political incorporation should be expanded to include both participation in electoral and nonelectoral forms of politics, and indeed, in forms of organizational life that might not be overtly considered political at all (Verba, Schlosman and Brady 1995; Jones-Correa 1998a; Wong 2002). Political incorporation might also refer not only to the incorporation of individual immigrants, but to their incorporation as a group. So it may be that political incorporation is reflected in the number of immigrant co-ethnics elected to office, appointed to administrative positions, or employed in government (McClain and Karnig 1990; McClain 1996). It might also be, however, that incorporation might best be measured not solely by representation, but by how immigrants' interests are reflected in political outcomes and policies (Browning, Marshall, and Tabb 1984).

How expansive a definition of 'politics' we choose shapes, of course, the extent to which we find immigrants are politically incorporated. The broader the definition, presumably the more likely we are to find immigrants involved in political life. If we look only at formal politics, clearly many immigrants have yet to naturalize—and once naturalized, may not fully exercise their right to vote. For example, while the number of naturalized citizens increased by 46 percent (from 6.2 million to 9 million) between 1970 and 1990, the increase in the total number of non-citizens was markedly greater—373 percent (from 3.5 million to 16.7 million) (Schmidley and Gibson 1999, 20). It appears that even when naturalized, immigrants do not vote at rates equal to the native born (DeSipio 1996; Bass and Casper 1999; Ramakrishnan and Espenshade 2000). However, if we look at political participation more broadly, immigrants might still register lower rates of nonelectoral participation, but their involvement in a much broader range of activities, particularly churches and ethnic organizations (de la Garza et al. 1992; Lien, Conway, and Wong 2003) might be seen as signs of incorporation.

WHY DOES INCORPORATION MATTER?

There are three principal arguments in favor of incorporation (see Jones-Correa 1998a, 46–48). First, there is the problem of representation and accountability. If non-participants hold views similar, and in similar proportions, to participants (Wolfinger and Rosenstone 1980, chapter 6; Bennett and Resnick 1990; Gant and Lyons 1993) then non-participation may not matter. But this is unlikely to be the case if a distinct *group* of people is underrepresented, rather than just random individuals, and if this group has special needs and unique views in a number of important areas (Verba et al. 1993). Immigrants are a case in point. While immigrants may hold representative views about, say, who should be elected president, they will probably have distinct views on a number of issues which affect them directly but affect most Americans only tangentially—questions of immigration restrictions, language policy, English as a second language, for example. Ignoring the question of representation means there is a widespread absence of accountability for the politicians and bureaucracies who purport to represent recent immigrants, and the inadequate representation of immigrants' views means many of their needs—in education, housing, and health—are poorly met.

Second and more importantly, inclusion of those on the margins of the polity is important because democratic decision making is not simply a matter of reflecting people's previously held views. If this were true, the argument above might be right—if participants and non-participants held the same views, then it might make little difference whether people participated or not. However, people do not enter the polity with their interests already formed and their minds already made up.[1] Participation is more than simply ensuring adequate representation; it is one of the key ingredients of democratic deliberation. In the process of deliberation, views are not only aired, but opinions changed, new options considered, old questions discarded. The political incorporation of immigrants matters because participation is about the *process* of democracy rather than about its outcome.[2]

Third, and most critically, the political marginalization of immigrants matters because they are all potential future citizens and future Americans. The absence of any mention of political incorporation from the immigration debate implies seeing immigrants only as "the other" not as potential members in a common polity. By focusing only on the economic costs or cultural dangers of immigration, the public discussion thus far has drawn a line between "us" and "them" not recognizing immigrants as being "one of us." To have a significant portion of the population remain inactive politically for most of their adult lives—participating in neither the formal political systems of the country they arrive from nor the country which takes them in—undermines the legitimacy of democratic institutions (Walzer 1983).

Reaching agreement on the importance of political incorporation still begs the questions of what incorporation might entail and how to go about carrying it out. What exactly should incorporation look like? The Americanization programs of the early twentieth century, with language and civic classes? Public services to mediate between immigrants and unfamiliar institutions? Ease of access to naturalization, registration, and voting, without regard to language?

WHO INCORPORATES?

The United States has no national policy or program for the incorporation of immigrants. The decision to naturalize, register, vote, or join associations is seen as an individual decision and immigrant incorporation is left largely in the hands of immigrants themselves. Any organized efforts at incorporation have been generated largely by the private sector, particularly by nonprofits. Both historically and contemporaneously, private associations such as political parties, labor unions, churches, and civic groups have been the primary actors engaged in immigrant incorporation (Putnam 2000; DeSipio 1996; Wong 2002).

Historically, political parties have been seen as the primary engine of political incorporation. But there is a debate about how effective parties ever were in incorporating immigrants. A generation of social scientists including Robert Merton, Robert Dahl, and Raymond Wolfinger generally portrayed the recruitment of immigrants by political parties in a positive light (Merton

1957; Dahl 1961; Cornwell 1964, 27–39; Wolfinger 1972). Their writing was deeply influenced by instrumentalist explanations for party politics like those of Joseph Schumpeter and Anthony Downs, who argued that given an environment with open elections and two political parties, parties will compete with one another to co-opt actors and issues so as to acquire and retain power (Schumpeter 1942, 279; Downs 1957). Theoretically, rivals and alternative programs will be co-opted since the alternative is that these might present the basis for subsequent challenges (Schumpeter 1942, 281).

In this view, because parties compete over votes, they will eventually mobilize potential or marginal players as well. Indeed, in the case of immigrants, "politicians took the initiative; they made it easy for immigrants to become citizens, encouraged ethnics to register, put them on the party rolls, and aided them in meeting the innumerable specific problems resulting from their poverty, strangeness and lowly position" (Dahl 1961, 34). Immigrants didn't even need to be citizens to be incorporated, because politicians guided them through the court system as fast as—or faster than—the law allowed, making them citizens and leading them to the polling booths. This made sense in the economy of machine politics, which traded in particularistic benefits (i.e. essentially trading favors for votes) for all parties involved (Wolfinger 1965, 898; Erie 1988, 192).

However, this argument only works if political parties are in fact competitive. Steven Erie argues that historically the goal of local parties was to become local hegemons. As long as local political machines were embryonic, he writes, they were mobilizers, facing competitive pressures to increase the number of partisan voters. Entrenched machines, on the other hand, were only selective mobilizers; as they nursed their limited resources, it was in their interests to turn out only minimal winning coalitions, so they had little incentive to mobilize newer ethnic arrivals (Erie 1988, 10). In this view, the incorporation of immigrants into politics can be explained by the timing and context of their arrival: Earlier immigrants like the Irish arrived to nascent urban political machines and were incorporated; later immigrants like the Italians and Jews arrived to cities with mature machines—and were largely marginalized. In competitive environments, immigrants were mobilized; in noncompetitive environments, they were not. Is there a similar dynamic today?

Contemporary parties are quite different from those of a hundred years ago. It is unclear whether parties could now play the role that proponents argue they did during the last wave of immigration—even if they wished. Parties function today as loose networks for candidate recruitment, as well as mechanisms for coordinated fundraising. Grassroots party organization has largely withered away. Professionalized interest group politics, targeting its audiences via mass mailings, has taken its place (Lowi 1979). With the removal of naturalization procedures from party-dominated local and state courts to specialized federal courts and the Immigration and Naturalization Service, it is unlikely, even if parties still had the local capacities they once did, that they could play the same role in incorporating immigrants into the political system. In addition, contemporary party politics at the state and local level are often not competitive—one or the other of the major parties often dominates. Party organizations understandably make choices about where to place scarce resources on the basis of where they believe their candidates might win, so resources go to areas of existing strength. Parties tend to leave their competitors' core areas of strength alone. As a result, few elections are won in close races and incumbents often go unchallenged.

However, national elections are a different story. Here the major parties continue to be competitive, and it is in national elections that parties are likely to have the greatest impact on mobilizing new ethnic voters. In the 2000 presidential election campaign, for example, both parties reached out to new Latino voters, with both Democrats and Republicans running Spanish-language ads in media markets across the country and their presidential candidates (particularly then-Governor Bush) making symbolic attempts (speaking Spanish, attending Catholic Mass) to reach out to these perceived swing voters. During the campaign, both Republicans and Democrats had operations to target Hispanic voters and donors, with steering committees, youth organizations, and materials and Web sites in English and Spanish, all targeting Latinos (Booth 2000).

The case of Latinos in the 2000 elections indicates that under competitive situations parties may, in fact, reach out to what they perceive as new swing constituencies. This implies, however, that the role of political parties in immigrant incorporation is likely to be quite uneven, with immigrants in competitive areas being contacted and mobilized, and those in non-competitive areas left to their own devices. In addition, in the 2000 elections, Latinos were a large enough population to potentially determine key state elections, and their voting patterns were indeterminate enough to make them appealing to both the Democratic and Republican national parties. This is not true of every immigrant or ethnic group. Some groups, because of their smaller size, or because they might be seen as too closely identified with one party, may not be the target of competitive mobilization.

Parties, however, are not the only mobilizing organizations—unions, religious and civic organizations, and ethnic groups all play a role in the political incorporation of immigrants. Some scholars (Mink 1986; Morawska 2001) have gone so far as to argue that historically, unions and churches did more to incorporate immigrants politically than did parties. Given the weakness of local party organizations, this should be even truer today. Union activism would seem to be an obvious alternative to party mobilization, but the percentage of the American workforce belonging to unions has been declining steadily for decades (Freeman and Medoff 1984; Troy 1990). There are some indications, however, that although unions are shrinking, they still play (or believe they can play) a significant role in those areas of economy where immigrants are concentrated. Among the most visible and active unions during the 1990s were those involved in unionizing largely immigrant workers in the service sector (Cranford 2000; Trumpour and Bernard 2002). These service unions were the only area of union expansion in the 1980s and 1990s. As a result, in a radical break from previous union policy, in 2001 the AFL-CIO officially adopted a policy advocating the legalization of undocumented immigrants in the United States (though older sentiments have not entirely disappeared;

see Briggs 2001). Whatever the impact of unions, however, they are unlikely to be the principal agent of incorporation. Most immigrants are more likely to come in contact with local non-profit organizations—churches, neighborhood groups, ethnic organizations, and so forth—in their own neighborhoods. Local non-profits are arguably more numerous and better organized than their counterparts during the last wave of immigration. The question is whether local non-profits are picking up the slack in incorporation efforts left by parties and unions, thereby serving to mobilize new immigrants. Some research suggests that they may be (Wong 2002). If so, what drives non-profit-led incorporation? If non-profit incorporation is not motivated by the competitive drive of politics, then is it driven by clientalist relationships with the immigrants non-profits serve (see, for example, Hamilton 1979)? Or is it driven by the goals of funding organizations like foundations or the state and local governments that back local non-profits? Will incorporation ebb and flow with the shifting interests (and endowments) of these funding organizations?

How different is political incorporation now than it was at the turn of the last century? The absence of governmental action and the involvement of the private sector in Americanization and political incorporation are striking, both in the past and present. In both eras, incorporation has been left to the private sphere—to immigrants themselves and to those organizations which, for one reason or another, found it in their interests to mobilize these new immigrants politically. But as noted earlier, incorporation seems to have shifted sites, or at least the emphasis among the sites of incorporation has shifted. What difference does this make to immigrants themselves? Do different sites of incorporation incorporate immigrants differently or incorporate different kinds of immigrants? For instance, those participating in church life might be engaged in quite different kinds of politics compared with those who are contacted and mobilized by political parties. It might also be, however, that incorporation in one site—labor activism, for instance—lends immigrants the skills and incentives to become politically incorporated in other ways—say, to naturalize or to vote.

WHO IS INCORPORATED?

Immigrants may share the sense of being strangers in a strange land, but they obviously do not have identical characteristics, histories, or experiences. Their prior socialization, their education, their occupations, and their English language skills all influence their incorporation into politics. By extension, differences in these areas translate into differential political incorporation. Similar to patterns found in the broader literature on political participation, the more educated immigrants are, the higher their income, and the greater their command of English, the more likely they are to be active in formal electoral politics (DeSipio 1996; Jones-Correa 1998a; Lien, Conway, and Wong 2003). The same is still likely to be true of informal politics (though less so) if findings for the population as a whole hold true for immigrants as well (Verba, Schlozman, and Brady 1995; Lien, Conway, and Wong 2003). Political incorporation also likely differs by gender, with women likely to be more engaged, or at least engaged differently, than men (Jones-Correa 1998b).

If individual characteristics shape political incorporation, so likely do those of groups. It seems to make a difference, for instance, whether immigrants come to the United States as political refugees or as economic migrants, not least because of the additional aid they receive upon arrival, but also because the reasons for migration shape their views of politics and its uses in the United States. Political migrants are more likely to see politics as central to their predicament and are therefore more likely to focus what resources they have on avenues of political mobilization. There is some evidence that political migrants become naturalized more quickly; presumably this would lead them to focus on politics in the United States quickly as well (Portes and Rumbaut 1990). This is an old story, but the effects of political exile can be seen in the mobilization of immigrant groups as disparate as Germans after 1848 (many of whom became active in the nascent labor movement) to Cubans after 1958 (who mobilized first as exiles, then as a foreign policy interest group).

The difference between political and economic migrants suggests that immigrants' ties (or lack of ties) to their home countries may affect their political incorporation in the United States. Sociologists and anthropologists have written extensively about the role of economic remittances, circular migration, and constant communication in the creation of a single social sphere for immigrants encompassing both sending and receiving countries (Smith 1993; Rouse 1996; Levitt 2001). If true, this transnational circuit would likely have effects on immigrant political incorporation in the United States. Some suggest the rise of expatriate politics, or, more precisely, of the extension of sending states' polities to include immigrants abroad (Guarnizo 1996, 2001). Others, myself included, have argued that these forms of politics, while playing an important role in the political incorporation of the first generation (Jones-Correa 1998a), will fade with subsequent generations in the United States (Jones-Correa 2002c). One might think that immigrants with greater ties to their countries of origin might be less incorporated, but this is far from certain. Research on dual nationality provisions (Jones-Correa 2001b) and language retention (Portes and Rumbaut 2001) both suggest otherwise. In either case, it is likely that immigrant experiences of transnationalism are likely to vary, both across groups and across time, and it would be worth the effort to know how these differences play out in the incorporation of immigrants into American politics.

It is also the case that different immigrant groups are likely to be received differently in the United States. This is not only because the native-born population evaluates immigrants from different countries of origin differently, though this is true as well. Latino immigrants are evaluated less highly than Asians, for instance, though both are often evaluated more highly (by employers at least) than native-born blacks (Waldinger 1996). Rather, it is also because some immigrants, upon entering the Unites States, are defined as minorities (immigrants from Latin American, Africa, Asia), whereas others are not (immigrants from Europe and the Middle East, for instance).

Coverage under statutes targeted for minorities may have a wide impact on incorporation—on immigrants' chances for education, business ownership, and access to public benefits, for instance. But inclusion as a "minority" has direct political consequences as well, including coverage under the Voting Rights Act. Though we have very little knowledge of the matter, presumably immigrants covered under the act will find it easier (and perhaps have more incentives) to incorporate politically than those who are not.

THE PARADOX OF CONTEMPORARY POLITICAL INCORPORATION

The discussion thus far suggests the paradoxical state of immigrant political incorporation. On the one hand, mobilizing institutions seem to be in decline and large numbers of immigrants remain outside the formal political system. Certainly two of the primary engines of mobilization in the past, parties and unions, are shadows of their former selves. And nearly half of all immigrants, almost twenty years after their arrival, have yet to naturalize. Yet by some measures, immigrants today, despite concerns from many quarters about their naturalization and participation as citizens, seem to be incorporating as quickly today (if not more quickly) as their counterparts in the past.

Take the case of Latinos, for instance: In the twenty years before the 1996 presidential election, the number of votes cast by Hispanics jumped 135 percent, compared with 21 percent for the rest of voters (Irvine 2000). Even in 1996, Latinos were still only 5 percent of the national electorate. In the 2000 elections—only four years later—Hispanics accounted for more than 7 percent of the electorate, a 40 percent increase. In California, the state with the largest number of electoral votes, 16 percent of registered voters—about 2.35 million people—were Latinos in 2000, compared with only 10 percent in 1990 (Jones-Correa 2002b). These increases are largely attributable to the naturalization of Latino immigrants. From 1991 to 2000, 5.6 million immigrants naturalized. Between 1994 and 1996, naturalization rates increased three-fold across all immigrant groups in the United States to 1.05 million per year.[3] In California, a record 879,000 immigrant adults were naturalized from 1994 to 1997 and another 623,000 had applications pending at the end of 1997. In 1997, the number of new citizens dropped off to 598,225 and then to 463,060 in 1998. But in 1999, the number again nearly doubled to 872,427, and by the fiscal year ending in September 2000, the number had risen even further, to 898,315 (Robinson 2000)—and rose again following the events of 9/11. Almost half of all recent new citizens were born in Latin America.

Forty-five percent of likely Latino voters in the 2000 election were foreign-born, compared with 20 percent in 1990 (Bustos 2000b). The mobilization of immigrant voters has meant that they are increasingly able to elect co-ethnics to office. Latinos have made significant inroads at every level, particularly in California. Haitians have been elected to office in North Miami, there are Dominican and West Indian city council members and state assembly members in New York City, and Asian Americans have been elected to school boards and city councils (for example, in Silicon Valley and the cluster of cities along the I-10 corridor between Los Angeles and Pomona). This is not to say that there has been a tidal wave of immigrants elected to office, but their numbers and impact have been steadily increasing. What is even more striking is that much of this success has been made within the *first* generation of immigrants—rather than their children's generation, as has been historically typical. At least in this respect, contemporary immigrants seem to be incorporating more quickly than immigrants in the past; few, if any, of the earlier immigrant groups, not even the Irish, were electing co-ethnic political representatives within the first generation of arrival. Yet among current immigrants, political representation, at some level of government, is not unusual.

How can we account for the disparity between the perspectives of immigrants as marginalized and immigrants as mobilized? The two seem at odds, but, in fact, both may be true. On the plus side, most immigrants are likely to encounter less overt discrimination in politics (and society) than previous migrants to the United States. There is little de jure exclusion and a great deal more institutional openness, thanks to the great social movements of the nineteenth and twentieth centuries—the push for abolition, women's suffrage, civil rights, and so forth. There is plenty of room for anti-immigration and anti-immigrant feeling to surface, but on the whole, at least in the public realm of politics, this is only occasionally directed directly at immigrants themselves. More often than not, in the public realm, immigrants are ignored rather than deprecated. This is not to suggest that immigrants do not face considerable hurdles to political incorporation, not the least from subtle (or not so subtle) forms of harassment and discrimination. But the passage of the Voting Rights Act and its subsequent implementation has opened opportunities for political representation that did not exist for previous immigrants.

There has been remarkably little evaluation of the Voting Rights Act and its effects on minority representation (though see Grofman and Davidson 1996; de la Garza and DeSipio 1997) and still less for immigrants. Yet it seems from the scattered evidence that does exist that immigrant and native-born minorities have both benefited from the implementation of the act, particularly when concentrated in sufficient numbers to warrant the creation of majority–minority political districts for political representation. The effects of redistricting allowing immigrant representation have been more evident at the local level than at the federal level—mainly because local politics offers a greater number of political openings. The fragmentation of local politics also makes it highly permeable, offering multiple avenues for incorporation, whether through school boards, city councils, county commissions, or other entities. All in all, the concentration of recent immigrants, the inclusion of many of them under the Voting Rights Act, and the multiplicity of local governments have enabled many immigrant groups to exercise a greater influence on politics than their historical counterparts at this stage in their migration.

This achievement should not ignore the fact that the election of immigrant representatives often occurs in the context of a broader alienation of immigrants from political participation of all kinds. Although more immigrants are naturalizing and voting, the rates of increase in formal politics are not keeping up with the rate of increase in immigration itself, so though more immigrants are participating in formal politics, many more remain outside it. It is also significant that the political representation of immigrants has occurred mostly at the local level. Political turnout in local elections (which are often non-partisan and off-cycle from national elections) is often quite low. In districts with a preponderance of immigrants, turnout is even lower. Under these circumstances, small organized electorates can successfully elect their representatives to office. While immigrants and other newcomers to the political system are trying to enter the political arena, the fact that small minimal-winning coalitions can capture and hold local offices is often problematic; many "immigrant" districts are represented by non-immigrants. Once mobilized, however, overall lower participation in local politics may work to immigrants' advantage, at least in the sense of getting co-ethnic candidates placed. The fact is that the Voting Rights Act facilitates political representation, but does not necessarily increase political mobilization.[4]

Hero suggests that minorities as a whole may suffer from a system of "two-tiered" pluralism in American politics (Hero 1992). That is, minorities are able to participate, vote, and elect representatives, but only up to a point; once political districts are no longer majority–minority (like most Congressional seats held by ethnic and racial representatives), or once they become de facto at-large districts (like most state-wide offices and Senate seats), then minorities are rarely elected to these offices. If this is true, then the Voting Rights Act and the opening of electoral politics to ethnic and racial minorities may lead only to the *limited* incorporation of immigrants in American politics. If so, then the success of certain immigrant groups in electing representatives at the local level will plateau, with increasing numbers of representatives elected where immigrants are concentrated, but little beyond that. Election of candidates in at-large districts may take much longer, depending on the racial and ethnic politics of the group in question. What may result is the political equivalent of what some sociologists have argued is the "segmented assimilation" of immigrants (Portes and Zhou 1993; Zhou 1998), with some (or all?) immigrant groups being trapped into electoral cul-de-sacs from which they can move no further. Is this true?

THE CONFUSION OF IMMIGRANT IDENTITIES

Despite the ease with which we talk about "Chinese," or "Asian American," or "Latino" immigrants, it is by no means clear to what degree we can talk about them as belonging to coherent ethnic groups. Immigrants, even immigrants from the same country, have as many differences among them as similarities (regional origin, occupation, education, status or class, to name a few). It is not clear why we should expect immigrants, even those from the same country, to share common interests and act as a group. Nonetheless— as also happened during the last wave of immigration as immigrants with very different regional identities became identified by nationality, for instance (Handlin 1973 [1951]), or as immigrants from Southern and Eastern

Europe became identified as "whites" (Jacobson 1998)—immigrants are often lumped together in categories not of their own making. Native-born Americans often see little to distinguish migrants from different parts of China (even though they may not share a common language), or immigrants from China from those of Taiwan or Hong Kong, or from ethnic Chinese immigrating from Vietnam or the Philippines. Once immigrants are in the United States, at least from many outsiders' perspectives, these differences seem trivial or irrelevant. Indeed, from outsiders' points of view, differences between ethnic Chinese and other Asian immigrants fade as well, though Asian immigration encompasses tremendous differences. The question is: When do identities, whether originating among immigrants or the host society, matter? To what extent do institutions in the United States shape immigrant identities? How do immigrants' identities affect their political incorporation? And do immigrant identities in turn shape political institutions?

Certainly the state plays a significant role in identity formation. Take, for example, the question of "race." The previous wave of immigration to the United States was overwhelmingly European. Most recent immigrants have come from either Asia or Latin America. In 2000, 14.5 million, or 51 percent of the foreign-born population was from Latin America, and an additional 24 percent, or 6.8 million people, were from Asia. These two regions accounted for the top ten countries of immigrants' origin (Mexico, China, Philippines, India, Vietnam, El Salvador, Korea, the Dominican Republic, Cuba, and Colombia; Schmidley and Gibson 1999, 2). Immigrants from Mexico accounted for about 29 percent of the foreign-born population alone, and the first-generation Mexican-American population is about six times as large as the next highest foreign-born population. On arrival, recent immigrants are seen through the prism of black/white relations in the United States. From the moment immigrants set foot in the country, the state—and the broader society at large—seeks to classify them by race and ethnicity. Immigrants arriving from Asia or Latin America, because of their origins, are considered "racial" or "linguistic" minorities. Congress enacted the Civil Rights Act (1964) and the Voting Rights Act (1965) primarily in response to the long-term exclusion of African Americans from full membership in the political, economic, and social spheres of life in the United States. However, in 1975, the Voting Rights Act was amended to include "linguistic minorities" like Asian Americans and Latinos. Since then, immigrants arriving to the United States from Africa, Asia, and Latin America have been included under this civil rights legislation.

Yet how do immigrants see themselves? Most Latinos (Jones-Correa and Leal 1996) and Asian Americans (Lien 2001; Lien, Conway, and Wong 2003) in the United States identify primarily by their national origins, not the panethnic labels (i.e "Asian American," "Hispanic") used by government agencies in the United States. But some identify panethnically exclusively while others are willing to use panethnic labels occasionally. Immigrants are asked to identify themselves in state, federal, and local documents according to the standard racial categories set out by the Office of Management and Budget's obscure Statistical Directive 15. This incessant classification—by the state, the media, and others—induces immigrants to adopt politically relevant identities, which to some extent they internalize (Jones-Correa and Leal 1996; Nobles 1999; Lien, Conway, and Wong 2003). There would appear to be some incentive for immigrants to use these identities, if only for instrumental purposes, because the state disburses funding and benefits in part according to its racial formulas. However, the little research on this topic suggests that panethnic identities for immigrants go beyond instrumentalism or ethnic solidarity, indicating that these identities shape orientations to politics more generally, and that individuals who use these identities have real attachments to these constructions (Jones-Correa and Leal 1996).

So do common identities lead to collective mobilization? In the case of African Americans, Michael Dawson has argued that collective action is facilitated by a common experience of discrimination, a sense of "linked fate" (what happens to one individual will happen to all), and shared institutions (Dawson 1994; see also Chong and Rogers, this volume). In the case of immigrants, there is a general absence of shared institutions and a dubious sense of linked fate. Perhaps the Catholic Church among Latinos could be said to be a shared institution and theoretically could play a role similar to the church in the African American community. But this is unlikely to happen (Jones-Correa and Leal 2001). Though there are national interest groups purporting to speak for Latinos and Asian Americans, their grassroots connections (and hence their legitimacy) have always been somewhat shaky. Both Asian Americans and Latinos identify somewhat with their co-ethnics of other national origins, but this does not lead to strong common positions on policy issues, except, unsurprisingly, on immigration issues. Even here, studies have found that earlier immigrants are often quite skeptical of continued immigration (Sierra 1987; de la Garza et al. 1991).

The majority of immigrants, like native-born minorities, indicates that they have encountered discrimination, and this experience of discrimination could be seen as a stepping stone to collective action. But for discrimination to lead to mobilization, it must not only be similarly experienced, but also similarly interpreted. Immigrants may fulfill neither of these conditions. Surveys clearly indicate that Latino and Asian immigrants are often discriminated against—but by whom and for what reasons? Contemporary surveys often use questions to illustrate interracial relations between blacks and whites that were designed in the 1950s and 60s. It is doubtful whether these questions fully capture the range of possibilities for discrimination existing in a multi-racial society. For instance, these surveys never ask who initiates the discrimination. A generation or two ago, it was assumed that whites were always the perpetrators and blacks always the targets of discrimination. This assumption is of course much less self-evident today. Immigrants from Latin America or Asia entering into the United States today might experience discrimination from any number of sources: from native-born whites, from native-born blacks, from other immigrants, and not least from their native born co-ethnics. To assume that native-born whites are the sole source of discrimination is an oversimplification at best.

Most surveys do not evaluate the root issue of the discrimination either. Did immigrants feel discriminated against for reasons of race or for reasons of language? If they answer the latter, then presumably discrimination will fade as an issue over time and generations. Most studies, though, have found that perceptions of discrimination in fact increase over time for immigrants, and some show increases over succeeding generations (Jones-Correa and Joyce 2001). This suggests that the discrimination immigrants perceive is not simply linguistic. However, "racial" discrimination can be tricky to pin down. Some scholars, for instance, point to Americans' perceptions of Asian Americans as "permanent foreigners" as a sign of racialization by the broader society (Lowe 1996). However, Asian Americans, as a whole, are currently overwhelmingly a first-generation population. Will this sentiment ease as more Asian Americans are native born? In short, are Asian Americans being targeted for their status as recent immigrants or for the colors of their skin?[5] In either case, while immigrants may experience discrimination as frequently as native-born minorities, they may interpret the experience quite differently. Immigrants may see discrimination as a sign of their own faults, or if they think it unjustified, may see it as the action of a particular unlikable individual, not as a systemic flaw. All this suggests that while immigrants may have identities and experiences in common, this may not guarantee common mobilization.

Once again, we are confronted by conflicting trends: On the one hand, immigrants come to the United States with disparate backgrounds and have quite different experiences when they arrive. On the other, immigrants receive common labels upon arrival, most say they experience discrimination, and their recognition of discrimination increases over time. How will immigrants' identities play out? Will they see themselves, over the long run, as part of an "immigrant" narrative in the United States, or rather as playing a role in the narrative of American race relations (Skerry 1993)? This question is complicated by the fact that the state-created "panethnic" categories of Hispanic and Asian American in fact include both narratives, in the sense that at least a portion among the native born in both groups was the subject of de jure racial discrimination while many Latinos and Asian Americans are also recent arrivals to the U.S. But the fact that these groups include both immigrants and minorities still does not meant that native-born and immigrant-born Asian and Hispanic Americans will see eye to eye; relations between the two are quite complicated (Gutierrez 1995, 1996).

Regardless of how immigrants in the end identify, there is no shortage of "ethnic entrepreneurs" seeking to mobilize immigrants and the native born into some broader panethnic coalition. And there is some evidence that immigrants and the native born falling under a panethnic umbrella will support co-ethnic candidates (de la Garza and DeSipio 1997; Lien, Conway, and Wong 2003). This suggests that whatever the ambivalence of immigrants about their shared identities, in this respect at least, these identities will have political effects. This is not dissimilar to what scholars found for the earlier wave of immigrants (Wolfinger 1965). The more ethnic strategies succeed politically, the more deeply entrenched they will become in the state. However, it may be that the strategies of ethnic entrepreneurship are only of limited use; that the two-tiered pluralism which may limit immigrant incorporation may in part reflect the choice of strategy for ethnic mobilization. It may be that the panethnic mobilization strategy that wins offices at the local level has counterproductive effects at the state level, for instance. At the state level, the broader pool of voters may not be able to disassociate the message of ethnic candidates running de-racialized campaigns in state-wide races from the message of candidates running more ethnically or racially specific campaigns at the local level.[6] Again, is this true?

This chapter thus far has set out general questions about immigrant political incorporation and has briefly explored two areas that seem particularly puzzling: the extent and limitations of immigrant political incorporation, and immigrants' ethnic and racial identities. The discussion thus far raises far more questions than it answers and, if anything, indicates how little we know about the political incorporation of immigrants. The rest of the chapter lays out what needs to be done—a possible agenda for the study of immigrant political incorporation.

As we gather more and better survey and fieldwork data, we will learn more about the political attitudes and behavior of individual immigrants and of individual groups of immigrants. But as the previous discussion has highlighted, immigrant incorporation is likely to be uneven, varying by institution, by group, and by generation, among other things. The unevenness of the immigrant experience underlines how much more we need to know about how and when political incorporation varies. There are at least four kinds of work needed to explore this variation adequately: We need more comparisons across groups, across places, across institutional levels, and across time periods. The sections which follow touch briefly on each of these areas.

COMPARISONS ACROSS GROUPS

Research on the new immigration has been increasing exponentially. Though the bulk of this research has been undertaken largely in the allied social sciences, political scientists too have begun to focus on these new immigrants and their politics. Most of this work has focused on particular immigrant groups, often in particular communities. We have studies of Caribbean immigrants in Brooklyn (Foner 1987; Kasinitz 1992), Asian Americans in Monterey Park (Fong 1994; Horton 1995), and Cubans in Miami (Portes and Stepick 1993), just to name a few. However, there is still very little comparative work across immigrant groups, say, comparing Chinese with Dominicans, or Russians with Haitians, even though different immigrant groups have very different immigration trajectories, socioeconomic characteristics, residential patterns, and more, each of which might presumably shape political incorporation.[7] There are increasing numbers of surveys of panethnic clusters: of Latinos (de la Garza et al. 1992; but see also the recent spate of surveys preceding the 2000 elections and the series of surveys conducted by the Kaiser Foundation and the Pew Hispanic Research Center) and of Asian Americans (Lien 1997, 2003), for example. These comparisons, while useful, unquestioningly accept the government's ethnic and racial classifications. It may indeed be useful to collect comparative data on Cubans, Puerto Ricans, and Mexicans in the United States, but it may be that something is lost by assuming that these comparisons are always automatically the best and most useful comparisons. As a result, we have little sense of how immigrant and ethnic groups compare or relate to one another.

This last is particularly important because immigrants are not living as isolated individuals, or even as isolated groups, but rather are often living in diverse ethnic settings. So how do individuals and groups relate to one another? How does the presence of one group affect the attitudes/identities/actions of others? There is a growing body of work on interethnic conflict, competition, and cooperation (McClain and Karnig 1990; Jennings 1994; McClain 1996; Saito 1998; Joyce 1999; Alex-Assensoh, Alex-Assensoh, and Hanks 2000; Jaynes 2000; Jones-Correa 2001c), though much of this literature does not address immigrants and immigration specifically. The fact is that we still know very little about the about how groups interact or how the presence of one group might shape or change the participation of another. Given that African Americans were at the forefront of the struggle for civil rights, for instance, what effect does the presence of a substantial native-born black population have on the political incorporation of immigrants? This chapter has already touched on the relation between native-born and immigrant co-ethnics, but it is worth reiterating that for the most part we know very little about what effect the presence of native-born co-ethnics, or even of a settled immigrant community, might have on the incorporation of new immigrants. How did the presence of the relatively large and well-placed Jewish population in New York City shape the process of incorporating the Russian Jewish population which began arriving to the city in the 1970s and 1980s? How did the presence of an established Cuban American population affect the reception accorded to the *Marielitos* and *balseros* who left Cuba in the 1980s and 1990s?

COMPARISONS ACROSS PLACES

The study of the political dimensions of the new immigration tends to focus either on the general national context or on particular local contexts. Both these approaches obscure what is one of the key characteristics of this immigrant wave (and probably of every immigration flow, for that matter): Immigrants and minorities are not arriving only to a national context but to specific local and state contexts as well, and these regional contexts vary considerably. Some states have many immigrants, some have almost none; and while immigration is largely urban, rural migration is changing the face of many small towns across the United States.

Most obviously, immigration is geographically concentrated. Six states had estimated foreign-born populations of 1 million or more in 2000: California (8.8 million), New York (3.6 million), Florida (2.8 million), Texas (2.4 million), New Jersey (1.2 million), and Illinois (1.2 million). Together these states accounted for 71 percent of the total foreign-born population in the United States. California's population is now about 26 percent first-generation immigrant, New York's is 20 percent. More than ten percent of the populations of Florida, Hawaii, New Jersey, Arizona, Massachusetts, and Texas is comprised of immigrants. At the other extreme, twenty-six states had fewer than five percent of foreign-born populations in 2000; these included most of the states in the Midwest and South. However, many of these states also had the fastest-growing immigrant populations. In relative terms, over the past ten years, immigration has had a greater impact on cities like Fayetteville, Arkansas, or Atlanta, Georgia, than it has on the immigrant gateway cities of New York and Los Angeles. We have very little sense of state level differences among immigrants, in part, again, because the data we have tends to be either national or local. The national data on immigrants are usually based on stratified samples that do not allow for genuine state by state comparisons (see, for example, the 1989 Latino National Political Survey). Only recently have scholars begun to take a closer look at census data for political questions (Ramakrishnan and Espenshade 2000) or undertaken smaller surveys of clusters of states that allow state-level comparisons (Barreto et al. 2002).

Recent immigrants to the United States, like their predecessors at the turn of the century, have also settled overwhelmingly in urban areas. Ninety-five percent of first-generation immigrants live in large metropolitan areas. About 60 percent of immigrants live in eight major metropolitan areas: Los Angeles (4.8 million), New York (4.6 million), Miami (1.4 million), San Francisco (1.4 million), Chicago (1.1 million), Washington, DC (677,000), Boston (610,000), and Houston (539,000; Schmidley and Gibson 1999, 16). More than a third lives in the New York and Los Angeles metro areas alone. In several key metro areas, first- and second-generation immigrants make up a substantial portion of the populations: 56 percent of metropolitan Miami, 53 percent of metropolitan Los Angeles, and 41 percent of metropolitan New York and San Francisco (Brookings 2004). Despite this concentration in urban areas, and in some metro areas rather than others (Frey 1995, 2001), comparisons of immigrant populations across cities or metropolitan regions are the exception, not the norm.[8]

Within metro areas, immigrants are disproportionately represented in central cities. Similarly, central cities have attracted the majority of ethnographic fieldwork examining the new immigration. But immigrants are increasingly residing in suburbia, and their presence in suburbs has approached, and in some cases surpassed, that of the population as a whole. About 53 percent of all Americans live in suburbs; so do 48 percent of immigrants. In 2000, 38 percent of blacks, 49 percent of Latinos, and 58 percent of Asian Americans lived in suburbs (Logan 2001). Yet suburbs with their distinctive spatial layout and politics are rarely studied as locuses of immigration. There are some exceptions (Fong 1994; Horton 1995; Mahler 1995; Saito 1998), but even these few cases place little emphasis on the *distinctiveness* of suburbia (for a preliminary discussion, see Jones-Correa 2002a).

The impact of local contexts on immigrant incorporation is important in and of itself. Urban areas provide immigrants' first sustained experience of government and its institutions in America—its role in policing, housing, health care, education, and the job market. These impressions are formative and lasting. Participation in a local context provides immigrants with the tools and skills of citizenship that lead to management of their relationships with their neighbors—and that serve as a gateway into participation in the larger national polity. Local contexts vary, however, in important ways: in their institutional structures, their ethnic makeup, and their history of immigration. Each of these factors shapes immigrant political incorporation and participation but has only rarely been systematically compared across cities (Joyce 1999; Jones-Correa 2001c; Joyce 2003). Local contexts matter—and not for local politics alone: National politics increasingly target specific state and local areas.

The decline of local political parties and the rise of a national media-driven interest group politics mentioned earlier suggest that state and local politics are less relevant in American politics today. But this is not quite true. National political campaigns are highly selective, investing resources by calculating gains, state by state, district by district. As polling and demographic mapping have become more reliable and precise, campaigns make highly targeted appeals to swing undecided voters, leaving less contested areas to one side. The 2000 elections provided a clear example of the localized strategies of national parties. At the beginning of the 2000 campaign, it appeared that Latinos would be targeted by both parties as key swing voters. They were seen as a fast-growing population concentrated in key electoral states with weak ties to either party. As it turned out, the concentrated Latino population was a double-edged sword. Their concentrated numbers made them a significant force in four critical states—New York (where they were 8 percent of voters), California (14 percent), Texas (10 percent) and Florida (11 percent). However only one of these states—Florida—was truly "in play" in 2000. The other states were seen as uncompetitive by one party or the other and were therefore (relatively) ignored.

In states where Latino voters had become powerful, the presidential race was not much of a contest; and in contested states there were few Latino voters (Bustos 2000a). As one prominent Latino political scientist noted, "You've got to have a very, very tight election for small groups to influence them. [Voters] would have to be divided [fifty-fifty]. If the majority population is going in one direction overwhelmingly, Latinos don't make much of a difference. It's only when the majority is divided can Latinos realistically hope to influence the outcome" (Herman 2000). Gilberto Ocanas, deputy director of the Democratic National Committee and the manager of the party's Latino campaign, pointed out: "It is one of the ironies of this race that it is not California or Texas or New York that matters most now. Now the emphasis [for Latinos] is on ... those states ... where the race is tight" (Booth 2000). In the closing weeks of the campaign, Bush and Gore concentrated their time and resources on ten battleground states (mostly in the Midwest) with 134 of the 270 electoral votes needed for victory— states like Pennsylvania, Michigan, and Missouri. The Latino voting-age population in these states was less than 3 percent of the total (Jones-Correa 2000–2001).

The unevenness of immigrant settlement patterns—across states, between metropolitan and rural areas, across metropolitan areas and within individual metro areas—suggests that immigrant political incorporation will most likely vary considerably. The nature of this variation is still largely unexplored. Does it make a difference whether immigrants reside in areas already comprised of large immigrant populations or in those areas where they are only one of a few? Does it make a difference whether immigrants live in the sprawl of suburbia or in compact central cities? Does it make a difference if immigrants live in key "battleground" states fought over in national elections rather than living in a relative electoral backwater that is taken for granted by one party or the other? Each of these variables probably has important effects and we may even hazard a guess at these effects. We won't know for sure, though, until we conduct more research and gather more data.

COMPARISONS ACROSS LEVELS OF INSTITUTIONS

Studies of immigrant and minority politics tend to focus on one level of policy/politics or another. Some levels of politics are relatively under-researched; research on immigrants and politics tends to be either on immigration policy at the federal level or immigrant politics at the local level. Little attention is paid, for example, to state policy and variations in "state citizenship"— state-supplied benefits and obligations immigrants receive that supplement or complement those they receive from the federal government. In addition, the U.S. federal government has layers of institutions with multiple actors that sometimes reinforce one another and at other times are in conflict. Politics and policies are often not isolated within a single layer of government, but have effects that touch other institutional actors. The Voting Rights Act is a perfect example of these kinds of interactions across institutional layers. The act was passed by Congress, interpreted by the courts, and implemented by state and local governments. We know much more about the congressional and judicial politics of the act, however, than we know about its implementation at the state and local levels (see, however, Grofman and Davidson 1996). The 1996 Welfare Reform Act also had significant implications for immigrants and presumably affected their decisions about political incorporation, but we know next to nothing about its impact (see, however, Singer and Gilbertson 2000, for a study of the effects of welfare reform on the naturalization of Dominican immigrants in New York City).

Immigrant political incorporation is influenced not only by federal, state, and local politics and policies, but by international politics and trends as well. Immigrant incorporation may well be affected by larger processes of the internationalization of trade and capital flows (Sassen 1991), the construction of an international human rights regime and the networks of non-governmental organizations that are its advocates (Soysal 1994), and the extension of immigrant identities and social spaces across national borders (Smith 1993; Basch, Schiller, and Szanton-Blanc 1994; Smith and Guarnizo 1998). This approach would argue for extending the study of immigrant political incorporation not just to different institutional layers within the state, but beyond the state altogether. Immigrants might be incorporated into political processes not wholly contained by any single state (Guarnizo 2001) or be affected in their host countries by policies adopted in their countries of origin (Jones-Correa 2001a).

COMPARISONS ACROSS TIME

Though the political incorporation process occurs through time, we have very little sense about precisely *how* immigrants are incorporated over time or in different historical periods. If spatial data are thin or underutilized, temporal data are almost non-existent. Most of the general population surveys (e.g., the General Social Survey, the National Election Survey) undersample immigrants and minorities, so even when pooled, the data is basically unusable for these purposes. As the amount of data on immigrants and immigration increases, however, there will inevitably be better data across time. The Census Current Population Surveys, for example, began asking about country of origin and citizenship status in the 1990s, and so we now have several years' worth of data on immigration status, naturalization, registration, and voting.

Despite the realization that the United States is experiencing its second (or third, depending on how one counts) great wave of immigration, we have almost no research comparing immigrant incorporation across these periods (though see Foner 2000; Gerstle and Mollenkopf 2001). Immigrant incorporation in the early twentieth century, for instance, was supposedly facilitated by the emphasis on Americanization and assimilation into American life and values; however, immigration transnationalism was independently curtailed by a number of factors: restrictions in immigration beginning in 1917, the Great Depression, and then the Second World War (Sterne 2001). The current immigration wave beginning in the 1960s commenced in a very different context, when the mobilization and display of ethnic and racial identities became part of the accepted repertoire of American politics. However, there is no guarantee that this period of acceptance will continue; indeed, following the destruction of the World Trade Center in September 2001, there have been some indications that this acceptance has diminished, with a resurgence of an emphasis on "American" identity and calls for reduced immigration. Nineteenth and early twentieth century immigration was also marked by very different attitudes and policies toward race, with immigrants trying to position themselves as "whites" to avoid the negative consequences of being seen as "non-white" (Haney Lopez 1996; Jacobson 1998). Most of these policies and some of the attitudes about race had changed by the late twentieth century. How do these shifts in national contexts play out in immigrant communities, and what is their impact on immigrant political incorporation?

Though we are not clear on how critical events might affect political incorporation, some studies have focused on the effect of anti-immigrant sentiment in California in the 1990s on immigrant incorporation and participation (Johnson et al.1999; Ramakrishnan and Espenshade 2000; Jones-Correa 2002b). California's state electorate passed Proposition 187 calling for an end to state assistance to undocumented aliens, followed by propositions ending state-sponsored affirmative action programs and English as a Second Language programs in public schools. Clearly these propositions, together with then-Governor Wilson's support for reduced immigration and his presidential run on that theme, all had an impact on immigrant incorporation in the state. The 1996 and 1998 elections gave evidence of the politics of immigration at work in Latino voting. A 1996 survey found that in California, 83 percent of the recently naturalized had registered to vote (International Migration Policy Program 1997), and in both 1996 and 1998, polls indicated that recently naturalized immigrants constituted nearly 40 percent of the 2 million Latino voters in the 1996 election in California.[9] As new citizens added their numbers to the growing Latino voter registration rolls, they also made up a sizeable percentage of those who cast ballots in those elections—12 percent of the state's voters by 1998, up from less than 8 percent in 1990.[10] The propositions passed in the 1990s also likely pushed Latinos toward the Democratic Party: in the California 1998 gubernatorial election, Latinos overwhelmingly supported Democrat Gray Davis over Republican Dan Lungren by a margin of 61 points. Latino voting in 1996 and 1998 signaled a repudiation of the tactics of Republican Governor Pete Wilson, who had championed Proposition 187 and adopted an anti-immigrant agenda during his brief presidential run in 1996. Though the political fallout of the Republican Party's anti-immigrant initiatives in California was significant, we still pay insufficient attention to the way in which critical events can shape immigrant political incorporation, or the way political incorporation plays out over time.

FINALLY, IT'S WORTH NOTING that if one were to take the effects of individual and group differences, place, institutional contexts, and time period seriously, one would quickly realize just how complex the study of immigrant incorporation could become. Each of the variables interacts with the others, and each of the variables, taken singly, also changes over time. Each element of the incorporation process overlaps in multiple ways such that no single causal process explains the political incorporation of immigrants. This is not to say that each study of immigrant incorporation is doomed to be an examination of a unique conjunction of variables, making it ungeneralizable. Studies can still strive for broader application without taking into account every variable, but most studies would be better off by acknowledging the interrelationships among variables.

CONCLUSIONS

The general contours of contemporary American immigration have been clear for at least two decades. Surprisingly, despite this, we have little more understanding of immigrant incorporation into American political life than we did a century ago after the last wave of immigration to this country. Most discussions concerning immigrants and politics either stick to generalities or seem unable to move beyond the description of narrow particularities. There has been little exploration of the patterns underlying immigrants' political lives and scant explanation of the variations that distinguish them. This chapter attempts some of both, although it remains more a roadmap to immigrant political incorporation in the United States than an exploration of that landscape itself. It lays out some questions guiding an examination of the political incorporation of contemporary immigrants into American politics and society. It suggests ways of thinking about what incorporation is, why it might matter, who incorporates, and who is incorporated. As might be expected, the chapter raises many more questions than it answers, for the study of contemporary immigrant political incorporation is still in its infancy and much remains to be done. As I argue in its second half, to answer these questions research must necessarily be comparative—across groups, across place, across layers of institutions, and across time. Immigrant political incorporation is extraordinarily complex, and it is easy to blunder (as this chapter no doubt does itself) into the pitfalls of oversimplification. However, without making explicit comparisons a central component of research design, it is impossible to avoid these pitfalls and to understand both the underlying patterns and variance of immigrant political incorporation.

NOTES

1. We cannot assume that if non-voters were to enter into the political sphere that their views would remain the same, or even that the menu of issues on the table would stay the same. Nor can we assume that the issues currently on the table accurately represent all the issues that might come to the fore if the process were more open. As Verba et al. note: "Comparisons between voters and non-voters in terms of their policy attitudes cannot fully address the issue of the representativeness of activist publics in that they focus only on differences in preferences as revealed in questions about public issues pre-selected by authors of surveys. These policy issues are not necessarily the matters of most concern to respondents" (1993, 304).

2. Many of the classic defenses of participation do so with the presumption that the main argument for participatory democracy is a moral one—people become better people if they participate. The argument presented here is somewhat different: the polity is a better polity as a result of participation and deliberation.

3. For further discussion of the impact of the 1996 Welfare Reform Act on the naturalization and voting rates of immigrants in the United States, see Jones-Correa (2002b).

4. Though the language provisions of the act probably make voting easier for language minorities in covered jurisdictions. On these points see de la Garza and DeSipio (1997) and Jones-Correa (2003).

5. The critique of the confusion between "racial" and "ethnic" identifications is at the core of Steinberg's discussion in *The Ethnic Myth* (1981). But with immigrants from Latin America, Asia, Africa, and the Caribbean, the two may remain more tangled than Steinberg was willing to concede.

6. For a discussion of the dilemma facing minority representatives seeking winning electoral strategies, see the discussion in Dench (1986, 138 ff).

7. Some exceptions are Portes and Rumbaut (2001), based on surveys of immigrant adolescents in different locations; the Second Generation Project directed by Mary Waters, John Mollenkopf and Peter Kasinitz, which collected data from different national origin

groups in the New York City metropolitan area; and Mollenkopf, Olsen and Ross (2001), which looks at immigrant voting by precinct in New York City.

8. The Multi-City Study of Urban Inequality funded by the Russell Sage Foundation, focused on race, not immigration, and included only one of the major immigrant gateway cities. In 2003, another Russell Sage funded project, the New York City Second Generation study, was extended to Los Angeles—this will allow the first in-depth comparisons of immigrant (second-generation) populations in the two primary immigrant gateway cities.

9. For 1996 election figures, see Tomás Rivera Policy Institute (1997).

10. For 1998 data, see "Profile of the Electorate," *Los Angeles Times*, June 4, 1998, and *The Latino Almanac, Special Report: 1998 Election Summary* (1998).

REFERENCES

Alex-Assensoh, Yvette, Marie Alex-Assensoh, and Lawrence J. Hanks, eds. 2000. *Black and Multiracial Politics in America*. New York: New York University Press.

Barreto, Matt, Rodolfo de la Garza, Jongho Lee, Jeasung Ryu and Harry Pachon. 2002. "A Glimpse Into Latino Policy and Voting Preferences." Tomás Rivera Institute.

Basch, Linda, Nina Glick Schiller, and C. Szanton-Blanc. 1994. *Nations Unbound: Transnational Projects, Postcolonial Predicaments, and Deterritorialized Nation-States*. Basel, Switzerland: Gordon and Breach Publishers.

Bass, Loretta E., and Lynne M. Casper. 1999. "Are There Differences in Registration and Voting Behavior Between Naturalized and Native-born Americans?" Working Paper 28, Population Division, U.S. Bureau of the Census.

Bennett, Stephen Earl, and David Resnick. 1990. "The Implications of Non-Voting for Democracy in the United States." *American Journal of Political Science* 34(3): 771–802.

Booth, William. 2000. "Impact of Latino Vote Shifts to Cities and the Southwest." *Washington Post*, October 6, A 18.

Briggs, Vernon. 2001. "American Unionism and U.S. Immigration Policy." Center for Immigration Studies Backgrounder, Washington DC. (August).

Brookings Institution. 2004. The Rise of New Immigrant Gateways: An Analysis of Immigration to Metropolitan Areas. Washington, DC: Brookings Institution, February. http://www.brookings.org/urban/publications/20040301 gateways.htm.

Browning, Rufus, Dale Rogers Marshall, and David Tabb. 1984. *Protest is Not Enough: The Struggle of Blacks and Hispanics for Equality in Urban Politics*. Berkeley: University of California Press.

———, eds. 1997. *Racial Politics in American Cities*. New York: Longman.

Bustos, Sergio. 2000a. "Hispanic Vote Key in Election." *Detroit News*, July 5. http://www.detnews.com/2000/politics/0007/05/a08-86270.htm.

———. 2000b. "Poll Finds a Shifting Hispanic Electorate." *USA Today*, June 30. p 12A.

Cornwell, Elmer E. 1964. "Bosses, Machines, and Ethnic Groups." *The Annals of the American Academy of Political and Social Science* 353 (May): 27–39.

Cranford, Cynthia. 2000. "Economic Restructuring, Immigration and the New Labor Movement: Latina/o Janitors in Los Angeles." Working Paper 9, Center for Comparative Immigration Studies, University of California, San Diego, pp. 1–34.

Dahl, Robert. 1961. *Who Governs?* New Haven: Yale University Press.

Dawson, Michael. 1994. *Behind the Mule: Race and Class in African-American Politics*. Princeton: Princeton University Press.

de la Garza, Rodolfo, Jerry Polinard, Robert D. Wrinkle, and Tomas Longoria. 1991. "Understanding Intra-Ethnic Attitude Variations: Mexican Origin Population Views of Immigration" *Social Science Quarterly* 72(2): 379–387.

de la Garza, Rodolfo, Louis DeSipio, F. Chris Garcia, John Garcia, and Angelo Falcon. 1992. *Latino Voices: Mexican, Puerto Rican, and Cuban Perspectives on American Politic.* Boulder, Colorado: Westview Press.

de la Garza, Rodolfo, and Louis DeSipio. 1997. "Save the Baby, Change the Bathwater and Scrub the Tub: Latino Electoral Participation after Twenty Years of Voting Rights Act Coverage." In *Pursuing Power: Latinos and the Political System*, edited by F. Chris Garcia, 72–126. Notre Dame: University of Notre Dame Press.

Dench, Geoff. 1986. *Minorities in the Open Society: Prisoners of Ambivalence.* New York: Routledge and Kegan Paul.

DeSipio, Louis. 1996. *Counting on the Latino Vote: Latinos as a New Electorate.* Charlottesville: University of Virginia Press.

Downs, Anthony. 1957. *An Economic Theory of Democracy.* New York: Harper and Row.

Erie, Stephen. 1988. *Rainbow's End: Irish Americans and the Dilemmas of the Urban Political Machine, 1840–1985.* Berkeley: University of California Press.

Foner, Nancy, ed. 1987. *New Immigrants in New York.* New York: Columbia University Press.

———. 2000. *From Ellis Island to JFK: New York's Two Great Waves of Immigration.* New Haven: Yale University Press.

Fong, Timothy. 1994. *The First Suburban Chinatown: The Remaking of Monterey Park.* Philadelphia: Temple University Press.

Freeman, Richard, and James Medoff. 1984. *What Do Unions Do?* New York: Basic Books.

Frey, William. 1995. "Immigration and Internal 'White Flight' from U.S. Metro Areas: Toward A New Demographic Balkanization." *Urban Studies* 32:733–757.

———. 2001. "Melting Pot Suburbs: A Census 2000 Study of Suburban Diversity." Center on Urban and Metropolitan Policy, Brookings Institution.

Gant, Michael M., and William Lyons. 1993. "Democratic Theory, Non-voting and Public Policy: The 1971–1988 Presidential Elections." *American Politics Quarterly* 21(2): 185–204.

Gerstle, Gary, and John Mollenkopf, eds. 2001. *E Pluribus Unum? Contemporary and Historical Perspectives on Immigrant Political Incorporation.* New York: Russell Sage Foundation.

———. 1996. *Quiet Revolution in the South: The Impact of the Voting Rights Act, 1965–1990.* Princeton: Princeton University Press.

Guarnizo, Luis Edwardo. 1996. "The Rise of Transnational Social Formations: Mexican and Dominican State Responses to Transnational Migration." *Political Power and Social Theory* 12:45–94.

———. 2001. "On the Political Participation of Transnational Migrants: Old Practices and New Trends." In *E Pluribus Unum? Contemporary and Historical Perspectives on Immigrant Political Incorporation*, edited by Gary Gerstle and John Mollenkopf, 213–263. New York: Russell Sage Foundation.

Gutierrez, David. 1995. *Walls and Mirrors: Mexican Americans, Mexican Immigrants and the Politics of Ethnicity.* Berkeley: University of California Press.

———. 1996. "Sin Fronteras? Chicanos, Mexican Americans and the Emergence of the Contemporary Mexican Immigration Debate, 1968–1978." In *Between Two Worlds: Mexican Immigrants in the United States*, edited by David Gutierrez, 175–212. Wilmington, Delaware: Scholarly Resources.

Hamilton, Charles. 1979. "The Patron–Client Relationship and Minority Politics in New York City." *Political Science Quarterly* 94(2): 211–227.

Handlin, Oscar. 1973 [1951]. *The Uprooted: The Epic Story of the Great Migrations that Made the American People*. Boston: Little, Brown.

Haney Lopez, Ian. 1996. *White By Law: The Legal Construction of Race*. New York: New York University Press.

Herman, Ken. 2000. "Hispanic Vote Unlikely to Swing Election." *Atlanta Journal-Constitution*, September 28. p 6A.

Hero, Rodney. 1992. *Latinos and the U.S. Political System: Two-Tiered Pluralism*. Philadelphia: Temple University Press.

————. 1998. *Faces of Inequality: Social Diversity in American Politics*. New York: Oxford University Press.

Horton, John. 1995. *The Politics of Diversity: Immigration, Resistance and Change in Monterey Park, California*. Philadelphia: Temple University Press.

International Migration Policy Program. 1997. "New American Co-Ethnic Voting." *Research Perspectives on Migration* 1(3): 10.

Irvine, Martha. 2000. "Midwest Hispanics May Be a Key Factor in Presidential Election." *Associated Press*, May 20.

Jacobson, Matthew F. 1998. *Whiteness of a Different Color: European Immigrants and the Alchemy of Race*. Cambridge: Harvard University Press.

Jaynes, Gerald, ed. 2000. *Immigration and Race: New Challenges for American Democracy*. New Haven: Yale University Press.

Jennings, James, ed. 1994. *Blacks, Latinos and Asians in Urban America*. Westport, CT: Praeger.

Johnson, Hans, Belinda Reyes, Laura Mameesh, and Elisa Barbour. 1999. "Taking the Oath: An Analysis of Naturalization in California and the United States." Working Paper, Public Policy Institute of California, San Francisco. Available on the web at: Public Policy Institute of California (http://www.ppic.org/publications/PPIC123/index.html). Accessed February 23, 2000.

Jones-Correa, Michael. 1998a. *Between Two Nations: The Political Predicament of Latinos in New York City*. Ithaca, NY: Cornell University Press.

————. 1998b. "Different Paths: Immigration, Gender, and Political Participation." *International Migration Review* 32(2): 326–349.

————. 2000–2001. "All Politics is Local: Latinos and the 2000 Elections." *Harvard Journal of Hispanic Policy* 13:25–44.

————. 2001a. "Under Two Flags: Dual Nationality in Latin America and Its Consequences for Naturalization in the United State." *International Migration Review* 35(4): 997–1029.

————. 2001b. "Institutional and Contextual Factors in Immigrant Citizenship and Voting." *Citizenship Studies* 5(1): 41–56.

————. 2001c. *Governing Cities: Inter-ethnic Coalitions, Competition and Conflict*. New York: Russell Sage.

————. 2002a. "Reshaping the American Dream: Immigrants and the Politics of the New Suburbs." Paper presented at the annual meeting of the American Political Science Association, Boston, MA, August 30–September 1.

————. 2002b. "Seeking Shelter: Immigrants and the Divergence of Social Rights in the United States." In *Dual Nationality, Social Rights and Federal Citizenship in the U.S. and Europe: The Reinvention of Citizenship*, edited by Randall Hansen and Patrick Weil, 233–263. New York: Berghahn Books.

————. 2002c. "The Study of Transnationalism among the Children of Immigrants: Where We Are and Where We Should Be Headed" In *The Changing Face of Home: The Transnational Lives of the Second Generation*, edited by Peggy Levitt and Mary Waters, 221–241. New York: Russell Sage.

————. 2003. "Language Provisions Under the Voting Rights Act: How Effective Are They?" Midwestern Political Science Association Meeting, Chicago, April 3–6.

Jones-Correa, Michael, and Patrick Joyce. 2001. "Discrimination and Its Effects on Mexican-American Political Preferences and Behavior." Western Political Science Association, Las Vegas, NV, March 15–17.

Jones-Correa, Michael, and David Leal. 1996. "Becoming 'Hispanic': Secondary Pan-Ethnic Identification among Latin American–Origin Populations in the United States." *Hispanic Journal of Behavioral Sciences* 18(2): 214–255.

————. 2001. "Political Participation: Does Religion Matter?" *Political Research Quarterly* 54(4): 751–770.

Joyce, Patrick. 1999. "Transforming Tensions: Politics, Protest and Violence in Black-Korean Conflicts." Ph.D diss., Harvard University.

————. 2003. *No Fire Next Time: Black-Korean Conflicts and the Future of America's Cities.* Ithaca, NY: Cornell Univeristy Press.

Kasinitz, Philip. 1992. *Caribbean New York: Black Immigrants and the Politics of Race.* Ithaca, NY: Cornell University Press.

The Latino Almanac, Special Report: 1998 Election Summary. 1998. San Antonio: The William C. Velásquez Institute.

Levitt, Peggy. 2001. *The Transnational Villagers.* Berkeley: University of California Press.

Lien, Pei-te. 1997. *The Political Participation of Asian Americans: Voting Behavior in Southern California.* New York: Garland Publishing.

————. 2001. *The Making of Asian America through Political Participation.* Philadelphia: Temple University Press.

Lien, Pei-te, M. Margaret Conway, and Janelle Wong. 2003. *Understanding Asian Americans.* New York: Routledge.

Logan, John. 2001. "The New Ethnic Enclaves in America's Suburbs." Report, Lewis Mumford Center for Comparative Urban and Regional Research, State University of New York, Albany.

Lowe, Lisa. 1996. *Immigrant Acts: On Asian American Cultural Politics.* Durham, NC: Duke University Press.

Lowi, Theodore. 1979. *The End of Liberalism: The Second Republic in the United States.* New York: Norton.

Mahler, Sarah. 1995. *American Dreaming: Immigrant Life on the Margins.* Princeton: Princeton University Press.

McClain, Paula. 1996. 'Coalition and Competition: Patterns of Black–Latino Relations in Urban Politics." In *From Polemics to Practice: Forging Coalitions Among Racial and Ethnic Minorities*, edited by Wilbur Rich. New York: Praeger, pp 52–63.

McClain, Paula, and Albert K. Karnig. 1990. "Black and Hispanic Socioeconomic and Political Competition." *American Political Science Review* 84(2): 535–545.

Merton, Robert K. 1957. Social Theory and Social Structure. Rev. ed. Glencoe, IL: Free Press.

Mink, Gwendolyn. 1986. *Old Labor and New Immigrants in American Political Development: Union, Party and State, 1875–1920.* Ithaca: Cornell University Press.

Mollenkopf, John, David Olson, and Timothy Ross. 2001. "Immigrant Political Participation in New York and Los Angeles." In *Governing Cities: Inter-Ethnic Coalitions, Competition and Conflict*, edited by Michael Jones-Correa, 158–180. New York: Russell Sage Foundation.

Morawska, Ewa. 2001. "Immigrants, Transnationalism and Ethnicization: A Comparison of This Great Wave and the Last." In *E Pluribus Unum? Contemporary and Historical Perspectives on Immigrant Political Incorporation*, edited by Gary Gerstle and John Mollenkopf, 175–212. New York: Russell Sage Foundation.

Nobles, Melissa. 1999. *Shades of Citizenship: Race and the Census in Modern Politics.* Stanford: Stanford University Press.

Plotke, David. 1999. "Immigration and Political Incorporation in the Contemporary United States." In *The Handbook of International Migration*, edited by Charles Hirschmann, Philip Kasinitz, and Josh DeWind, 294–318. New York: Russell Sage Foundation.

Portes, Alejandro, and Ruben Rumbaut. 1990. *Immigrant America: A Portrait.* Berkeley: University of California Press.

————. 2001. *Legacies: The Story of the Immigrant Second Generation.* Berkeley: University of California Press.

Portes, Alejandro, and Alex Stepick. 1993. *City on the Edge: The Transformation of Miami.* Berkeley: University of California Press.

Portes, Alejandro, and Min Zhou. 1993. "The Second Generation: Segmented Assimilation and Its Variants." *The Annals of the American Academy of Political and Social Science* 530:74–96.

"Profile of the Electorate." 1998. *Los Angeles Times*, June 4. p 30.

Putnam, Robert D. 2000. *Bowling Alone: The Collapse and Revival of American Community.* New York: Simon and Schuster.

Ramakrishnan, Karthick. 2001. "Immigrant Incorporation and Political Participation in the United States." *International Migration Review* 35:870–910.

Ramakrishnan, S. Karthick, and Thomas J. Espenshade. 2000. "Political Participation and Immigrant Behavior in U.S. Elections." Paper presented at the Conference of the Population Association of America, Los Angeles, March.

Robinson, Walter. 2000. "Immigrant Voter Surge Seen Aiding Gore." *Boston Globe*, November p A1.

Rouse, Roger. 1996. "Mexican Migration and the Social Space of Postmodernism." In *Between Two Worlds: Mexican Immigrants in the United States*, edited by David Gutierrez, 247–264. Wilmington, DE: Scholarly Resources.

Saito, Leland. 1998. *Race and Politics: Asian Americans, Latinos, and Whites in a Los Angeles Suburb.* Urbana: University of Illinois Press.

Sassen, Saskia. 1991. *The Global City: New York, London, Tokyo.* Princeton: Princeton University Press.

Schmidley, Diane, and Campbell Gibson. 1999. *Profile of the Foreign-Born Population in the United States, 1997.* U.S. Census Bureau Current Population Reports, Series P23–195. Washington, DC: Government Printing Office.

Schumpeter, Joseph. 1942, 1975. *Capitalism, Socialism, and Democracy.* New York: Harper and Row.

Sierra, Christine Marie. 1987. "Latinos and the 'New Immigration': Responses From the Mexican American Community." In *Renato Rosaldo Lecture Series Monograph*, vol. 3 (1985–1986), edited by Ignacio M. Garcia, 33–61. Tucson: Mexican American Studies and Research Center, University of Arizona.

Singer, Audrey, and Greta Gilbertson. 2000. "Naturalization in the Wake of Anti-Immigrant Legislation: Dominicans in New York City," Working Paper 10, International Migration Policy Program, Carnegie Endowment for International Peace.

Skerry, Peter. 1993. *Mexican Americans: The Ambivalent Minority.* New York: Free Press.

Smith, Michael Peter, and Luis Guarnizo, eds. 1998. *Transnationalism from Below.* New Brunswick: Transaction Publishers.

Smith, Robert. 1993. "'Los Ausentes Siempre Presentes': The Imagining, Making, and Politics of a Transnational Community between New York City and Ticuani, Puebla," unpublished Ph.D diss., Columbia University.

Soysal, Yasemin. 1994. *Limits of Citizenship: Migrants and Postnational Membership in Europe.* Chicago: University of Chicago Press.

Steinberg, Stephen. 1981. *The Ethnic Myth: Race, Ethnicity and Class in America*. Boston: Beacon Press.

Sterne, Evelyn Savidge. 2001. "Beyond the Boss: Immigration and American Political Culture From 1880 to 1946." In *E Pluribus Unum? Contemporary and Historical Perspectives on Immigrant Political Incorporation*, edited by Gary Gerstle and John Mollenkopf, 175–212. New York: Russell Sage Foundation.

Tómas Rivera Policy Institute. 1997. "Press Release: Latino Electorate Continues to Speak Out On Issues; Tomas Rivera Policy Institute, La Opinion and KVEA-TV Reveal Results of New Poll." February 6. http//www.azteca.net/aztec/immigrat/trc_poll.html (accessed December 13, 2004).

Troy, Steven. 1990. "Is the U.S. Unique in the Decline of Private Sector Unionism?" *Journal of Labor Research* 11(2): 111–143.

Trumpour, John, and Elaine Bernard. 2002. "Unions and Latinos: Mutual Transformation." In *Latinos: Remaking America*, edited by Marcelo Suarez-Orozco and Mariela M. Paez, 126–145. Berkeley: DRCLAS/University of California Press.

Verba, Sidney, Kay Lehman Schlozman, and Henry Brady. 1995. *Voice and Equality: Civic Voluntarism in American Politics*. Cambridge: Harvard University Press.

Verba, Sidney, Kay Lehman Schlozman, Henry Brady, and Norman H. Nie. 1993. "Citizen Activity: Who Participates? What Do They Say?" *American Political Science Review* 87:303–318.

Waldinger, Roger. 1996. *Still the Promised City? New Immigrants and African Americans in Post-Industrial New York*, Cambridge, MA: Harvard University Press.

Walzer, Michael. 1983. *Spheres of Justice: A Defense of Pluralism and Equality*. New York: Basic Books.

Wolfinger, Raymond. 1965. "The Development and Persistence of Ethnic Voting." *American Political Science Review* 59(4): 896–908.

———. 1972. *Politics of Progress*. Englewood Cliffs, NJ: Prentice Hall.

Wolfinger, Raymond, and Steven J. Rosenstone. 1980. *Who Votes?* New Haven: Yale University Press.

Wong, Janelle. 2002. "The Role of Community Organizations in the Political Incorporation of Asian American and Latino Immigrants." Paper presented at the Conference on Race and Civil Society; Racine, Wisconsin, January.

Zhou, Min. 1998. "Segmented Assimilation: Issues, Controversies and Recent Research on the New Second Generation." In *The Handbook of International Migration*, edited by Charles Hirschmann, Philip Kasinitz, and Josh DeWind, 196–211. New York: Russell Sage Foundation.

II. Mediating Institutions

Christina Wolbrecht

MEDIATING INSTITUTIONS—social movements, political parties, and interest organizations—sit at the intersection between the public and the institutions that govern them. As such, they play a central role in American democratic functioning: Mediating institutions help educate citizens about political processes and policy issues. They socialize the public as to its civic duties. They mobilize people into political activity and involvement. They provide vital information about public debates. They recruit and promote political candidates. They influence and organize the activities of government officials. They provide representation of diverse issues and interests.

These roles and contributions—how well they are performed, what bias exists, how they shape outcomes—make mediating institutions fundamental to democratic governance and thus to democratic inclusion. Indeed, it is only a slight exaggeration to say that the original pluralists believed that understanding the interaction of organized interests revealed all one needed to know about American politics (e.g., Truman 1951), while others have argued, (in)famously, that "modern democracy is unthinkable save in terms of parties" (Schattschneider 1942, 1). However, one need not assume mediating institutions are the *sine qua non* of American politics to recognize their important role in interceding between citizens' interests and the formal institutions of government.

As a result of their deep and broad influence in American politics, mediating institutions potentially can contribute to the pursuit of each benchmark of democratic inclusion noted in this volume's introduction. As agents of political mobilization and socialization, mediating institutions can help or hinder disadvantaged groups in their quest to achieve and then take advantage of *full access to political participation* (benchmark 1). Mediating institutions influence whether group members achieve *representation in important decision-making processes and institutions* (benchmark 2). Social movements provide opportunities for the development of group leadership (e.g., the number of black members of Congress with a background in the civil rights movement). Interest groups can support group representatives' bids for election financially and otherwise. Most importantly, political parties serve as the primary mechanisms for candidate recruitment and promotion, structure the electoral process by their control over candidate selection and ballot access, and so on. Mediating institutions also help determine the amount of *influence in/power over government decisions* (benchmark 3) disadvantaged groups might enjoy and whether or not government will *adopt public policies that address group concerns* (benchmark 4). Political parties structure the terms of the debate and decision making both within Congress and between Congress and the President. Social movement demands create a context that encourages greater influence for group interests in government decisions. Interest organizations shape government decisions both as petitioners on the outside (through groups like the NAACP) and as a way to organize group members from the inside (e.g., through the Congressional Black Caucus). It is typically the stated goal of interest organizations and social movements to seek and achieve greater *socioeconomic parity* (benchmark 5) for disadvantaged groups both through political demands and other advocacy.

Mediating institutions often are given credit for playing a central role in helping disadvantaged groups attain greater democratic inclusion. Yet, while the papers in this section note the potential for mediating institutions to play such a role, they also emphasize how institutional structures often mean that parties, interest organizations, and social movements do not have the incentive, ability, or opportunity to provide effective representation of the interests of those excluded from political power. Costain's work on social movements in many ways offers the most positive assessment of mediating institutions' potential for facilitating democratic inclusion. She notes that while scholars have often expressed concern that social movements are a destabilizing threat to democracy, in the American experience movements often have functioned as effective mechanisms for those excluded from the promise of democratic equality to press for and achieve "new arrangements of power" (119). As Costain acknowledges, not all movements have sought greater equality and power for the powerless, but their adaptability and responsiveness means that they are at least capable of serving that purpose.

Other authors in this section are less optimistic about mediating institutions' potential to contribute to greater democratic inclusion. For example, Frymer notes that scholars traditionally have maintained a very favorable view of the way political parties and the two-party system facilitate the inclusion of minorities. Yet, both he and Leighley argue that institutional incentives discourage strategic party elites from placing racial concerns on the agenda or mobilizing black, Hispanic, or poor voters. This may not be unintentional: Frymer notes that many basic dimensions of the American political system were constructed in an attempt to dissipate and avoid fundamental conflicts over race; as a result, office-seeking, strategic party politicians rarely have an incentive to appeal to African American voters by making their concerns central to political campaigns. Similarly, the incentives parties face to mobilize supporters, rather than all voters, likely leads to systematic bias against the mobilization of disadvantaged groups.

As with the volume as a whole, the authors in this section given particular attention to institutions. For example, Leighley notes that the dominant socioeconomic status model of turnout downplays or ignores, among other things, contextual and institutional effects. These effects, such as the role of political parties in mobilizing voters, are particularly problematic vis-à-vis democratic inclusion because the lesser resources of disadvantaged groups means that their members are in greater need than are other citizens of the "subsidization of costs" offered by parties' mobilization efforts. Andersen and Cohen detail how the complex and changing immigration policy regime, combined with an evolving U.S. economy and labor market, has dramatically shaped immigration patterns, immigrant political identities, and the prospects for meaningful political incorporation and representation of immigrant interests.

As highlighted in the chapters in the previous section, *Diversity within and across Groups*, the unique characteristics of different disadvantaged groups can lead to diverse politics of democratic inclusion. Andersen and Cohen, for instance, note that current immigrant populations differ from their predecessors in their continuing ties and close geographic proximity to their home countries, as well as the complicating racial issues faced by Latino and other more-recent immigrants as compared to earlier white ethnics. Thus, while parties are believed to have played a facilitative role in incorporating earlier immigrants, racial and cultural differences may discourage them from performing such a task for contemporary immigrant populations. Kittilson and Tate observe that the different historical experiences of people of color in the United States, where slavery and the civil rights movement are central, and Great Britain, where racial issues are linked to voluntary immigration, contribute to differences in the demands and positions of blacks in those two political systems. Group identity (see Chong and Rogers in the previous section) is also consequential for mediating institutions. Costain suggests social movement effectiveness requires the creation of what she terms *oppositional consciousness* or a collective identity that can link group members across generations and other differences, and provide an alternative perspective to the dominant negative cultural stereotypes that justify political exclusion.

The chapters in this section also provide a useful link to those in the next section, *Governing Institutions*. As Canon discusses in detail, a prime aspect of democratic inclusion is group members' presence in political (particularly legislative) office. The recruitment of candidates for political office is perhaps the central task of political parties; thus, Kittilson and Tate's examination of models of the opportunities for inclusion provided by political parties provides considerable insight into the role parties can play in both hindering and facilitating greater group representation. Likewise, Frymer's analysis of the institutional disincentives parties face in confronting racial issues in (particularly presidential) campaigns provides a useful segue into Conley's consideration of the constraints and opportunities for presidents to contribute to democratic inclusion. Overall, the authors show how mediating institutions link the processes of democratic inclusion at the mass and elite levels. As Leighley points out, for example, we have reason to expect that members of Congress provide better representation to populations that turn out to vote; if parties do not mobilize racial minorities, it is unlikely that governing institutions will respond to their concerns and needs.

Finally, these chapters frame the question of mediating institutions within the broader literature on American politics and political science, highlighting in many cases the inattention to or inadequacy of previous analyses of democratic inclusion. For example, Frymer points out that the basic faith in parties and the two-party system as a mechanism for democratic inclusion can be traced back to foundational works in political science, including Schattschneider (1942), Key (1949), and Dahl (1961), as well as more recent work across rational choice, behavioral, and historical institutional traditions. Leighley discusses parties as potential mobilizing mechanisms for disadvantaged groups within the context of our central theories and empirical models of mass behavior (e.g., Rosenstone and Hansen 1993; Huckfeldt and Sprague 1995; Verba, Schlozman, and Brady 1995). What Leighley and the other chapter authors tend to find is that much of the dominant literature commonly overlooks questions of democratic inclusion, leaving important questions for American democracy less than fully explored, much less answered, by our current body of research. These chapters are part of an attempt to encourage greater attention to these crucial issues.

REFERENCES

Dahl, Robart A. 1961. *Who Governs*? New Haven: Yale University Press.

Huckfeldt, Robert, and John D. Sprague. 1995. *Citizens, Politics, and Social Communication: Information Influence in an Election Campaign*. New York: Cambridge University Press.

Key, V. O., Jr. 1949. *Southern Politics in State and Nation*. Knoxville: University of Tennessee Press.

Rosenstone, Steven J., and John Mark Hansen. 1993. *Mobilization, Participation, and Democracy in America*. New York: Macmillan.

Schattschneider, E. E. 1942. *Party Government*. New York: Holt, Rinehart, and Winston.

Truman, David. B. 1951. *The Governmental Process: Political Interests and Public Opinion*. New York: Alfred A. Knopf.

Verba, Sidney, Kay Lehman Schlozman, and Henry Brady. 1995. *Voice and Equality: Civic Volunteerism in American Politics*. Cambridge: Harvard University Press.

ANNE N. COSTAIN

5   Social Movements as Mechanisms for Political Inclusion

FOR DECADES, SOCIAL MOVEMENTS as *political* forms flew largely underneath the radar of scholarly investigation. Sociologists, historians, and psychologists studied movements and their members, but tended to focus on their social rather than political features. Early work by LeBon (1895), Blumer (1939), Kornhauser (1959), Selznick (1960, 1970) and others, identified movements as outgrowths of crowd behavior, irrationally carried out by individuals who were isolated from the rest of society. The Nazi overthrow of the Weimar republic in Germany prior to the onset of the Second World War, along with the Bolshevik takeover of the Soviet Union in the war's aftermath were seen as emblematic of a phenomenon known as "mass society," where individuals were uprooted from friends, family, churches, and rural communities and sent to urban areas to work in the growing factory economy of Europe. It was believed that the alienation of these individuals drove them into movements, which then projected the anger of their members onto the greater society with destructive force. These anti-democratic movements seemed to taint the social movement form as inherently anti-democratic. This view was only reinforced in academic circles in the United States with the appearance of Senator Joseph McCarthy and the advent of McCarthyism, with its disregard for civil liberties in its search for communist spies and domestic fellow travelers in America (Hofstadter 1965; Lipset and Raab 1970).

Such a politically one-sided view of social movements seems particularly surprising in the U.S. context where, historically, most of America's experience with social movements have been as catalysts for democratic inclusion, seeking to broaden democratic forms rather than restrict them. The populist, progressive, women's suffrage, and civil rights movements of the late nineteenth and early twentieth centuries played major roles in extending the franchise to women, African Americans outside the South, and poor and rural populations. Yet, political scientists have often viewed this increase in voter eligibility—along with the democratizing of elections through the addition of party primary votes, introduction of direct democracy including the initiative, referendum, and recall, and the initiation of direct popular election of U.S. senators—as weakening the two-party system in the United States rather than as widening the realm of politics. Academics have also often viewed the wave of anti-imperialist movements in Africa and Latin America as introducing instability and spawning autocratic leaders rather than as bringing previously excluded populations into politics (see Huntington 1968). Without going into detail, social movements became swallowed up in a pluralist/elitist debate in which a well-informed and politically engaged electorate was viewed as countering the "mass" electorate, which was more likely to be unattached to either major party, relatively ignorant of the political issues of the day, and electorally "up for grabs." The writings on social movements of the fifties and sixties seemed to reflect this fear of the potential for social movements to challenge basic democratic values.

This has been part of a long tradition of valuing democracy in the United States more for its stability than its adaptability. When the American Revolution became embodied in a constitution and national institutions of government, awareness of the revolution as a major social movement was overwhelmed by fascination with what replaced it. Even during the decades of institution-building following the revolution, including Shay's rebellion over collection of debt and imprisonment of debtors, the competition between agrarian and business interests over government preferences, and on-going religious ferment, emphasis remained on the institutionalizing of the Presidency, Supreme Court, and Congress, not on the resolution of revolutionary concerns. Sidney Tarrow (1998) has noted that when as astute a political commentator as Alexis de Tocqueville visited America in the 1830s, against the blazing backdrop of social movements in his native France, he completely failed to recognize their American counterparts, including the religious revivalism of the period which would quickly lead to anti-Catholic violence as well as the mounting contention over the institution of slavery which would soon plunge the United States into its own civil war. De Tocqueville missed the passions simmering in the moral beliefs of the abolitionists and in the efforts of evangelical Protestantism to appropriate interpretation of democracy to itself, while moving to stem the inflow of Catholic immigrants. American history was viewed more as a search for equilibriums than as a crucible for change.

REFRAMING SOCIAL MOVEMENTS

With the focus of this volume on the politics of democratic inclusion, I argue for reframing the study of social movement politics to re-emphasize their role as mechanisms for incorporating marginalized groups into the polity. Social movements historically have been recognized for their representation of the excluded. Yet as research on movements has mushroomed, this characteristic has been largely overshadowed by emphasis on movement success in mobilizing resources and sustaining contentious interaction with elites. A noteworthy exception to this trend is the recent Mansbridge and Morris (2001) edited volume, which draws attention back to what the editors label "oppositional consciousness." Mansbridge and Morris call again for the exploration of the way movements foster the "empowering mental state that prepares members of an oppressed group to act to undermine, reform or overthrow a system of human domination" (4–5). This emphasis is consistent with much of the earlier research on social movements. William Gamson (1975) used the term challenging rather than excluded groups in his classic examination of their role in the United States between 1800 and 1945, as he measured their degree of success in achieving stated goals. Doug McAdam

(1982, 23–32) similarly stressed the centrality of exclusion for generating movement forms of political activism. He argued to modify the then dominant theory of resource mobilization by adding a specific emphasis on the "cognitive liberation" necessary for individuals to sustain high risk challenges to existing power structures. He further critiqued resource mobilization for its overemphasis on elites as providers of these resources and organizational strengths. His challenge, which gave rise to a political opportunity theory of social movements, developed less as an effort to trace power and became instead an effort to understand the importance of timing and tactics for achieving success. By re-emphasizing political exclusion as an (if not *the*) essential feature of movement behavior, a different understanding of social movement activity emerges.

Quickly reviewing the history of social movement theory building shows how this reintroduction of political exclusion shifts some fundamental assumptions concerning movement behavior. Mass society theory lost influence in the 1960s, as empirical studies showed that most of the individuals who participated in social movements, including Nazism and Bolshevism, could be more accurately characterized as "joiners," belonging to more organizations than the average citizen, rather than as social isolates (see Jenkins 1983). Similarly, although there was a scholarly debate, which still continues, over the exact worth of organization for attaining movement success, the option of ignoring organization as a key factor became unsupportable within social movement theory (Piven and Cloward 1977; McAdam 1982). Resource mobilization sought to overcome the shortcomings of mass society theory by reintroducing the presumption that social movement participants are rational political actors, who seek greater power through coalition formation and the accumulation of resources. Emphasis shifted from marginalized populations to all political actors seeking to bring about change through successfully wielding power using a mixture of institutionalized and noninstitutionalized actions (Zald and Ash 1966; McCarthy and Zald 1973, 1977; Mueller 1992).

Political opportunity theory pressed for acknowledgment that more than gathering resources was needed to create a successful social movement. Movements must have the political savvy to create psychological readiness for their adherents while using indigenous resources effectively to press for change during times of political flux (Tilly 1978; McAdam 1982; Tarrow 1993).

Both resource mobilization and political opportunity theories deserve credit for bringing social movements back into the study of politics. Their stress on rational rather than irrational behavior, goal-seeking through tactical and strategic means, and the mobilization of resources to attain a particular end allowed movements to be compared with the actions of other political actors. The theories did this, at least in part, at the cost of blunting the edge that movements possess to challenge domination and oppression.

McAdam, Tarrow, and Tilly (2001) in a recent re-formulation of social movement theory, argue for blending social movements into the broader category of contentious politics, including revolutions and collective behavior more generally. This step clearly re-establishes the notion of agency for movement actors. Social movements are no longer seen as waiting for political opportunities, which may or may not appear, but as creating and exploiting them. The real advantage of this reformulation of social movement theory is in its redirection of attention to the fluidity and dynamism of the movement form as well as the built-in advantages that form brings to a political system where economic and social institutions generally change so much more quickly than political ones.

As helpful as this reformulation of social movements is, it still does not fully address the blurring of conceptual lines created when its precursor theories ignored the link between the movement and excluded interests. Paul Burstein (1998, 1999) challenges both sociologists and political scientists to acknowledge that separating social movement organizations from interest groups and political parties is extremely difficult given current usage. He recommends the alternative of treating the excluded, the average, and the elite all as interest organizations. This, along with the suggestion of McAdam, Tarrow and Tilly (2001) to fold social movements into the broad category of contentious politics, adds urgency to the need to reclaim social movement theory as a mechanism uniquely tailored to the needs of the politically marginalized. Through this reformulation, I do not suggest that the rhetoric, tactics, or claims characteristic of social movements are not frequently appropriated by elites. President Ronald Reagan asserted that he was leader of a "conservative revolution" in the same way that pro-business political action committees sometimes adopt names that evoke radical environmentalism, while opposing most state controls on the environment. The difference lies in the essential characteristics of social movements. At the core, they are not simply efforts to use terminology to put a particular "spin" on politics. If a hypothetical interest has access to significant resources, wields political influence through control of elected offices, or emerges on the scene when political opportunities for this interest to gain power are optimal, why should such a group spend decades in movement activities, gathering recruits, building solidarity, educating the public, re-framing issues and public perceptions, rather than following more conventional routes to power in interest group, electoral, or partisan politics?

What makes movements unique and worthy of study is their demonstrated capability to deliver access to the excluded. This should be integral to defining what a social movement is. Such inclusion has never been granted easily. It is a dynamic, long-term process, often putting its members as well as the larger society at risk. Yet, perilous as the social movement path may be, it is sometimes able to provide citizenship, voice, political legitimacy, publicity, and institutional responsiveness to those issues and individuals who have been without it for protracted periods of time. Therefore, defining social movements as large-scale, enduring mobilizations of excluded populations—which, through developing awareness of their own marginalization and experience of injustice, utilize protest as well as conventional politics to mount sustained challenges to those in power—acknowledges their most salient political characteristics.

Even in democratic societies such as the United States, movements occupy a tenuous space. Excluded groups and ideas are usually kept outside the polity for a reason. Historically in the American case, immigrants, freed slaves, and native peoples, along with many other groups, were not trusted to honor and preserve the U.S. legacy of a stable democracy. De Tocqueville could see and celebrate participation in voluntary organizations by American citizens, recognizing the way that the federal structure encouraged the rapid growth of groups representing ethnic, religious, trade, affinity, and other interests, without recognizing the capacity of these interests (using this same federal structure) to transform local discontents into more widespread political conflicts through the medium of social movement (de Tocqueville 1838). That is why distinctions between interest groups, political parties, and social movements are important to preserve.

To provide empirical support for this theoretical argument, this chapter uses the U.S. civil rights and women's movements to focus on some of the ways that movements bring about democratic inclusion. Although the civil rights movement is paradigmatic as a successful movement and the women's movement, to an extent, emulated many of its tactics, these two, in some ways quite similar movements, also show the adaptability of movements as mechanisms for overcoming very different barriers to political inclusion. Because they are two of the most successful movements in American history, I use them to establish what it is possible for movements to accomplish, not what movements are likely to achieve.

For any who doubt the success of these two movements, I propose Carol Mueller and John McCarthy's (2003) division of movements into their structural and cultural aspects as a way to trace social and political impact. Mueller and McCarthy note that complex and long-lasting movements develop structural patterns (including resources, repertoires of contention, targets, and mobilization methods) that point toward successes and failures. Similarly, the cultural aspects of such movements display patterns of "identifying injustices, movement goals, and coherent activist identities" (222) that furnish locales for finding political and social impacts. A large body of scholarship exists on both the civil rights and women's movements, assessing and cataloging the substantial electoral, programmatic, policy, and social successes attributable to each movement's structural elements (Lawson 1976; McAdam 1982; Burstein 1985; Mueller 1988; Costain 1992; Epp 1998; Katzenstein 1998) A slightly smaller, but still extensive, literature focuses on the cultural influences these two movements have produced (McAdam 1988, 2000; Costain 1992; Katzenstein 1998; Rochon 1998).

EXISTENCE SURVIVING AT THE MARGINS

In most societies, social movements mobilize out of divisions over emotionally charged and enduring factors such as race, ethnic origins, sex, religion, or class/economic barriers. Although hostility to democratic government characterizes some movements (as discussed earlier), embracing democratic forms has been the more common posture of U.S. movements (see Polletta

2002). This means that there is likely to be recurrent movement formation among groups on the losing side of these historic cleavages. Groups themselves are likely to possess a history, a vocabulary, and sometimes potent symbols which can be drawn upon by new movements to frame public discourse on the injustices claimed by these excluded groups. Movements too are often able to use public policies remaining after the work of earlier movements to draw attention to their continuing political marginalization and the grievances flowing from it. For example, the civil rights movement in the 1950s could point to the fourteenth amendment to the Constitution, guaranteeing equal protection under the law, along with anti-lynching and other anti-discrimination laws that were on the books, but that were not being enforced. Similarly, interest groups remaining after previous mobilizations often continue to provide training, access, and resources to new movements pursuing long-standing causes. In the case of the civil rights movement, the National Association for the Advancement of Colored People (NAACP) and the Urban League were two groups organized nationally during previous mobilizations in support of African American civil rights. They, along with black churches, formed networks of activists, leaders, expertise, and resources that could be absorbed into the emerging civil rights movement (see McAdam 1982).

In the case of the women's movement in the United States, there were not only numerous groups that were either left over from the suffrage movement or spurred to form when women acquired the vote (such as the League of Women Voters, the National Woman's Party, the American Association of University Women, and the National Federation of Business and Professional Women's Clubs), but there were also aging suffragist leaders such as Alice Paul of the National Woman's Party and activists ready to take up the struggle for women's equality once again (Costain 1992). Feminism as a justification for women to occupy more equal private and public roles was also developed and available to be adapted to contemporary concerns (Cott 1987). In addition, public interest groups, descended from progressive era allies of woman's suffrage interests, including the Women's International League for Peace and Freedom and newer groups such as Common Cause and Public Citizen, which carry forward the values of "good government," traceable back to the progressive era, were also ready to assist in training and forming coalitions with women's liberation groups emerging as part of the women's movement in the late 1960s.

The multi-generational recurrence of certain types of movements, particularly those of the politically excluded, provides a cumulative power to their demands. Governments and the public have to realize that if the movement is ignored, turned away, or defeated in a particular manifestation, it will be back again in future decades. Political opportunity theory used this insight into the frequent recurrence of political movements of certain types within a given society to search for external factors, which produced opportunities for diverse movements to re-emerge years later. In a chilling way, efforts to "ethnically cleanse," or to commit genocide against particular populations may be a perverse attempt by elites to halt such recurrences.

DYNAMIC ENDURANCE

The dynamism of recurrent movement re-emergence is especially critical in achieving the mobilization and ultimately the inclusion of marginalized populations within American society. Consider the situations of African Americans and women and the efforts of other mediating institutions (i.e., political parties) to champion their causes. For both African Americans and women, the Republican Party was their initial supporter (with President Lincoln's "Emancipation Proclamation" and passage of the thirteenth, four-teenth, and fifteenth amendments to the Bill of Rights after the civil war, establishing the framework for black civil rights in America and Republican Party support for addition of an Equal Rights Amendment to the U.S. Con-stitution to extend legal equality to women after passage of the nineteenth amendment granted suffrage). This Republican support was then followed by a fifty- to seventy-year-long Republican disengagement from the goals and objectives of both women and blacks (Lawson 1976; McAdam 1982; Costan 1992; Wolbrecht 2000). As the Republican Party moved away from these historic commitments, the Democratic Party altered its own position over this same time, with both women and African Americans becoming key components of the Democratic Party's electoral base.

This is not an unreasonable time span for a major U.S. political party to re-shape its underlying policies and consequently its electoral coalition. Contrast it, however, with the relative speed and ease with which the civil rights and women's movements "jumped ship," after the parties reversed positions on their willingness to advocate legal and social equality for women and blacks. African Americans moved out of the Republican Party to vote for Franklin Roosevelt in the 1936 election (McAdam and Sewell 2001, 93). In a similarly dramatic move, women rejected Ronald Reagan in the 1980 election to vote for the Democratic ticket of Jimmy Carter and Walter Mondale opening a gender gap which more than twenty years later is still a factor in American electoral politics (Mueller 1988). Both movements were able to move rapidly from one party to the other, despite past ties, because of their focus on the issues, including legal equality and provision of an economic safety net, which meant most to their members. Had their timeframes to switch allegiances come close to paralleling those of the political parties, they might never have caught up with each other. Social movements might have spent decades trying to influence parties that no longer valued their support.

Being on the wrong side of the divides of race, religion, sex, gender, and ethnic origin denies access for these groups to the very institutions of govern-ment with the power to change conditions. Social movements have become an alternative means to confront institutions, achieve access, and bring about change. The cases of the civil rights and women's movements illustrate this adaptability. For the civil rights movement, the limited access of Southern black citizens to the ballot box meant that Southern Senators could use the veto to defeat legislation in Congress extending civil rights to African Americans. With many of its members effectively denied the vote, it was hard to gain the attention of politicians in the executive or legislative branches of national government. So, the federal court system became a preferred target to apply pressure for change. The movement used the legitimacy inherent in forceful Supreme Court opinions, such as *Shelley v. Kraemer* (1948), which barred government from enforcing restrictive real estate covenants based on race, *Brown v. Board of Education* (1954), which rejected the doctrine of "separate but equal," and *Swann v. Charlotte-Mecklenburg* (1971), which upheld the use of forced busing as part of court-ordered remedial action to end segregation in public schools, to pull public attention toward rights unconstitutionally denied. In the era of the Cold War, the civil rights movement was able to connect to liberation movements world-wide, invoking the words of Gandhi, and in the process interfering with U.S. foreign policy, which positioned itself as the champion of individual liberty against communist dictatorship (McAdam 1998).

With many of the normal routes to influencing government blocked, the civil rights movement employed many innovative tactics ranging from the Montgomery bus boycott, to the Greensboro, North Carolina, lunchroom sit-ins, to the Mississippi Freedom Rides. The media provided an outlet to demonstrate the denial of access to public facilities based on the mere fact of race. Similarly, the unleashing of police dogs, use of billy clubs, and imprisonment of individuals for attempting to demonstrate peacefully and exercise their civil rights, evoked sympathy for the movement from around the nation. Scenes from the southern states particularly showed the futility of working with local and state governments to bring about change. The civil rights movement helped to pass federal legislation guaranteeing voting rights, access to employment, and public accommodations by demonstrating how these rights were denied on a daily basis to African Americans.

The women's movement profited from the work done by the civil rights movement to educate the nation about the extent to which America's promise of democracy was routinely denied to many individuals on the basis of their membership in a social group. The women's movement also inherited activists trained in the tactics of the civil rights struggle (Evans, 1980). Some of the earliest activists in the women's movement fled sexist treatment in the civil rights movement, with Student Nonviolent Coordinating Committee (SNCC) leader Stokely Carmichael's now infamous statement that the place for women in his organization was "prone." Finally, some of the major laws guaranteeing equality, such as the 1964 Civil Rights Act and Title IX of the 1972 Education Amendments Act, included protection from discrimination based on sex as well as race.

Yet, most of the obstacles that the women's movement faced lacked parallels to the problems of the civil rights movement. Consequently, they demanded new tactical solutions. Feminists recognized early in their struggle that much of the exclusion of women was embedded in culture and language. The creation of consciousness-raising groups had no parallel in the civil rights movement, but was necessary for women, since exclusion from jobs, as one example, was often explained away as either making sure that men would be employed so they could support families or as protecting women from long hours and harsh working conditions so that their reproductive health would not be impaired. When more women began to be admitted to graduate and professional schools in the 1960s, it was bemoaned that these programs were being filled with "4 Fs." To local draft boards the notation "4 F" simply meant excused from military service, because of poor health or disability. The black humorists of the day, however, made up varied lists of all those whom the military did not want even in wartime, including females, the "feeble-minded" (a derogatory term for those afflicted by some types of mental illness or impairment), foreigners, and "fags" (an insulting term for homosexuals). African Americans knew that they were denied education, jobs, and access to public accommodations. They had no delusions that this was for their benefit. Since English uses the male pronoun as universal and identifies women so that their marital status is apparent (*Miss* or *Mrs.*), these usages were also consistent targets of the women's movement. Not only were consciously degenerative terms (e.g., *slut, bitch, dyke*) fought against, as racial slurs such as *nigger* had been, but language was seen as putting women in their place through both ordinary usage and occupational terms which seemed to exclude women (e.g., *fireman, congressman,* and *postman*). The use of Ms. for a woman's formal title and an effort to search out sexually unspecific occupational titles, such as *representative* or *legislator* rather than *congressman,* and server rather than *waiter* or *waitress,* sought to change language as a way of altering thinking.

The women's movement also rejected the model of designating leaders and consistent "spokesmen" [*sic*] for the movement. The argument was that organizations with designated leaders and followers paralleled a male model of dominance rather than one of more equal relationships, which the movement favored. Models of groups with rotating leadership, co-leaders, and limited term elected leaders all become part of the movement's attack on organizational and cultural patterns that seemed to build in a male perspective. Men took part in virtually every aspect of the women's movement, from Richard Graham, former member of the Equal Employment Opportunity Commission (EEOC), who urged women to organize to protect their interests, to many men, including Graham, who served on the national boards of leading feminist organizations. It was not men that the movement rejected, but male hierarchy and dominance. The women's movement also needed to devise new terms for offensive activities that previously were unnamed, such as sexual harassment. These requests for sexual favors as a condition of employment, had often been viewed either as a reason not to have married women in the work place, or as a type of "office romance." Attacks on dress codes, which sometimes kept women from wearing the attire most appropriate to the work they were doing were also common. The effort was to persuade companies and managers to come up with rules of attire that were reasonable in relation to the work, rather than assigned based on one's sex.

A number of cultural icons were also challenged, ranging from the Miss America contest to bridal fairs. In efforts to mock the early women's movement, the media reported that women burned bras outside the Miss America pageant in Atlantic City. This "bra burning" was actually a collection of feminine objects, including underwear, cosmetics, hosiery, and so forth, which were deposited in garbage cans as a rejection of the cultural construction of what it meant to be a woman. In another famous incident, activists released mice at a bridal fair in New York City, to protest the commercial exploitation of marriage.

The women's rights movement confronted many legal challenges, which included sex-segregated publicly funded education programs, public restaurants or bars that were open only to men, limitations on the types, places, and hours of work for which women could apply, help wanted advertising that specified whether men, women, or both sexes might apply, and lower wages paid to women in predominantly male occupations. Women as a group might have been able to win these battles using only their votes, lobbying and organizing skills, and economic clout. Yet, there was much more to the effort to redefine women's place in American society than the differential treatment described above; changes in language, public discourse, education, and intellectual debate presented other challenges that a social movement form was better able to address. In a provocative study of how movements influence culture, Thomas Rochon (1998) uses the women's movement as one of his primary cases for asserting that movement transformation of culture may be even more powerful than successes in altering laws and policies.

It is evident that movement commitment to specific goals has to endure long enough for political institutions to take up their cause and win their support. Marginalized groups come from their place astride long-held social and political cleavages. Social movements take these sources of contention, infuse them with meaning, and then, in the most successful cases, create change. Although they may be tactically swift, their objectives are constant, sometimes over extremely long periods of time.

OPPOSITIONAL CONSCIOUSNESS

A key to this multi-generational commitment to challenge established power is the construction of a positive identity for the excluded group (see Chong and Rogers, this volume, on group consciousness). Taylor and Whittier (1992) suggest a definition of identity broad enough to encompass movements of the excluded: "Collective identity is the shared definition of a group that derives from members' common interests, experiences, and solidarity" (105).

Both the women's and civil rights movements confronted social realities replete with stereotypes of how members of these groups were thought to behave. When the movements first mobilized in the fifties and sixties both groups were widely regarded as intellectually inferior to white males. Women were portrayed as preferring private life to public. African Americans were represented as sexually promiscuous and lacking ambition. Each group had to reclaim its past and internally re-define its situation, before it could effectively compete for political power. African Americans used the movement form to reclaim their past, understanding how the legacy of slavery severed family ties, denied blacks fundamental academic skills including reading and writing, devalued the worth of individuals, and produced levels of poverty and segregation that separated their members from the wider society. For women, in addition to the cultural issues discussed above, it was necessary to understand how the biology of child-bearing and child-rearing often removed women from education early in their lives and kept them close to their homes caring for a succession of babies and small children. Similarly, the labor-intensive nature of much housework prior to the period of the two world wars severely limited the time women had to spend on political causes and community activities.

Individuals and collective groups of the excluded go through periods of oppositional consciousness or cognitive liberation as part of the movement experience. This process moves them from understanding that they have legitimate grievances that deserve addressing, to acknowledging that as individuals or as individuals in a group they are capable of taking action, which will lead to redressing these grievances. Identity building helps create the capacity to act.

LINKS BETWEEN SOCIAL MOVEMENTS AND DEMOCRATIC INCLUSION

The cases of the civil rights and women's movements suggest how movements become mechanisms for the democratic inclusion of excluded groups. Both populations benefited from recurrent movements, capable of moving quickly to exploit political opportunities, to build oppositional consciousness, to create and leave behind laws and organizations with the potential to support future efforts, and to build a history and community capable of sustaining struggle. Both moved from an early emphasis on protest and confrontation, to a sustained period of institutionalizing. Although processes of institutionalizing are among the least studied in the literature on social movements, there is an emerging consensus concerning the meaning of institutionalizing (see Meyer and Tarrow, 1998). It consists of three components: routinization, inclusion and marginalization, and cooptation. *Routinization* permits both challengers and authorities to follow a common script, recognizing both acceptable and inherently dangerous interactions between them. *Inclusion and marginalization* allow challengers who adhere to these pre-established routines to sustain a dialog with mainstream institutions, while those who do not can be repressed or neglected. Finally, *cooptation* is the point at which challengers change their claims and tactics so they can pursue them within the orbit of conventional politics. Both women and African Americans as political actors follow a political path that is routinized, sometimes inclusive and at others marginal, and with a few exceptions, too distant from mainstream discourse to be considered coopted.

The social movement mechanism itself is highly fluid. Even taking two movements with overlapping time frames and a fundamental shared interest in achieving legal equality, their tactical differentiation is noteworthy. For the civil rights movement, pressure on the major institutions of government to pass legislation, enforce existing laws, and protect black Americans from hostile state and private actions lay at the core of its success. The women's movement, by contrast, directed more of its effort toward restructuring social norms and a culture that largely devalued women and their contributions. Had either the women's or civil rights movements retained their traditional allegiances to the Republican Party, held rigidly to political demands such as an Equal Rights Amendment to the constitution for women or monetary reparations for slavery for African Americans, or waited to challenge the political system until they had overwhelming resources, they would certainly have achieved less than they have.

Social movements further display a cumulative and enduring power, both in their re-emergence from the ashes of earlier mobilizations and in their participation in social movement cycles such as America experienced in the sixties and seventies. This endurance of struggle, balanced on the great cleavages of society, has created a political form, which has been among the most effective historically for winning political access for excluded groups.

The partial incorporation of two excluded groups through the social move-ment form in no way denies that most efforts of this type by marginalized groups will fail. Indeed, earlier mobilizations of women and blacks were less successful in gaining access to the political arena than the more contempo-rary movements. Perhaps one of the reasons for defining the movement form more broadly than just applying to the marginalized is that it then would allow for a higher rate of success. For example, a "revolutionary" effort by a party-controlling government, such as the highly touted "Reagan revolution," is far more likely to achieve victories than a black civil rights movement. Yet, does the behavior of the Republican Party in recruiting conservative can-didates for office, winning elections, governing the country, and rewriting public policy look more like a social movement than it does a political party? By the term social movement, is not more implied than changing policies and restructuring partisan politics? Is not the struggle for a new collective identity, sustained contention between the oppressed and dominant groups, and efforts to construct a political landscape populated by interests that previously were not part of the political community what are commonly viewed as political actions of social movements? When the new identity is realized, contention leads to new arrangements of power and the community includes the movement that had been excluded, this is arguably more mean-ingful for movement success than policy change or control of a political office.

REFERENCES

Blumer, Herbert. 1939. "Collective Behavior." In *Principles of Sociology*, edited by Robert E. Park, 219–288. New York: Barnes and Noble.

Brown v. Board of Education of Topeka, 347 U.S. 483 (1954).

Burstein, Paul. 1985. *Discrimination, Jobs, and Politics: The Struggle for Equal Employment Opportunity in the United States Since the New Deal*. Chicago: University of Chicago Press.

———. 1998. "Interest Organizations, Political Parties, and the Study of Democratic Pol-itics." In *Social Movements and American Political Institutions*, edited by Anne N. Costain and Andrew S. McFarland, 39–56. Lanham, MD: Rowman and Littlefield.

———. 1999. "Social Movements and Public Policy." In *How Social Movements Mat-ter*, edited by Marco Guigni, Doug McAdam, and Charles Tilly, 3–21. Minneapolis: University of Minnesota Press.

Costain, Anne N. 1992. *Inviting Women's Rebellion: A Political Process Interpretation of the Women's Movement*. Baltimore: Johns Hopkins University Press.

Cott, Nancy F. 1987. *The Grounding of Modern Feminism*. New Haven: Yale University Press.

de Tocqueville, Alexis. 1838. *The Republic of the United States of America and Its Political Institutions, Reviewed and Examined*. New York: A. S. Barnes and Company.

Epp, Charles R. 1998. *The Rights Revolution: Lawyers, Activists, and Supreme Courts in Comparative Perspective*. Chicago: University of Chicago Press.

Evans, Sara. 1980. *Personal Politics: The Roots of Women's Liberation in the Civil Rights Movement and the New Left*. New York. Vintage Books.

Gamson, William. 1975. *The Strategy of Social Protest*. Homewood, IL: Dorsey Press.

Hofstadter, Richard. 1965. *The Paranoid Style in American Politics*. New York: Knopf.

Huntington, Samuel P. 1968. *Political Order in Changing Societies*. New Haven: Yale University Press.

Jenkins, J. Craig. 1983. "Resource Mobilization Theory and the Study of Social Movements." *Annual Review of Sociology* 9:527–553.

Katzenstein, Mary Fainsod. 1998. *Faithful and Fearless: Moving Feminist Protest Inside the Church and Military*. *Princeton*: Princeton University Press.

Kornhauser, William. 1959. *The Politics of Mass Society*. Glencoe, IL: The Free Press.

Lawson, Steven F. 1976. *Black Ballots: Voting Rights in the South, 1944–1969*. New York: Columbia University Press.

LeBon, Gustave. 1895. *The Crowd. A Study of the Popular Mind*. London: Ernest Benn.

Lipset, Seymour Martin, and Earl Raab. 1970. *The Politics of Unreason*. New York: Harper and Row.

Mansbridge, Jane, and Aldon Morris. 2001. *Oppositional Consciousness: The Subjective Roots of Social Protest*. Chicago: University of Chicago Press.

McAdam, Doug. 1982. *Political Process and the Development of Black Insurgency, 1930–1970*. Chicago: University of Chicago Press.

———. 1988. *Freedom Summer*. New York: Oxford University Press.

———. 1998. "On the International Origins of Domestic Political Opportunities." In *Social Movements and American Political Institutions*, edited by Anne N. Costain and Andrew S. McFarland, 251–267. Lanham, MD; Rowman and Littlefield.

———. 2000. "Movement Strategy and Dramaturgic Framing in Democratic States: The Case of the American Civil Rights Movement." In *Deliberation, Democracy, and the Media*, edited by Simone Chambers and Anne Costain, 117–34. Lanham, MD; Rowman and Littlefield.

McAdam, Doug, and William H. Sewell, Jr. 2001. "It's About Time: Temporality in the Study of Social Movements and Revolutions." In *Silence and Voice in the Study of Contentious Politics*, edited by Ronald R. Aminzade, Jack A. Goldstone, Doug McAdam, Elizabeth J. Perry, William H. Sewell, Jr., Sidney Tarrow, and Charles Tilly, 89–125. New York: Cambridge University Press.

McAdam, Doug, Sidney Tarrow, and Charles Tilly. 2001. *Dynamics of Contention*. Cambridge: Cambridge University Press.

McCarthy, John D., and Mayer N. Zald. 1973. *The Trend of Social Movements in America*. Morristown, NJ: General Learning Press.

———. 1977. "Resource Mobilization and Social Movements." *American Journal of Sociology* 82:1212–1242.

Meyer, David S., and Sidney Tarrow. 1998. "A Movement Society: Contentious Politics for a New Century." In *The Social Movement Society: Contentious Politics for a New Century*, edited by David S. Meyer and Sydney Tarrow, 1–28. Lanham, MD; Rowman and Littlefield.

Mueller, Carol M., ed. 1988. *The Politics of the Gender Gap: The Social Construction of Political Influence*. Newbury Park, CA: Sage.

————. 1992. "Building Social Movement Theory." In *Frontiers in Social Movement Theory*, edited by Aldon D. Morris and Carol McClurg Mueller, 3–25. New Haven: Yale University Press.

Mueller, Carol M., and John D. McCarthy. 2003. "Cultural Continuity and Structural Change: The Logic of Adaptation by Radical, Liberal, and Socialist Feminists in State Reconfiguration." In *Women's Movements Facing the Reconfigured State*, edited by Lee Ann Banaszak, Karen Beckwith, and Dieter Rucht, 219–241. Cambridge, England: Cambridge University Press.

Piven, Frances Fox, and Richard Cloward. 1977. *Poor People's Movements: Why They Succeed, How They Fail*. New York: Vintage Books.

Polletta, Francesca. 2002. *Freedom is an Endless Meeting: Democracy in American Social Movements*. Chicago: University of Chicago Press.

Rochon, Thomas R. 1998. *Culture Moves: Ideas, Activism, and Changing Values*. Princeton: Princeton University Press.

Selznick, Philip. 1960. *The Organizational Weapon*. New York: The Free Press.

————. 1970. "Institutional Vulnerability in Mass Society." In *Protest, Reform and Revolt*, edited by Joseph R. Gusfield, 258–274. New York: John Wiley.

Shelley v. Kraemer, 334 U.S. 1 (1948).

Swann v. Charlotte-Mecklenburg Board of Education, 402 U.S. 1. (1971)

Tarrow, Sidney. 1993. *Power in Movement: Social Movements, Collective Action and Politics*. New York: Cambridge University Press.

————. 1998. "'The Very Excess of Democracy': State Building and Contentious Politics in America." In *Social Movements and American Political Institutions*, edited by Anne N. Costain and Andrew S. McFarland, 20–38. Lanham, MD; Rowman and Littlefield.

Taylor, Verta, and Nancy E. Whitter. 1992. "Collective Identity in Social Movement Communities: Lesbian Feminist Mobilization." In *Frontiers in Social Movement Theory*, edited by Aldon D. Morris and Carol McClurg Mueller, 104–30. New Haven: Yale University Press.

Tilly, Charles. 1978. *From Mobilization to Revolution*. Reading, MA: Addison-Wesley.

Wolbrecht, Christina. 2000. *The Politics of Women's Rights: Parties, Positions, and Change*. Princeton: Princeton University Press.

Zald, Mayer N., and Roberta Ash. 1966. "Social Movement Organization: Growth, Decline, and Change." *Social Forces* 44:327–341.

6   Race, Parties, and Democratic Inclusion

FEW INSTITUTIONS OF AMERICAN DEMOCRACY enjoy more reverence from political scientists than the two-party system. E. E. Schattschneider's (1942, 1) claim that the two-party system "created democracy" and that "modern democracy is unthinkable save in terms of the parties" remains widely cited and adhered to. Among its most important attributes, the two-party system is thought to promote the inclusion of racial minorities and groups otherwise disadvantaged in terms of wealth, resources, and power because its existence "enable[s] the many to pool their resources to offset the advantages of the few" (Dahl 1967, 245). In his famous study of urban politics in New Haven, Robert Dahl (1961, 34) found that party competition was critical for the incorporation of new immigrant groups into American politics because "whatever else ethnics lacked they had numbers." V. O. Key (1949, 310), writing in reaction to African American disfranchisement in the one-party South, argued that the development of a two-party system in the region would ensure that one political party "of necessity must pick up whatever issue is at hand to belabor the 'ins.' " The belief that a competitive two-party system is inclusive so dominates the discipline today, including rational choice scholars, behaviorists, and historical institutionalists (e.g., Wattenberg 1990; Rhode 1991; Reichley 1992; Shefter 1994; Benoit and Shepsle 1995; Bibby 1997; Milkis 1999; Cain 2001; Sabato and Larson 2002),[1] that debate about the role parties play in American democracy "has been reduced to a matter of particulars, not theory" (White 1992, 170; also see Epstein 1986).[2]

It is perhaps surprising, then, that scholars of African American politics make dramatically different arguments about the two-party system's impact for democratic inclusion, emphasizing its limits and exclusionary nature (Walton 1972; Holden 1973; Pinderhughes 1984; Walters 1988; Guinier 1991; Tate 1993; Smith 1996; Lusane 1997; Frymer 1999; Eldersveld and Walton 2000; Kim 2001; Marable 2002).[3] In turn, these scholars tend to explore strategies that in different ways involve the *weakening* of two-party politics. Some have raised the possibility of strategic voting, forming third parties, and changing electoral laws to allow for greater proportional representation (Walton 1972; Walters 1988; Guinier 1991; Tate 1993). Others have focused on the implementation of the Voting Rights Act and the potential of race-conscious congressional redistricting (Grofman and Davidson 1992; Swain 1993; Whitby 1997; Cannon 1999; Gay 2001; Tate 2003). Still other scholars focus on local politics where racial demographics provide more frequent opportunities for African Americans to win elections (Eisinger 1982; Browning, Marshall, and Tabb 1984; Pinderhughes 1987; Bobo and Gilliam 1990; Sonenshein 1993; Reed 1995; Hajnal 2001), courtroom litigation (e.g., Ely 1980; see, however, Rosenberg 1991 and Lovell and McCann of this volume as powerful counters to this argument), social movement activism (Piven and Cloward 1977; Chong 1991; Lee 2002; Costain, this volume), or political empowerment through changes in popular culture (Gilroy 2000).

Why this discrepancy between scholars who study parties and those who focus on African American politics? In part, it is simply a point of emphasis and priorities. Within the recent major edited volumes on U.S. party politics, for example the most recent editions of *The State of the Parties* (Green and Shea 1999) and *The Parties Respond* (Maisel 2002), not a single chapter or subchapter is devoted to the intersection of race and party dynamics. But this is just symptomatic of a larger reason: While party scholars recognize the importance of race in American politics, they do not see it as a central or fundamental feature of American politics or as intrinsic to understanding two-party dynamics.[4] Following the famous traditions of de Tocqueville (2001), Myrdal (1944), Dahl (1961), and today's leading racial attitude scholars (e.g., Kinder and Sanders 1996; Sears, Sidanius, and Bobo 2000), party scholars treat race and racism as a set of ideas largely reducible to psychologically driven prejudice that exists independent of elite actors and institutions. Accordingly, these scholars believe that parties will sometimes manifest specific racist expressions, but they are not thought to independently further racial inequality; they merely echo existing views in society. And no matter how often parties manifest societal racism, it is thought that as long as two-party competition exists, black Americans will have an opportunity to provide an opposing view. Indeed, Key's (1949) argument mentioned above is typical of how party scholars understand the role of parties with regards to racial equality—it is only when the two-party system fails to be competitive that African American interests suffer inadequate representation: it is not something more intrinsic to party competition and institutional dynamics.

Recent attention to American political development challenges this conventional view. Rogers Smith (1997), for instance, has argued that racism is best understood as part of an essential ideological element of the American creed and nation building. If racism is recognized as an ideology, and as such, a structural or organizing principle of American politics (Bobo 1988; Omi and Winant 1994; Bonilla-Silva 1996), then it cannot be dismissed as irrational or meaningfully separate from the workings of our political institutions. A number of scholars have made great advances in intersecting race with institutional dynamics, arguing that institutional rules and procedures not only provide avenues for racist actors to operate, but also have independent consequences by influencing individual preferences, privileging some groups over others, and providing "rational" incentives that motivate political actors to either behave in a racist manner or behave in a manner that motivates others to do so (Katznelson 1973; March and Olsen 1984; Lieberman 1998; Marx 1998; Kryder 2000; Skrentny 2002). Specific to the study of parties, scholars argue that electoral institutions provide incentives for party politicians to represent specific types of politics, ideologies, and groups, reshaping societal divisions in the process (Shefter 1993; Aldrich 1995; Valelly 1995; Bridges 1997; Frymer 1999; James 2000; Wolbrecht 2000).

In the rest of this chapter, I argue both why we should pay closer attention to the links between race and party dynamics, even in periods when race is seemingly not on the public agenda, and why these links have profound implications for efforts at greater African American inclusion. I begin with a discussion of why party institutional design matters. I then look at the activities of the Democratic Party over the past two decades to illustrate how electoral incentives and the increasing success of the party went hand-in-hand with its efforts to distance itself from black voters.

THE TWO-PARTY SYSTEM, RACE, AND INSTITUTIONAL DESIGN

When we think about race mixing with politics we tend to focus on dramatic events. Americans fought a civil war over slavery and arguably fought a second war during the civil rights movement. Race issues have had huge consequences for national politics, precipitating at least one, may be two, electoral realignments (Sundquist 1983; Cowden 2001), the decline of urban political machines (Katznelson 1973; Kleppner 1985; Marable 1985), and the decline of the New Deal welfare state (Edsall with Edsall 1991; Quadagno 1994; Sugrue 1996; Lieberman 1998). The moments when race issues have dominated the political agenda, from the Civil War to the civil rights movement to the Rodney King beating and subsequent riots in Los Angeles, are indelibly etched in our memory.

In terms of understanding politics and democratic inclusion, however, it is problematic to consider race solely in terms of dramatic moments. Yet scholars have tended to do just that, creating a dichotomy between moments when race is not a part of public debate—and institutions and politicians seemingly function in a "normal" manner—and moments when race dominates the public sphere, and institutions and politicians behave irrationally because they are motivated by prejudice and anti-individualistic notions (e.g., Carmines and Stimson 1989; Poole and Rosenthal 1991). For these scholars, race matters—but only sometimes. It comes and goes, explosive when it is on the agenda, but then disappears and loses not only salience, but relevance. I argue alternatively that race should be understood as mattering not just in irrational acts of prejudice but in the day to day maneuverings of our political elites. Even when race is not publicly manifested in politics, its underlying presence has great consequences for both party leaders and the possibility of democratic inclusion as these party leaders work actively to keep race off the agenda to the direct detriment of African American representation.

Throughout the period when the founders were forming national political institutions, racial considerations were foremost on their minds. Starting with the Constitutional Convention, southern whites long maintained an effective veto power over proposed institutional designs that would threaten slavery (Freehling 1990; Finkelman 1996). Prior to the Civil War, this institutional design consistently benefited southern whites politically, enabling slaveholders to hold the presidency for 50 of the nation's first 62 years, the Speaker of the House for 41, and a majority of federal judgeships and appointments

(Richards 2000; Wills 2003). Although the Civil War ended slavery, many of the institutions that this original compromise birthed have proven stalwart. Whether it is the creation of the Senate, the Electoral College, the Full Faith and Credit Provision, or the Commerce Clause, the implications of institutional design remain significant. Initially designed to mitigate racial conflict, many of these institutions remain a powerful method of denying democratic inclusion because they privilege white and often specifically conservative white voters, resulting in a discourse and political agenda that gives primacy to white interests.[5]

The two-party system is a perfect example of an institution that was initially designed to alleviate the effects of racial conflict, and continues to have significant implications for democratic inclusion. Scholars have traditionally viewed the rise of the two-party system to be in accordance with the nation's "exceptionalism" of Liberal-individualism, moderate political tastes, and the absence of great conflicts (e.g., Dahl 1966; de Tocqueville 2001; Huntington 1968). As an electoral institution, however, the two-party system first developed in the 1820s when political leaders believed that such a system could effectively side-step divisiveness over a fundamental conflict—slavery—and refocus national attention through partisan competition around moderate voters with appeals to nationalism, economic populism, and stylistic vagaries (Remini 1963; Aldrich 1995). Party leaders, and most notably the leading influence behind the two-party system's development, Martin Van Buren, at the time recognized that institutional engineering could determine what Americans thought about and acted on. By creating two majority-seeking party coalitions, each party necessarily needed to appeal to centrist voters who did not feel strongly about slavery in order to win the election. Writes John Aldrich (1995, 125) in discussing the formation of the Democratic Party: "The assurance that no one person or faction could become dominant also meant that no one region, even one holding a majority of the nation, could dominate. . . . 'States Rights' in the structure of the Democratic Party meant controls to ensure national unity in the party, and in particular, controls to keep the 'peculiar institution' of slavery off the national political agenda for as long as institutionalized partisan politics could do so." As Van Buren wrote, "Instead of the question being between a northern and Southern man, it would be whether or not the ties, which have heretofore bound together a great party should be severed" (Remini 1963, 5). Van Buren selected Andrew Jackson to be the party's first candidate because he was perfect for avoiding ideological and regional conflicts. He was personally popular, unspecific in his ideas, and a war hero that Americans could unite around. "Indeed," Van Buren wrote, "Genl. Jackson has been so little in public life, that it will be not a little difficult to contrast his opinions on great questions with those of Mr. Adams" (Remini 1963, 6).

The two-party system may have, at least temporarily, saved a nation from civil war. But its development had both short- and long-term implications for the role of parties as agents of democratic inclusion. Most nations that have developed party systems in the context of racial and ethnic division have institutionalized some form of minority voice and power-sharing, usually through a form of proportional representation (Lijphart 1977, 1984). The U.S. party system was designed in a similar historical and political context of racial division but with a far different outcome. Instead of creating a system of representation for all groups, the two-party system was designed to deflect the voices in the debates over slavery by attempting to remove the issue from political contestation. Proclamations of ideological consensus and liberal creed aside, the development of this institutional dynamic, has contributed a significant role in engineering this consensus on a national scale. By creating an incentive system for party leaders to campaign around moderate/median voter causes, at a time when society was highly polarized over slavery, the two-party system was understood to manufacture which elements of public opinion would be amplified and represented by politicians. Party competition around the median voter influenced the types of ideologies that could be generated and which groups would be mobilized and demobilized.

The primary features of the nation's two-party system, the necessity of attracting the support of the median voter to win elections and the resulting emphasis on moderation and nonideological campaigns, remain in place today. In this system, party scholars widely assume that a group's simple presence in the electorate should be sufficient for democratic inclusion. All groups are not considered equal, of course, and groups that have more people, higher turnout rates, more money, and are strategically located within the Electoral College, will get more attention from party leaders than will other groups. At the same time, as long as a group's votes are available, the voter median (and thus the expected place of party contestation) ought to move in the direction of the group's interests and at least one party ought to reach out for the group's support (Key 1949; Shefter 1994; Benoit and Shepsle 1995). To lure the group to its party, leaders are expected to bestow the group with promises of policy promotion and representation.

But throughout much of U.S. history, party leaders have perceived the potential support of black voters as not simply leading to more votes in their electoral coalition but as destabilizing and divisive for winning elections. In part this is because many civil rights policies are unpopular with a majority of Americans, and in part because African American voters tend to be more liberal on many issues than the median voter.[6] But racism encourages party leaders to treat African Americans differently from other liberal and conservative groups that find themselves in the midst of party competition despite their ideological preferences. The presence of African Americans in the party coalition is often seen by party leaders as divisive for attracting the support of white voters, and hence the median voter. For instance, after African Americans entered the party system in large numbers during the 1960s, the voter median shifted but not in the direction expected by party theorists: Whites who saw themselves as economic liberals moved to the Republican Party in opposition to civil rights programs and because their perceptions about programs they once supported, such as welfare and active federal spending, changed as the programs became associated with blacks (Edsall with Edsall 1991; Kinder and Sanders 1996; Gilens 1999).

The combination of racism and electoral incentives leads parties to treat black voters differently than other similarly liberal or conservative groups. As long as African American votes are perceived as divisive to the building of party coalitions, their votes will not "count" in the same way as other groups. While black voters often make the statistical difference in election outcomes (Walters 1988), they are rarely given the political credit. In part this is because of party leaders' assumptions that black voters will vote Democrat regardless of any specific appeal; in every national election since 1964, African Americans have voted for the Democratic Party at rates higher than 80 percent (Tate 1993). But it is also because politicians perceive their votes as destabilizing the broader party coalition.[7] Recognizing this, the Democratic Party tries to win elections by keeping race off the political agenda (in order to remain appealing to conservative white voters) while delicately balancing subtle race-specific appeals at different moments to both black and white voters. The Republican Party, meanwhile, tries to win elections by making direct appeals to white voters without portraying the party as out of the mainstream on race matters. Both strategies leave African American interests severely underrepresented.

The resulting capture of black interests within the Democratic Party places the representatives of African American voters in a quandary. While these representatives push for civil rights goals as emphatically as they can, at the same time they have little choice but to ultimately unite behind party strategy designed to appeal to white swing voters. They oppose many of the specific actions of the Democratic Party leadership but endorse the party come election time because it remains a better choice than the Republican Party. The quandary becomes further apparent when African American political leaders attempt to promote greater black representation through the Voting Rights Act in a manner that seemingly hurts the Democratic Party. The drawing of congressional districts with black majorities has had many positive benefits for African American inclusion (Whitby 1997; Cannon 1999); at the same time, Democratic Party leaders fear that the drawing of such districts has hurt their broader electoral chances, leading to a loss of power in the House of Representatives and further marginalization of black political interests (Hill 1995; Lublin 1995). This same battle has arisen within the party over its congressional rules: Most white members of the House Democrats, for instance, want an organization that empowers the majority of the party over the preferences of individual members. The Congressional Black Caucus, in contrast, has consistently favored devices such as seniority and committee autonomy—devices that once benefited southern Democrats who opposed civil rights reforms. Support of such devices reflects recognition on the part of the Black Caucus that rules that benefit the majority of the party are often at odds with the interests of its black constituency.

Before moving on, let me address two counterarguments. First, one might well argue that while this institutional dynamic might marginalize the voice of black voters, it has also quite often muted and marginalized the interests of other groups, including the very same white racists who would deny African

Americans the right of political participation. In this sense, one could identify an important democratizing function of the two-party system—it keeps extremists of all stripes out of mainstream political debate. Rabid pro-slave politicians were no more electable in the post-1820s two-party system than were passionate abolitionists. In the election of 1948 and again in the 1960s, supporters of southern segregation were effectively marginalized because they could not find direct expression within the two-party system and had to opt for third-party alternatives. George Wallace's 1968 third-party campaign endorsing racial segregation, for instance, captured 15 percent of the national vote and 46 of the 538 Electoral College votes and yet he gained no political power from this because of our winner-take-all electoral system.

Still, there are many reasons why African Americans might find a political system that provides a greater voice to explicitly racist third parties in exchange for a greater voice to African Americans preferable to one that denies opportunities to both. One reason is that two-party politics already centers on white voters, enabling racist expression to remain viable in partisan politics. For much of America's history, this racism was quite explicit (Mendelberg 2001). But even since the civil rights era of the 1960s, a period in which racist hate speech is no longer an acceptable element in public discourse, code words with racial implications—such as "crime," "welfare," and "affirmative action"—have taken their stead (Kinder and Sanders 1996; Gilens 1999; Mendelberg 2001). Conservative political leaders utilized these code words during the seventies and eighties, engendering the support of large number of middle and working class white voters to dismantle many key New Deal social welfare programs (Edsall with Edsall 1991). Even when politicians are less subtle in their use of racism—for example, the Willy Horton commercial of 1988 or the Trent Lott comments of 2002—the Democratic Party has generally been reluctant to respond critically. By institutionalizing proportional power for African American voters with a multi-party system, African Americans would by no means be guaranteed policy victories, but they would be ensured a "voice" that could keep issues on the agenda and be confident that there would always be at least one political party with the incentive to mobilize black voters during campaign season.

The second counterargument asks: What explains the dramatic inclusion of African Americans during the 1860s and 1960s, as championed by first the Republican and later the Democratic Party? Three factors are notable about these two periods. First, African American interests were championed by a political party in each period during historically exceptional moments of weak two-party competition. In 1860, Abraham Lincoln won with less than 40 percent of the popular vote in a closely fought multi-party race; the passage of the Reconstruction Amendments subsequently occurred during a time when large numbers of southern whites were disenfranchised and the nation effectively had a one-party system. In 1964, Lyndon Johnson won with the largest popular vote percentage in American history; passage of much of the critical civil rights legislation during these years was marked not by competitive party dynamics so much as overwhelming bipartisan support. Second, in both cases, dramatic events outside of the control of party actors were underlying the election. Outsider social movements, in particular, were influential—abolitionists emerged from a third party and civil rights groups were organizing largely in areas where the right to vote was denied African American citizens. Third, as two-party competition returned in both periods—as the Democrats reemerged as a powerful electoral counter between 1866 and 1876, and as the Republican Party won a very close 1968 presidential election—the party that opposed further civil rights reform used race as a wedge while the party that represented black interests attempted to distance itself from the issue. African American inclusion, then, came at moments of great instability; as the party systems returned to "normal" African Americans in both periods would find their interests less central to national debate.

The process by which parties returned to close competition by removing race from the national political agenda was in both cases halting and uneven. Parties in the United States are neither hierarchical nor unified. They are democratic organizations with many different voices and it is often ambiguous who represents the party, especially at the national level. The closest thing that each party has to an official leader—the elected chair of the Democratic National Committee and Republican National Committee—is rarely of much consequence in terms of power and strategy. At different times, national party power has been centered in city mayors, congressional committee leaders, populist outsider candidates, and small interest groups (Polsby 1983; Ware 1985; Shefter 1994). More often, and particularly in the recent decades since the McGovern-Fraser reforms mandated the use of primaries in picking presidential nominees, no one individual or group has held command of the national parties. As a result, party strategy has moments when it lacks coherence, as many different groups and individuals vie for leadership and have alternative goals and opinions about how to achieve those goals. This strategic incoherence can provide moments of opportunity for black representation. Jesse Jackson, for instance, capitalized on the Democratic Party's nominating rules in the 1980s to push an active civil rights agenda from within the party.

But what is historically striking is how the need for parties to win national elections to remain politically viable eventually encourages unity among its members. Whether one believes that parties are simply instrumental in their desire to win elections or whether parties are composed of ideological individuals desiring policy agendas, winning elections remains essential to the goal. When parties lose elections, particularly when they have sustained losing streaks, the necessity to win becomes more and more dominant, and the party tends to unify more clearly around strategies directed at changing their losing ways (Klinkner 1994). Ideologically driven people who prefer to maintain policy agendas at the cost of winning are marginalized by those who can emphatically proclaim that winning through compromise is better than ending up with nothing at all. It is this dynamic—the need to win elections by attracting a majority of votes, combined with a perception among party elites that the median voter is opposed to discussions of racial equality—that leads black voters to be continually excluded from the benefits of party contestation. Prior to 1964, this dynamic led to the denial of civil and voting rights for most black Americans. Since 1964, much has changed and improved—black voting rights remain protected and even privileged by Congress and the courts, and their political interests institutionalized in different and important ways in the Democratic Party and the federal bureaucracy. Nonetheless, party dynamics continue to affect black political interests in powerful and important ways. After losing in the 1980s, for instance, the Democrats changed party nominating rules to try to prevent Jackson-type candidacies from having too much success and influence (Frymer 1999). Those efforts by the party are not foolproof, but there is a consistent and identifiable logic that works consistently to winnow out opportunities for the inclusion of black political interests. As we'll see in the following section, it was the return of close two-party contestation in the 1990s that most notably led the Democratic Party to distance itself from black voters and interests, leading to a significant decline in civil rights promotion on a number of critical issues from welfare and crime policy to school quality and job programs.

COMPETITIVE ELECTIONS AND AFRICAN AMERICAN REPRESENTATION, 1992–2000

The 2000 presidential election was among the closest in American history and followed similarly close elections in 1992 and 1996 in which no national party received a majority of the popular vote. According to conventional party scholarship, these three elections ought to have provided ideal conditions for the advancement and inclusion of African American voters and political interests (indeed, regarding the positive impact of these close elections for the inclusion of Latino voters, see Jones-Correa of this volume). First, the more competitive and closely fought the election, the more that any and all swing groups ought to be pivotal and subject to party appeals. African Americans were a critical group for Democratic Party success. No Democrat has won a presidential election with a majority of the white vote since 1964 and black voters in critical electoral college states such as Michigan, Illinois, Ohio, and (dare we say) Florida have frequently determined those states' outcomes. Second, none of the elections were dominated by racial animosity and they were certainly not elections that scholars would identify as particularly divisive. In the 2000 election, for instance, George Bush seemed sincere in his efforts to make blacks, as well as Latinos and Asian Americans, more visible in his campaign; even Patrick Buchanan nominated an African American woman as his vice presidential candidate.

Both the closeness of partisan electoral conflict in the last three presidential elections and the lack of prominence of racial divisiveness were marked changes from the prior two decades. Between 1968 and 1988, the Republicans dominated presidential contests, winning 5 of 6 elections. Democrats found their party under attack by the Republicans for policies that were perceived as simultaneously pro-black and anti-white. Party support for controversial issues such as government-enforced school busing to end racial segregation in schools, affirmative action, welfare rights, criminal procedure protections, and general government spending on national social programs was blamed for the swing of white voters to the Republicans. Republican race baiting further fueled this exodus of white voters. Richard Nixon centered his campaign around two distinct groups whose identities were embedded in racial significance: the "silent majority," the group of voters who were portrayed as not protesting, not breaking the law, and who had jobs, families, and home mortgages; and a southern strategy which targeted whites opposed to school integration policies and in favor of state rights. Ronald Reagan courted the same groups, promoting states rights from a lectern in Mississippi and appealing to working class "Reagan Democrats" who were dissatisfied with welfare, crime, and affirmative action policies. George Bush, Sr., followed in their footsteps, as during the 1988 election he continually equated the Democratic Party with Jesse Jackson and was linked to a Willy Horton television ad in which Horton's face was shown to American voters as representative of what happens when Democratic Party politicians are soft on black criminals.

While Republicans race baited, the Democratic Party was subject to internal criticism for being too beholden to special interests and increasingly irrelevant as an electoral institution. In response to controversies within the party during the 1960s over the incorporation of African Americans into its nominating delegation (as exemplified in the battle over the Mississippi Freedom Democrats in 1964 and the powerful position of the Daly Administration in 1968), the party changed the rules that governed the way, its members, nominated presidential candidates. To mobilize the party's base, the McGovern-Fraser reforms made primaries central to the nomination of the party's presidential candidate, removing power from the hands of urban mayors and other regional leaders and giving it to rank-and-file voters and party delegates—delegates who were racially diverse as a product of strict quotas (Crotty 1978). These reforms greatly increased the numbers of blacks, women, and other previously underrepresented groups in the party's delegation. They were also criticized as making the party less competitive and leading its strategically important white base from the South and northern urban areas to flee to the Republican Party (Baer 2000). Nelson Polsby (1983, 147) described the Democrats after the McGovern-Fraser reforms as a party of crazes, manias, and fads. Byron Shafer (1983, 252) claimed that "at bottom, the result of all these reforms was *the diminution, the constriction, at times the elimination, of the regular party in politics of presidential selection*" (emphasis in original).

Fractured over race, policy, and electoral strategy, Democratic Party elites argued vociferously with each other as electoral defeats mounted. There was plenty to argue about in the interpretation of electoral results. On the one hand, until 1994, Democrats continued to win a majority of seats in the House and often in the Senate, producing less of a Republican realignment than a period of divided government. Public opinion polls, moreover, were not showing a great deal of depth among voter preferences in their shift toward the Republican Party. Perhaps as a result of the polls that showed voters continuing to support Democrats on issues most closely identified with the New Deal economic coalition, the conventional wisdom in strategic circles quickly became that it was the party's civil rights policies, particularly on busing, affirmative action, crime, and welfare that were leading to its electoral demise (Edsall with Edsall 1991). A study by one of the party's leading pollsters, Stanley Greenberg, of traditionally white Democrats who were voting Republican in the suburbs of Detroit reported that the voters "express[ed] a profound distaste for blacks, a sentiment that pervades almost everything they think about government and politics. . . . These sentiments have important implications for Democrats, as virtually all progressive symbols and themes have been redefined in racial and pejorative terms" (Greenberg 1985, 13). These policies allowed Republicans to win by luring white working and middle class voters in the North and South without making economic appeals (Black and Black 1987; Edsall with Edsall 1991).

Whether this conventional wisdom was the product of campaign and public opinion realities or some of the party leaders' personal ambivalence about race, it resulted in successful efforts to make counterinstitutional reforms to the McGovern-Fraser rules so that the party could be more competitive in presidential elections with white voters. After the party's landslide defeat to Reagan in 1984, moderates created the Democratic Leadership Council with the intent of changing the party's agenda and moving it away from the civil rights and social spending goals of previous decades (Hale 1995; Baer 2000). "Super Tuesday," a one-day primary involving fourteen southern states, became the signature of the party's effort to return to electoral success. By grouping these southern primaries together early in the nominating season, party leaders hoped to provide a strategic advantage to candidates who were appealing to the region's conservative white voters and lead to the nomination of a candidate who would appeal nationally. If a conservative southern candidate ran in Super Tuesday (Al Gore was the initial target of party strategists), he or she would most likely exit with a commanding lead over other Democratic candidates; even if no southern candidate ran for president, theoretically Super Tuesday should force all candidates to adopt policy positions consistent with southern voters. Super Tuesday did not work as expected right away. In 1988, Jesse Jackson's candidacy mobilized black voters who became a disproportionately large part of the Democrat's southern base when most southern white voters (the group that the party was trying to target) ended up participating in the Republican primaries instead. Jackson won a majority of southern states that day with Gore and Michael Dukakis splitting the white vote.

But calls by leading Democrats to change the party's electoral strategy only became louder with Jackson's success and the party's eventual loss to George Bush, a candidate thought by Democrats as very beatable. By 1992, even progressive party leaders came to be persuaded by the importance of winning over ideological purity and leading members of the party's left wing became critical in legitimating the promotion of centrist candidates Bill Clinton and Al Gore. Former civil rights activist John Lewis typified this response when he said of Clinton in 1992, "in the communities I deal with, people want to win, they want to see a Democrat in the White House. . . . They understand that in order to win, it's necessary to bring back those individuals who had left the party" (quoted in Edsall 1992). Party leaders, whites and blacks united, convinced Jackson to stay out of the race and unify the party around Clinton in order to defeat Bush. When Jackson made overtures to third-party candidate Ross Perot, claiming that he could bring with him large portions of the black voting bloc, Perot wasn't interested.

The Clinton strategy of distancing the party from its black constituency both during the campaign and during his presidency has been well argued elsewhere (Frymer 1999; Klinkner 1999; Kim 2001). Clinton's election in 1992 and eventual success in office was seen as part of the triumph of "third way" candidates throughout the United States, United Kingdom, and across the globe. He was tough on crime, making sure to participate in the execution of a mentally disabled African American man earlier on in his first presidential bid, and later making anti-crime legislation a major tenet of his legislative agenda. He criticized Jesse Jackson, Sister Soulja, and Lani Guinier, and ended "welfare as we know it" just prior to his 1996 reelection bid, effectively taking away one of the leading ways in which Republicans were able to race bait Democrats. Clinton's strategy was certainly a "third way" as opposed to a straightforward cooptation of conservative causes. He stood behind affirmative action programs with a typically moderate but politically successful "mend, don't end" solution, he promoted social spending and programs in a way far different from the Republicans, and he promoted an ambitious if merely symbolic and substantively empty dialogue on race (Kim 2001). In the course of his impeachment hearings, he was even labeled by the famous African American writer, Toni Morrison, as the first black president and received overwhelming support from the black community.

Nonetheless, important concerns for large numbers of black voters—racial segregation in housing and schools, unequal access to health care and other important social services, and dramatic disparities in arrests and sentencing for nonviolent crimes—were largely ignored by the President and other leaders of the Democratic Party. Leading African American supporters of Clinton who promised opportunities for a race agenda after he was elected would be hard pressed to argue that Clinton at any time turned to such an agenda. Members of the Congressional Black Caucus were continually at odds with the President in his early years regarding welfare, crime, and social spending. The Caucus had some success during these years—they pushed the President to invade Haiti and increased spending provisions in some of the budget debates (Boyler 1994). But in a moment that in many ways symbolized the conflict between the Caucus and Clinton, when key members of the Caucus balked at a Clinton-sponsored Crime Bill in 1994 that they opposed because it failed to contain a provision about racial justice and the death penalty, Clinton simply moved further to the right to find additional votes to pass the legislation. He rarely went back in his subsequent years in office.

That Clinton made it safe for Democrats to be conservatives on civil rights is undeniable. Labeled "the president of a rational choice theorist's dreams" (Rockman 2000, 288), he was exceptional at balancing acts that alienated African American voters with acts that won wide approval, such as his attendance at all-black events, his symbolic yet earnest appeals at dialogue on national race issues, and his endorsement of black politicians for high-ranking political posts—many of whom he was close friends with as he was arguably the first U.S. president to have close African American friends. He also made it safe for Republicans to make symbolic gestures at inclusion toward black voters. With the promise of a substantive discussion of racial issues no longer a primary point of division between the parties, candidates Bob Dole and Jack Kemp in 1996 and George Bush in 2000 found it safe to speak of the possibility of African American involvement in the Republican Party. Bush, in fact, seemed fairly successful with a balancing act of his own—opposing affirmative action, welfare, and federally mandated school integration, but equally emphatic in his support of basic civil rights principles, his endorsement of black politicians for high ranking political posts, and his campaign promise to leave no child behind.[8]

Al Gore's strategy in 2000, however, reinforced the problematic nature of the Democratic Party's efforts to return to competitiveness by denying the salience of racial matters. Most notable about the election campaign were not the brief moments of controversy over George Bush's visit to Bob Jones University or the numbers of black faces at the Republican Convention; it was how infrequently race came up as a point of discussion during the Gore campaign. Consider just two examples when Gore avoided raising racial issues when it seemingly made at least short-term political sense to do so. Months before the election, Texas governor George Bush approved the execution of convicted murderer Gary Graham. Graham's execution caused a great deal of outrage and controversy. Graham was convicted in a trial with little evidence and a single self-doubting witness, his lawyers were woefully unprepared for the case, and he had emphatically maintained his innocence until his death. Graham's execution symbolized the unfairness underlying the criminal legal system in which African American men are sentenced to the death penalty in grossly disproportionate numbers (Cole 1999). Graham defiantly declared at his execution that "this is what happens to black men in America," and the NAACP called the execution "a gross travesty of justice" (Mitchell 2000). Even a majority of Texas citizens believed Graham was innocent, notable in a state that executes far more people than any other state in the nation. But Gore remained silent throughout the controversy, maintaining his personal support for the death penalty, and stating on the day of the execution, "I do not know the record in Texas. I have not examined the cases. I've always tried to stay away from issues in criminal courts" (Moret and King 2000).

The second example involves African American voters in the state of Florida who may or may not have been denied their right to vote on the day of the election, or had their votes voided by confusing ballots and "hanging chads." Newspaper articles at the time reported widespread complaints by African Americans in the state. Some were stopped at roadblocks and prevented from voting. Some were told at polling booths that they were ineligible to vote because they were incorrectly labeled felons (and thus denied by law the right to vote in Florida) or because they simply were not on the relevant voter registrars. For whatever reason, African American ballots in the state were also disproportionately voided for having holes punched incorrectly. Yet, while more than 90 percent of African Americans voted for Gore nationally, and while the missing votes in Florida surely would have favored Gore and probably would have provided the difference in the state and national election results, the Gore campaign did not precipitate these accusations or demand investigations into potential violations of the Voting Rights Act. In fact, when African American politicians such as Jesse Jackson and Al Sharpton attempted to rally public support around the potential voting rights violations, they were quietly asked by leaders of the Gore campaign to tone down their complaints (Crowley 2000).

CONCLUSION

In some ways, we ought to be celebrating the relative absence of race from the 2000 campaign. An election that is unremarkable on race issues is indeed remarkable given the historical context. In past decades, the Republican Party too easily used race to drive a wedge into the Democratic Party's once reliable electoral coalition, a coalition unified on issues of economic liberalism but deeply fractured on issues pertaining to race. The absence of race in the 2000 campaign meant voters who agree that they want better health care, more social services, and improved labor conditions did not end up splitting their vote because of their differences on affirmative action, welfare, immigration, and crime. The lacunae of divisive race issues allowed Democrats to promote a modern-day twist on the New Deal economic liberalism that made the party so successful at the polls earlier in the twentieth century. Moreover, it is certainly a step in the right direction that the Republican race-baiting strategies of the 1980s and early 1990s have been replaced by at least a skin-deep effort at inclusion. National leaders of both political parties seem to recognize that explicit racism is unappealing to the mainstream American voter. In a nation that fought a civil war over the issue of slavery, and followed this war with another century of legal racial apartheid, this newly found consensus is not to be minimized.

But while this silence over race issues can be interpreted as an achievement in terms of national politicians maintaining civility, it is also a cause of concern for those interested in promoting a more vibrant and inclusive democracy. Racial harmony in our national election campaigns has come at a cost; it has meant avoiding discussion of causes and solutions to pressing policy issues concerning racial inequality, particularly with specific regard to African American voters. The major party candidates do not discuss critical issues of concern to African Americans such as racial segregation in housing and schools, the increasing racial divides in wealth and resources, and the continuing inequalities in criminal justice, health care, labor rights, and equal access to a clean environment. African American voices and interests have been largely ignored during recent campaigns as the parties focus on various groups deemed by party strategists to be potentially determinative of the election campaign. White Americans, moreover, are told little about race matters from political leaders and as a result remain largely ambivalent toward and unaware of critical inequalities. Even in the most civil of elections (such as 2000), national political discourse is merely racially generic—the parties focus on narrow sets of issues that are believed to be without any racial content.

While this might seem good in theory, in practice it amounts to a discourse that is quite race-specific, as it focuses on issues that can be discussed in white households without implicit connections to racial minorities.

Consistent with the institutional focus of this volume, I have argued that this racialized discourse is a direct result of U.S. electoral institutions. The ballot system, the rules governing the number of votes needed to win the election, and the number of parties favored by such rules, play significant roles in determining which issues are discussed during political campaigns. To win elections, politicians must appeal to swing voters. In recent U.S. elections, it has seemed political suicide for national politicians to discuss racial inequality, racism, or civil rights because Reagan Democrats, Perot supporters, soccer moms, and Nascar dads have a significant interest in maintaining the status quo. In a historically white majority nation with racially conservative swing voters, parties have little incentive—in fact, they often have great disincentive—to appeal to black voters. In the current context, this has resulted in a defensive politics: Democrats appeal to African American issues at the base level calculated to keep blacks in the party, and Republicans address racial issues with only enough care not to frighten white voters with unattractive racism. Discussion of race by both parties is minimal and centers largely on the symbolic. The result is that race issues have been institutionalized outside of the electoral arena, creating a large and problematic void in democratic politics in this country.

Given the historical context of racism in the United States, African Americans need affirmative government measures to rectify a long history of past wrongs. The political incorporation of African Americans has, in fact, arguably been the most dominant and important task in making American democracy a reality. The two-party system is hardly the only explanation for why equality has been so elusive, but it does provide us with arguably the primary engine that drives American democracy. While we should not minimize the myriad ways in which parties encourage greater democracy throughout the country, it is only when we recognize a significant irony—that this essential engine of democracy only works when we suppress national divisions over race—that we can confront its constant impact on the possibilities that exist for policy reform and democratic inclusion.

NOTES

1. This is not to say that all U.S. party scholars agree. See Amy (1993), Lowi (2001), and Disch (2002). In his more recent work, Dahl (1989, 2001) has also become more critical of the U.S. two-party system.

2. Legal scholars are increasingly making similar arguments in defense of the two-party system (Kramer 2000; Persily 2001; Garrett 2002) while the U.S. Supreme Court over the last decade has cited these arguments in denying opportunities to third parties and citizen groups to gain greater representation in electoral politics (see *Timmons v. Twin Cities Area New Party*, 520 U.S. 351 (1997); *California Democratic Party v. Jones*, 530 U.S. 567 (2000)).

3. I focus specifically on African American representation and not the broader category of racial minorities in the United States not because the inclusion of other racial minorities

has necessarily been better or easier but simply because the inclusion of African Americans into the party system is meaningfully different than that of other racial and ethnic minorities (see Frymer and Skrentny 1998; Kim 1999; Fields 2002).

4. This seems to be a viewpoint specific to the understanding of U.S. politics. Scholars of comparative parties tend to see racism and ethnic conflict as far more fundamental and systematic and thus recognize that party institutions are both built around and constantly affecting these fissures (see Kymlicka 1995; Lijphart 1995; Horowitz 2000). Ironically, many scholars of American parties agree with this assessment when they confront what they identify to be racially and ethnically divided societies elsewhere. Dahl (1971, 116), for example, argued at the same time that he was promoting two-party politics in the United States that the two-party system will fail to adequately represent all of its members when racial cleavages are fundamental: "If a country is divided into majority and minority subcultures, then members of the majority have less need to be conciliatory toward the minority, since they can form a majority coalition among themselves. As a consequence, members of the minority may see no prospect of ever freeing themselves from the political domination of the majority; hence they, too, have little incentive to be conciliatory." Anthony Downs (1957, 121) agreed; while he argued that opportunities will exist for all groups to obtain majority status for at least the short term in a society with pluralistic divisions where no one group is consistently in the majority and no one group is consistently in the minority, he contrasts that with societies in which there is a fundamental cleavage and one side is consistently in the minority—"fear of this is precisely what caused many European aristocrats to fight the introduction of universal suffrage" (also see Epstein 1967).

5. Although certainly not all of these institutions continue to have the same impact. The Commerce Clause, for example, while initially protective of slave interests because it disallowed opportunities for northern anti-slave interests to tax slave-made commercial goods, later became a critical engine in the fight against southern civil rights violations (e.g., *Heart of Atlanta Motel v. United States*, 379 U.S. 183 [1968]).

6. Though as David Cannon (1999, 28–30) has recently shown, on non–civil rights issues, African American voters are not as liberal and are actually quite similar to whites in their political beliefs.

7. When African American political leaders have reached out to the Republicans and third parties in moments when those parties were behind in the electoral polls, they have been rebuffed despite their votes seemingly making a difference in the electoral calculus. In the 1990s, for instance, Jesse Jackson reached out to Ross Perot (1992) and Bob Dole (1996) without interest from either candidate.

8. Of course, this balancing act was not persuasive with black voters, as he was summarily rejected by more than 90 percent of black votes nationwide and in his home state of Texas. In fact, Bush received a smaller percentage of the black vote (8 percent nationally) than any Republican candidate since 1964.

References

Aldrich, John H. 1995. *Why Parties? The Origin and Transformation of Party Politics in America.* Chicago: University of Chicago Press.

Amy, Douglas J. 1993. *Real Choices/New Voices.* New York: Columbia University Press.

Baer, Kenneth S. 2000. *Reinventing Democrats: The Politics of Liberalism from Reagan to Clinton.* Lawrence: University of Kansas Press.

Benoit, Kenneth, and Kenneth A. Shepsle. 1995. "Electoral Systems and Minority Representation." In *Classifying by Race*, edited by Paul E. Peterson. Princeton: Princeton University Press, ch. 3.

Bibby, John F. 1997. "In Defense of the Two-Party System." In *Multiparty Politics in America*, edited by Paul S. Herrnson and John C. Green. Lanham, MD: Rowman and Littlefield, 45–58.

Black, Earl, and Merle Black. 1987. *Politics and Society in the South*. Cambridge: Harvard University Press.

Bobo, Lawrence. 1988. "Group Conflict, Prejudice, and the Paradox of Contemporary Racial Attitudes." In *Eliminating Racism: Profiles in Controversy*, edited by Phylis Katz and Dalmas A. Taylor. New York: Plenum, 85–116.

Bobo, Lawrence, and Franklin D. Gilliam. 1990. "Race, Sociopolitical Participation, and Black Empowerment." *American Political Science Review* 84:377.

Bonilla-Silva, Eduardo. 1996. "Rethinking Racism: Toward A Structural Interpretation." *American Sociological Review* 62:465.

Boyer, Peter J. 1994. "The Rise of Kweisi Mfume," *New Yorker* (August 1).

Bridges, Amy. 1997. *Morning Glories: Municipal Reform in the Southwest*. Princeton: Princeton University Press.

Browning, Rufus, Dale Rogers Marshall, and David Tabb. 1984. *Protest is Not Enough: The Struggle of Blacks and Hispanics for Equality in City Politics*. Berkeley: University of California Press.

Cain, Bruce. 2001. "Party Autonomy and Two-Party Electoral Competition." *University of Pennsylvania Law Review* 149:793–814.

Cannon, David T. 1999. *Race, Redistricting, and Representation: The Unintended Consequences of Black Minority Districts*. Chicago: University of Chicago Press.

Carmines, Edward G., and James A. Stimson. 1989. *Issue Evolution: Race and the Transformation of American Politics*. Princeton: Princeton University Press.

Chong, Dennis. 1991. *Collective Action and the Civil Rights Movement*. Chicago: University of Chicago Press.

Cole, David. 1999. *No Equal Justice: Race & Class in the American Criminal Justice System*. New York: New Press.

Cowden, Jonathan A. 2001. "Southernization of the Nation and Nationalization of the South: Racial Conservatism, Social Welfare and White Partisans in the United States, 1956–92." *British Journal of Political Science* 31:277.

Crotty, William J. 1978. *Decision for the Democrats: Reforming the Party Structure*. Baltimore: The Johns Hopkins University Press.

Crowley, Michael. 2000. "Why Feminism Wins Elections; Why Blacks Want Gore to Keep Fighting." *The New Republic* (December 18).

Dahl, Robert A. 1961. *Who Governs?* New Haven: Yale University Press.

———. 1966. "The American Oppositions: Affirmation and Denial." In *Political Oppositions in Western Democracies*, edited by Robert A. Dahl. New Haven: Yale University Press.

———. 1967. *Pluralist Democracy in the United States*. Chicago: Rand McNally.

———. 1971. *Polyarchy*. New Haven: Yale University Press.

———. 1989. *Democracy and Its Critics*. New Haven: Yale University Press.

———. 2001. *How Democratic is the American Constitution?* New Haven: Yale University Press.

de Tocqueville, Alexis. 2001. *Democracy in America*. New York: Signet.

Disch, Lisa Jane. 2002. *The Tyranny of the Two-Party System*. New York: Columbia University Press.

Downs, Anthony. 1957. *An Economic Theory of Democracy*. New York: Harper.

Edsall, Thomas Byrne with Mary D. Edsall. 1991. *Chain Reaction: The Impact of Race, Rights, and Taxes on American Politics*. New York: Norton.

Edsall, Thomas Byrne. 1992. "Black Leaders View Clinton Strategy with Mix of Pragmatism, Optimism." *Washington Post* (October 28): A16.

Eisinger, Peter. 1982. "Black Empowerment in Municipal Jobs: The Impact of Black Political Power." *American Political Science Review* 76:380.

Eldersveld, Samuel J., and Hanes Walton, Jr. 2000. *Political Parties in American Society*. Boston: Bedford/St. Martin's.

Ely, John Hart. 1980. *Democracy and Distrust: A Theory of Judicial Review*. Cambridge: Harvard University Press.

Epstein, Leon D. 1967. *Political Parties in Western Democracies*. New York: Praeger.

————. 1986. *Political Parties in the American Mold*. Madison: University of Wisconsin Press.

Fields, Barbara J. 2001. "Whiteness, Racism, and Identity." *International Labor and Working-Class History* 60 (Fall): 48.

Finkelman, Paul. 1996. *Slavery and the Founders: Race and Liberty in the Age of Jackson*. Armonk, NY: M.E. Sharpe.

Freehling, William W. 1990. *The Road to Disunion: Secessionists at Bay, 1776–1854*. New York: Oxford University Press.

Frymer, Paul. 1999. *Uneasy Alliances: Race and Party Competition in America*. Princeton: Princeton University Press.

Frymer, Paul, and John David Skrentny. 1998. "Coalition-Building and the Politics of Electoral Capture during the Nixon Administration: African-Americans, Labor, Latinos." *Studies in American Political Development* 12:131.

Garrett, Elizabeth. 2002. "Is the Party Over? Courts and the Political Process." *The Supreme Court Review* 2002:95.

Gay, Claudine. 2001. "The Effect of Black Congressional Representation on Political Participation." *American Political Science Review* 95:589.

Gilens, Martin. 1999. *Why Americans Hate Welfare: Race, Media, and the Politics of Antipoverty Policy*. Chicago: University of Chicago Press.

Gilroy, Paul. 2000. *Against Race: Imagining Political Culture Beyond the Culture Line*. Cambridge: Harvard University Press.

Green, John C., and Daniel M. Shea. 1999. *The State of the Parties: The Changing Role of Contemporary American Parties*. Lanham, MD: Rowman and Littlefield.

Greenberg, Stanley B. 1985. "Report on Democratic Defection." (report to the Democratic Party, April 15, 1985).

Grofman, Bernard, and Chandler Davidson. 1992. "Postscript: What is the Best Route to a Color-Blind Society?" In *Controversies in Minority Voting: The Voting Rights Act in Perspective*, edited by Grofman and Davidson. Washington, DC: Brookings, 300–17.

Guinier, Lani. 1991. "The Triumph of Tokenism: The Voting-Rights Act and the Theory of Black Electoral Success." *University of Michigan Law Review* 89:1077.

Hajnal, Zoltan L. 2001. "White Residents, Black Incumbents, and a Declining Racial Divide." *American Political Science Review* 95:603.

Hale, Jon. 1995. "The Making of the New Democrats." *Political Science Quarterly* 110: 207–32.

Hill, Kevin A. 1995. "Does the Creation of Majority Black Districts Aid Republicans? An Analysis of 1992 Congressional Elections in Eight Southern States." *Journal of Politics* 57:384.

Holden, Matthew. 1973. *The Politics of the Black "Nation."* New York: Chandler Publishings.

Horowitz, Donald L. 2000. "Provisional Pessimism: A Reply to Van Parijs." *Nomos* 42: 321–28.

Huntington, Samuel P. 1968. *Political Order in Changing Societies*. New Haven: Yale University Press.

James, Scott C. 2000. *Presidents, Parties and the State: A Party System Perspective on Democratic Regulatory Choice, 1884–1936*. New York: Cambridge University Press.

Katznelson, Ira. 1973. *Black Men, White Cities: Race, Politics, and Migration in the United States and Britain*. Chicago: University of Chicago Press.

Key, Vladimir O. Jr. 1949. *Southern Politics in State and Nation*. New York: Vintage.

Kim, Claire Jean. 1999. "The Racial Triangulation of Asian Americans." *Politics and Society* 27(1): 105.

———. 2001. "Managing the Racial Breach: Clinton, Black–White Polarization, and the Race Initiative." *Political Science Quarterly* 117(1): 55.

Kinder, Donald R., and Lynn Sanders. 1996. *Divided by Color: Racial Politics and Democratic Ideals*. Chicago: University of Chicago Press.

Kleppner, Paul. 1985. *Chicago Divided: The Making of a Black Mayor*. DeKalb: Northern Illinois University Press.

Klinkner, Philip A. 1994. *The Losing Parties: Out-Party National Committees, 1956–1993*. New Haven: Yale University Press.

———. 1999. "Bill Clinton and the Politics of the New Liberalism." In *Without Justice for All: The New Liberalism and the Retreat from Racial Equality*, edited by Adolph Reed. Boulder: Westview Press.

Kramer, Larry D. 2000. "Putting the Politics Back into the Political Safeguards of Federalism." *Columbia Law Review* 100:215.

Kryder, Daniel. 2000. *Divided Arsenal: Race and the American State During World War II*. New York: Cambridge University Press.

Kymlicka, Will. 1995. *Multicultural Citizenship*. New York: Oxford University Press.

Lee, Taeku. 2002. *Mobilizing Public Opinion: Black Insurgency and Racial Attitudes in the Civil Rights Era*. Chicago: University of Chicago Press.

Lieberman, Robert C. 1998. *Shifting the Color Line*. Cambridge: Harvard University Press.

Lijphart, Arend. 1977. *Democracy in Plural Societies: A Comparative Explanation*. New Haven: Yale University Press.

———. 1984. *Democracies: Patterns of Majoritarian and Consensus Government in Twenty-One Countries*. New Haven: Yale University Press.

———. 1995. "Self-Determination versus Pre-Determination of Ethnic Minorities in Power-Sharing Systems." In *The Rights of Minority Cultures,* edited by Will Kymlicka, 275–97. New York: Oxford University Press.

Lowi, Theodore J. 2001. "Political Parties and the Future State of the Union." *In American Political Parties: Decline or Resurgence?* edited by Jeffrey E. Cohen, Richard Fleisher, and Paul Kantor, 229–240. Washington, DC: Congressional Quarterly Press.

Lublin, David Ian. 1995. "Race, Representation, and Redistricting." in *Classifying by Race*, edited by Paul Peterson. Princeton: Princeton University Press.

Lusane, Clarence. 1997. *Race in the Global Era: African Americans at the Millenium*. Boston: South End Press.

Maisel, L. Sandy. 2002. *The Parties Respond: Changes in American Parties and Campaigns*. Boulder CO: Westview.

Marable, Manning. 1985. *Black American Politics: From the Washington Marches to Jesse Jackson*. New York: Verso.

———. 2002. *The Great Wells of Democracy: The Meaning of Race in American Life*. New York: Basic Civitas.

March James G. and Johan P. Olsen. 1984. "The New Institutionalism: Organizational Factors in Political Life." *American Political Science Review* 78:734.

Marx, Anthony W. 1998. *Making Race and Nation: A Comparison of the United States, South Africa, and Brazil*. New York: Cambridge University Press.

Mendelberg, Tali. 2001. *The Race Card: Campaign Strategy, Implicit Messages, and the Norm of Equality*. Princeton: Princeton University Press.

Milkis, Sidney M. 1999. *Political Parties and Constitutional Government: Remaking American Democracy*. Baltimore: The Johns Hopkins University Press.

Mitchell, Alison. 2000. "Response Polite as Bush Courts the N.A.A.C.P.," *New York Times* (July 11), A1.

Moret, Jim and John King. 2000. "Vice President Reluctant to Join Debate on Capital Punishment," *CNN The World Today* (June 21), Transcript #00062109V23.

Myrdal, Gunnar. 1944. *An American Dilemma*. New York: Harper & Row.

Omi, Michael, and Howard Winant. 1994. *Racial Formation in the United States*. Philadelphia: Temple University Press.

Persily, Nathaniel. 2001. "Toward a Functional Defense of Political Party Autonomy." *New York University Law Review* 76:750–824.

Pinderhughes, Dianne. 1984. "Political Choices: A Realignment in Partisanship Among Black Voters?" In *State of Black America*, edited by James Williams. New York: National Black Urban League.

———. 1987. *Race and Ethnicity in Chicago Politics*. Urbana: University of Illinois Press, 85–113.

Piven, Frances Fox, and Richard A. Cloward. 1977. *Poor People's Movements: Why They Succeed, How They Fail*. New York: Pantheon.

Polsby, Nelson W. 1983. *The Consequences of Party Reform*. New York: Oxford University Press.

Poole, Keith T. and Howard Rosenthal. 1991. "Patterns in Congressional Voting," *American Journal of Political Science* 35:228–78.

Quadagno, Jill. 1994. *The Color of Welfare: How Racism Undermined the War on Poverty*. New York: Oxford University Press.

Reed, Adolph, Jr. 1995. "Demobilization in the New Black Political Regime: Ideological Capitulation and Radical Failure in the Post-Segregation Era." In *The Bubbling Cauldron: Race, Ethnicity, and the Urban Crisis*, edited by Michael Peter Smith and Joe R. Feagin. Minneapolis: University of Minnesota Press, ch. 9.

Reichley, A. James. 1992. *The Life of the Parties: A History of American Political Parties*. Lanham, MD: Rowman and Littlefield.

Remini, Robert. 1963. *The Election of Andrew Jackson*. Philadelphia: Lippincott.

Rhode, David W. 1991. "Something's Happening Here, What It Is Ain't Exactly Clear: Southern Democrats in the House of Representatives," In *Home Style and Washington Work*, edited by Morris P. Fiorina and Rhode. Ann Arbor: University of Michigan Press.

Richards, Leonard L. 2000. *The Slave Power*. Baton Rouge: Louisiana State University Press.

Rockman, Bert. 2000. "Cutting *With* the Grain: Is there a Clinton Leadership Legacy?" In *The Clinton Legacy*, edited by Colin Campbell and Rockman. New York: Chatham.

Rosenberg, Gerald N. 1991. *The Hollow Hope: Can Courts Bring About Social Change?* Chicago: University of Chicago Press.

Sabato, Larry J., and Bruce Larson. 2002. *The Party's Just Begun: Shaping Political Parties for America's Future*. New York: Longman.

Schattschneider, Elmer E. 1942. *Party Government*. Westport CT: Greenwood Press.

Sears, David, Jim Sidanius, and Lawrence Bobo, eds. 2000. *Racialized Politics: The Debate about Racism in America*. Chicago: University of Chicago Press.

Shafer, Byron E. 1983. *Quiet Revolution: The Struggle for the Democratic Party and the Shaping of Post-Reform Politics*. New York: Russell Sage.

Shefter, Martin. 1994. *Political Parties and the State: The American Historical Experience*. Princeton: Princeton University Press.

Skrentny, John D. 2002. *The Minority Rights Revolution*. Cambridge: Harvard University Press.

Smith, Robert C. 1996. *We Have No Leaders: African Americans in the Post–Civil Rights Era*. Albany: State University of New York Press.

Smith, Rogers M. 1997. *Civic Ideals: Conflicting Visions of Citizenship in U.S. History*. New Haven: Yale University Press.

Sonenshein, Raphael J. 1993. *Politics in Black and White: Racial Power in Los Angeles*. Princeton: Princeton University Press.

Sugrue, Thomas J. 1996. *The Origins of the Urban Crisis: Race and Inequality in Postwar Detroit*. Princeton: Princeton University Press.

Sundquist, James L. 1983. *Dynamics of the Party System: Alignment and Realignment of Political Parties in the United States*. Washington, D.C.: Brookings.

Swain, Carol M. 1993. *Black Faces, Black Interests: The Representation of African Americans in Congress*. Cambridge: Harvard University Press.

Tate, Katherine. 1993. *From Protest to Politics: The New Black Voters in American Elections*. Cambridge: Harvard University Press.

———. 2003. *Black Faces in the Mirror: African Americans and their Representatives in the U.S. Congress*. Princeton: Princeton University Press.

Valelly, Richard M. 1995."National Parties and Racial Disenfranchisement." In *Classifying by Race*, edited by Paul E. Peterson. Princeton: Princeton University Press, ch. 8.

Walters, Ronald W. 1988. *Black Presidential Politics in America: A Strategic Approach*. Albany. State University of New York Press.

Walton, Hanes Jr. 1972. *Black Political Parties*. New York: Free Press.

Ware, Alan. 1985. *The Breakdown of Democratic Party Organization 1940–1980*. New York: Oxford University Press.

Wattenberg, Martin P. 1990. *The Decline of American Political Parties: 1952–1988*. Cambridge: Harvard University Press.

Whitby, Kenny J. 1997. *The Color of Representation: Congressional Representation and Black Interests*. Ann Arbor: University of Michigan Press.

White, John K. 1992. "E. E. Schattschneider and the Responsible Party Model." *PS* 25: 167–71.

Wills, Gary. 2003. "The Negro President." *New York Review of Books* 50(17).

Wolbrecht, Christina. 2000. *The Politics of Women's Rights: Parties, Positions, and Change*. Princeton: Princeton University Press.

7 Race, Ethnicity, and Electoral Mobilization
Where's the Party?

FEW WOULD DISAGREE that a fundamental indicator of democratic inclusion in a representative democracy is the extension of full electoral rights and privileges to racial and ethnic minorities. The history of the civil rights movement in the United States, as well as continuing legal conflicts over racial redistricting, voting systems, and election administration underscore the multiple dimensions of this central feature of democratic politics.

Various chapters in this volume speak to the importance of political institutions such as voting rights and legal systems in structuring the representation of racial and ethnic minorities in the United States, with some conclusions more optimistic than others. George Lovell and Michael McCann, for example, counter the notion that the federal courts are effective guardians of minority rights, while Canon details the normative and empirical evidence for redistricting as an instrument for enhancing minority representation. Kittilson and Tate discuss the role of the party in enhancing representation, focusing on whether such representation is elite driven ("top down," by elected party officials) or a reflection of societal change ("bottom up," by mass identifiers). Their comparative historical analysis suggests that neither model is fully satisfactory.

Yet the political process of including and representing racial and ethnic minorities in our political system surely also depends on political processes beyond those centered in the formal institutions of government or a conceptualization of political parties as either mass identifiers or elected officials. Having achieved the right to vote and gained a voice in national party institutions, an important question for racial and ethnic minorities then becomes what informal political processes facilitate or impede participation. These informal processes are especially important for previously disenfranchised groups that might lack information or skills relevant to electoral participation, resources that are gained through the exercise of the right to vote. Alternatively, weaker norms and social pressures to participate—given previous barriers to participation—might otherwise result in newly, enfranchised groups participating less than other groups who have historically enjoyed the privilege of electoral eligibility.

The importance of the black church to the civil rights movement and as a source of political mobilization for African Americans is one example of how social institutions have helped to politicize previously disenfranchised groups (see, e.g., Dawson, Brown, and Allen 1990; Harris 1994; Calhoun-Brown 1996; Alex-Assensoh and Assensoh 2001). Similarly, historical analyses often point toward political parties providing selective incentives (e.g., jobs, food, assistance in times of unemployment) to racial and ethnic minorities and the poor in an effort to secure their votes at the polls (Riordan 1963; Wilson 1973; Bridges 1984; Erie 1988; Maisel 1999, 68–69; White and Shea 2000, 448–52; also see Andersen and Cohen, and Costain, this volume).

These studies suggest that the parties play an important role in mobilizing the participation of racial and ethnic minorities and in minimizing participation differences between racial and ethnic minorities and Anglo-whites. And both of these expectations would seem to be important aspects of a democratic politics that includes racial and ethnic minorities. That is, in a truly inclusive democratic system, mobilizing or linkage institutions would be expected to seek out the participation of minorities as much as (or perhaps more than) majorities and, as a consequence, participation differences across these groups should be minimal.

Contemporary evidence, however, suggests that racial and ethnic minorities are less likely than Anglo-whites to exercise their right to vote by showing up at the polls. African Americans and Latinos in particular tend to vote less than Anglo-whites as a group. In the 2000 presidential election, for example, 62 percent of non-Hispanic Anglo-whites reported voting compared with 57 percent of African Americans, 45 percent of Hispanics, and 43 percent of Asian and Pacific Islander citizens (U.S. Census Bureau 2002). Since voting electorates are not fully representative of all citizens and underrepresent racial and ethnic minorities in particular,[1] the political parties do not apparently "deliver" on the expectation that they act as linkage institutions generally.

My explanation for why political parties do not equalize participation is that they are strategic political institutions. Normative arguments suggest that political parties are especially critical in stimulating the participation of individuals whose own (social status) resources make them less likely to participate. This is the standard that parties are typically expected to uphold, reflecting the belief that parties are "equalizing" (and, therefore, "democratizing") institutions in American political life.

Yet this expectation ignores the essential electoral goal of political parties: to win electoral contests. With the goal of winning office in mind, political parties seek to mobilize not *voters* in general but rather *supporters* in particular (Huckfeldt and Sprague 1992, 1995; Rosenstone and Hansen 1993; Brady, Schlozman, and Verba 1999). Once these strategic considerations are acknowledged, expectations of the political party's role in mobilizing mass participation and reducing racial/ethnic participation disparities are substantially reduced.

Nonetheless, it is still important to understand the conditions under which parties mobilize racial and ethnic minorities and the conditions under which such mobilization effectively enhances participation. Although the scholarly literature on these questions is limited, it provides some initial answers and also suggests further avenues for future research. Importantly, these initial answers help us assess the actual and potential roles of political parties in fostering democratic inclusion of racial and ethnic minorities. And the additional scholarly work that follows will enhance our understanding of democratic inclusion even further.

I begin by discussing the conceptualization of mobilization and participation levels as indicators of democratic inclusion and by reviewing recent research on mobilization and participation differences across racial and ethnic groups. I then discuss two distinct models of political participation, one individual, driven and the other elite, driven. Next, I discuss the various ways in which political parties have been overlooked, understudied, or poorly conceptualized as mobilizing institutions. Finally, I suggest the critical questions that future studies of partisan mobilization must address and follow that with a brief research proposal.

Mobilization and Participation as Democratic Inclusion

The beginning and endpoint of many discussions of participation as an indicator of democratic inclusion is the simple observation that policymakers reward those who participate. From a historical perspective, of course, it is clear that groups excluded by law (or practice) from the electorate sought the right to vote because they believed that the franchise offered them the potential for specific, if not more diffuse, benefits from political power.

Yet the expectation that specific (material) benefits are derived from electoral participation has also been affirmed. Near-legendary accounts of the role of the party machine in organizing politics—and turning out the vote—focus anecdotally on the provision of material benefits such as food, clothing, and fuel. More systematic scholarship also bears out the expectation that voting has its rewards. Hill and Leighley (1992), for example, demonstrate that higher lower-class turnout levels are associated with greater state welfare policy expenditures. And, more recently, Martin (2003) shows that members of Congress do not just bring the pork home to their districts—but they bring it home to the high-turnout precincts within their districts. Martin's argument is that the electoral benefits of pork are greater when delivered to constituencies that pay more attention to member behavior and that are more likely to formally register their preference (i.e., vote) for who represents them in Congress. Because turnout levels vary across precincts within Congressional districts—and members of Congress and their campaign staff are well aware of this—the policy benefits of Congressional representation are targeted to those precincts that can deliver the most on election day.

At the same time that elites reward those who participate, they also seek to mobilize participation—not in general, but rather those individuals who provide the greatest potential electoral benefits. According to Rosenstone and Hansen, "Political leaders mobilize citizens strategically. Constrained by limited money, limited time, and finite other resources, they target their efforts and time their efforts carefully. Anxious to involve the greatest number of the right people with the least amount of expense, they mobilize people who are known to them, who are well placed in social networks, whose actions are effective, and who are likely to act" (1993, 162).

Rosenstone and Hansen's analysis of American National Election Study 1956–1988 (NES) data suggests that education, income, and age are typically the most important predictors of individuals' reporting that they have been contacted by a political party; strength of partisanship and concurrent political races (e.g., senatorial or gubernatorial races) are also associated with a greater likelihood of being contacted. This general argument is likewise advanced by Wielhouwer (1995, 1999) whose analyses of the NES data support many of these claims, especially regarding education and partisanship as predictors of being contacted (see also Caldeira, Clausen, and Patterson 1990; Wielhouwer and Lockerbie 1994).

Further, Leighley (2001, 82–84) demonstrates that income and race are associated with self-reported party contact, with wealthier individuals and Anglo-whites being more likely to be contacted than poorer individuals and non-Anglos, respectively. The importance of the parties' immediate electoral incentives in structuring their mobilization efforts is also clear: Anglo-whites are more likely to be contacted by the Republican Party than are non-Anglos, whereas no race-related differences emerge for the Democratic Party. Importantly, these patterns remain when controlling for region, party identification, and election year.

Thus, key to viewing racial and ethnic differences in participation as indicators of democratic inclusion is the observation that political elites both reward and seek to mobilize participants. To the extent that such mobilization efforts (and subsequent participation) are relatively equal across racial and ethnic groups, we can conclude that parties foster democratic inclusion by virtue of their mobilization activities.

ELITE AND MASS MODELS OF PARTICIPATION

How are we to describe current levels of democratic inclusion, as represented by mobilization and participation differences across racial and ethnic groups? Verba, Schlozman, and Brady's (1995) national Citizen Participation Study (CPS) provides the most systematic response to this question with oversamples of African Americans, Latinos, and political activists. Using the CPS data, Leighley (2001, 42) reports that "the level of campaign mobilization that racial/ethnic minorities are exposed to is substantially lower than that reported by Anglo-whites: only 27.4 percent of African Americans, 14.4 percent of Latinos, and 16.8 percent of Latino citizens report being asked to become involved in campaign work or contribute money, compared to 47.1 percent of Anglo-whites."

Consistent with this pattern of mobilization is the fact that African Americans and Latinos are less likely than Anglo-whites to report participating in most electoral activities, with the possible exception of campaign work. According to the CPS data, about 18 percent of Anglo-whites and blacks report engaging in campaign work, compared to approximately 8 percent of Latinos (Leighley 2001, 32–33). Multivariate analyses typically draw the same conclusions: Turnout and campaign work differences between Anglo-whites and African Americans are eliminated once education and

TABLE 7.1. Percentage of Participation by Education, Controlling for Race/Ethnicity

	Less than high school	High school	Some college	College degree
Campaign work				
Anglo-whites	2.2	11.3	21.8	25.8
African Americans	8.7	11.4	19.2	37.4
Latinos	5.9	5.6	14.1	10.3
Latino citizens	7.7	4.7	16	5.6
Contributing				
Anglo-whites	5.6	19.5	37.9	59
African Americans	8.7	18.1	32.5	54.5
Latinos	5.9	4.5	18.3	24.1
Latino citizens	6.2	4.7	24	27.8
Voted in Local Election				
Anglo-whites	61.4	68.8	72.7	81.2
African Americans	69	55.6	73.8	80.5
Latinos	62.5	55.3	55.3	77.8
Latino citizens	56.3	51.4	53.3	76.9
Registered to vote				
Anglo-whites	62.9	82.5	88.3	90.8
African Americans	70.7	76.5	85	91.9
Latinos	46.1	59.6	63.4	65.5
Latino citizens	60	62.5	70	83.3

Note: Data are unweighted. Table entries indicate the proportion of each racial/ethnic group at each level of education that reports having engaged in each political activity.
Source: Citizen Participation Study (CPS). Reprinted from Leighley, *Strength in Numbers?* (Princeton: Princeton University Press, 2001), 35, with permission from the publisher.

income differences are taken into account, but Latino participation is still significantly less than Anglo and African American participation (see, e.g., Cain, and Kiewiet 1989; Tate 1991, 1993; Uhlaner 1991; Uhlaner, Verba, Schlozman, Brady, and Nie 1993; Arvizu and Garcia 1996; Hero and Campbell 1996; Leighley and Vedlitz 1999; Shaw, de la Garza, and Lee 2000). As an example of these race-related differences persisting despite controls for social status, Table 7.1 presents self-reported participation levels for African Americans, Latinos, Latino citizens, and Anglo-whites at four different levels of education. The conclusion is, again, that for most types of participation and most levels of education, we see African Americans and Latinos participating less than Anglo-whites.

These persistent lower levels of electoral activity of African Americans and Latinos are indeed troublesome with respect to normative concerns about democratic inclusion.[2] Yet they also seem to indict the performance of political parties as mobilizing institutions. As Verba, Nie, and Kim argue:

Lower status groups, in contrast, need a group-based process of political mobilization if they are to catch up to the upper-status groups in terms of political activity. They need a self-conscious ideology as motivation and need organization as a resource. The processes that bring them to political activity are more explicit and easily recognized. They are more likely to involve explicit conflict with other groups. Our argument is consistent with Michels's contention that organization—and we might add ideology—is the weapon of the weak. (1978, 14–15)

Despite general agreement that lower-status individuals in effect require mediating institutions to subsidize the costs of participating, studies of political participation over the past several decades have often ignored such institutional effects (see Hill and Leighley [1994] for an exception). The dominant model in the study of participation over the past several decades is the *socioeconomic status model*, first described in Verba and Nie (1972), extended further in Wolfinger and Rosenstone (1980), and most recently embellished by Verba, Schlozman, and Brady (1995); for an extended discussion, see also Leighley (1995).

The socioeconomic status, or SES, model argues that individuals with greater resources are more likely to participate because they are able to overcome the costs associated with participation. The standard analytical approach is to use individuals' education, income, age, and civic orientations (i.e., political efficacy, strength of partisanship, political interest) as indicators of status. Across a wide range of studies, time periods, and model specifications, consistent empirical evidence supports the SES model (for a recent example, see Timpone 1998).

One of the shortcomings of the SES model, however, is that it is, simply, a very *apolitical* model of *political* participation. Little attention is devoted to participation as an instrumental act on the part of individuals (i.e., the benefits of participation); nor does the SES model explain why certain individuals choose to expend resources in the political realm as opposed to other pursuits.

Verba, Schlozman, and Brady (1995) address some of these issues more explicitly in *Voice and Equality: Civic Voluntarism in American Politics.* The contributions of this study are numerous and I mention only a few here. First, they develop the notion of resource differences more fully, considering time and money, for example, as individual-level resources structuring individuals' propensity to engage in civic activity. Second, they contrast individuals' choices to engage in political, as opposed to voluntary, activity, to offer some leverage on what is different about political participation as compared to voluntary activity. And third, they examine the extent to which individuals' institutional contexts (i.e., their jobs, churches, and voluntary associations) enhance their participatory skills (another type of resource) and directly mobilize them to participate.

Verba, Schlozman, and Brady's findings on mobilization differences across racial/ethnic groups are quite interesting when considering mobilization differences across institutional contexts versus types of political participation. As shown in Figure 7.1, there are at best minimal differences across racial/ethnic groups in the probability of being mobilized at church, on the job, in a voluntary organization or in any of these institutions.[3] Being asked to engage in any political activity within these contexts is relatively uncommon and differences between groups are smaller than differences across these three institutions.

In contrast, when individuals reports whether they had been asked to participate in certain types of political activity, racial/ethnic group differences are significant (see Figure 7.2). Anglo-whites are nearly twice as likely as

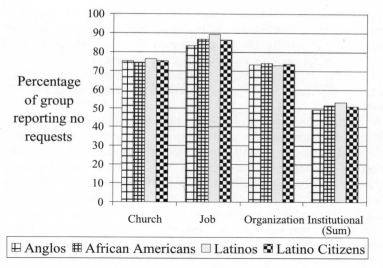

FIGURE 7.1. Institutional Mobilization, Controlling for Race/Ethnicity.
Note: Data are unweighted.
Source: Citizen Participation Study (CPS). Reprinted from Leighley, *Strength in Numbers?* (Princeton: Princeton University Press, 2001), 39, with permission from the publisher.

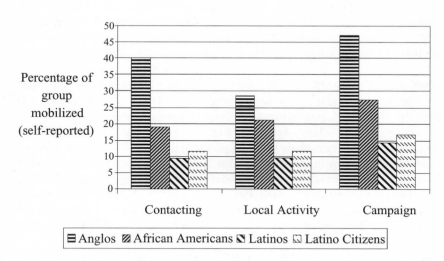

FIGURE 7.2. Mobilization to Particular Activities, Controlling for Race/Ethnicity.
Note: Data are unweighted.
Source: Citizen Participation Study (CPS). Reprinted from Leighley, *Strength in Numbers?* (Princeton: Princeton University Press, 2001), 41, with permission from the publisher.

African Americans or Latinos to report being asked to contact a government official and nearly one-third as likely to be asked to engage in some sort of local political activity. For the purposes of this essay, the most important disparity is that for campaign activity: Over 45 percent of Anglo-whites report being asked to engage in campaign activity, in contrast to about 25 percent of African Americans, and approximately 15 percent of Latinos and Latino citizens.

The paradox here is twofold. First, that an in-depth study of the institutional and organizational bases of civic involvement focuses explicitly on nonpolitical institutions. And, second, that race-related differences in mobilization are evident in the very *political* institutions that we expect to help overcome resource-based differences in participation. The first point here likely reflects a reasoned choice made in the course of designing a very complex, yet manageable, research project. The second point, I would argue, reflects the fact that scholars in general have not seriously considered the consequences of party activity and mobilization with respect to racial and ethnic groups.[4]

This is not to say, of course, that we have completely ignored the concept of mobilization in studies of participation. In fact, a variety of studies over the last two decades have indicated that mobilization is an important factor in understanding mass political participation. Party-related characteristics such as competitiveness, organization, and ideology, for example, and candidate spending are also associated with voter turnout (see, e.g., Patterson and Caldeira 1983; Caldeira, Patterson, and Markko 1985; Cox and Munger 1989; Leighley and Nagler 1992b; Hill and Leighley 1993, 1994; Jackson 1993, 1996, 1997). And, more specifically, there is some evidence that candidate spending on political advertising boosts turnout as well (see, e.g., Jamieson 2000).[5]

Scholars of minority participation have focused largely on the effects of political empowerment on minority participation. Bobo and Gilliam (1990) argue that blacks residing in areas of minority empowerment—where blacks serve as elected officials—are more likely to participate, largely because empowerment enhances their sense of political efficacy. They acknowledge, however, that empowerment might also be linked to greater participation through the existence of stronger political institutions (e.g., political parties, candidate and community organizations) in areas of black empowerment. More recently, Leighley (2001) confirms Bobo and Gilliam's conclusions for African Americans, but not for Latinos (see also Gilliam 1996; Gilliam and Kaufman 1998; Gay 2001).

Only recently have scholars of minority politics begun to focus on mobilization efforts specifically directed toward minority groups (see de la Garza and DeSipio 1992; Pinderhughes 1992; de la Garza, Menchaca, and DeSipio 1994; Pantoja and Woods 1999; Michelson 2002; Ramirez 2002; but also see Carton 1984 and Krassa 1988, 1989 for rare examples of earlier work on the mobilization of blacks). Although these studies are promising and indeed suggestive that mobilization efforts enhance the participation of Latinos and African Americans, much of the evidence offered is limited in either time or space (i.e., focusing on specific communities or regions or a particular election) or suggests that mobilization effects depend on other social or political factors. Thus, drawing broad generalizations from these studies is difficult.

The significance of mobilizing institutions is underscored by Rosenstone and Hansen's (1993) analysis of the post-1960 decline of voter turnout in the United States, and of the first increasing, then decreasing, turnout of blacks in the United States over the same time period. Rosenstone and Hansen argue that the decline in voter turnout since the 1960s did not result from changes in individuals' resources, but instead declining party mobilization, social movement activity, party competitiveness, and the increasing number of primaries that both elites and the mass public were required to attend to. Similarly, they conclude that *changes* (both positive and negative) in black voter turnout between the 1950s and 1980s likewise reflect changes in partisan and social movement mobilization rather than changes in the personal resources of blacks.

THEORETICAL BASES OF MOBILIZATION EFFECTS

These assorted approaches to studying political mobilization suggest that we have quite limited evidence regarding how individuals are mobilized and for whom mobilization makes a difference. Related, we know even less about how mobilization works. That is, what mechanism accounts for the relationship between mobilization and participation? Rosenstone and Hansen (1993) argue that party mobilization is associated with greater turnout because, first, it reduces the costs of voting through the provision of information about the election and voting. Second, it "occasions the creation of selective social incentives for political involvement" (176). It does not, they claim, increase turnout by enhancing individuals' perceptions of the costs and benefits (i.e., enhancing individuals' political efficacy or modifying their views of the parties or candidates).

While the evidence they present on this point is thin, it is not inconsistent with a number of related research traditions and findings. Numerous studies have demonstrated that when the costs of voting associated with voter registration decrease, voter registration increases (see, e.g., Oliver 1996). Thus, the easier it is to register, the more likely individuals are to do so.

This suggests that mobilization efforts aimed at getting people registered reduce informational costs associated with election rules and registration—likely a first step toward increased participation. However, fairly consistent evidence further suggests that lowering these information costs (i.e., registration reform) has not resulted in greater turnout (Knack 1995, 1999; Highton 1997; Highton and Wolfinger 1998; Wolfinger and Hoffman 2001). This latter finding suggests that successful mobilization requires something in addition to information.

An emphasis on the social incentives associated with mobilization is also consistent with Brady, Schlozman, and Verba's (1999) findings that mobilization is more effective when the target of the mobilization request knows the initiator. Moreover, Leighley (2001) reports that this finding is robust across racial/ethnic groups (see also Huckfeldt 1979; Zipp, Landerman, and Luebke 1982; Smith and Zipp 1983; Zuckerman and West 1985). Gerber and Green's (2000) finding that face-to-face contacts are more effective than telephone or direct-mail contacts likewise suggests the importance of social incentives as a mechanism linking mobilization to participation (but does not rule out the possibility of mobilization enhancing individuals' psychological orientations toward politics as well).

The importance of social incentives in structuring behavior is also underscored in various analyses and discussions of minority participation. Chong's (1991) discussion of participation in the civil rights movement, for example, emphasizes the importance of small groups, reputation, and selective (social) incentives in overcoming the collective action problems associated with movement participation. Similarly, Uhlaner's (1989) formal *relational goods* model predicts that individuals will contribute to collective action problems when leaders devote resources to mobilization efforts that seek to enhance individuals' sense of group identity change their perceptions of the costs and benefits of participating; and enhance the perceived benefits of relational goods such as social approval, identity aspects of sociability, and the desire to be accepted by others, among others.[6]

Thus, Uhlaner (1989) emphasizes the social incentives identified by Rosenstone and Hansen (1993), as well as Chong (1991), but also underscores group identity as a psychological mechanism linking mobilization to participation. This is of course a familiar argument to scholars who emphasize the importance of group identity, consciousness, or awareness as stimulating political participation (see, e.g., Shingles 1981; Tate 1993; Dawson 1994).

More broadly, the social aspects of political communication have been underscored by scholars studying contextual effects on political participation. In this research tradition, political campaigns are inherently social events as they stimulate political discussion, political activity such as the display of yard signs and bumper stickers, and individuals' search for relevant electoral information. Thus, formal and informal social networks emerge in the campaign context and these social influences structure individuals' political involvement and vote choices. Party contacting is thus just one aspect of party mobilization, which occurs both formally and informally.

According to Huckfeldt and Sprague (1995, 5), political campaigns are "socially coercive, interactive and dynamic," national in scope, yet fundamentally dependent on individuals' locally supplied flow of information. This local flow of information is structured by both social and political institutions:

> By political organization we include electoral laws, levels of partisan competition and control, and the locally specific strategies of party organizations—factors that affect the political communication that occurs between political parties and citizens. By social organization we include all the factors that affect the transmission of political information through social communication—churches, secondary organizations, work groups, families, networks of political discussion.

Huckfeldt and Sprague (1992) analyze the party canvass in their study of sixteen purposively chosen neighborhoods in South Bend, Indiana, during the 1984 presidential election. They find that the parties' reliance on primary voting records (as an efficient means of identifying supporters) is more efficient for Republicans (the political minority) than for Democrats. Indeed, because of the Democrats' dominance in local politics, many Republican voters actually participated in the Democratic primary. In relying on primary lists, then, the Democratic Party was more likely than the Republican Party to actually contact a Republican identifier.

More important, however, Huckfeldt and Sprague (1992) note how the use of primary voting records to identify supporters (and supportive neighborhoods) introduces a class bias into the parties' mobilization efforts. Rather than target their political constituency—lower-class individuals—the Democratic Party in South Bend instead devoted its resources to those individuals who had already demonstrated an interest in voting—those with higher education and income. They conclude that "social structure tends to lose out to political structure . . . the unintended consequence of party mobilization activity is an aggregate structure of contacting that is only weakly related to the social structure underlying party support" (243). While Huckfeldt and Sprague are quick to point out these findings are premised on the political context of South Bend, it is surely intriguing to wonder whether similar dynamics would hold more broadly in locales also dominated heavily by Democrats (and, conversely, perhaps those dominated by Republicans as well).

Huckfeldt and Sprague's (1992) assessment of the effects of party contacting on turnout is rather different from those relying on NES data and reported above. Huckfeldt and Sprague report that party contacting has little effect on individuals who have already participated in party primaries—such individuals voted in the general election campaign at a rate of around 98 percent, party contact aside. At the same time, they report that party contacting— direct contact of the individual as well as a contextual effect of the proportion of the neighborhood that was contacted—has no effect as well. They do find, however, that party activity is associated with vote choice. That is, individuals' reported vote choices are structured by the presence of party canvass activities in their neighborhoods.

Thus, in contrast to the standard approach to thinking about party contacting and its effects, Huckfeldt and Sprague (1992) conclude that individual-level consequences are minimal, but that there are substantial aggregate-level consequences. The aggregate-level effects result largely from how the party canvass structures the flow of political information (e.g., political discussion, display of yard signs, perceptions of election outcomes, etc.) by stimulating party activists. These findings might be interpreted as supporting either information provision or selective incentives as the mechanisms that link party contacting and voter turnout.

WHERE'S THE PARTY?

The implication that can be drawn from this overview of what we know about political participation, mobilization, and minority political behavior as aspects of democratic inclusion is that the political party as a mediating institution has been overlooked and understudied. In this sense the question, "Where's the Party?" is multifaceted and requires serious scholarly attention.

Where's the Party—from a Normative Perspective?

The dominant view of the role of political parties in democratic politics has been that of a linkage institution, serving to connect citizens with the political system. In this sense, political parties are viewed by many as essential to democratic politics as they aggregate the interests of like-minded citizens and represent them in the formal institutions of government. And the expectation is that this linkage function enhances opportunities for mass participation and the clarity with which the electorate's views are represented, as well as subsidizes the costs of participation for all.

This normative perspective pervades historical descriptions of the political parties, especially the days of the party machine. These often anecdotal accounts tend to be drawn from periods of high levels of immigration and suggest that the party has played an important historical role in incorporating newly arrived (and franchised) immigrants into democratic politics. These portrayals also emphasize the role of the party in providing selective incentives to encourage the participation of immigrants.

Another important aspect of these portrayals, however, is that of party strategy. Indeed, party organizations provided transportation to the polls or food to needy families. But in return they expected a vote (or two) on election day. Our normative expectations of the political parties have, by and large, ignored, even shunned, this notion that the parties' activities might be motivated by their return in electoral success.

Perhaps the one exception to this point is Downs' (1957) formulation of rational political parties. Although not writing from a normative perspective, his formalization of the incentives facing rational actors in a representative democracy in fact implies that parties as vote-seeking institutions perform a positive function: "The party which runs this government manipulates its policies and actions in whatever way it believes will gain it the most votes without violating constitutional rules. Clearly, such behavior implies that the governing party is aware of some definite relationship between its policies and the way people vote" (31).

This aspect of political parties as electoral institutions is perhaps the focus of minority leaders' criticisms of political parties in contemporary politics. The Democratic Party is often criticized for taking the black vote for granted, or for moderating its racial policy positions so as not to lose white votes. In the context of American politics, then, this strategic function of the party is viewed as a detriment to racial and ethnic minorities. But this specific claim has not been addressed fully by normative theorists.

Where's the Party—from an Empirical Standpoint?

The field's major study of the impact of institutions on mass political participation explicitly focuses on *apolitical* institutions. It is time to systematically study *political* parties and their role in mobilizing participation. Previous research has focused primarily on the mobilization of the mass electorate, relying on individuals' self-reports of having been contacted. A useful shift would be to study the parties as organizations, and how they respond to their specific strategic environment. Data collected from state and local (i.e., county) party leaders, supplemented by archival data on voting records and population data, would be a good start in this direction. We first need to know who is doing what under what circumstances.

Yet that is just the descriptive part of the research agenda. Several theoretical issues also need to be addressed. First, studies of the effectiveness of party contacting in mobilizing participation must incorporate specific arguments regarding the mechanism that links mobilization efforts to voter turnout and campaign activity. As noted above, Rosenstone and Hansen (1993) suggest that the linkage is based primarily on the provision of information and the development of social incentives. They claim that mobilization has no effect on individuals' perceptions of the parties, candidates, or the efficacy of participating. This is a strong claim, and one that needs further investigation.

It is especially important to examine Rosenstone and Hansen's claim more closely as it seems that either of the mechanisms they identify might affect individuals' assessments of political issues, political identities, or participatory attitudes—all factors that have been identified in studies of minority political behavior. Without conceptualizing this linkage mechanism more carefully and designing research to distinguish among these three—issues, identities, and attitudes—we cannot be confident in our understanding of party mobilization, minority participation, or mass political behavior.

Second, future research must consider more directly whether the mobilization of minority participation is internally or externally generated—or in this respect dependent on both group characteristics as well as institutional efforts. By group characteristics I refer to the nature of social networks in local neighborhoods, the structure of minority political leaders' organizations, and the activity of church and voluntary associations. This might be a chicken-and-egg problem, but it is an important one nonetheless: Are "well-organized" minority communities likely to seek inclusion in local political parties, or vice versa? To what extent is the effectiveness of party mobilization (i.e., contacting) efforts dependent on informal social networks—or constrained by local electoral conditions (e.g., competitiveness)?

Third, the strategies and consequences of party mobilization must be evaluated in the context of what many view to be an era of party decline. News of the demise of the political party—in the electorate, in government, as an organization—may be premature. But how are we to conceptualize and assess the consequences of party mobilization in a period of candidate-centered elections? And how are we to model the various mobilization "layers" to which individuals are exposed?

Rigorous research designs will necessarily investigate the relationship between candidate and local party organizations. But, too, what about statewide or presidential campaigns? Studies of party mobilization must clearly address the issue of multiple layers of party organization. Are all politics local? Key (1949) and Hero (1998) pose questions about state-level party systems. But when thinking about the strategic mobilization of racial and ethnic minorities, do we not have to think more carefully about local parties? Probably so, because it is in localities that minorities are capable of being political majorities.

Another aspect of the layering of mobilization efforts is the recognition that other institutions also seek to mobilize electoral involvement. Unions, single issue groups and other organized interests often make substantial monetary contributions to parties and candidates, as well as mobilize their members to vote and offer "free" labor to political campaigns. More specifically in the case of racial and ethnic minorities, numerous organized groups seek to mobilize their members and engage them in a variety of civil rights, health, and community issues (see Anderson and Cohen, this volume). Whether national or local in scope, these associations likely offer significant opportunities and incentives for participation. How they modify or mediate the role of party mobilization is a question worth addressing.

And, fourth, studies of party mobilization need to conceptualize party strategy in a more sophisticated manner. Party contacting studies emphasize that parties mobilize strategically, but strategy in the extant literature is based solely on demographics and attitudes to identify supporters. What about the broader contextual aspects of party strategy associated with competitiveness and ideology? Shouldn't even party contacting reflect the strategic use of party resources premised on competitiveness and/or ideology? For example, shouldn't supporters be more likely to be contacted when they reside in competitive districts? Or when money is more plentiful? And are conservatives more likely to be mobilized if they reside where pro-life groups are well-organized?

A PROPOSED RESEARCH AGENDA

Successfully addressing these questions requires scholars dedicated to developing more systematic evidence regarding the individual and institutional factors associated with mass political mobilization and participation. It also requires being willing to ask important questions about the racial aspects of these social and political processes. I have identified numerous questions that must be addressed for us to understand more fully the politics of mobilization and participation as it relates to racial and ethnic groups. Certainly, questions beyond these remain and must also be addressed.

But I also offer a broader argument here. Our current understanding of political mobilization and participation is that both reflect the incentives faced by elites as well as individuals. Understanding democratic inclusion thus requires that we explicitly study both elite and mass political behavior. The fundamental question is this: How do class, race/ethnic, and political structures interact to structure the flow of political information available to individuals during election campaigns? And what are the direct and indirect racial and ethnic consequences of these information flows?

I propose that the best approach to addressing these questions is to adopt a research design strategy reflecting Huckfeldt and Sprague's (1995) sociologically based model of mobilization, where individuals' political beliefs and electoral choices are structured by their social environment, both directly and indirectly. Thus, individuals' social contexts provide politically relevant information and interactions and, as a result, significantly influence individuals' political attitudes and behaviors, i.e., individual-level attitudes and behaviors "adjust" toward the neighborhood context in which they reside (see, e.g., Huckfeldt and Sprague 1995, chapter 5).

In addition, social contexts structure institutional efforts to mobilize individuals into politics. In South Bend, a predominantly Democratic community, the Republican Party has an advantage in effectively contacting supporters because many Republicans cross over to vote in Democratic primaries. Thus, lists used by Democrats to contact "their own" are not as useful as those used by Republicans; as a result the majority party is less effective in directly mobilizing their supporters. More importantly, however, Huckfeldt and Sprague (1994) emphasize that the second-order effects of party contacting—the discussion or yard signs that it stimulates—are more effective, and have greater reach, than the specific contacts themselves. In this sense, according to Huckfeldt and Sprague (chapter 12), the social structure—and the way it structures information diffusion and personal interaction—dominates political structure. Yet Huckfeldt and Sprague consciously chose to study only the white population in South Bend: "Social influence in politics operates among both Anglo-whites and blacks, but one project cannot study both populations successfully due to the social fissure separating racial groups in American society, and in South Bend as well" (37).

What should we expect when we move on to consider racial structure? Will class also trump politics—and how can race be disentangled from the two? These are critical questions to be addressed in this new line of research. Importantly, what we do not know is how individuals' class and racial context structure formal (i.e., institutional) and informal (i.e., social) mobilization. My sense is that we will most fully address this question if we continue to be guided by the same assumptions that guided Huckfeldt and Sprague's research design. First, that all politics are local; thus, a community-specific (or communities-specific) research design is appropriate. And, second, it is likely that both class and race effects operate at multiple levels in community politics, with both individual- and contextual-level factors influencing the behavior and attitudes of citizens.

Engaging in such a research agenda must necessarily address two aspects of social influence that Huckfeldt and Sprague were able to ignore. First, previous research has demonstrated an important effect of racial context and interracial contact in determining individuals' political attitudes and electoral choices (see, e.g., Stein, Post, and Rinden 2000) and these findings lead to important new research questions. Does interracial contact magnify or suppress the effects of political discussants on individuals' political attitudes and vote choices? Does the neighborhood racial context exert an independent influence on individuals' political attitudes and vote choices? To what extent do individuals control their exposure to interracial contact and thus limit racially relevant informational cues?

Second, such a research agenda must consider the extent to which political institutions and social organizations structure racial differences in mobilization and participation—that is, whether their efforts magnify or suppress the individual-level differences in political behavior. This is especially important given Oliver's (2001) finding that mobilization differences among Anglo-whites, blacks, and Latinos are fairly constant across different racial contexts. That is, blacks are about equally likely to report being mobilized in predominantly white communities as they are in predominantly black communities (122–129). This is a curious finding, so much so that Oliver acknowledges that it might well reflect the fact that communities at the aggregate level, rather than neighborhoods within them, are the inappropriate racial context to consider.

Other questions about political institutions and social organizations must also be considered. Are political parties equally as active and effective in their canvassing efforts in racially diverse neighborhoods as in racially homogeneous neighborhoods? How do racially diverse and racially homogeneous neighborhoods differ with respect to political and social organization?

Addressing this wide range of important questions will substantially enhance what we know about the individual- and institutional-level determinants of both mobilization and participation. And such knowledge will provide us with a much clearer understanding of how today's political and social processes systematically include or exclude racial and ethnic minorities. Only then—when we understand the informal processes of political mobilization by parties, groups, and the social context—will scholars have a complete picture of democratic inclusion in the United States.

NOTES

1. Evidence also suggests that the poor are underrepresented in today's electorates (see, e.g., Leighley and Nagler 1992a; Rosenstone and Hansen 1993; Lijphart 1997; Shields and Goidel 1997). Of course, to the extent that minorities are disproportionately poor, class bias in the electorate likely exacerbates their underrepresentation.

2. One might also be concerned about the generally low levels of participation of Anglo-whites—which is our baseline. But that is not central for this discussion of democratic inclusion of excluded groups. On the importance of voter turnout and the significance of low voter turnout, see Lijphart (1997).

3. The mobilization measure graphed in Figure 7.1 represents the proportion of the racial/ethnic group reporting no requests for political activity—specifically, that they had not been asked to: vote for a specific candidate in church or a voluntary organization; take some other political action either in church or a voluntary organization; or asked to contribute money to an election campaign at work.

4. A more serious theoretical and empirical treatment of these issues, of course, is what I propose as an important research agenda in the study of democratic inclusion. I offer some ideas for this research program in the last section.

5. The reference to campaign advertising brings to mind an alternative thesis—that some candidates and campaign organizations actually seek to depress turnout (see, e.g., Mendelberg 2001).

6. Uhlaner (1989) formally defines relational goods as those which can "only be 'possessed' by mutual agreement that they exist after appropriate joint actions have been taken

by a person and non-arbitrary others. . . . Moreover, the others must either be specific individuals or drawn from some specific set" (254).

REFERENCES

Alex-Assensoh, Yvette, and A. B. Assensoh. 2001. "Inner-City Contexts, Church Attendance and African American Political Participation." *Journal of Politics* 63 (August): 886–901.

Arvizu, John R., and F. Chris Garcia. 1996. "Latino Voting Participation: Explaining and Differentiating Latino Voting Turnout." *Hispanic Journal of Behavioral Sciences* 18:104–128.

Bobo, Lawrence, and Franklin D. Gilliam, Jr. 1990. "Race, Sociopolitical Participation, and Black Empowerment." *American Political Science Review* 84:377–393.

Brady, Henry E., Kay Lehman Schlozman, and Sidney Verba. 1999. "Prospecting for Participants: Rational Expectations and the Recruitment of Political Activity." *American Political Science Review* 93:153–168.

Bridges, Amy. 1984. *A City in the Republic: Antebellum New York and the Origins of Machine Politics*. New York: Cambridge University Press.

Caldeira, Gregory A., Aage Clausen, and Samuel Patterson. 1990. "Partisan Mobilization and Electoral Participation." *Electoral Studies* 9(3): 191–204.

Calhoun-Brown, Allison. 1996. "African American Churches and Political Mobilization: The Psychological Impact of Organizational Resources." *Journal of Politics* 58(4): 935–953.

Carton, Paul. 1984. *Mobilizing the Black Community: The Effects of Personal Contact Campaigning on Black Voters*. Washington, DC: Joint Center for Political Studies.

Chong, Dennis. 1991. *Collective Action and the Civil Rights Movement*. Chicago: University of Chicago Press.

Cox, Gary W., and Michael C. Munger. 1989. "Closeness, Expenditures, and Turnout in the 1982 U.S. House Elections." *American Political Science Review* 83:217–231.

Dawson, Michael C. 1994. *Behind the Mule: Race and Class in African-American Politics*. Princeton: Princeton University Press.

Dawson, Michael C., Ronald E. Brown, and Richard L. Allen. 1990. "Racial Belief Systems, Religious Guidance, and African-American Political Participation." *National Political Science Review* 2:22–44.

de la Garza, Rodolfo O., and Louis DeSipio. 1992. *From Rhetoric to Reality: Latino Politics in the 1988 Elections*. Boulder, CO: Westview.

de la Garza, Rodolfo O., Martha Menchaca, and Louis DeSipio. 1994. *Barrio Ballots: Latino Politics in the 1990 Elections*. Boulder, CO: Westview.

Downs, Anthony. 1957. *An Economic Theory of Democracy*. New York: Harper and Row.

Erie, Steven. 1988. *Rainbow's End: Irish-Americans and the Dilemmas of Urban Machine Politics, 1840–1985*. Berkeley: University of California Press.

Gay, Claudine. 2001. "The Effect of Black Congressional Representation on Political Participation." *American Political Science Review* 95:589–602.

Gilliam, Frank D. 1996. "Exploring Minority Empowerment: Symbolic Politics, Governing Coalitions, and Traces of Political Style in Los Angeles." *American Journal of Political Science* 40(1): 56–81.

Gilliam, Franklin D., Jr., and Karen M. Kaufman. 1998. "Is There An Empowerment Life Cycle? Long-Term Black Empowerment and Its Influence on Voter Participation." *Urban Affairs Review* 33(6): 741–766.

Harris, Fredrick C. 1994. "Something Within: Religion as a Mobilizer of African-American Political Activism." *Journal of Politics* 56:42–68.

Hero, Rodney E. 1998. *Faces of Inequality: Social Diversity in American Politics*. New York: Oxford University Press.

Hero, Rodney E., and Anne G. Campbell. 1996. "Understanding Latino Political Participation: Exploring the Evidence from the Latino National Political Survey." *Hispanic Journal of Behavioral Sciences* 18:129–141.

Highton, Benjamin. 1997. "Easy Registration and Voter Turnout." *Journal of Politics* 59(2): 565–575.

Highton, Benjamin, and Raymond E. Wolfinger. 1998. "Estimating the Effects of the National Voter Registration Act of 1993." *Political Behavior* 20:79–104.

Hill, Kim Quaile, and Jan E. Leighley. 1992. "The Policy Consequences of Class Bias in American State Electorates." *American Journal of Political Science* 36 (May 1992): 351–365.

———. 1993. "Party Ideology, Organization and Competitiveness as Mobilizing Forces in Gubernatorial Elections." *American Journal of Political Science* 37:1158–1178.

———. 1994. "Mobilizing Institutions and Class Representation in U.S. State Electorates." *Political Research Quarterly* 47:137–150.

Huckfeldt, Robert. 1979. "Political Participation and the Neighborhood Social Context." *American Journal of Political Science* 23:579–592.

Huckfeldt, Robert, and John D. Sprague. 1992. "Political Parties and Electoral Mobilization: Political Structure, Social Structure and the Party Canvass." *American Political Science Review* 86:70–86.

———. 1995. *Citizens, Politics, and Social Communication: Information Influence in an Election Campaign*. New York: Cambridge University Press.

Jackson, Robert A. 1993. "Voter Mobilization in the 1986 Midterm Election." *Journal of Politics* 55:1081–1099.

———. 1996. "A Reassessment of Voter Mobilization." *Political Research Quarterly* 49:331–350.

———. 1997. "The Mobilization of U.S. State Electorates in the 1988 and 1990 Elections." *Journal of Politics* 59 (May): 520–537.

Jamieson, Kathleen Hall. 2000. *Everything You Think You Know about Politics . . . And Why You're Wrong*. New York: Basic Books.

Kenny, Christopher B. 1992. "Political Participation and Effects from the Social Environment." *American Journal of Political Science* 36:259–267.

Key, V. O., Jr. 1949. *Southern Politics in State and Nation*. New York: Knopf.

Knack, Stephen. 1995. "Does 'Motor Voter' Work? Evidence from State Level Data." *Journal of Politics* 57(3): 796–811.

———. 1999. "Drivers Wanted: Motor Voter and the Election of 1996." *PS: Political Science and Politics* 32:237–243.

Krassa, Michael A. 1988. "Context and the Canvass: The Mechanisms of Interaction." *Political Behavior* 10:233–246.

———. 1989. "Getting Out the Black Vote: The Party Canvass and Black Response." In *New Perspectives in American Politics: National Political Science Review*, edited by Lucius J. Barker, 1. New Brunswick, NJ: Transaction Publishers.

Leighley, Jan E. 1995. "Attitudes, Opportunities and Incentives: A Field Essay on Political Participation." *Political Research Quarterly* 48:181–209.

———. 2001. *Strength in Numbers? The Political Mobilization of Racial and Ethnic Minorities*. Princeton: Princeton University Press.

Leighley, Jan E., and Jonathan Nagler. 1992a. "Socioeconomic Class Bias in Turnout, 1964–1988: The Voters Remain the Same." *American Political Science Review* 86(3): 725–736.

————. 1992b. "Individual and Systemic Influences on Turnout: *Who Votes*? 1984." *Journal of Politics* 54:718–740.

Leighley, Jan E., and Arnold Vedlitz. 1999. "Race, Ethnicity and Political Participation: Competing Models and Contrasting Explanations." *Journal of Politics* 61 (November): 1092–1114.

Lijphart, Arend. 1997. "Unequal Participation: Democracy's Unresolved Dilemma." *American Political Science Review* 91(1): 1–14.

Maisel, L. Sandy. 1999. *Parties and Elections in America: The Electoral Process*. 3rd ed. Lanham, MD: Rowman and Littlefield.

Martin, Paul. 2003. "Voting's Rewards: Voter Turnout, Attentive Publics and Congressional Allocation of Federal Money." *American Journal of Political Science* 47:110–127.

Mendelberg, Tali. 2001. *The Race Card: Campaign Strategy, Implicit Messages and the Norm of Equality*. Princeton: Princeton University Press.

Michelson, Melissa R. 2002. "Getting Out the Latino Vote: How Door-to-Door Canvassing Influences Voter Turnout in Rural Central California." Presented at the Western Political Science Association meeting, Long Beach, CA, March 22–24.

Oliver, J. Eric. 1996. "The Effects of Eligibility Restrictions and Party Activity on Absentee Voting and Overall Turnout." *American Journal of Political Science* 40:498–513.

————. 1999. "The Effects of Metropolitan Economic Segregation on Local Civic Participation." *American Journal of Political Science* 43:186–212.

————. 2001. *Democracy in Suburbia*. Princeton: Princeton University Press.

Pantoja, Adrian D., and Nathan D. Woods. 1999. "Turnout and the Latino Vote in Los Angeles County: Did Interest Group Efforts Matter?" *The American Review of Politics* 20:141–162.

Patterson, Samuel C., and Gregory A. Caldeira. 1983. "Getting Out the Vote: Participation in Gubernatorial Elections." *American Political Science Review* 77:675–689.

Pinderhughes, Dianne M. 1992. "The Role of African American Political Organizations in the Mobilization of Voters." In *From Exclusion to Inclusion: The Long Struggle for African American Political Power*, edited by Ralph C. Gomes and Linda Faye Williams, 35–52, New York: Greeenwood.

Ramirez, Ricardo. 2002. "Getting Out the Vote: The Impact of Non-partisan Voter Mobilization Efforts in Low Turnout Latino Precincts." Paper presented at the American Political Science Association meeting, September, Boston.

Riordan, William L., ed. 1963. *Plunkitt of Tammany Hall*. New York: Dutton.

Rosenstone, Steven J., and John Mark Hansen. 1993. *Mobilization, Participation, and Democracy in America*. New York: Macmillan.

Shaw, Daron, Rodolfo O. de la Garza, and Jongo Lee. 2000. "Examining Latino Turnout in 1996: A Three-State, Validated Survey Approach." *American Journal of Political Science* 44:332–340.

Shields, Todd G., and Robert K. Goidel. 1997. "Participation Rates, Socioeconomic Class Biases, and Congressional Elections: A Crossvalidation." *American Journal of Political Science* 41:683–691.

Shingles, Richard D. 1981. "Black Consciousness and Political Participation: The Missing Link." *American Political Science Review* 75:76–91.

Smith, Joel, and John F Zipp. 1983. "The Party Official Next Door: Some Consequences of Friendship for Political Involvement." *Journal of Politics* 45:959–78.

Stein, Robert, Stephanie Shirley Post, and Allison L. Rinden. 2000. "Reconciling Context and Contact Effects on Racial Attitudes." *Political Research Quarterly* 53(2): 285–303.

Tate, Katherine. 1991. "Black Political Participation in the 1984 and 1988 Presidential Elections." *American Political Science Review* 85:1159–1176.

————. 1993. *From Protest to Politics: The New Black Voters in American Elections*. New York: Russell Sage Foundation.

Timpone, Richard J. 1998. "Structure, Behavior and Voter Turnout in the U.S." *American Political Science Review* 92(1): 145–158.

Uhlaner, Carole J. 1989. "Rational Turnout: The Neglected Role of Groups." *American Journal of Political Science* 33:390–422.

————. 1991. "Political Participation and Discrimination: A Comparative Analysis of Asians, Blacks and Latinos." In *Political Participation and American Democracy*, edited by William Crotty, 139–170. New York: Greenwood Press.

————. 1991. Uhlaner, Carole J., Bruce E. Cain, and D. Roderick Kiewiet. 1989. "Political Participation of Ethnic Minorities in the 1980s." *Political Behavior* 11:195–231.

U.S. Census Bureau. 2002. "Registered Voter Turnout Improved in 2000 Presidential Election, Census Bureau Reports." Press Release embargoed until February 27, 2002. Accessed at www.census.gov/Press-Release/www/2002/cb02-31.html on February 21, 2003 at 10:30 a.m.

Verba, Sidney, and Norman H. Nie. 1972. *Participation in America: Political Democracy and Social Equality*. New York: Harper and Row.

Verba, Sidney, Norman H. Nie, and Jae-on Kim. 1978. *Participation and Political Equality*. Cambridge: Cambridge University Press.

Verba, Sidney, Kay Lehman Schlozman, and Henry Brady. 1995. *Voice and Equality: Civic Voluntarism in American Politics*. Cambridge: Harvard University Press.

Verba, Sidney, Kay Lehman Schlozman, Henry Brady, and Norman H. Nie. 1993. "Race, Ethnicity, and Political Resources: Participation in the United States." *British Journal of Political Science* 23:453–497.

White, John Kenneth, and Daniel M. Shea. 2000. *New Party Politics: From Jefferson and Hamilton to the Information Age*. Boston: Bedford/St. Martin's.

Wielhouwer, Peter W. 1995. "Strategic Canvassing by the Political Parties, 1952–1990." *American Review of Politics* 16:213–238.

————. 1999. "The Mobilization of Campaign Activists by the Party Canvass." *American Politics Quarterly* 27:177–200.

Wielhouwer, Peter W., and Brad Lockerbie. 1994. "Party Contacting and Political Participation, 1952–1990." *American Journal of Political Science* 38:211–229.

Wilson, James Q. 1973. *Political Organizations*. New York: Basic Books.

Wolfinger, Raymond E., and Jonathan Hoffman. 2001. "Registering and Voting with Motor Voter." *PS: Political Science and Politics* 34:85–92.

Wolfinger, Raymond E., and Steven J. Rosenstone. 1980. *Who Votes?* New Haven: Yale University Press.

Zipp, John F., Richard Landerman, and Paul Luebke. 1982. "Political Parties and Political Participation: A Reexamination of the Standard Socioeconomic Model." *Social Forces* 60:1140–1153.

Zuckerman, Alan S., and Darrell M. West. 1985. "The Political Bases of Citizen Contacting: A Cross-National Approach." *American Political Science Review* 79:117–131.

8   Political Parties, Minorities, and
     Elected Office

*Comparing Opportunities for Inclusion in the
United States and Britain*

IN LIGHT OF THE LONG HISTORIES of racial violence, discrimination, and organized protest by racial and ethnic minority groups in both the United States and across established democracies, it is increasingly imperative to examine how minority groups achieve democratic inclusion, particularly how they achieve greater voice in the regular channels of the democratic process. The growing literature on minority group politics focuses chiefly on the grassroots level. Previous research asks how racial and ethnic minorities groups achieve a critical mass, win numerical representation, and realize their policy goals (Browning, Marshall, and Tabb 1984; Gurin, Hatchett, and Jackson 1989; Hero 1992, 1998; Tate 1994; Leighley 2001).

We examine the role of political parties in the process of racial and ethnic minority democratic inclusion in the United States and Britain.[1] Comparison between these two democratic systems illuminates some common characteristics that have led to increased numerical representation, while exposing other features that are unique to the American case. By examining major parties in the two countries, we isolate the dynamic effects of both political environments and group strategies. How have minorities groups in these two democracies pressed for more representation, and how have their party systems responded to such demands? How have minorities groups been incorporated into the political parties and their national legislatures, and how have the political and institutional environments facilitated their inclusion? There are many paths toward democratic inclusion; this chapter focuses on one in particular—the role parties play in mediating greater representation for minorities groups in national legislatures.

Scholars have begun to identify factors that facilitate government responsiveness to citizens and groups (Powell 2000). We contend that the numerical representation of minorities in legislatures is important to the quality of the democratic process and an important aspect of democratic inclusion. Yet this assumption has been a continuing source of debate among political theorists. In her seminal book, *The Concept of Representation*, Hannah Pitkin (1967) contends that representation based on issue position, not demographics, produces a more favorable outcome for constituents. Anne Phillips (1995), however, attacks the traditional view that political representation was attained by one's vote for candidates and parties offering different sets of issue positions. On the contrary, Phillips argues marginalized groups need to be present at the agenda-setting stage of policy making in order to raise issues that might otherwise be ignored in legislatures represented only by members of the racial or ethnic majority group. Similarly, Jane Mansbridge (1999) contends that issues raised and acted upon are also shaped by the descriptive composition of the legislative body, not exclusively by its ideological character.

In addition, scholars engaged in empirical research on this question are finding strong support for why descriptive representation is an important component of democratic practices. In communities where blacks are elected to Congress, for example, black voters are more likely to be knowledgeable and feel better represented in government (Gay 2002; Tate 2001, 2003). At the presidential level, research shows that turnout among blacks was stimulated by Jesse Jackson's presidential campaign (Tate 1991, 1994). Lawrence Bobo and Frank Gilliam (1990) show that African American participation rates are higher in communities represented by African Americans. The mechanism behind this increase in participation appears to be the engagement of the marginalized group through the introduction of a symbolic cue of likely responsiveness to racial concerns. Descriptive representation, therefore, is an important indicator of to what degree democratic inclusion is occurring among racial and ethnic minority groups. While many legal barriers to minority political participation and office holding have been dismantled, this project will examine more subtle structural barriers in the nomination process and within political parties.

Political party responsiveness to minority mobilization has received less systematic attention than has the impact of minority mobilization on election and governmental outcomes. We focus on minority efforts to gain power in the top echelons of the party and in the national legislature. A substantial body of research exists on how women have increased their numbers among elected officeholders, both in the United States and in comparative perspective. While many scholars point to the importance of the electoral system, others have also pointed to the critical role political parties play in electing women (Darcy, Welch, and Clark 1991; Lovenduski and Norris 1993; Caul 1999; Caul Kittilson 2001). Recognizing the wealth of the work on gender and politics in the comparative field, we turn our attention to the question of race and ethnicity.

Two theoretical approaches to understanding the role parties play in minority inclusion can be extracted from the broad literature on political change and adaptation. The *elite model* views parties as rational actors who alter their environment through a top-down process. The elite model suggests that party leaders promote and field minority candidates in order to attract votes. The *societal change model* theorizes that parties and other political institutions react to new challenges through a bottom-up process. Certainly both processes are evident within the dynamics of party politics. In the case of women's integration and advancement in European political parties, Miki Caul Kittilson (2001) finds evidence for both analytical models. From the societal perspective—in a more permeable party structure—rising support from women and women's groups pressure the party from below to promote women candidates for office. From the elite-led perspective—in a more centralized party organization—women in top party leadership posts encourage greater numerical representation in national legislatures. These two models differ in terms of how they explain the sequence of change but are not necessarily rival theories.

While substantial evidence now details the process through which women have gained greater influence in party structures and increased numerical representation, we still expect the process to be different for racial and ethnic minority groups. As normative theorists point out, the problem of race and ethnicity in democratic states is quite distinct from that of gender. Certainly in the United States, for example, the social and political divisions between whites and blacks are significantly greater than are those found between men and women. In addition, minority claims to equality are often perceived by the majority as more threatening than are those presented by women. As Anne Phillips (1995) argues, policies aimed toward advancing minority rights and equality threaten the status quo because ultimately minority groups are asking for a greater share of power and autonomy in that society. She notes:

> The historical experience of slavery; the continuing and grotesque disparities between black and white Americans in levels of poverty, unemployment, educational qualifications, housing conditions, drug abuse, prison sentences, and infant mortality; the often stark geographic separation between black and white communities—all these combine to create a very different context from the power struggles between men and women. (1995, 95–96)

Gender equality demands, in contrast, may be less threatening precisely because they are interpreted as appeals for greater power "sharing" and are therefore less disruptive of the status quo. One consequence of the less sharp political divide between men and women in some western democracies has been the ready adoption of quotas for women as candidates. Quotas for minorities are fiercely resisted on the grounds that such quotas would reify race and ethnicity and their divisions.

Because the politics differ for minorities versus women seeking advancement in political parties, we expect that the top-down and societal models that have successfully explained women's political gains will not fully account for the political gains realized by minority groups. The key to opening up the party structure to minority groups will depend on the political environment in addition to elite behavior and grassroots mobilization. Following on the research of Doug McAdam (1999) and Sidney Tarrow (1983), we argue that the "political opportunity structure" shapes the degree to which efforts from the top or bottom to include minority citizens in elected office will succeed or fail.

BACKGROUND: MINORITY REPRESENTATION IN THE POLITICAL PARTIES

Race relations in the United States and United Kingdom have been quite different, and remain unique, even as Great Britain has witnessed increasing racial diversity since World War II. Representing only 1 percent in 1961, by the 1991 census, approximately 5 percent of the U.K. population was "non-white" and this proportion is currently estimated to have grown to 10 percent. The largest minority groups in Britain are Afro-Caribbean, African, Indian, Pakistani, and Bangladeshi (Saggar 2000). The United Kingdom's expanding diversity has been accompanied by new restrictions on immigration, racially motivated violence against minority residents, and race riots. Despite their strikingly different racial histories, including the long enslavement of blacks in the United States, minority groups in both countries have organized politically to press for greater political rights. The campaign for black political empowerment took off in the 1970s in the United States as the civil rights movement formally ended (Smith 1981; Tate 1994). British minorities engaged in a similar campaign for greater inclusion in the 1970s in the United Kingdom, a campaign that has since gained additional momentum. Although significantly more muted than campaigns in the United States, Britain stands out in comparison with other continental European nations for its relatively higher level of ethnically based mobilization (Nelson 2000; Saggar 2000).

Broad similarities make the United States and Britain ripe for comparison on this issue. The two nations share common Western values, historical political trajectories, and levels of socioeconomic development. Politically, both hold elections under single-member district systems where the winner of the plurality of votes takes office. In both cases, these electoral rules have yielded two-party systems, although in the British case the persistence of a third party makes it a "two-and-one-half-party system."

Case studies of the politics of minority inclusion in Britain and the United States imply that U.S. blacks are the most politically engaged and best numerically represented in government (Lublin 1997; Tate 1994, 2003; Whitby 1998; Canon 1999), while British minority groups are less collectively engaged and represented (Nelson 2000; Saggar 2000). This presents a paradox because racial conflict has been, in a relative sense, less overt in the United Kingdom. Black political empowerment in the United States appears largely based on the strength of the racial solidarity and group consciousness. Racial group consciousness appears to be the key variable that accounts for black political empowerment in the United States.

Minorities groups in both nations feel slighted by their parties and by the party system. In the United Kingdom, minorities voters were more likely than white voters to feel that their vote was taken for grant by the major parties. For example, while only 23 percent of the mostly white respondents in the regular British Election Study disagreed with the statement that "political parties care what people think," 54 to 62 percent of the minority respondents surveyed in the supplemental minority survey agreed with the statement that the political parties are "only interested in votes." Blacks, and especially those from the Caribbean, are less trusting of politicians and more likely to claim that there is "a lot" of prejudice against minorities in the United Kingdom. In a 1984 survey of African Americans, one-quarter of the respondents felt that the Democratic Party did not work very hard on issues blacks cared about (Tate 1994, 57). Black Americans' political alienation was a factor that black civil rights activist Jesse Jackson successfully exploited in his 1984 and 1988 bids

TABLE 8.1. Black Numerical Representation in the U.S. House and Senate
(Black Members of Congress), 1971 to 1999

Year	Number of black members of Congress	Percentage of black members of Congress
1971	14	2.6
1973	17	3.2
1975	18	3.4
1977	17	3.2
1979	16	3.0
1981	18	3.4
1983	21	3.9
1985	21	3.9
1987	23	4.3
1989	24	4.5
1991	26	4.9
1993	40	7.5
1995	40	7.5
1997	39	7.3
1999	38	7.1

Note: Includes District of Columbia's nonvoting delegate, thus percentages calculated are based on a number of 536.
Source: Tate (2003), table 2.3.

for the Democratic Party's presidential nomination. The partisan alienation that U.K. citizens of color have expressed in political surveys has not been yet skillfully exploited by their political leaders.

The U.S. Congress better mirrors its population in terms of racial minority groups than does the British House of Commons. Table 8.1 presents the number and percentage of black members of the U.S. Congress from 1971 to 1999. Of the 38 black members of the U.S. House of Representatives (including the nonvoting D.C. delegate) serving in 1999, all but one belong to the Democratic Party. Taken together, blacks, Latinos, and Asian American minority members today represent approximately 12 percent of the U.S. Congress, the vast proportion of whom serve in the lower House.[2]

Racial and ethnic minorities[3] are severely underrepresented in the British House of Commons. Table 8.2 displays the trends in the percentage of minority members of Parliament (MPs) from 1970 to 2001. While the racial

TABLE 8.2. Minority Numerical Representation in the British House of Commons, 1970 to 2001

Year	Number of minority members of Parliament	Percentage of minority members of Parliament
1970	0	0
1974	0	0
1979	0	0
1983	0	0
1987	4	0.6
1992	6	0.9
1997	10	1.5
2001	12	1.8

Source: Norris and Lovenduski 1995; Rich 1998; Saggar 2000.

and ethnic minority proportion of the British population has grown from less than 1 percent in 1961 to an estimated 10 percent in 2001, the proportion of "non-white" minorities in parliament has only risen from 0 to almost 2 percent over the same period. Of the twelve minority MPs in 2001, all are from the Labour Party. In 1987, minorities achieved a breakthrough in representation: Of the fourteen minority Labour candidates, four were elected. During this period, the Conservatives could only claim one minority MP in 1992. Although the Tories fielded sixteen minority candidates in the 2001 election, all but one were candidates in hopeless contests.

PREVIOUS APPROACHES TO PARTY CHANGE: THE SOCIETAL CHANGE MODEL

The societal change model emphasizes the direct role of citizens in effecting party change. From this perspective, social movements and citizen groups pressure parties into incorporating new demands. The party responds—or does not respond—to those challenges at its own peril. At its core, the societal change model views the party as a set of institutions that reflects changes in the environment (Katz and Mair 1992).

Ron Inglehart's (1997) research on political change across advanced industrial societies exemplifies this perspective. He finds considerable evidence of a shift in citizen values and the emergence of a set of new citizen demands such as women and minority rights, often represented by organized groups. In response, many established parties have repositioned themselves ideologically, adopting some of the new issues. In research on women's issues and parties in the United States, Wolbrecht (2000) finds a similar bottom-up pattern. She concludes that with the rise of the women's movement, the Democrats and Republicans absorbed and channeled demands from their existing constituencies and shifted their positions on women's rights. Similarly, seminal studies of party transformation in Europe depict parties changing in response to shifts in society. Underpinning both Otto Kirchheimer's (1966) catch-all prophecy and Leon Epstein's (1980) theory of a contagion from the right is a common theme in which the attenuation of links between social groups and parties is followed by changes in party behavior, most notably a shift toward pursuit of the median voter in a race for electoral success.

The general societal change model may provide a framework for understanding how political parties respond to public pressure for minority representation. It suggests that increased minority representation can result from changing demographics, values, and demands by activists at the party's grass roots. Increasing minority participation at the grassroots level may increase minorities' power, resources, and opportunities to pressure from below for representation in the legislature.

In the U.S. context, the civil rights movement provides strong evidence for the efficacy of organized groups pressing their demands from the bottom up in the Democratic Party system. The roots of the Democrats' move toward more inclusive delegation selection rules certainly lay in the civil rights struggle. At the Democrats' 1964 convention, the Mississippi Freedom Democratic Party

(MFDP), an offshoot of a multi-racial civil rights organization, objected to the all-white delegation representing Mississippi. (The challenge was dramatically conveyed in Fannie Lou Hamer's famous nationally televised speech.) At the convention, the MFDP was offered two at-large seats and was promised future party rules that would prevent the seating of groups that discriminated against minority groups. However, all-white delegations from Mississippi would continue to be sent to the national conventions (although the national party refused to seat them) until 1976.

Because of civil rights issues as well as protests against the Vietnam War, important reforms were initiated by the Democratic Party that changed the delegation selection process. The McGovern–Fraser Commission specified that convention delegations had to be chosen in an open and representative process. Ninety percent of pledged delegates must either reflect the results of the state's presidential primary, or delegates must be selected by party caucuses open to all Democrats. To achieve the "representativeness" standard, delegations had to include more minorities, women, and young adults in "reasonable relationship to their proportion in the state." State delegations that discriminated, as in the case of the all-white Mississippi state delegation, would not be seated under the 1968 rule changes. Whereas men dominated state delegations in the past, women have now achieved numerical parity with men as a direct result of the 1968 reforms. The conversion of the black civil rights movement into organized electoral politics pressured the Democratic Party into increasing black representation. In 1973, a black Democratic Caucus had formed that was more radical and influential than the previous black caucus (Walters 1988, 60–61). Black membership on key standing committees of the party increased on average from 7.7 percent in 1972 to 20 percent in 1984 (Walters 1988, 65). Jesse Jackson's two presidential bids in 1984 and again in 1988 put tremendous pressure on the party, but with little tangible effects. Jackson obtained over 3 million votes in the 1984 Democratic nomination contest, but all his political planks fell to defeat by the Mondale–Hart forces at the convention (Barker 1989).

In contrast to the United States, past research in Britain provides little support for either an ethnic minority voting bloc or representation of minority issues (Crewe 1983; McAllister and Studlar 1984; Studlar 1986; Studlar and Layton-Henry 1990). Recent research suggests that ethnicity indeed "counts" and that an ethnic minority identity exists (Saggar, 2000). Shamit Saggar (2000) concludes that the "interaction between ethnicity and ideology . . . best captures the essence of racial and electoral politics in Britain" (237). While there is little evidence of a discrete ethnic agenda, William Nelson (2000) argues that because certain issues are conditioned by ethnic and racial components, minorities in Britain have formed a consciousness of solidarity, albeit indirectly.

At the level of citizen support for parties, a pattern well established by national survey data in both the United States and Britain is minority identification with the nation's leftist political parties—the Democratic and Labour parties. Table 8.3 shows that even during the Labour Party's successive electoral defeats (from 1979 to 1992), more than 50 percent of minorities

TABLE 8.3. British Major Party Identification by Race, 1979 to 2001 (in percentages)

	Labour		Independent		Conservative	
	Minority	White	Minority	White	Minority	White
1979	52.6	38.2	8.8	5.3	22.8	40.7
1983	50.5	30.2	13.1	10.5	12.1	36.7
1987	53.7	29.1	16.9	10.7	19.1	37.8
1992	50.0	32.9	11.2	4.9	30.6	41.4
1997	63.7	44.0	11.9	6.9	11.9	28.1
2001	53.2	41.6	16.7	13.2	8.7	24.1

Note: "Minority" refers to self-identified respondents of Asian, African, and mixed heritage.
Source: British Election Studies.

identified themselves as Labour supporters or independents leaning toward Labour ideologies.[4] With the "New Labour's" newfound popularity in 1997, minority identifiers rose to almost 64 percent. During this period, minority identification with the Conservative Party remained well below white identification. Strikingly, the proportion of minority Independents remained higher than that of whites. The greater propensity among minorities to remain unattached to a party may signal a higher degree of dissatisfaction with party politics and a perceived reluctance of parties across the ideological spectrum to address minority issues.

The survey data from the United States shown in Table 8.4 show a similar pattern. In the 1950s and early 1960s, about 56 to 66 percent of blacks identified themselves as Democrats or independents leaning toward the Democratic Party. Largely because of events leading up to and during the 1964 national elections, a full 80 percent of blacks came to identify with the Democratic Party. This high percentage of black identification has persisted ever since, in fact. In 2000, 83 percent of blacks claimed identification with the Democratic Party. Since the 1970s, conservative parties in both countries have rarely been able to win more than 10 percent of the minority vote. In short, high levels of minority attachment to the more leftist party and the relatively higher level of descriptive representation in the legislature by leftist parties in both countries provide some support for the bottom-up theory. It appears that minority support in the electorate is reflected in minority inclusion in the legislature.

While a bottom-up process explains how minorities have won political office in the United States and United Kingdom, there is still ample evidence favoring an elite or top-down approach. First, in the United States, the electoral mobilization of minorities did not automatically translate into party and governmental. Rather, the demand–protest process at the level of the political elite in addition to electoral mobilization was key. And second, special legislation and litigation rather than elite capitulation to minority pressure were crucial for minorities to win seats in state and national legislatures. The elite model garners even stronger support in the U.K. case than in the United States. After all, U.K. minorities have met with much less success as their numbers in the population have greatly expanded and their rate of voter participation nearly matches that of the white British population (Saggar 2000).

TABLE 8.4. U.S. Major Party Identification by Race, 1952 to 2000 (in percentages)

	Democrats		Independents		Republicans	
	Black	White	Black	White	Black	White
1952	63	56	4	6	17	36
1954	58	56	5	7.5	22	34
1956	56	49	7	9	19	39
1958	56.5	55	5	7	19	35
1960	53	53	11.5	9	22	37
1962	63	53	6	8	16	36
1964	82	59	6	8	8	33
1966	72	53	14	12	11	34.5
1968	91	51	3	11	3	36
1970	85	51	10	13	4	35.5
1972	76	48.5	12	13	11	37
1974	83	48	10	14	4	36
1976	85.5	46	8	15	6	38
1978	82	50	9	14	7.5	33
1980	81	48	7	13.5	8	37
1982	90.5	50	5	11	3	37
1984	76	43	11	10	11	45
1986	84	44	8	11	6	43
1988	80	39	6	12	11.5	48
1990	78.5	47	8	11	12	41
1992	77	45	13	11.5	8	43
1994	81	42	8	10	10	47
1996	81	47	11	8	9	44
1998	84	45	6.5	10.5	7	43
2000	83	44	10	11.5	7	44

Note: Independent leaders are grouped with their partisans, and the percentages of "apolitical" respondents are not shown.
Source: American National Election Study 1948–2000, Cumulative Data File (Sapiro et al., 2002).

The mismatch between minority population and minority seats can be illustrated more clearly by examining the demographic composition of minority and non-minority MP's constituencies. Theories of critical mass suggest that once a minority group reaches a certain numerical threshold, the status quo will be altered. Table 8.5 compares the characteristics of constituencies represented by minority MPs against constituencies represented by white MPs that have 10 percent or more minority citizens. Overall, minority MP constituencies are socioeconomically similar to their white MP counterparts. The citizens in the minority MP constituencies are not more likely to depend on government programs nor more likely to be out of work than citizens in constituencies represented by white MPs. These constituencies are also as likely as those in districts led by white MPs to vote. In short, the differences in the demographic and political characteristics of the constituencies cannot explain how minority MPs got their seats. Other factors must explain how they came to represent the party; we discuss these factors in our discussion of how elites can promote minority incorporation.

TABLE 8.5. 2001 British Constituency Comparison of Average Constituency Demographics

Variable name	Minority MP* constituency	White MP constituency with minority population of 10% or more
Total number of constituencies	12	86
Percentage of constituency Greater London region	41.6	52.8
Turnout	53.3	53.4
Percentage of Labour members of Parliament	100.0 (12/12)	90.7 (78/86)
Percentage of Labour vote	54.9	54.8
Percentage of Conservative vote	22.7	25.5
Party seat change from 1997	0	0
White residents	70.3	78.9
Black residents	8.7	7.0
Indian, Pakistani, Bangladeshi residents	10.1	10.5
Other non-white residents	2.9	3.6
Minority residents (total)	29.7**	21.1
Economically active residents	75.4	76.4
Full-time work	61.2	63.3
Part-time work	13.5	11.6
Single parent households	26.8	27.0
Migrants	10.1	11.3
Professional occupation households	5.4	7.0
"On the dole"	15.9	13.6

Source: Data collected from Pippa Norris. British Parliamentary Constituency Database, 1992–2001.
* MP = Member of Parliament
** Data for constituency Glasgow Govan Include "white" and "non-white" totals: missing entries for ethnic breakdown. As a result, category averages do not total to zero.

THE ELITE-LED MODEL

From the elite-led perspective, politicians drive political change. Seminal works by Anthony Downs (1957) and William Riker (1965) portray political actors as rational decision makers who calculate their actions and positions to win elections. Recently John Aldrich (1995) applied this core principle of self-interest to his study of the development of the American party system. He contends that politicians create and maintain parties only because parties are useful vehicles for politicians to further their own individualistic goals and ambitions. Under this logic, in competition with other parties, parties strategize and manipulate their policy stances in order to win elections. Thus, the party itself initiates change, marketing its new ideas to the electorate. By promoting minorities for office, parties may "advertise" to potential voters their support for minority issues.

The elite perspective of party change is adopted by Carmines and Stimson's (1989) research on race and political parties in the United States. They theorize that although many issues compete for recognition, those that become salient are those prompted by strategic politicians. The electorate responds to some issues, but to not others, in a manner analogous to natural selection in the biological world. Carmines and Stimson measure party positions over time and find that changes in the popular perceptions of where parties stood on civil rights and race registered only after the parties took polarized positions on civil rights and race. They conclude the following: "The origin of the policy dialogue between politicians and voters must lie, we believe, with the former, who provide definition to a multitude of issue conflicts" (1989, 179).

Recent comparative party literature emphasizes the role of parties as agents of change and treats parties as coalitions of competing factions rather than as unitary actors (Berman 1997; Wilson 1994; Panebianco 1988). According to these theorists, the key to change lies in the behavior of party leaders and reformers who make deliberate policy choices. Party leaders perceive a need to adopt new issues and then choose among a variety of tactics and strategies. Thus, change is not reduced to a stimulus—response dynamic, but rather the outcome of the redistribution of power among contending intra-party factions.

This process of top-level intra-party interest group lobbying is evident in both the United States and Britain. As a consequence of the civil rights and anti-war movements, the Democratic Party had adopted rules to achieve greater diversity at its national conventions. Fairly quickly, however, the Democratic Party began backing away from its new "representativeness" standard. In 1973, the burden of proving that racial discrimination existed at the state level was shifted from the state party to challengers. The draft proposal read, "If a State Party has adopted and implemented an approved Affirmative Action Program, the Party shall not be subject to challenge based solely on delegation composition or primary results" (Walters 1988, 58). This meant that unrepresentative state delegations could be seated at the national convention, as long as minorities or some other group did not successfully object. With women having achieved numerical parity, in fact, the implications of this rule change was effectively that the imbalance in minority representation could continue to exist as long as the state party had adopted an affirmative action plan.

In response, in 1973, black Democrats formed a new caucus group, the Black Democratic Caucus (BDC), replacing an older one. The BDC's threats yielded increases in the numbers of blacks within the key standing committees of the Democratic Party, from an average of 7.7 percent in 1972 to 20 percent in 1984 (Walters 1988, 65). Jesse Jackson would challenge the delegation selection rules with limited success in both his 1984 and 1988 bids. His delegates would meet with a striking lack of success in adopting liberal policy planks at the conventions (Tate 1994). However, the Democratic Party responded to these internal lobbying pressures from blacks by selecting its first black national chairman in 1992, the late Ronald H. Brown. Democratic leaders made changes, but not necessarily in strategic anticipation to the changing electoral environment. Changes were made as a response to demands by blacks placed on the party at its top echelons. Thus, top-level efforts combined with simultaneous bottom-up agitation (black political loyalty combined somewhat later by their overwhelming support for Jackson's presidential bids) forced the Democrats to take concrete steps toward bringing more blacks into leadership positions within the organization.

In Britain, demands for greater minority representation emerged in the 1970s, and activists targeted their efforts on the Labour Party. Black activists formed the Labour Party Black Section (LPBS) in 1983. Top leaders took charge of the group's goals and strategy and lobbied the Party through inside channels. Although the LPBS never gained official recognition, organizers never wavered in their loyalty to the Labour Party. In a political compromise during the Labour Party's march toward a centrist ideology in the early 1990s, the new Black and Asian Socialist Society (BASS) gained official recognition in 1993. Most of the former LPSB activists redirected their efforts toward this new, more pragmatic organization (Shukra 1998). The black sections' efforts focused minority mobilization on electoral channels of participation, and support for the Labour Party, rather than grassroots protest (Shukra 1998, see chapter 5). Neither LPBS nor BASS acted as protest organizations in the larger society. Rather, these groups pressured at the top echelons of the party organization, seeking change through bargaining and coalition formation.

Indeed, the Labour Party made a concerted effort to offer more minority candidates, beginning in 1983. These "efforts" initially proved more rhetorical than substantive, as most minority candidates were put up in hopeless seats (see Anwar 1986; Norrisand Lovenduski 1995, 104). Yet in subsequent elections leaders were able to subtly prod the local party constituencies in winnable open seats to nominate minority candidates, and minorities eventually won twelve seats. Further, following the image-building success of visible promotions for women (dubbed "Blair's Babes") in the previous cabinet, after the 2001 victory, Tony Blair appointed two minority candidates to his government—as Chief Secretaries of the Treasury and the Health Ministry. The Conservative Party has more recently tried to improve its image among minority voters by promoting a few minority candidates to highly visible party offices. Most notably, in the wake of their second loss to Labour in October 2001, Conservative leaders appointed their first Asian vice-chair. The Conservatives have avoided anything akin to a black section within the party, preferring a more centralized approach, most recently in the form of the One Nation Forum, which is designed to recruit minority members and voters. Membership in this forum is by party leader invitation only (Rich 1998). The failure of the Labour Party to achieve greater gains in increasing the number of minority MPs, in spite of pressure from organized internal groups, reveals the serious limitations of the elite model.

APPLYING A NEW APPROACH: THE POLITICAL OPPORTUNITY STRUCTURE MODEL

Taken together, the elite and societal models go far in explaining the sequence of change in minority representation. Yet both are inadequate in explaining where and when minority inclusion occurs (or does not occur). Previous research on parties and minority candidacies largely ignores the opportunity structure in which events take place (for an exception, see Geddes 1998). The political opportunity structure model describes the political and institutional environment within which actors–either at the elite or mass level–operate. Although contextual characteristics may not act as agents of change, they do act as intervening variables that make it more likely for groups or leaders to take strategic action.

We conceptualize the political opportunity structure as a political party's receptivity to the demands placed on it by either minority political leaders or by the masses below. This structure includes changes in the institutional "rules of the game"—formal rules, practices, or norms that act as constraints and incentives within an organization. Sidney Tarrow (1983, 1989, 1998) has applied the political opportunity structure to explain why collective action arises in some instances and not others. Doug McAdam (1999) employs the political opportunity structure in his analysis of the rise and decline of the black civil rights movement. Analytically, an improved political opportunity structure implies a decrease in the power disparity between the group seeking power and the majority in power; it also implies that the cost of keeping the insurgent group in its place has increased (McAdam 1999, 43). McAdam puts it this way:

> Any event or broad social process that serves to undermine the calculations and assumptions on which the political establishment is structured occasions a shift in political opportunities. Among the events and processes likely to prove disruptive of the political status quo are wars, industrialization, international political realignments, prolonged unemployment, and widespread demographic changes. (1999, 41)

For example, the delegation selection rules were changed not only because of the efforts of MFDP leaders, or because of the civil rights movement taking place at the grass roots, but also because of anti-Vietnam War protests and the women's movement. The Democratic Party was effectively forced to respond to minorities because they also needed to respond to the demands placed on it by women and anti-war activists as well. Broad social and political processes are key agents that can improve or restrict the political opportunities of insurgent groups. Thus, for example, the Cold War enhanced the opportunities for black civil rights, as the USSR frequently pointed to the second-class citizenship of blacks in America for propaganda purposes.

Following the contours of the political opportunity structure approach, we apply three broad categories that condition the receptivity of parties to minority demands: (1) the legal structure, (2) the intra-party organization, and (3) the ideological climate.

Legal Environment

The legal system in the United States certainly contributed importantly to blacks' political gains. The civil rights movement led Democratic Party leaders to make new laws and policies that advanced blacks politically. Yet, these actions were not independent of the external environment, and indeed, one could argue only came about because of the great political pressures the civil rights movement and the threat of litigation created. The affirmative racial gerrymandering that Democratic Party officials have engaged in—either in response to litigation or the threat thereof—explains in part how black Americans have made significantly greater strides in winning elective office than have minorities in the United Kingdom. In 1965, the Voting Rights Act was passed by a nearly all-white Congress (there were five black members in Congress out of 535 members at that time) as a direct result of President Johnson's response to the civil rights movement. The judiciary ruled that election systems shown to discriminate against minorities are unconstitutional only when minorities can show that those systems were created purposefully with a racial animus against them. Voting rights activists responded to a more liberal judicial environment by pressing for the modification of the 1965 Voting Rights Act in 1982 (Grofman, Handley, and Niemi 1992; Pinderhughes 1995). The modification expressly prohibited voting procedures that afforded minorities fewer "opportunities than other members of the electorate to participate in the political process and to elect representatives of their choice" (Grofman, Handley, and Niemi 1992; Davidson and Grofman 1994). Democrats in Congress were most likely reluctant to amend the Voting Rights Act but nevertheless went along fearing further intra-racial strife and litigation within the party. Republicans also went along with the amendment in 1982 because of the electoral benefits to their party in drawing new minority-majority congressional districts.

In their effort to gain representation in mainstream party politics, minorities in Britain also utilized litigation. Minority litigants brought suit against political parties, claiming barriers to the election of minorities included unclear ad hoc selection rules and inherent ethnic biases in the selection criteria. The litigants argued that because minorities, in aggregate, lack the resources and connections of the traditional party nominee, they stand at a disadvantage in the process. In *Ishaq v. McDonagh*, an employment tribunal ruled Labour's selection procedures discriminatory. Likewise, in *Sawyer v. Ashan*, a tribunal ruled that the Race Relations Act, designed to prohibit discrimination on the basis of nationality, applies to candidate selection. Notably, the British cases have not been nearly as extensive in the United States, and the British claims have been framed in terms of equal opportunity employment rather than political rights.

Intra-Party Organization

The rules and norms within a party certainly shape receptivity to minority demands. Specific to promoting minorities for office, the party's ideology, degree of centralization, and level of candidate nomination may prove most important.

A more leftist ideology appears conducive to minority office holding. Leftist parties (*liberal* in American terms) espouse more egalitarian ideologies in general, and traditionally offer more support to underrepresented groups. In both cases, the Democrats and Labour have more support from minorities in the electorate, and send more minorities to the legislature. These parties' traditional distributive economic policies naturally overlap with minority interests in many ways. In addition, Labour has supported anti-discrimination laws and the expansion of the powers of Britain's Commission for Racial Equality (Messina 1998).

Both the Republican and Conservative Parties espouse ideologies based on "merit" and oppose "special interest" politics. For example, in the 1983 campaign, the British Conservative Party designed a poster to connote its "colorblind" perspective. The poster's slogan read, "Tories say he's British, Labour says he's black" (Saggar 2000, 200). The Conservatives have alienated many minority voters with anti-immigration campaigns ("race-card politics") and have been characterized by their "indifference and/or explicit hostility" toward minorities (Messina 1998, 100). Party elites in both the Republican and Conservative parties have been publicly chastised for making anti-minority comments. Certainly this has hurt the party's image with minority voters. In the United States, the Republican Party's Majority Senate Leader Trent Lott made remarks endorsing Strom Thurmond's 1948 Presidential bid as a segregationist. His comments caused a major public furor which led to his resignation as party leader. In a similar scandal, before the June 2001 election, Conservative MP John Townend stated immigration was creating "a mongrel race" in Britain (Travis 2001). Although the national party leader, William Hague, promptly forced Townend to retract his statements, Townend, however, was not expelled from the party. Moreover, Hague himself made highly publicized remarks that appeared to have racist overtones. In a speech, Hague warned that under Labour leadership Britain would become a "foreign land." In another instance, Britain's Commission for Racial Equality drafted and circulated a pledge for candidates from all parties to sign on a voluntary basis. By signing the declaration, candidates promised not to stir up anti-ethnic sentiment during the 2001 election. After having issued an anti-"race-card" declaration, some Tory MPs very publicly stated their opposition to it and refused to sign.

Similar to ideology, the degree of centralization within a party structure may shape minority efforts for inclusion. On the one hand, more decentralized parties, with several levels of organization, may offer more points of access for organized groups to press their claims on the party. On the other hand, a more centralized party might allow party leaders leeway to create openings and enact rules to promote minority candidates—when the leadership perceives the need to do so. As Paul Frymer notes in an earlier chapter, American parties are neither unified organizations, nor hierarchical ones. In contrast, British parties, based on the model of accountability in government, are clearly more centralized and cohesive. Therefore, American parties may be more permeable and receptive to demands from below (societal change model), while British parties may be more amenable to top-down efforts led by strategic party leaders (elite-led model).

Certainly the degree of centralization and cohesion within a party is shaped by, and in turn shapes, the level of candidate selection. The rules of candidate nomination in the United States differ greatly from those in Britain. Through primary elections, the American nomination system places the impetus on the potential candidate. In contrast, in Britain, the local political parties determine nominations (Gallagher and Marsh 1988). The central party organization in London maintains a list of approved candidates, and can veto a nomination, but this right is rarely exercised (at least overtly). In short, although British candidate selection is decentralized, it still remains within the party, and the central party retains greater control over the process, relative to national party control in the United States.

Theoretically, there are conflicting expectations as to whether a strong or weak party role might facilitate the nomination of minorities. In primary systems where candidates generally self-select, personal resources are essential. The entrepreneurial nature of the process depends on the individual candidate's resources. Because minorities as a group are less likely to possess these resources, they are at a disadvantage to potential competitors. The heavy reliance upon large sums of campaign money, especially personal wealth, may preclude many potential minority candidates from entering the nomination race and from advancing to the general election. With regard to the underrepresentation of women, research on differences in primary systems within the United States suggests that the weaker the party's role in the nominating process, the more difficult women find it to run for public office due to the need to raise their own funds (Caul Kittilson and Tate 2002).

Minorities in the United States, however, possess a stronger foundation of constituents on the basis of race and ethnicity than do women on the basis of their gender (Tate 1997). Thus, in contrast to women, minority candidates, while lacking greatly in personal wealth, have political advantages over women in having this ready-to-mobilize constituency. Moreover, having the power nomination in the hands of party gatekeepers means that these activists have the power to discriminate against minority candidates. In a study of Conservative Party selectors in the early 1980s, Bochel and Denver (1983) found evidence that selectors perceived minority candidates as an electoral handicap for their party. Furthermore, the Conservative Party has publicly recognized discrimination within the electorate and has sent special instruction to selectors to minimize bias in the selection process. The greater strides made by minorities in the United States lend support to the superiority of the open primary system in gaining numerical representation. However, pressure on parties to nominate more women took the form of adopting gender quotas in several European democracies (Caul Kittilson 2001). Quotas for minorities is presently politically infeasible; thus, opening up nominating pressure control to the electorate is the most likely way minorities can win greater numerical representation in government.

The two-party system that emerges under majoritarian electoral systems, which characterizes both the American and British party systems, is another factor that impedes minority political incorporation. As Paul Frymer (1999; see also his chapter in this volume) argues, in a two-party system, minority voters lack alternatives to and are therefore made captives of the more liberal party precisely because the parties on the Right (i.e., the Republican Party) do not want their votes. Consequently, the Labour and Democratic parties do not necessarily have to reward minority voters for their loyalty by offering them more seats. The two-party system does not mean that minority voters are entirely ignored by party leaders. Presidential candidates in the United

States on the left and right must publicly embrace minority voters because of their expansion in the national electorate. This is vividly demonstrated at recent presidential nominating conventions and in the conscious efforts of recent presidents to ensure minority representation in their administrations.

Ideological Climate

According to McAdam (1999), causal forces that can improve the political climate for minorities seeking greater representation include wars, demographic and social change, international political realignments, or concerted political pressure from outside actors, notably international groups.

Demographic changes are critical transformers of the political opportunity structure. As minorities become citizens, they can more effectively seek the end of legal barriers to equal opportunity. As they move closer to the majority's socioeconomic elite, minorities can apply greater pressure on parties for their incorporation and political advancement. Moving up the ranks in the country's economic order is more critical for advancing political change for minorities than increasing their numbers and collective voting strength in the population. Party and political change is not possible without minorities first winning some integration into the socioeconomic order. Economic and social power can expand their opportunities for political change.

The argument that minorities need economic empowerment in advance of political empowerment is not new, but nonetheless represents a break from the societal model insofar as it underscores the fact that parties do not court votes equally or operate as equal opportunity organizations. Groups with social power are more favored than groups lacking power. Viewing parties in this fashion makes it easier to understand why minorities are disproportionately underrepresented in established democracies and will remain so until and unless they effectively scramble up the socioeconomic ladder.

The political opportunity structure approach also emphasizes the importance of political realignment and a shifting ideological environment in creating openings for minority empowerment. This is most clearly demonstrated in the American case, where separate-but-equal, made legitimate in the *Plessy* (1896) ruling, was ultimately declared unconstitutional in the 1954 *Brown* decision. As a precursor to *Brown, in Smith v. Allwright*, the white-only primary system was declared unconstitutional in 1944. These Supreme Court rulings not only transformed electoral arrangements, but also gradually helped in the liberalization of whites' racial attitudes. These new liberal attitudes on race were politically critical if the numerical underrepresentation of minority groups were to be seen as a real political problem that needed to be addressed. The challenge facing minorities today is that after having realized significant gains in their numbers in the U.S. House, their continued exclusion in the U.S. Senate, for example, is no longer seen as serious problem for American democracy. The liberal racial attitudes of whites, in fact, have been used to deny charges that whites still discriminate against candidates of color in the voting booth. Because Americans today are "colorblind," there is little ideological goodwill left in the United States toward promoting minority candidates as a matter of principle in the parties or in the courts. The strategy of advancing minority political empowerment as a vehicle of furthering the cause of racial equality is no longer legitimate in the new racially conservative but colorblind environment. Thus, currently, it is ironically *more* difficult for minorities in the United States to collectively organize and press for further change because of the new colorblind ideology that has become dominant political discourse.

Broad changes in the British electoral landscape have reshaped party strategy and have created new opportunities for minority advancement in the near future, particularly on the Left. While British politics was traditionally rooted in social class divisions, class structure has weakened in its ability to structure electoral behavior (Franklin et al. 1992; Norton 1994). A decline in the industrial sector and the subsequent attenuation of the relationship between the Labour and the trade unions has opened up space for new groups of Labour supporters and new group representatives at the party's top levels. As union representatives have lost favor and power among the party elite, space has opened up for newcomers. Specifically, in the wake of several embarrassing electoral defeats, Labour's shift toward the ideological center, and its efforts to centralize and "professionalize" party operations, has shaken up the ideological environment. The "politics of ideology" that once characterized British politics has the potential to be supplemented with the "politics of identity" that is more common in the American political arena. It is important to note that Labour's centrist drift has meant that in order to achieve goals, minority groups within Labour must align themselves with centrist factions and make more moderate claims, rather than align with the more leftist sections that controlled the party up to the mid-1980s.

Finally, the salience of minority politics on the national political agenda may be on the rise. Concurrent with the very recent rise in minority MPs in Britain, racial and ethnic issues have risen dramatically in the electoral landscape. Urban disorder in 1980 and 1981 brought attention to incorporating minorities into the mainstream channels of participation (Geddes 1998). Following several race riots, increasing percentages of Brits cited in a 2001 poll the importance of issues of immigration and race relations as opposed to the economy, education, poverty, or the European Union. In 1996, only 3 percent highlighted racial issues as the most pressing problems facing the country, and yet by 2001, 19 percent cited such issues (Branigan 2001).

The diminishing illegitimacy of race-card politics in the United Kingdom may yield a more conducive environment to the election of minority MPs. Party leaders have an important role here in setting forth the party's strategy in terms of the salience of racial issues. As yet, in British politics, anti-race and anti-ethnic minority sentiment still underscore mass electoral behavior to a degree (Saggar 2000). In combating this form of racism, U.K. minorities may ultimately elect to organize more forcefully around their identity as blacks, and press more aggressively and assuredly for inclusion in spite of the dominant group's denouncement of race-card politics. Thus, cultural interpretations of the validity of empowering minorities through structural reform are as important as the electoral structures for impeding or facilitating minority empowerment. Whether groups believe in the legitimacy of political change and the degree to which minorities share a collective consciousness are important political forces separate from the electoral arrangements and the political opportunity structure.

CONCLUSION

In sum, our review of party responsiveness to minorities in the United States and United Kingdom finds elements of support for both societal change and elite top-down accounts of party change. Whereas the process of party change in the United States best fits the societal change model, efforts in Britain have relied more on elite groups within party politics. In the American case, minority political gains have come about through a demand-protest process at the grassroots level. Localized, decentralized politics shape this process. In the British case, through efforts to shore up support from minority groups (especially the more conservative South Asian groups) Labour party leaders want to hasten progress in minority representation, but must drag the local party selection committees along. A similar process characterizes the Conservatives in the post-1997 election defeat. The Conservatives revealed a new initiative in which they would "train" selection committee members to recognize potential biases in the candidate nomination process. In both parties, minorities have gained the ear of party leaders by forming coalitions—lending their potential support for powerful positions. Certainly, the more centralized party structure in the United Kingdom renders this a more effective strategy than in the United States.

Neither account, on its own, can fully explain why certain political parties have been more or less receptive at particular points in time—that is, when and why parties will function as mechanisms for democratic inclusion. The fact that American minorities have had to rely heavily on forces outside the standard political channels for their inclusion and empowerment reveals the inadequacies of both the elite-led and societal change models. The failure of U.K. minorities to win more seats in Parliament speaks volumes about how elites are simply not responsive to changing electoral constituencies.

Through comparison, we highlight some conditions under which minority groups may find inclusion in the democratic system, specifically in terms of finding access in a party system and increasing their numerical representation in the legislature. Certain institutional structures create incentives for underrepresented groups to pursue top-down or bottom-up strategies in their efforts for democratic inclusion.

For parties to be willing to truly include racial and ethnic minorities, the political opportunity structure must change. Minorities must accumulate a greater share of societal power to better press their demands for greater political inclusion. Minorities must have opportunities to circumvent control at the top through more open electoral procedures. In addition, transformative racial ideologies that challenge the racial status quo are critical stimuli for political change. In short, our analysis of party change in the United States and United Kingdom strongly contests the view that standard democratic processes are enough to ensure that racial and ethnic minorities will eventually become equal and full players in the political process. Minorities can make important political strides, but not automatically, and only, it seems, under specific historical conditions.

Future research on minority representation through partisan channels may benefit from a stronger focus on political opportunity structure, both in terms of institutional constraints and political environment. The impact of these forces is best isolated through cross-temporal and cross-national comparison. Industrialized democracies, especially in Europe, face new challenges with substantial rises in minority populations. Certainly the efforts of U.S. minorities and parties offer insights into effective (and not so effective) strategies. We must not forget that even in an increasingly candidate-centered political landscape, the political party is still an effective vehicle for minority inclusion. By offering forums for organizing and lobbying on racial and ethnic bases, and by heightening the salience of racial issues on the agenda, parties can promote both substantive and descriptive representation.

NOTES

Acknowledgments. We would like to thank the conference participants. An earlier version of this chapter was also presented at the 2001 Western Political Science Association meeting, Long Beach, CA, March 21-24. Finally, we wish to thank Pippa Norris at Harvard University for making her 2001 British Parliamentary Constituency Database, analyzed here, publicly available.

1. We define political minority groups broadly as groups that are subjected to social, political, and economic discrimination in society. A narrow definition of a political minority group is one that has been subjected historically to legally different standards.

2. For the United States, we concentrate on African Americans in party politics and elected office. Ideally, we would add Latinos and Asian Americans to our analysis. However, this would also greatly expand the scope of the chapter, beyond what could be clearly and thoroughly presented within the parameters of one chapter. Of the twenty Latino representatives serving in the U.S. Congress, the vast majority are Democrats. The two Cuban Americans elected to the 107th Congress, however, are Republicans. Seven Asian-Pacific Islanders serve in the 107th Congress, including two U.S. Senators from the State of Hawaii. As in the case of Latino legislators, most Asian-Pacific Islanders are Democrats.

3. We use the term *minority* in the British case to include both black and Asian groups. Although these two groups certainly come to the political arena with different group-based interests and values, it is difficult to examine each group individually for two major reasons. First, the British census has made little distinction here, reporting statistics in what they term "white" and "non-white" groups. (We prefer the term *minority*.) Second, these two groups have forged alliances when lobbying within the Labour Party with the Black and Asian Socialist Society (BASS).

4. Party identification trends date back to 1979. While a longer time series is desirable, the low proportion of minority respondents in the British National Election Study before 1979 makes data analysis unreliable.

REFERENCES

Aldrich, John H. 1995. *Why Parties? The Origin and Transformation of Party Politics in America*. Chicago: University of Chicago Press.

Anwar, M. 1986. *Race and Politics*. London: Tavistock.

Barker, Lucius J. 1989. *Our Time Has Come*. Urbana and Chicago: University of Illinois Press.

Berman, Sheri. 1997. "The Life of the Party." *Comparative Politics* 30(1): 101.

Bochel, J. and D. Denver, 1983. "Candidate Selection in the Labour Party: What the Selectors Seek" *British Journal of Political Science*. 13:45–59.

Bobo, Lawrence, and Franklin D. Gilliam, Jr. 1990. "Race, Sociopolitical Participation, and Black Empowerment." *American Political Science Review* 84:377–393.

Branigan, Tania. 2001. "Race Relations High on List of UK Concerns." *The Guardian*, 22 June.

Browning, Robert P., Dale Rogers Marshall, and David H. Tabb. 1984. *Protest is Not Enough*. Berkeley and Los Angeles: University of California Press.

Canon, David T. 1999. *Race, Redistricting and Representation: The Unintended Consequences of Black Majority Districts*. Chicago: University of Chicago Press.

Carmines, Edward G., and James A. Stimson. 1989. *Issue Evolution: Race and the Transformation of American Politics*. Princeton: Princeton University Press.

Caul, Miki L. 1999. "Women's Representation in Parliament: The Role of Political Parties." *Party Politics* 5(1): 79–98.

Caul Kittilson, Miki. 2001. *Challenging the Organization, Changing the Rules: Women, Parties, and Change in Western Europe, 1975 to 1997*. Unpublished dissertation thesis, University of California Irvine.

Caul Kittilson, Miki, and Katherine Tate. 2002. "Thinner Ranks: Women and the Blanket Primary in California." In *Voting at the Political Fault Line: California's Experiment with the Blanket Primary*, edited by Bruce E. Cain and Elisabeth R. Gerber, 234–247. Berkeley: University of California Press.

Crewe, Ivor. 1983. "The Electorate: Partisan Dealignment Ten Years On." *West European Politics* 6:183–215.

Darcy, R., Susan Welch, and Janet Clark. 1991. *Women, Elections, and Representation*. Lincoln: University of Nebraska Press.

Downs, Anthony. 1957. *An Economic Theory of Democracy*. New York: Harper and Row.

Epstein, Leon. 1980. *Political Parties in Western Democracies*. New Brunswick, NJ: Transaction Books.

Franklin, Mark, Thomas T. Mackie, Henry Valen, with Clive Bean. 1992. *Electoral Change: Responses to Evolving Social and Attitudinal Structures in Western Countries*. New York: Cambridge University Press.

Frymer, Paul. 1999. *Uneasy Alliances: Race and Party Competition in America*. Princeton: Princeton University Press.

Gallagher, Michael, and Michael Marsh. 1988. *Candidate Selection in Comparative Perspective*. London: Sage Publications.

Gay, Claudine. 2002. "Spirals of Trust? The Effect of Descriptive Representation on the Relationship between Citizens and Their Government." *American Journal of Political Science* 46(4): 717–732.

Geddes, Andrew. 1998. "Inequality, Political Opportunity, and Ethnic Minority Parliamentary Candidacy." In *Race and British Electoral Politics*, edited by Shamit Saggar, 145–174. UCL Press. London: University College of London Press.

Grofman, Bernard, Lisa Handley, and Richard G. Niemi. 1992. *Minority Representation and the Quest for Voting Equality*. New York: Cambridge University Press.

Gurin, Patricia, Shirley Hatchett, and James S. Jackson. 1989. *Hope and Independence: Blacks' Response to Electoral and Party Politics*. New York: Russell Sage Foundation.

Hero, Rodney. 1992. *Latinos and the U.S. Political System: Two-Tiered Pluralism*. Philadelphia: Temple University Press.

———. 1998. *Faces of Inequality: Social Diversity in American Politics*. New York: Oxford University Press.

Inglehart, Ronald. 1997. *Modernization and Postmodernization*. Princeton: Princeton University Press.

Katz, Richard, and Peter Mair, eds. 1992. *Party Organizations: A Data Handbook*. London: Sage Publications.

Kirchheimer, Otto. 1966. "The Transformation of Western European Party Systems." In *Political Parties and Political Development*, edited by Joseph LaPolombara and Myron Weiner, 177–200. Princeton: Princeton University Press.

Leighley, Jan. 2001. *Strength in Numbers? The Political Mobilization of Racial and Ethnic Minorities*. Princeton: Princeton University Press.

Lovenduski, Joni, and Pippa Norris. 1993. *Gender and Party Politics*. London: Sage Publications.

Lublin, David. 1997. The Paradox of Representation: Racial Gerrymandering and Minority Interests in Congress. Princeton: Princeton University Press.

Mansbridge, Jane. 1999. "Should Blacks Represent Blacks and Women Represent Women? A Contingent 'Yes.'" *Journal of Politics* 61(3): 628–657.

McAdam, Doug. 1999. *Political Process and the Development of Black Insurgency, 1930– 1970*, 2nd ed. Chicago: University of Chicago Press.

Messina, Anthony. 1998. "Ethnic Minorities and the British Party System in the 1990s and Beyond." In *Race and British Electoral Politics*, edited by Shamit Saggar, 47–72. London: University College of London Press.

Nelson, William E., Jr. 2000. *Black Atlantic Politics, Dilemmas of Political Empowerment in Boston and Liverpool*. Albany, NY: SUNY Press.

Norris, Pippa and Joni Lovenduski, 1995. *Political Recruitment: Gender, Race & Class in the British Parliament*. NY: Cambridge University Press.

Norton, Philip. 1994. *The British Polity*. London: Longman.

Panebianco, Angelo. 1988. *Political Parties: Organization and Power*. Cambridge: Cambridge University Press.

Phillips, Anne. 1995. *The Politics of Presence*. New York: Oxford University Press.

Pinderhughes, Dianne M. 1995. "Black Interest Groups and the 1982 Extension of the Voting Rights Act." In *Blacks and the American Political System*, edited by Huey L. Perry and Wayne Parent, 203–224, Gainesville: The University of Florida Press.

Pitkin, Hanna. 1967. *The Concept of Representation*. Berkeley: University of California Press.

Powell, G. Bingham, Jr. 2000. *Political Responsiveness and Constitutional Design*. In *Democracy and Institutions: The Life Work of Arend Lijphart*, edited by M. M. L. Crepaz, T. A. Koelble, and D. Wilsford. Ann Arbor: University of Michigan Press.

Rich, Paul B. 1998. "Ethnic Politics and the Conservatives in the Post-Thatcher Era." In *Race and British Electoral Politics*, edited by Shamit Saggar, 96–116. London: University College London Press.

Riker, William H. 1965. *Democracy in the U.S.* New York: MacMillan Co.

Saggar, Shamit. 2000. *Race and Representation, Electoral Politics and Ethnic Pluralism in Britain*. Manchester and New York: Manchester University Press.

Sapiro, Virginia, Steven J. Rosenstone, and the National Election Studies. 2002. American national election studies cumulative data file, 1948–2000 [Computer File]. 11th ICPSR version. Ann Arbor: University of Michigan, Center for Political Studies [producer]. Ann Arbor: Inter-University Consortium for Political and Social Research [distributer].

Shukra, Kalbir. 1998. *The Changing Pattern of Black Politics in Britain*. London: Pluto Press.

Smith, Robert C. 1981. "Black Power and the Transformation from Protest to Politics." *Political Science Quarterly* 96(3): 431–443.

Studlar, Donley. 1986. "Non-White Policy Preferences, Political Participation, and the Political Agenda in Britain." In *Race, Government, and Politics in Britain*, edited by Z. Layton-Henry and P. Rich, 159–186. London: Macmillan.

Studlar, D., and Z. Layton-Henry. 1990. "Non-White Access to the Political Agenda in Britain." *Policy Studies Review* 9(2): 273–293.

Tarrow, Sidney. 1983. *Struggling to Reform*. Ithaca, NY: Center for International Studies, Cornell University.

———. 1989. *Struggle, Politics, and Reform: Collective Action, Social Movements, and Cycles of Protest*. Ithaca, NY: Center for International Studies, Cornell Univ.

———. 1998. *Power in Movement* Cambridge, UK: Cambridge Univ. Press 2nd Edition.

Tate, Katherine. 1991. "Black Political Participation in the 1984 and 1988 Presidential Elections." *American Political Science Review* 85(4): 1159–1176.

———. 1994. *From Protest to Politics, The New Black Voters in American Elections*, Enlarged ed. Cambridge: Harvard University Press and the Russell Sage Foundation.

———. 1997. "African American Female Senatorial Candidates: Twin Assets or Double Liabilities?" In *African American Power and Politics*, edited by Hanes Walton, Jr., 264–281. New York: Columbia University Press.

———. 2001. "African Americans and their Representatives in Congress: Does Race Matter?" *Legislative Studies Quarterly* xxvi: 623–638.

———. 2003. *Black Faces in the Mirror: African Americans and Their Representatives in the U.S. Congress*. Princeton: Princeton University Press.

Travis, Alan. 2001. "Losing His Grip." *The Guardian*, May 1.

Walters, Ronald W. 1988. *Black Presidential Politics in America: A Strategic Approach*. Albany: State University of New York Press.

Whitby, Kenny J. 1998. *The Color of Representation: Congressional Behavior and Black Constituents*. Ann Arbor: The University of Michigan Press.

Wilson, Frank L. 1994. "The Sources of Party Change: The Social Democratic Parties of Britain, France, Germany and Spain." In *How Political Parties Work*, edited by Kay Lawson, pp. 263–284, Westport, CN: Praeger.

Wolbrecht, Christina. 2000. *The Politics of Women's Rights: Parties, Positions and Change*. Princeton: Princeton University Press.

KRISTI ANDERSEN AND ELIZABETH F. COHEN

9 Political Institutions and Incorporation of Immigrants

THE MEMBERSHIP OF ANY POLITICAL SYSTEM evolves over time. People who are part of the system—as voters, activists, or leaders—are replaced by new generations. Written and unwritten rules change: Eligibility to vote or serve in electoral office is altered, acceptance of diverse kinds of people (women, for example) in high office expands, changes in public policy (e.g., with regard to campaign finance or the status of nonprofits) pull different actors into the system. Beyond normative and structural factors in political change are changes to membership from external sources such as immigration. The American polity in particular has seen successive waves of immigration since its founding.

The inclusion of immigrants in the American political system has been a subject of contention throughout the whole of American history. Decisions about controlling immigration have always been controversial and have become even more so since the September 11th attacks (Schuck 1998). Once immigrants arrived on American shores and worked in American cities, their roles in social and political life were still matters of heated debate. The Know-Nothing Party of the 1850s was famously concerned with limiting immigration and marginalizing the immigrant population (they proposed prohibiting immigrants from holding public office and increasing the length of the naturalization period). The ways in which immigrants have been (or might be) included or excluded, the extent to which their roles in the political system have been limited (to voting rather than leadership, for example), the potential for change implicit in the addition of large new groups of citizens or potential citizens have all been recurrent questions in our political history. The present moment is no exception: The recent upsurge of journalistic interest in the political involvement, partisan tendencies, and voting behavior of immigrant groups clearly reflects these groups' potential political importance in many areas of the country.

In this chapter we describe three factors that may shape the democratic inclusion of immigrants process—public policy, characteristics of immigrant populations, and attributes of political and civic institutions—and we try to put into historical perspective the present situation with regard to the political inclusion of immigrants. We focus in particular on the third factor, as the role of parties and other groups in structuring the contemporary politics, mobilization, and participation of immigrants remains a subject of debate among immigration experts and students of American politics.

What do we mean by *democratic inclusion?* It is certainly not a binary concept, where an individual or a group is either included or not. We can think of several indicators of the extent to which a group is included in our democracy such as the group's naturalization, registration, and voting rates; the extent to which the group can make its demands and interests known; the extent to which members of the group serve in elective and appointive office; and the density of civic and voluntary associations within the group. Just as sociologists have approached immigrant "assimilation" and "acculturation" from various conceptual viewpoints, political scientists have debated the meaning of inclusion (Wong 2002). A legalistic definition might see inclusion as dependent on naturalization and voting. While many scholars would agree with Michael Jones-Correa (1998) that "naturalization and voting do not by any means exhaust the full range of immigrant political participation" (42), such a conceptualization of inclusion—if often implicit— is widespread. Yet it is legitimate to criticize this definition on several counts. Many native-born Americans do not vote, of course, and even more important, politics neither begin nor end at the voting booth. Most of us would agree that political participation also includes such activities as writing letters to public officials, organizing with others to change local policies, or joining marches or demonstrations (Verba, Brady, and Schlozman 1995). One can engage in these activities, and others, without registering or voting. The line between incorporation into politics and incorporation into politically relevant elements of civil society is a fine one. It is not always clear where one ends and the other takes up. The activities of various community organizations, nongovernmental organizations (NGOs), and religious groups often have political overtones, are politically relevant, or impart political skills.[1] This consideration is particularly important given the increasingly central role of community groups and NGOs in the process of immigrant incorporation. In this chapter, however, we assume a fairly narrow notion of democratic inclusion that focuses primarily on the electoral system—and thus on the processes of naturalization, registration, and voting. A final definitional note: We use the terms *inclusion* and *incorporation* more or less interchangeably here. The theme of the book is democratic inclusion, an appropriately broad concept, but since our particular focus is largely on the intentional actions of policy makers and organizational actors, we think of their behaviors as being more or less "incorporative" toward immigrants.

PUBLIC POLICY ON IMMIGRATION

From 1850 to 1930 (the period of large-scale immigration from Europe), the foreign-born population in the United States increased steadily, from 2.2 million to 14.2 million. Foreign-born residents constituted just under 10 percent of the population in 1850 (the first year census data were collected on the nativity of the population) and varied between about 13 and 15 percent from 1860 to 1920. Immigration slowed markedly after this point; the foreign-born population fell to 9.6 million, or only 4.7 percent of the population, in 1970. Since 1970, immigration, primarily from Latin America and Asia, has increased rapidly. The 2000 Census counted more than 31 million foreign-born people, or 11.1 percent of the population. The rate at which immigrants have naturalized has varied over time, roughly conversely with the rate of immigration. The naturalization rate was 49.5 percent in 1920, rose steadily to 78.7 percent in 1950, and then dropped just as steadily to its current low point of 40.5 percent (Gibson and Lennon 1999).

These changing patterns of immigration have shaped and been shaped by significant alterations in immigration policies. Public opinion and public policy have been characterized at different times by quite different visions of the extent to which immigrants were expected to become a part of the polity and how that vision could best be achieved. In general, the metaphor of the "melting pot" (though with a strong assumption that the dominant ingredients would consist of Anglo-American and northwest European peoples and cultures) prevailed during the nineteenth century and public policy was consistent with this outlook. Restrictions on immigration were not enacted until the 1880s (with the Chinese Exclusion Acts) and legislation structuring the naturalization process was not adopted until 1906.

Before the Second World War, temporary immigration was seen as problematic and was the source of policy prescriptions specifically designed to encourage immigrants to naturalize, rather than working for a few years and then returning to their home countries. The infamous Dillingham Report, which was motivated by immigration restrictionists, and which ultimately culminated in the 1924 legislation restricting immigration to the United States, targeted the immigration of temporary workers as one of the problems with the supposed "new" wave of immigration Americans experienced in the late nineteenth and early twentieth centuries (King 2000). Temporary immigrants were considered to be parasitical on the U.S. economy, benefiting from their jobs without making an effort to assimilate and participate in U.S. society. *Americanization* was a policy undertaken to combat these and other pathologies of early twentieth century immigrant life in the United States. Beginning in 1916, agencies including the Bureau of Education, the Council of National Defense, the Department of the Interior, and the Committee on Public Information headed a national campaign to inculcate American social and political values into immigrants. At its height, Americanization employed federal, state, and locally mandated programs to assimilate and incorporate the vast numbers of immigrants that were considered to be living outside the American polity.[2]

Since World War II, both European nations and the United States have moved toward immigration models that do not merely tolerate temporary migrants but encourage them. Beginning in the 1960s, France and Germany were early pioneers in recruiting guest workers to do primarily manual labor. Germany recruited heavily from Turkey, while the French government took advantage of colonial ties with Algeria to bring in Maghreb workers. Germany later became the target of criticism for not only failing to politically incorporate their guest workers, but for actively cleaving to policies that made such incorporation impossible.[3] The French case was more complex—naturalization was possible, but assimilation was problematic, thus indirectly complicating political incorporation.

In recent decades, the United States has moved toward a guest-worker economy as well (Cohen 2003). While immigration to the United States has skyrocketed following the 1965 Immigration and Nationality Act (INA), much of this is commonly attributed to the generous family reunification allowances provided for by the INA (Zolberg 1999, 79). However, in the 1980s and 1990s, selective recruitment of workers with skills needed by American industries began to increase. Technologically skilled workers brought in on H-1B visas populated Silicon Valley and the pharmaceutical industry in New Jersey, among other places. Workers qualified to enter the home health care and nursing industries have also been sought with special visa programs facilitating the entry of anyone willing to do these kinds of work. More recently, President Bush has proposed that undocumented workers already living in the United States, as well as an unspecified number of new recruits, be allowed to apply for visas permitting them to stay and work in the United States for up to 6 years (Dewar 2004).

Currently, U.S. Citizenship and Immigrations Services defines temporary workers as "non-immigrants" who have "specialty occupations" or who "perform temporary services or labor if persons capable of performing such services or labor cannot be found in this country" (see 101[8 u.s.e. 1101]). The Immigration and Naturalization Service (INS) stated that around 260,000 non-immigrants were approved for H-1B visas in 2000 (U.S. Immigration and Naturalization Service 2002, 121, 134). Similar statistics for H-2B visas, which provide for the entry of mostly unskilled (and often migrant) labor are noticeably absent from the INS yearbook.[4] However, it seems clear just from these numbers that, in addition to a rise in traditional immigration, there has been a rapid increase in the number of people being admitted into the United States under conditions that structurally exclude the possibility of traditional political inclusion.[5] Were the recent Bush plan enacted, the number of structurally excluded immigrants would grow at an even more rapid clip.

Exacerbating official policies that create a class of unincorporated immigrants is the fact that the United States has one of the world's more benignly neglectful policies toward undocumented immigrants. Although the 2001 terrorist attacks led to increasing scrutiny of immigration laws and how they are enforced, the general stance toward illegal immigration has not been as rigorous as that of our European counterparts. Laws passed in 1986 and 1996 that were intended to give teeth to enforcement agencies have extended their mandate without adequately (and permanently) extending the resources needed to realize these goals. Daniel Tichenor (2001) reports that "tellingly, $34 million was spent on enforcing sanctions fiscal year 1987, $59 million in fiscal year 1988, and below $30 million annually in ensuing years" (263). In large part this may be attributed to the simple fact that, much as was the case in Europe following World War II, a good deal of the work being done by undocumented workers would not get done if they were ejected from the country (see, e.g., Cleland 1999). Furthermore, if Americans were to do those jobs, labor and consumer costs would skyrocket in many areas.

As temporary labor has become an increasingly important and permanent part of the U.S. economy and society, the lives of immigrants who are not institutionally incorporated have become more difficult. The Illegal Immigration Reform and Immigrant Responsibility Act (IIRIRA) of 1996 weakened the civil and social rights of non-citizens in a number of ways. It allows for the summary removal of people that INS inspectors believe hold fraudulent documents. Since the *Plyler v. Doe* ruling, most resident aliens in the United States had come to depend upon a relatively expansive range of civil rights, particularly due process and equal protection rights.[6] The sudden and retroactive nature of IIRIRA sent many eligible aliens scrambling to apply for citizenship. Those not fortunate enough to be able to naturalize were left in many cases with no protection against summary deportation. The restrictions of IIRIRA were exacerbated by the changes made to welfare laws in the same year, which made it harder for aliens to receive the legal aid necessary to pursue cases against deportation.

The extensive provisions of IIRIRA are too complex to be analyzed here, and some of the more egregious sections were—after protracted battle—declared illegal. However they are widely cited as a cause for the spike in naturalizations that followed their enactment (Schuck 1998). Similar effects are being seen in the wake of civil rights restrictions of non-citizens following the terrorist attacks of September 11, 2001. Increases in naturalization have also been a consequence of other recent public policies. In particular, in the last two decades, one of the most powerful tools in the incorporation of immigrants has been amnesty to allow undocumented immigrants to become "legal" and eventually to naturalize. In 1986, the Immigration Reform and Control Act (IRCA) set into effect policies that would ultimately naturalize 3 million formerly illegal aliens (Brimelow 1996, 28).

In summary, relatively little federal action has been taken to reduce illegal immigration. Moreover, since 1996, important rights and benefits immigrants could once count on have been withdrawn. With the exception of Bush's none too generous recent proposal to offer temporary visas to some undocumented workers, few have been extended. Because the United States does not consider itself to have an official guest-worker policy, the political incorporation of the people who make up this class, along with many of their more permanent immigrant counterparts, is not central to the political concerns of either political parties or national political institutions.

Federal policies toward immigrants and immigration have changed markedly in the period following World War II. Whereas the state once took a strong, frequently even paternal, hand in the process of incorporating immigrants, it now turns the other cheek. While this has had the positive effect of altering expectations regarding the degree to which assimilation is expected in order to achieve political standing, it also indicates a worrisome degree of indifference toward new and potential members of the polity. As a nation, we no longer care *for* our immigrants with social programs to aid their social welfare, and it is not clear how much we care *about* them as political beings either. While a return to the "melting pot" model would not be advisable, both from a practical and a normative standpoint it would seem advisable for the federal government to stand up and take note of immigrants in ways that go beyond their economic usefulness or their potential to pose a political threat.

CHARACTERISTICS OF THE IMMIGRANT POPULATION

While policies that limit or encourage the immigration of specific groups place general constraints on the possibilities for immigrant political inclusion, the nature of the immigration streams have given more concrete shape to the ways in which immigrants to the United States have become involved in politics and civic life. The middle of the nineteenth century saw an enormous influx of Irish immigrants, followed by Germans and Scandinavians and then, around the turn of the century, by Eastern and Southern Europeans including Italians, Poles, Czechs, and Russians.

Recent years have again seen a rapid increase in the number of immigrants entering the United States, and a similarly stark shift in the countries of origin most immigrants come from. The period of time between the implementation of the National Origins Quota Act in 1924 and the Immigration and Nationality Act of 1965 had been marked by a steady decline of immigration (Schmidley 2001, 15). Yet the U.S Census reports that by 2000 the percentage of the population that was foreign born was 11.1, up from 6.2 in 1980 and 7.9 in 1990.[7] Several dramatic internal patterns have accompanied and shaped this overall increase in immigration. In particular, in contrast to nineteenth century immigrants who often settled in farm or rural areas and were quite dispersed, these newer immigrants are concentrated in several states (California, Texas, Illinois, New York, Florida, and New Jersey), though there are smaller pockets in other areas. Furthermore, while the politics of early twentieth century immigrants in the United States were traditionally studied as an urban phenomenon, recent trends indicate shifting patterns of settlement. Michael Jones-Correa's (2002) recent research indicates that "the suburbanization of immigrants and minorities is approaching, and in some cases has surpassed, that of the population as a whole" (3, 4). The suburbanization of politics, and in particular politics that hold the possibility of racial and class conflicts, raises a host of issues that have not been studied by urban ethnographers and political scientists.

In addition to changes in settlement patterns, more often noted changes in the racial and ethnic makeup and immigrants' countries of origin have impacted the makeup, and consequently processes of incorporation, of immigrants crossing U.S. borders today. While immigrants earlier in the century were likely to arrive here on boats from Europe, a large proportion of contemporary immigrants come from, and maintain strong ties to, home countries in the Americas. An Irish immigrant at the turn of the century would have had a difficult time maintaining political or other ties to her homeland. A Mexican immigrant who arrived in 1990 has greater opportunity to travel home, maintain ties with friends and relatives in Mexico, and keep abreast of Mexican local and national politics. In addition, we must consider the fact that, while white ethnic immigrants entering the United States were often seen as racially distinct and inferior, the vast majority of contemporary immigrants are people of color, and as such, inherit a legacy of powerful ascriptive exclusion and exploitation.

Thus, the nature of the immigrant stream has changed in important ways over the past century. Though we are arguably a more tolerant society today, the "otherness" of immigrants from the Americas and from Asia, as opposed to Europe, means that racial categorizations and racial attitudes complicate an already complicated process. More generally, the diversity of current immigrants means that "they take on more-varied legal statuses [and] work in more-varied economic sectors," (Morawska 2001, 192), which suggests that group-based mobilization of immigrants may be more difficult than in the past.

Because immigrants have concentrated their settlements in particular states and cities, the politics of immigration is really often local politics elevated to a national stage (cf. Proposition 187 in California). Obviously *which* local political situations are important in this regard has changed over time and will continue to do so. Finally, particularly given the changes in transportation and communication, political experience in non-natives' homeland and in the immigration process should be taken into account and will have an important impact on the way individuals and groups encounter the American polity. On this score, there may be important distinctions between refugees and immigrants, or between those who arrive in the United States with political skills useful in a democracy and those who do not.[8]

NATIONAL AND LOCAL INSTITUTIONS

Though an important function of political parties is understood to be the mobilization of mass publics, American parties' overriding interest in winning elections has usually meant that they concentrate their energies on mobilizing those who are already party supporters, as Leighley points out in her chapter in this volume. Rosenstone and Hansen (1993), among others, make it clear that parties act strategically to target those whose behavior is predictable (and thus who are already participants in the political system). This produces a "rich get richer" situation where those with resources, for whom political participation is already less costly, are encouraged by parties to participate, and those for whom the costs of participation would need to be subsidized are ignored. But there are clearly times when parties need to expand their base to head off an electoral threat or are otherwise trying to increase the size and solidity of their coalition.[9] Thus our expectations about party behavior with regard to groups of new citizens (including immigrants) will be affected by the political context and, of course, by our understandings of the changes which have taken place in the nature of parties as organizations.

The Historical Role of Parties and Groups

It is certainly fair to say that in the late nineteenth and early twentieth centuries, concerns about the impact of immigration on American society and politics, while producing a number of anti-immigrant spokesmen and initiatives, also generated a number of institutional efforts to "Americanize" immigrants—

that is, to acculturate, assimilate, and incorporate immigrants into American society and politics.

To place the current situation into historical context, it is useful to look at the roles parties and other political and civic institutions played in the political incorporation of the last big wave of immigrants to the United States, which began in the late 1800s, peaked in the first two decades of the twentieth century, and was curtailed by the quota-based immigrant control legislation of the 1920s. Prior to the 1870s, the major source of immigration had been from northwestern Europe, and once arrived in the United States, many of these people dispersed to rural areas and small communities across the country. Rules governing naturalization and voting were lax; local parties may have been easily able to mobilize immigrants. In fact, in ten states prior to 1910 (primarily in the South and Midwest), aliens were permitted to vote if they merely declared their intention to become citizens (Gavit 1922, 217). Partially in reaction to the new streams of immigrants from southern and Eastern Europe beginning roughly in the 1880s, and partly as a function of the general Progressive desire toward rationalization, laws and practices were tightened. For example, in all but two of the ten states mentioned above, aliens' voting privileges were revoked via constitutional amendment.

The common image of machine politicians providing coal, food baskets, and patronage jobs to immigrants in return for votes—which figured prominently in Progressives' critical views of party politics in the early twentieth century—did have much truth to it.[10] For immigrants (and in-migrants from rural areas) the urban party organizations served as intermediaries between the citizen and the state. Though there are many examples of urban organizations dominated by a particular group (often WASPs or Irish) that ignored newer immigrants' interests, the organizations' desires to increase their electoral strength usually pushed them to make some accommodation to these groups. They typically recruited precinct leaders and other party workers who "shared the race, religion, and national origins of their constituents" (Allswang 1977, 28). At the same time, of course, these organizations were rife with corruption, committed to preserving the status quo and their own privileged position, and often quite resistant to thoroughgoing "incorporation" of immigrants. Thus the extent to which the urban party organizations—and electoral politics more generally—also served as channels of upward mobility for successive groups of immigrants has been a matter of debate. Nonetheless, as new groups did become involved in politics, it was primarily the parties that performed the function of providing them with connections to local and national government and with civic and political life more broadly.[11]

At the state and national levels, the political parties created "committees and bureaus to assist the alien in getting naturalization" (Gavit 1922, 32). To what extent the party efforts at various levels were mostly symbolic is not clear. Certainly in the press coverage of the elections of the 1920s and 1930s one can find frequent mention of efforts made by parties to secure the votes of various ethnic groups, speeches to nationality-based organizations, and so forth.

The 1932 presidential campaign saw the Democrats distributing three million pieces of foreign-language literature throughout the country in Italian, German, Polish, Russian, French, Yiddish, Hungarian, Slovene, Czech, Norwegian, and Swedish.[12] In the summer of 1936, Jim Farley, Roosevelt's campaign manager, announced the organization of a "foreign-language citizens' division" to include eighteen units. Periodically after this announcement, the Democrats sent out press releases to the effect that various prominent Greeks, Hungarians Italians, Germans, and so on had agreed to head the particular divisions.[13]

The resources targeted toward foreign-stock voters on behalf of the national party and the presidential campaigns were, by most indications, not generous. But FDR's campaigns could increasingly rely on the work of the local Democratic Party organizations, which worked to help immigrants become citizens and then register them to vote. Historical studies of urban Democratic and Republican organizations can illuminate the extent to which these local parties worked to incorporate new immigrants into the electoral process and into the national parties' constituent bases.

For example, Lizabeth Cohen's work on Chicago in the 1920s and 1930s describes how "ethnic politicians established such entities as the Polish Democratic Club of the 7th Ward or the Lithuanian Democratic League to help their constituencies exact their due from the party and the new agencies of government.... Ethnic organizations proved to be crucial conduits providing new members and resources to the CIO" and to the Democratic party (Cohen 1990, 362–363). Allswang describes Cermak's attempts to build local Democratic organizations—and loyalty—within the Italian and Black communities, the only two ethnic groups that had not supported him in the Chicago mayoral election of 1931 (Allswang 1971, 160–162). In Chicago, as in other big cities during the Depression, important issues were being nationalized and the local party organizations were building stronger ties with the national Democratic Party. Cohen describes this change:

> Even those ethnic workers who voted during the 1920s did not often identify politically beyond their local community. The kind of machine politics that flourished in Chicago during the twenties kept people dependent on a very local kind of political structure not tightly bound to any one major party.... Alliances developed around personalities, not policies.... There were general patterns, of course, in the voting of blacks and "new immigrant" groups who dominated Chicago's industrial work force—blacks and Yugoslavs strongly Republican; Poles, Czechs, Lithuanians and eastern European Jews frequently Democratic; Italians often split—but no party could count on a particular group's votes, except the Republicans on the blacks. It was a rare ethnic worker in Chicago who had a strong identity as either Democrat or Republican before the late 1920s.... All this changed at the end of the decade. Workers became drawn into an interethnic Democratic machine in Chicago under the leadership of Czech politician Anton Cermak that connected them not only to a unified Democratic Party on the city level but also to the national Democratic Party. (Cohen 1990, 254–255)

The local Democratic Party under Cermak utilized the issue of Prohibition (in referenda of 1919, 1922, 1926, 1930, and 1933, the city voted 72 percent to 92 percent against Prohibition) to "unite ethnic Chicagoans around Democratic politics [and] particularly to attract the workingmen and women among them" (Cohen 1990, 255; see also Kantowicz 1975).

Many other institutions and groups helped to integrate immigrant populations into American politics. If we assume that for most new arrivals, naturalization is a necessary first step toward political incorporation, a logical first question to ask is about the institutional pressures and channels through which immigrants were encouraged to naturalize in the early twentieth century. Pressure to naturalize often came from employers or unions: During and after World War I in particular, many companies demanded at least first papers for employment, and some unions required citizenship or intention for membership. And there was "wholesale naturalization" of immigrants in the U.S. Army during the war, as well (Cohen 1990, 213).

A number of civic groups emerged to provide naturalization assistance to immigrants. Some of these were nationality-based clubs and groups, as comprehensively described in the case of New York City by Roy Peel in *The Political Clubs of New York City* (1935). Fundamentally, these organizations (he studied 750 of them) aimed at integrating new citizens into political parties and thus into the polity. Some of these clubs were essentially either subsidiaries or affiliates of the political parties, but Peel argues that even the primarily social or recreational clubs "gradually, almost unconsciously, acquire political interests and attitudes" (Peel 1935, 262). Other groups, such as the National League for American Citizenship and the National Council on Naturalization and Citizenship, collected information on immigration and naturalization, took positions on issues involving immigration, and provided various resources to help in the naturalization process.

To summarize, in the early twentieth century, local Democratic and Republican Party organizations prospered in situations where dependent populations could be motivated (by means of service provision and jobs) to supply votes and political manpower. At the same time, the strong traditions of associationalism within immigrant communities made it easier for local and state party organizations to use existing organizational networks to bring these groups into their electoral coalitions. During the transformation of the Democratic Party between the 1920s and the 1930s, those dynamics were especially beneficial to the national Democratic Party, whose constituency was significantly reshaped with the incorporation of first and second generation immigrants. From that point until the late 1960s, immigration declined dramatically and the political incorporation of immigrants faded from national consciousness.

THE CURRENT ROLES OF PARTIES AND GROUPS

Though there is a great deal of scholarly debate about the extent to which parties have "declined" on various dimensions, there is consensus to the effect that the level of individual identification with the parties has decreased. Studies of realignment, failing to accurately predict shifts in partisanship, have moved toward trying to explain "dealignment." Political scientists have marked a distinct negative trend in attitudes toward parties, increased ticket splitting, and a lessening of identification with the parties (Wattenberg 1986). Election campaigns (and voter decision making) are more "candidate-centered" than in the past, and parties' power increasingly derives from their important roles as providers or services and funds to candidates rather than from their grassroots organizational vigor. At the same time that parties' roles in democratic politics have been shrinking, interest groups are widely being recognized as ever more plentiful and important to elections, grassroots organizations, and national politics. Campaign finance changes in the 1970s fed the growth of political action committees that represented narrow (often business oriented) interests or concentrated on single issues (Loomis and Cigler 1991, 11). The combination of a broad national stage and focused issue orientation has enabled interest groups to relate to their constituencies in ways quite distinct from political parties. Particularly for immigrant groups, who may understand their interests in ways that set them apart from broader class or interest affiliations, issue-oriented groups may offer opportunities for democratic inclusion and participation that parties, by virtue of their broad appeal, cannot. Theories that predict cyclic changes in the character of group-based politics in the United States may imply that this change is temporary, but it nonetheless has great relevance for the study of contemporary processes of incorporation.

Given this general context, we should not be surprised to find scholars arguing that political parties no longer serve the important role they once did either in naturalizing immigrants or including new citizens in political activities. Michael Jones-Correa's (1998) study of Latin American immigrants in Queens gives evidence of this shift. Jones-Correa's research indicates that, "Rather than lowering the costs for marginal political players, the Queens Democratic Party . . . raises them." Jones-Correa explains, "If actors are at the margins of electoral politics, as immigrants are, then they are ignored; if political players rise to the challenge of the machine, they are thwarted. Only if the new political actors succeed in mobilizing themselves on their own does the party organization attempt to bring them into its cycle" (Jones-Correa 1998, 70). In similarly directed comparative work on community organizations in New York City and Los Angeles, Janelle S. Wong concludes that, "mainstream political machines and party organizations are not the driving force towards participation in minority immigrant communities today" (Wong 2002, 4).

Further study will be required to confirm whether these conclusions about political parties apply nationally and to the full range of immigrant communities currently living in the United States. In the next few pages we will discuss some of our preliminary investigations of this question and consider the other institutions—NGOs, community groups, and immigrant advocacy groups—that appear to be playing important roles in the process of immigrant political inclusion.

One reason generalizations are difficult in the U.S. context is our federal structure. In a federal system, incorporation will naturally be complicated by the multiple locations of politics into which immigrants and other political outsiders must be incorporated. Much recent research focuses on the local level: voids left by the diminished strength of party machines and the degree to which these voids have been filled (to some extent) by NGOs and community-based organizations (CBOs), many of which are locally rather than nationally based (Wong 2002). But local citizenship, even though it may lead to the acquisition of nationality—a characteristic of and precondition for national citizenship—nonetheless does not constitute the entirety of citizenship in a federal system. CBOs and NGOs that incorporate immigrants into local politics are not necessarily well positioned to facilitate similar processes of incorporation at the national level. In order to fully understand how immigrants are being incorporated, we need to conduct and then integrate research on actions being taken at the local, state, regional, and national levels.

Looking at the national picture, it seems clear that political parties are not silent on either questions of interest to immigrants and new citizens or immigration and citizenship itself. Both national parties discuss immigration in their platforms; their stance on issues related to immigration and their rhetorical choices are similar: they welcome the "newest Americans," endorse family reunification, and stress the importance of English as a common language. Party platform differences include a commitment by Democrats to restore welfare benefits to legal immigrants and Republican's endorsement of more funding for border control. In our initial research we were particularly interested in evidence that the national and state parties were engaged in outreach activities involving immigrant communities. The Democrats, for example, broadcast a weekly radio address in Spanish; their website includes a "voter outreach" page which lists leaders and contact information for groups including African Americans, Asian–Pacific Islander Americans, Latino/Hispanic Americans, and "Ethnic Americans." The Republicans launched a monthly Spanish language TV show in May 2002. The first show focused on ways to reduce the school dropout rate among Latinos and increase the number of Latinos in college. The GOP also has a Hispanic Training Program for recruiting and training candidates.

Examination of party Web sites in states (in the fall of 2002) with significant numbers of recent immigrants (California, Texas, Florida, Illinois, New Jersey, New York, Arizona, New Mexico) suggests both symbolic and material efforts to reach out to immigrant groups and also suggests that there may be a good deal of variation among states and state parties. In New York, for example, the Republicans have links to newspaper stories on Latino appointed and elected officials; the Democrats have nothing more than a link to translate the main page into Spanish. California Republicans include a photo with the caption, "newly registered Republicans pose after a new citizen naturalization ceremony in July." They link to a state government Web site that explains how to register and include an email contact for information on participating in a number of voter registration drives. California Democrats have a Latino chairman as well as criticisms of the GOP gubernatorial nominee for his anti-immigrant stances and excerpts from their platform about protecting immigrant rights and reinstating welfare benefits for undocumented immigrants. In Florida, on the other hand, neither party's

Web site has immigrant-related references, links, or registration information. Illinois parties' Web sites are similarly uninformative. But both Democrat and Republican Web sites in Arizona include voter registration information, including (for Democrats) a link that lets the user register online and finds the correct polling location and (for Republicans) ways to get information about the Hispanic Coalition and the Asian American Coalition.[14]

Without further research, it seems impossible to say with certainty that political parties have rejected their former role as incorporators of aliens. Furthermore, if in fact political parties are no longer serving an important role in the incorporation of immigrants it may not be a result of inaction on the part of political parties. Instead, non-citizens may be following the lead of many citizens in rejecting political parties as a major form of entrée into politics.

It is therefore not surprising to find scholars concluding that national institutions and political parties are no longer serving immigrants in the ways they once did: Political parties no longer serve most people living in the United States in the ways typical of the period between the end of the Civil War and the middle of the twentieth century. A veritable army of political scientists is currently studying issues related to civic disengagement with institutional politics and the role that both intermediary institutions and civil society can play in reconstituting the political lives of American citizens. Perhaps some of the conclusions they make about the relationship to political parties of native-born Americans will also hold true for immigrants.

At the same time, it is clear that a wide range of local, state, and regional organizations are working to incorporate immigrants into American civic and political life. Even if immigrant registered voters are "off the radar screens" of campaigns, unions, and party organizations (Minnite and Mollenkopf 2001), they are definitely on the radar screens of many religious organizations, labor unions, ethnic associations, and service-providing organizations.

Labor unions, following years of ignoring immigrants or supporting anti-immigrant legislation through their desire to protect the jobs of their members, have recently begun to shift their position. The AFL–CIO decided several years ago to begin making efforts to organize immigrants (Jencks 2001a, 60). Religious organizations have historically and currently provided immigrants with social services, ways to maintain ethnic ties, and civic skills—though churches vary greatly in the extent to which they take explicitly political positions or even encourage political participation on the part of their members (Wong 2002, 19–23).

At least three other types of organizations are important features in the landscape of current immigrant politics and political involvement: local non-profit (largely service-providing) organizations, ethnic voluntary organizations, and groups explicitly organized to mobilize immigrant or ethnic voters. Chi-kan Richard Hung's research documents the substantial growth of Asian American nonprofit groups (including religious, cultural, service agencies, and activist associations) in eight metropolitan areas over the last ten years (Hung 2002). Janelle Wong's research illustrates the reach of some of these groups—a Los Angeles organization that provides legal education (including help with citizenship applications) to over 40,000 immigrants annually, for example. Wong states, "While not every community-based organization has an explicitly political agenda, many leaders see their organizations as having a political role in immigrant communities" (Wong 2002, 24). Certainly in providing assistance with finding jobs, obtaining social services, and naturalizing, these groups are playing an important role in the process of civic (if not political) incorporation.

Ethnic voluntary organizations play many roles in immigrant communities, from maintaining homeland (even town or village) ties to raising money for political causes related to homeland politics, to preserving cultural traditions, to protecting the civil rights of group members. The Chinese Progressive Association (CPA) of New York City, for example, conducts English and citizenship classes, as well as tenants' rights clinics, services for senior citizens, and recreational programs: "The CPA has recently moved into voter education and registration" (Lin 1998, 131).

Finally, voter education groups often target immigrants, sometimes in response to particular threats such as Proposition 187 in California. Ramakrishnan's recent research investigates the mobilization activity in 1994 and 1998 of groups such as the Southwest Voter Research and Education Project, the Mexican American Legal Defense and Education Fund, and the Salvadoran American Legal and Education Fund, all of which targeted newly registered voters, many of them first generation (Ramakrishnan 2001). Some groups with mobilization agendas are organized within particular immigrant groups. The Organizacion Salvadorena Americana (OSA) in Los Angeles, for example, aims to promote participate of Salvadorans, "first as informed voters and eventually as candidates" (Guarnizo 2001, 242).

The Southwest Voter Registration Education Project (SVREP), which "dispatches organizers to work with church and civic groups to register Latino voters," is attempting to mobilize 400,000 Latino voters in fifteen states in the South, the Southwest, and the West. "The hope is to work with these people through three election cycles, eventually turning them into habitual voters." We could not want a clearer statement of incorporativist intentions. "We do what political parties used to do two generations ago," says Antonio Gonzalez, president of SVREP (Freedman and Johnson 2002, 10–11).

Increasing use of the Internet has meant that organizations attempting to mobilize immigrants are not necessarily based in a single geographic locale. The 80–20 Initiative, for example, was an attempt to mobilize Asian Americans in the 2000 election. A small group formed a PAC (political action committee) in 1999 and then worked to develop as large an e-mail list as possible and invite these additional people to join. They maintained a Web site and sent out semi-monthly messages to raise political knowledge and build cohesion. By November 2000, 80–20 had more than 300,000 valid e-mail addresses and had raised $400,000. In August of 2000, members of the group met, argued, and decided to support Al Gore in the presidential election. The 80–20 Initiative made reasonably good progress toward its goal of getting 80 percent of Asian Americans to vote as a bloc for Gore (Davis, Elin, and Reeher 2002, 205–210).

Comparing the situation today with that of seventy-five years ago, it appears that parties no longer play the same central role in socializing and mobilizing new citizens they did in previous years. In Peel's (1935) book on political and civic clubs in New York (discussed above), he found that any organization that wanted to have some political impact or wanted to communicate demands to the political system would—probably sooner rather than later—come under the influence of or connect itself with a political party. It was simply the case that the points of entry into political decision making, in most cases, were controlled by party organizations and partisan officials. Today, lobbying groups, nonprofit organizations, and candidate organizations, among others, may encourage involvement of immigrants independent of any involvement in parties, and they may act as conduits by which immigrant groups can express their political interests and demands—again, independent of party organizations. There are a greater number of effective points of entry today. In our conclusion, we raise some questions about the normative implications of these changes for the nature of political access available to new (and old) groups in the population.

VARIATION IN INDICATORS OF DEMOCRATIC INCLUSION

One way to begin to develop a picture of the ways in which immigrants are—or are not—becoming involved in American political and civic life is to focus on the over-time, group-based and politico-geographic variations in the extent of that involvement. For example, are naturalization rates higher in some states than others? Are some immigrant groups voting at higher rates than others? How can we characterize the political jurisdictions where immigrants have achieved political influence? What are the connections between policy shifts at the national and state levels and increased immigrant naturalization, voting, and political organization?

Consistent with the policies of benign neglect with regard to immigration we have discussed above, we find a huge segment of the immigrant population that is, at least by many standards, unincorporated. Based on the census bureau's 1994 Current Population Survey Registration and Voting Supplement, of the total number of residents who were foreign born, only about 34 percent reported being naturalized.[15] Of these, about 64 percent were registered to vote and less than half of these reported voting in the 1994 elections. There are some variations in these rates by state. For example, the naturalization rate ranges from 23 percent in Texas to 43 percent in Massachusetts. Texas also ranks lowest in terms of registration of naturalized citizens at 57 percent, compared to Florida at 70 percent. Florida has the highest voting rate also, while Illinois' turnout is the lowest.

There are a number of possible explanations regarding the failure of large numbers of aliens to incorporate. First, it may be that the critical first step—naturalization—is seen by many immigrants as unnecessary. Peter Schuck advanced this view in his 1989 essay, "Membership in the Liberal Polity: The De-valuation of American Citizenship." What this perception of naturalization says about incorporation more broadly is not entirely clear. Schuck's thesis suggests that the rights that constitutional law and public policy make available to non-citizens tend to reduce "the value of citizenship as compared to resident alien status. These changes have not only minimized the alien's incentive to naturalize; they have also altered the social significance of citizenship" (1998, 164).[16] Essentially, Schuck suggests that institutional incorporation in the form of naturalization will continue to be viewed as unnecessary by a large proportion of aliens because they feel their social and civil rights are adequately protected. Schuck's normative judgment is that viewing naturalization as unnecessary means that immigrants will be perpetually unincorporated in ways that devalue American citizenship (or at least nationality). Alternately, some might argue that these immigrants are well incorporated in ways not necessitating naturalization.

This thesis is complicated by evidence that, during periods in which immigrant rights are threatened, mobilization rates rise dramatically (Ramakrishnan and Espenshade 2001, 870–910). Similar spikes are noted after the 1996 immigration and welfare legislation and are emerging in the wake of the recent terrorist attacks. The fact that immigrants do incorporate when they are faced with the possibility of diminished rights suggests that, rather than having a sense that citizenship and political incorporation into U.S. politics is without value, immigrants recognize its value but are deterred from incorporating by other factors.

Consistent with this, we would suggest that political incorporation is an act with high costs for some immigrants. In particular, moving toward political incorporation in the U.S. system requires the rejection of other affiliations and attachments. Long-standing prohibitions against dual citizenship have established U.S. citizenship as a zero-sum game. Until very recently, Mexican, Salvadoran, and Dominican citizens, who together make up a significant proportion of immigrants to the United States, were forbidden from holding dual citizenship (Martin 2002). For these and many others who arrived here from countries that prevent dual citizenship, institutional incorporation came at a high cost: not only were they far from their homeland with its many emotional attachments, but they would have to sever their official connections as well in order to incorporate in the United States. Naturalization and other forms of institutional political incorporation therefore came at a high cost, even for those who did not have immediate plans to return to their homelands.

CONCLUSION

Bringing these intermediary institutions into focus as important in the process of political incorporation raises a host of issues. Are immigrants being mobilized by groups that have relatively few resources and little power, as opposed to the groups who contribute to campaigns and are wooed by parties? How do we understand the complex relationships among party organizations at various levels, including campaign organizations, and the groups that work to mobilize immigrants? Getting back to our initial discussion of the concept of "incorporation," how do we fit not-explicitly-electoral mobilization of immigrants into our thinking about the process of incorporation, which has so often been conceptualized (even by us) as including naturalization, registration, and voting? What are the implications of the very issue- or candidate-specific incorporative strategies that non-party groups often undertake for long-term socialization and incorporation?

A discussion of various political institutions' relative roles in the incorporation of immigrants into U.S. politics would not be complete without a discussion of the normative merits of various conduits to incorporation. While there is a growing awareness within the academic and policy communities that the process of immigrant incorporation is changing as both the immigrant community and its relationship to incorporative institutions changes, the normative implications of these changes have not been fully explored. What do the shifts we have catalogued mean for democratic politics? Political parties were traditionally an important means through which immigrants became involved in American politics, and there is an implicit sense in much of the incorporation literature that parties ought to be taking a more active role in these processes. Democratic theorists credit parties as having crucial effects on the political incorporation of the entire population, including but not limited to segments likely to be disenfranchised by traditional routes to power such as wealth and birth. In *Polyarchy*, Robert Dahl (1971) argues that contestation, which generally takes place through party competition, is a crucial and decisive process for the incorporation of all strata of a populace. The right of franchise alone is not enough to guarantee incorporation; in some cases it may not be necessary, and in no case is it sufficient. Individuals need conduits through which they can come to identify, understand, and advocate their own interests within the larger context of democratic politics. This sets up a unique relationship between parties and the newly incorporated. Outside of the public education system, political parties are the closest thing Americans have to a nation-wide institutional framework for the pursuit of such knowledge and activities. "As a system becomes more competitive or more inclusive, politicians seek the support of groups that can now participate more easily in political life" (Dahl 1971, 23). Additionally, this effect is not unidirectional. Newly included people tend to alter the agendas and even existence of parties once they have been included in democratic (or polyarchic) politics. Dahl's observations about the role of parties in inclusion suggest that the weakening of ties between immigrants and political parties may mean that immigrants are being excluded from an important facet of the democratic process. Yet even a brief glance into the past, particularly into the Americanization period, demonstrates that parties did not always have the best interests of their immigrant members at heart—inclusion often came at the price of conformity that bordered on undemocratic. With the developing role of interest groups in the politics of inclusion, new questions must be raised regarding whether non-party institutions will perform these functions in more or less effective and desirable ways. Only then will we be in a position to evaluate the future of the democratic incorporation of immigrants into the American polity.

NOTES

1. A conceptualization that took into account the connections between nonelectoral and electoral activities might demand that to be deemed "incorporative," organizations and institutions would have to demonstrate that their activities help immigrants and new citizens to acquire lasting political self-sufficiency. In other words, even if the organization ceased to exist, its members would have acquired a legacy that allowed them to seek out and participate in other political activities. Included in this idea of an incorporative legacy might be organizing or participatory skills that could be applied in other political arenas as well as institutional affiliations including (but not limited to) U.S. citizenship, party identification, or other official political membership.

2. Americanization was also directed at native-born minorities including African Americans and Native Americans (King 2000, 92).

3. It was only in 2001 that the German government finally made changes to their citizenship laws that enabled children born in Germany to non-native parents to acquire citizenship.

4. These statistics may be hard to gather because H-2B visas bring many migrant workers to this country; however, it is equally possible that the statistics that could be gathered would be embarrassing, since compared to the median income of H-1B visa holders, many migrant workers earn very little.

5. This is fairly historically anomalous; in the past only prohibitions on the naturalization of Chinese workers who were already living in the United States (contained in the Chinese Exclusion Act which barred further Chinese immigration) and the Bracero program created similar structural exclusions.

6. *Plyler v. Doe* (457 U.S. 202, 1982).

7. Data for these estimates can be found at the U.S. Census website (www.census.gov).

8. In a Syracuse case study, officials of social service agencies serving refugees described Vietnamese and Sudanese, who were vitally interested in the politics of their homelands, as consequently being particularly politically "savvy" (Jessica Wintringham, final paper for WSP 615, Syracuse University, December 2002).

9. For example, Republicans in Oregon in the early twenties successfully mobilized women to counter the Ku Klux Klan's support of Democratic candidates (see Andersen 1994).

10. For a good, concise survey of this literature, see Allswang 1977.

11. The machines certainly did not value diversity for its own sake, and came only later to the habit of balanced slate-making, but Allswang (1977) points out about Tammany Hall that while they "did not really try very hard to get representatives of the new immigrant groups into elective office, its opponents went so far in the other direction as to make the Hall look good by comparison" (Allswang 1977, 75). For a critical view of parties during this period, see, e.g., Erie 1990.

12. FDR Governorship Papers, Box 866, FDR Library.

13. *New York Times*, 7 August 1936:6; 8 August 1936:2; 9 August 1936:25.

14. Obviously the lack of Web-based outreach indications for any given state or party does not allow us to infer that such outreach efforts do not exist. We were simply interested in getting a sense of the extent to which reaching out to immigrant groups seemed to be an accepted part of state parties' self-descriptions.

15. Comparisons are difficult, but in John P. Gavit's *Americans by Choice* (1922), he reports naturalization rates (for those in the country more than five years) of 74 percent for

northern and western European immigrants, and 38 percent for those from southern and southeastern Europe (210–211).

16. Schuck originally published this essay in 1989. He later recanted some of what he wrote after the 1996 changes demonstrated the fragility of the status of most immigrants in the United States.

REFERENCES

Allswang, John M. 1971. *A House for All Peoples: Ethnic Politics in Chicago 1890–1936.* Lexington: University Press of Kentucky.

——. 1977. *Bosses, Machines, and Urban Voters.* Baltimore: Johns Hopkins University Press.

Andersen, Kristi. 1994. "Women and the Vote in the 1920s: What Happened in Oregon." *Women and Politics* 14(4): 43–56.

Brimelow, Peter. 1996. *Alien Nation.* New York: Random House.

Chi-kan, Richard Hung. 2002. "Asian American Participation in Civil Society in U.S. Metropolitan Areas." Presented at Meetings of American Political Science Association, Boston, 2002.

Cohen, Elizabeth F. 2003. *The Myth of Full Citizenship.* (Dissertation manuscript on file with author.)

Cohen, Lizabeth. 1990. *Making a New Deal: Industrial Workers in Chicago, 1919–1939.* New York: Cambridge University Press.

Dahl, Robert A. 1971. *Polyarchy.* New Haven: Yale University Press.

Davis, Steve, Larry Elin, and Grant Reeher. 2002. *Click on Democracy: The Internet's Power to Change Political Apathy into Civic Action.* Boulder, CO: Westview Press.

Dewar, Helen. 2004. "2 Senators Counter Bush on Immigrants." *Washington Post*, January 22, A04.

Erie, Steven. 1990. *Rainbow's End: Irish Americans and the Dilemma of Urban Machine Politics, 1840–1985.* Berkeley: University of California Press.

Freedman, Dan, and Sasha Johnson. 2002. "New Voters: Shadow Falls Between Registration and Voting," *National Voter* (September/October).

Gavit, John P. 1922. *Americans by Choice.* New York: Harper & Bros.

Gibson, Campbell J., and Emily Lennon. 1999. "Historical Statistics on the Foreign-Born Population of the United States: 1850–1990." Working Paper No. 29, Population Division, U.S. Bureau of the Census, Washington, DC.

Guarnizo, Luis Eduardo. 2001. "On the Political Participation of Transational Migrants: Old Practices and New Trends." In *E Pluribus Unum? Contemporary and Historical Perspectives on Immigrant Political Incorporation*, edited by Gary Gerstle and John Mollenkopf. New York: Russell Sage Foundation.

Jencks, Christopher. 2001a. "Who Should Get In?" *New York Review of Books*, November 29, 57–63.

Jones-Correa, Michael. 1998. *Between Two Nations.* Ithaca: Cornell University Press.

——. 2002. "Reshaping the American Dream: Immigrants and the Politics of the New Suburbs." Paper prepared for the Annual Meeting of the American Political Science Association.

Kantowicz, Edward R. 1975. *Polish-American Politics in Chicago 1888–1940.* Chicago: University of Chicago Press.

King, Desmond. 2000. *Making Americans.* Cambridge: Harvard University Press.

Lin, Ran. 1998. *Reconstructing Chinatown: Ethnic Enclaves and Global Change.* Minnesota: University of Minnesota Press.

Loomis, Burdett A. and Allan J. Cigler. 1991. *Interest Group Politics*, 3rd ed. Washington, DC: Congressional Quarterly Press.

Martin, David A. 2002. "New Rules for Dual Nationality." In *The Reinvention of Citizenship: Dual Nationality and Federal Citizenship in the U.S. and Europe*, edited by Randall Hansen and Patrick Weil, 54–60. New York and Oxford: Berghahn Books.

Minnite, Lorraine C., and John H. Mollenkopf. 2001. "Between White and Black: Asian and Latino Political Participation in the 2000 Presidential Election in New York City." Presented at the meetings of the American Political Science Association, San Francisco.

Morawska, Ewa. 2001. "Immigrants, Transnationalism, and Ethnicization: A Comparison of This Great Wave and the Last." In *E Pluribus Unum? Contemporary and Historical Perspectives on Immigrant Political Incorporation*, edited by Gary Gerstle and John Mollenkopf, 175–212. New York: Russell Sage Foundation.

Peel, Roy V. 1935. *The Political Clubs of New York City*. New York: G. P. Putnam's Sons.

Ramakrishnan, S. Karthick. 2001. "Unpacking the Backlash: Political Threat, Institutional Mobilization and Immigrant Electoral Participation in the Mid-1990s." Paper presented at the meetings of the APSA, San Francisco.

Ramakrishnan, S. Karthick, and Thomas J. Espenshade. 2001. "Immigrant Incorporation and Political Participation in the United States." *International Migration Review* 35 (Fall): 870–910.

Rosenstone, Steven J., and John Mark Hansen. 1993. *Mobilization, Participation, and Democracy in America*. New York: MacMillan.

Schmidley, Dianne A. 2001. "Profile of the Foreign-Born Population of the United States: 2000." Washington DC: U.S. Government Printing Office.

Schuck, Peter H. 1989. "Membership in the Liberal Polity: The Devaluation of American Citizenship." In *Immigration and the Politics of Citizenship in Europe and North America*, edited by William Rogers Brubaker. Lanham, MD: University Press of America. Chapter 21.

———. 1998. *Citizens, Strangers, and In-Betweens: Essays on Immigration and Citizenship*. Boulder, CO: Westview Press.

Simon, Julian, 1999. The Economic Consequences of Immigration, Ann Arber: Universtiy of Michigan Press.

Tichenor, Daniel J. 2001. *Dividing Lines: The Politics of Immigration Control in America*. Princeton and Oxford: Princeton University Press.

U.S. Immigration and Naturalization Service. 2002. *Statistical Yearbook of the Immigration and Naturalization Service, 2000*. Washington, DC: U.S. Government Printing Office.

Verba, Sidney, Henry Brady, and Kay Lehman Schlozman. 1995. *Voice and Equality: Civic Voluntarism in American Society*. Cambridge: Harvard University Press.

Wattenberg, Martin P. 1986. *The Decline of American Political Parties*. Cambridge: Harvard University Press.

Wong, Janelle. 2002. "The Role of Community Organizations in the Political Incorporation of Asian American and Latino Immigrants." Paper Prepared for the Conference on Race and Civil Society, Racine, WI. Jan 11–12

Zolberg, Aristide. 1999. "Matters of State: Theorizing Immigration Policy." In *The Handbook of International Migration*, edited by Charles Hirschman, Philip Kasinitz, and Josh DeWind, 11–93. New York: Russell Sage Foundation.

III. GOVERNING INSTITUTIONS

PERI E. ARNOLD AND RODNEY E. HERO

A CENTRAL THEME of this volume is that institutions matter for the prospects of democratic inclusion in American society. The chapters in this concluding section address the significance of formal institutions for democratic inclusion in the United States.

For both citizens and political scientists, the term *institution* is associated first and foremost with governmental structures—legislatures, executives, agencies, and courts. Operating at the several levels of the federal system, these formal institutions authoritatively formulate and implement policies that allocate benefits and costs across society and its varying interests. As Harold Laswell (1958) famously asserted, political institutions determine "who gets what, when, and how." In particular, how these institutions intersect and interact with members of marginalized groups substantially affects the status and prospects of these groups.

The effects of institutions on democratic inclusion are twofold. Institutions shape and define the arenas of politics and the opportunities to access government that are available to marginalized groups. In turn, the rules and structures of formal political institutions influence the kinds of public policies produced by government. On the demand ("input") side, institutional processes and rules affect the activities of the diverse minority groups, social movements, and other mediating institutions as they seek to influence public policy making. On the policy ("output") side, institutions do not just process-aggregated demands as if they were political calculating machines. Institutions respond unevenly to different influence seekers because those making demands upon government vary in their political status. Additionally, institutions' responses to demands are constrained by their own organizational interests and collective conceptions of purposes and goals. The introduction to this volume refers to benchmarks of inclusion by which we can assess the status of marginalized groups in America. Most of those benchmarks require some acquiescence by or adjustment to the functioning of formal political institutions, whether it be legal actions to guarantee full access to political participation (benchmark 1) or the adoption of public policies that address group interests (benchmark 4). Ultimately, formal institutions are the critical channeling or filtering mechanisms whose actions may be more or less consistent with the democratic inclusion of disadvantaged groups.

Institutions matter, but can we identify regularities of *how* they matter? Or, are institutions just agglomerations that are accidents of politics and history? The new institutionalism, or its subspecies termed *the new institutional economics*, is instructive in this regard (Mayer 2001, 24). This perspective conceives of institutions as purposeful and rationally designed to fulfill given goals. As Terry Moe (1999) explains, the "structures that define an institution derive from the choices of individuals, while the choices of individuals derive from incentives and resources that are shaped by the institutional context itself" (145). In this perspective, those with authority design and alter institutions, guided by rational expectations and responding to opportunities and challenges in the political environment. From a new institutional perspective, how institutions work for democratic inclusion is a reflection of their designs, purposes, and control.

While the methodological approaches in the following five chapters on formal institutions vary, the new institutionalism is a useful heuristic for organizing and generalizing their insights. With that heuristic, we can consider how the institutions are constructed to intersect with new and marginalized groups. And we can inquire, diagnostically, what alterations of rules and structures would enhance an institution's role in democratic inclusion?

The first two chapters of this section probe local governmental institutions' impact on democratic inclusion. Susan Clarke argues that urban governmental institutions may have lost efficacy as mechanisms for democratic inclusion because radically changed social and economic urban contexts have had a splintering effect that institutions of urban governance have not yet managed to overcome. Kenneth Meier focuses on local governmental institutions responsible for public education—school districts. Education is typically perceived as pivotal to achieving a host of goals relevant to social equality. Meier shows how various factors associated with school district processes and governance—including electoral structures for the selection of school boards and the role of school bureaucracies—affect the possibilities and limitations of education as an instrument of democratic inclusion.

The final three chapters of this section examine institutions of national government. David Canon's assessment of minority groups' congressional representation focuses closely on debates over the legal and political dimensions of enhanced representation of African Americans in Congress. His discussion particularly illuminates the links between institutional changes (such as the evolution of reapportionment, voting rights, and campaign finance reform systems) and a more effective political voice for black Americans. Patricia Conley characterizes the presidency as institutionally ill suited for the politics of democratic inclusion. On the one hand, she notes, the presidency is potentially the most prominent point for advocacy of democratic inclusion. However, she argues, presidents typically have incentives that run contrary to furthering the interests of democratic inclusion. Concluding this section, George Lovell and Michael McCann examine the federal courts as institutionally prone to maintaining the political, economic, and social status quo. In this view, despite the courts' moments of almost mythic triumph in securing the rights of marginalized people, their norm is to produce a quite different kind of outcome.

Seen through the heuristic of the new institutionalism, these chapters portray American formal institutions as operating with relatively low attention to—or capacity for—democratic inclusion. America's democratic and constitutional aspirations take democratic inclusion as an ongoing and normal dimension of its politics. However, this analysis of formal institutions teaches the more realistic, if pessimistic, lesson that, by and large, these institutions are not well designed for the tasks entailed in democratic inclusion. But there is an insight here that is consistent with a fundamental element of America's constitutional aspiration. David Canon observes that ensuring representation and voice in Congress for African Americans changed the very institution of Congress. In effect, the structural changes that could ensure fuller representation in turn could make possible substantive consequences for democratic inclusion.

This section is an appropriate place to conclude our volume. Both politics and institutions matter. The way the American political system will become more inclusive is through a politics that can change institutions and, subsequently, through the policies consequent of those changed institutions.

REFERENCES

Laswell, Harold. 1958. *Politics: Who Gets What, When, and How?* New York: Meridian Books.

Mayer, Kenneth R. 2001. *With the Stroke of a Pen: Executive Orders and Presidential Power*. Princeton: Princeton University Press.

Moe, Terry. 1999. "The Politicized Presidency." In *The Managerial Presidency*, edited by James P. Pfiffner, pp. 144–161. College Station: Texas A & M University Press.

SUSAN E. CLARKE

10   Splintering Citizenship and the Prospects for Democratic Inclusion

TRENDS CONTRIBUTING TO THE SPLINTERING of American cities— and, by implication, to the splintering of citizenship itself—increasingly constrain the prospects for greater democratic inclusion of underrepresented groups in subnational settings. These splintering processes signal a reconfiguration of the relationships of the state, market, and civil society—relationships that have been presumed, in previous models of political incorporation, to shape the politics of democratic inclusion. Rethinking political incorporation models primarily in terms of the characteristics of underrepresented groups and new immigrants overlooks critical changes in the context in which these processes operate.

This chapter argues that these contextual features significantly influence contemporary incorporation processes and their subsequent impacts on policy responsiveness at least as much as the features of the groups themselves. In particular, our current understanding of local political incorporation tends to assume a state-centric polity, the preeminence of electoral institutions, the construction of racial and ethnic identities within a societal context bounded by national borders, and the eventual responsiveness of lagging political institutions to political competition and, on occasion, to social protest. Many of these assumptions are now open to question.

This chapter sketches some of these contemporary conditions and assesses the extent to which models of local political incorporation continue to be adequate for understanding the processes by which traditionally underrepresented groups gain representation and influence in local politics. Particular attention is given to the ways in which new economic growth processes, city competitiveness agendas, complex identities, weaker proximity and contact among diverse groups, the emergence of new governance arrangements, and the United States' "inequality-inducing" variant of federalism complicate democratic inclusion. In distinguishing between political incorporation models and more dynamic concepts of democratic inclusion, the conclusion argues for greater attention to three transformative factors: (1) the political geography of democratic inclusion, (2) the institutional attributes of governance arrangements, and (3) the discursive dimensions of democratic inclusion processes. Arguments to think of democratic inclusion in terms of local regimes of incorporation or local governance ecologies are put forward to indicate the type of research strategies that might overcome the shortcomings of existing models.

Splintering Citizenship and Democratic Inclusion

"Fragmentation" is a well-worn adjective to use in describing power and politics in American cities. Cities' contested roles in American federalism, the separation of their executive, legislative, and judicial powers alongside independent local government bodies for everything from schools to sports stadiums and, especially, the generations of struggle to reform and then un-reform local political institutions make this an apt descriptor.

To some, this fragmentation contributes to the "ungovernability" of American cities (Yates 1977). The conventional fragmentation argument centers on electoral institutions, public bureaucracies, and special governments; the ungovernability charge stems from the difficulties of coordinating these islands of dispersed power for larger policy agendas. But historically, under-represented groups potentially gained greater chances of access with frag-mented institutions. Cities with large, district–based city councils and many appointive positions in city agencies offered more opportunities for under-represented groups to gain a hold in the political system. Indeed, political reform campaigns sought to remove these footholds and make city govern-ment processes less easily accessible. In pushing for nonpartisan ballots, at–large elections, civil service rosters, and smaller city councils, reformers' goals of removing politics from city government meant less democratic voice for city residents but more influence for those able to navigate this cue-less political landscape.[1]

More recently, urban scholars see institutional fragmentation as only one element in the growing complexity and interdependence of urban life in the twenty-first century (Mayer 1994, 1995; Stone et al. 2001). The fragmen-tation of formal political institutions can pale in significance relative to the growing disjuncture of economic power and local political influence. For underrepresented groups, the shifting of key policy decisions to informal, shadow regimes of business and government elites presents daunting prob-lems in gaining democratic voice. As a result, scholarly attention has been directed to how informal governing coalitions and regimes form to over-come the collective action problems created by this disjuncture (Stone 1989, 2001).

These features profoundly affect the prospects for democratic inclusion at the local level. Using democratic processes to make a difference—to bring about changes desired by citizens—is at the heart of debates on democratic inclusion. Indeed, the norm of inclusion is often the criteria used to char-acterize the extent of democratic practice and the legitimacy of decisions made through democratic processes (Young 2000, 5). Inclusionary practices, whereby those affected by decisions are included in the decision-making pro-cesses in ways that allow them the opportunity to influence outcomes, are more democratic and more likely to be perceived as more legitimate than less-inclusionary practices. In the absence of inclusion, voting rights alone present a thin measure of citizenship to most democratic theorists although, as Hochschild (2003, 344) notes, even nominally inclusive citizenship is a relatively recent feature of American politics. As Suleiman (2003) puts it,[2] democratic society means inclusive citizenship—not just political participation and voting equality, but also control over the agenda. Inclusive citizenship encompasses opportunities for collective problem solving and deliberation, drawing on both public and private institutions to express and mediate diverse voices.

Political incorporation models bring this concern with democratic inclusion into the study of local politics, shifting attention away from democratic theorists' focus on democratic processes to consider local institutional frameworks.[3] Whether inclusive citizenship is structured around individuals or groups (Hochschild 2003, 340) is at the heart of many debates about pluralism, two-tiered pluralism, and political incorporation processes. Whether extant political incorporation models remain adequate for understanding how contemporary contextual features shape the prospects for inclusive citizenship is the question addressed here.

Fragmented Cities and Splintering Urbanization Processes

"Splintering" suggests something more than fragmentation. Graham and Marvin (2001) use the metaphor of "splintering urbanism" to characterize the unbundling of urban infrastructures into public and private segments. This resonates with our sense of fragmentation of local political authority but the splintering metaphor highlights the increasing divisions and demarcations attendant to the unbundling of public authority and the growing disconnect between local residency and local political voice. It is not merely a matter of policy tools such as privatization or vouchers, although they play a part in these processes. Rather, contemporary processes unbundling local public authority also selectively reconnect some people and some places to political power in advantageous ways. Thus, globalization and the disjuncture of economic power and local political authority in themselves do not lead to the diminishment of local political power. More precisely, local power is reconfigured in new networks and structures that extend political power differentially—and in ways that complicate issues of political incorporation. The splintering metaphor, therefore, directs attention not just to the fragmentation of public authority, but to the unbundling and reconfiguration of public and private spheres and the new linkages and network attendant to these processes.

Splintering complicates the familiar equations of more fragmentation leads to greater representation and incorporation prospects, while more reformed local institutions result in fewer representation and incorporation prospects. Generally, this overall pattern may hold if we "count" representation in terms of individual access to formal political institutions and modest gains in distributional benefits. The historical gains from access to these formal institutions, however, are undermined by the changing conditions in American cities and the potentially diminishing salience of formal electoral positions.

Beyond Fragmentation: The Splintering of the Urban Landscape

Splintering urbanism reflects an urban landscape where economic processes and political power increasingly transcend the local scale, and indeed may be independent of scale. In this splintering economic landscape, the bulky city government form of the industrial age is giving way. A leaner governmental structure—once again mimicking economic changes—features a specialization of urban political authority and a reconfiguration of political power that complicates political incorporation processes. Bringing political mobilization and participation in this new landscape into question suggests that the reformed/un-reformed nature of local political institutions may be less critical for political incorporation than the less-obvious features of these new power configurations.

TRENDS AND CONDITIONS CONTRIBUTING TO SPLINTERING PROCESSES

Although this brief sketch may seem to imply deterministic processes— economic splintering causes political splintering—they are, of course, contingent processes and context-specific. Political incorporation processes in different cities will take different forms, with different consequences for underrepresented groups.

New Economic Growth Processes Fracture Localities

If we think of local economies in terms of their contribution to the splintering of urban political life, several features stand out. In contrast to the expanding local presence of firms, utilities and transport, and retail markets in an industrial era, new economic growth is in specialized sectors—especially knowledge- and information-based sectors- and distinguished by links to more distant production and distribution points rather than local presence. Wealth is not derived from standardization of production processes and homogenization of factor costs and product lines at a particular locale but from flexible production and differentiated locations and products (Reich 1991; Clarke and Gaile 1998). The sources of value added, and profitability shift from internal economies of the firm—gained through more efficient use of the factors of production in any one location, as in the high volume industrial model—to production economies gained from minimizing transaction and linkage costs among a dispersed array of firms, suppliers, outsourcers, innovators, and so on (Scott 1992).

While few would be nostalgic for the noxious, toxic, and unhealthy neighborhood conditions of industrial cities, the workplace itself and industrial production processes provided grounds for organizing around common concerns. Ethnic conflicts and violence created "fault lines" (Katznelson 1981) hampering collective action; few political demands incorporated concerns of blacks or women. But the contrast between the proximity of work and community in the old economy and the fractures separating jobs from communities, new from old economy sectors, skilled from unskilled workers, and workers from each other in the new economy is telling.

The local reality of globalization flows and economic restructuring in most cities is an overlay of increasingly specialized new economy sectors and employment structures on old economy forms. The spatial and social consequences of these changes further divide neighborhoods, workers, and citizens. For most cities, the impacts of economic change have been partial and spatially specific. That is, the renaissance in downtowns such as Cleveland and Chicago occurs alongside areas, as in most cities, where "work disappears" (Wilson 1997). Furthermore, many features of the new economy make workers and local residents more vulnerable. Low-skilled non-unionized service jobs are the first victims of recessions. The wage structures in new economic sectors tend to be more polarized than in industrial occupations. And employment itself is now "flexible" and often episodic. For poor people, it takes two wage earners making minimum wages to support a family at the poverty level. Under these conditions, participating in local politics may demand more time and energy than is available; work, not political demands, may seem the pathway to a better life. In this "new politics of work and time" (Staeheli and Clarke 2003), the likelihood of political mobilization and participation cannot be read off of historical experiences, particularly to the extent those models reflect the experiences of white, male, industrial workers with standardized jobs and wages.

The sectoral shifts to a service and information-based economy may promote new economic growth, but they also generate growing inequalities. In some ways, the inequalities stemming from these economic changes are more invidious and difficult to confront than racial or gender discrimination because they appear to reflect a meritocratic distribution of rewards (Bluestone 1995). By valuing and rewarding education and training, these new sectors act as "the inequality express" (Bluestone 1995): They privilege those individuals with the proper credentials and distribute earnings in line with formal education. As the gap between the earnings of the more and less educated grows, inequalities escalate.

City Competitiveness Agendas Trump Social Concerns

Given the imperatives of interjurisdictional competition for investment, few local officials can be expected to put a priority on addressing a splintering local economy and weakened social fabric driven by factors beyond their control (Clarke and Gaile 1998). Instead, the emphasis is on ensuring the competitiveness of the city as a whole, a concept with enough plasticity to accommodate most political agendas (Sousa 2002). Somewhat paradoxically, there is a growing consensus that globalization does not mean "the death of distance" and the irrelevance of place (Cairncross 2001). Instead, cities and regions are seen as key locales for innovation, business incubation, cultural heritages, and development of human capital. Cities are viewed as central to national economic competitiveness, rather than the drags on competitiveness envisioned by the Reagan and Thatcher administrations in the early 1980s.

In Europe, more so than in the United States, problems of social inequalities and poverty are redefined as potential sources of "economic inefficiency" hindering national competitiveness in a global economy (Harloe 2001, 890). This offers a rationale for addressing the consequences of a splintering economy, not as an end in itself but as a means of advancing economic growth. But to Harloe and other critical theorists, the language of social inclusion is grounded in meritocratic assumptions and an emphasis on new linkages integrating productive (as compared to nonproductive) members of society. City competitiveness agendas, therefore, redefine poverty and exclusion policies in economic terms and leave aside political dimensions along with any significant role for public authority.

Translocal Identities and Bounded Democratic Institutions

The 2000 Census revealed the startling demographic and social changes in many cities that had resulted from new immigration patterns (e.g., Lewis Mumford Center 2001; Suro 2002). The political implications are less apparent, particularly if the links between ethnic and racial identity and political participation do not operate as in the past. Whereas immigrants and racial minorities historically used their ethnic identities and citizenship status to mobilize for local political incorporation, the contemporary arenas are more ambiguous.

Rather than constructing identities in the context of American society, recent immigrants—and to some extent, African Americans (Hochschild 2001) and Latinos (Jones-Correa 1998)—construct their ethnic and racial identities beyond the boundaries of the American nation state. To many, immigration is not an act of forsaking their homes but of moving within diasporas linking their American community and their home community (Jones-Correa 1998). As a result, their identities and their sense of citizenship are translocal—citizenship sentiments are dual or even multiple (Held 1999). Slow rates of naturalization and political participation may be less a function of lack of resources, time, or information than a reluctance to take on a citizenship that requires them to abandon these ties to family, friends, and home communities (Jones-Correa 1998). Thus, political incorporation may be stalled or partial or even segmented (Jones-Correa 1998).

This mobility and simultaneity makes the notion of political community a contested one. As Held points out, we've traditionally relied on jurisdictional boundaries to demarcate "the basis on which individuals are included and excluded from participation in decisions affecting their lives" (1999, 105). But when these boundaries no longer encompass the processes and decisions most critical to daily lives—now translocal if not transnational—the nature of constituencies, and the meaning of representation, not to mention the possibilities of political participation, are undermined. While Held's solution of cosmopolitan democracy appears remote, the diagnosis of the problem is immediate—the growing translocal nature of local politics in the face of territorially bounded democratic institutions (Smith 2001).

The Passing of Proximity?

Although "the death of distance" (Cairncross 2001) due to globalization appears overstated, splintering trends suggest the passing of proximity is more likely. Spatial segregation by class, race, and ethnicity is increasing in many cities, with modest declines for some groups (Lewis Mumford Center 2001). Indexes of dissimilarity show that many larger metropolitan areas continue to encompass groups with very little contact with each other. Though this was also true historically the scale today is larger and the consequences more troubling.

This decline of proximity stems from more than differential mobility patterns, however. Graham and Marvin (2001) underscore how universal provision of some public goods historically created a sense of connection and community. At both the neighborhood and city level, proximity meant similar services and similar citizenship. While careful not to romanticize a past solidarity and coherence in American communities—women and ethnic and racial minorities rarely shared these privileges—Graham and Marvin emphasize the ways in which common infrastructure supports the urban fabric. As these infrastructures become splintered and public goods are privatized or selectively distributed, the disconnect between proximity and coherence increases. New networks emerge, selectively connecting favored people and places rather than territorially cohesive places (16); by implication, less-favored people and places are hived off to lesser levels and quality of services—and inclusion.

By treating privatization issues in terms of social and spatial segregation rather than as matters of bureaucratic efficiency, Graham and Marvin highlight the normative citizenship dimensions of the growing trend of privatizing previously public goods and services.[4] This is especially significant when considering local schools: The universal provision of public education has been a deliberate citizenship strategy since the turn of the last century.[5] But many schools remain independent from local political systems; this legacy of the Progressive reforms means that the issues most important to parents of color—issues potentially capable of mobilizing them for political participation—are not accessible or accountable through conventional political incorporation. Latino and Asian representation on school boards, as well as in school administrations and classrooms, is weak relative to their majority status in public school populations. Even mechanisms such as site-based management arrangements do not appear adequate means of voicing the concerns of parents of color, especially in the absence of bilingual staffing and appropriate meeting schedules.

Splintering of public education is most obvious in the wake of the school reform movements. Support for school reforms from parents of color is likely to vary by city and school district: National public opinion data indicate little understanding of what charter schools and vouchers mean or of their consequences for public schools (see www.publicagenda.org). To claim that some reform will benefit or harm Latinos or Asians or blacks or whites, is to overlook the multiple identities and situations within those groups; a simple argument about distributional consequences of school reforms is unwarranted. Notably, views of these new constituencies on school reform are not stable over time: During the last decade, for example, many Latino organizations have moved from ambivalence toward charter schools toward advocacy of small charter schools geared toward supporting bilingual, culturally grounded education for Latino students.[6]

To date, there is little evidence of multi-ethnic cooperation on local school reforms. This may seem surprising since the "decentralization" elements of systemic reforms are portrayed as a means of providing more context-sensitive resources and services that respond to the needs of particular groups and neighborhoods. But to many parents of color, the educational reforms often introduced by state governments and the courts further weaken their voice in educational policymaking and enhance the exit options available to white middle class families (see Chambers 2002).

More Governance, Less Government

Governance dilemmas rather than fragmentation of government authority are the preeminent feature of this new political context. It is fair to say the "governance" concept is widely used but infrequently defined by urban scholars.[7] The scholarly emphasis increasingly is not on who governs per se but on how governance occurs (Rhodes 1996; Stone 2002), signaling a shift from analyzing the representation of groups in discrete political institutions to their involvement in more diffuse governance processes.[8]

The governance notion stems from the premise that governments are increasingly interdependent with other public and private actors—governance processes require that actors seeking mutual gains find ways to coordinate their efforts. In contrast to earlier views of the city as limited by jurisdictional boundaries and operating essentially as a closed system (e.g., Peterson 1981), cities now appear to be open systems in which the problems, actors, and potential solutions are not bounded by the city limits. External actors intervene in local decisions, advocating policy solutions for motives that may have little to do with the local situation. Nonprofit organizations, rather than government agencies, often bear responsibility for carrying out policy decisions and have become political actors as well as service providers (see Smith and Lipsky 1993; Hula and Jackson-Elmoore 2000).[9] State and federal governments both create and contribute to local problems as well as constrain the solutions possible at the local level. Reaching consensus on appropriate policy solutions becomes that much more difficult with multiple actors involved at different scales.[10]

This open, fluid setting—interdependent, complex, loosely linked actors and institutions with shared purposes but no shared authority—creates new conditions under which decisions must be made and renders such decision making more problematic. The governance dilemmas facing local officials are distinctive—many times local officials will be one of many actors with stakes in local decisions; no one actor will be able to produce the desired outcomes due to interdependent resources and actions; coordination of networks spanning public and private sectors will be critical to leadership; there is value added in combining resources rather than acting alone; local officials face shared purposes among multiple actors but in the absence of any hierarchy of control—and as a result, decisions are made by negotiations and inter-active processes, building on trust and consensus. And while the outcomes may be similar to those produced in the past by traditional governmental institutions—and can include governance failure—the processes are distinc-tive (Clarke 2000).

Democratic inclusion issues can be obscured by this emphasis on networks, coalitions, and strategic capacities. In the absence of a larger theoretical framework explicitly introducing such concerns, issues of race, ethnicity, and inequality are rarely addressed in governance analyses. Jones-Correa (2000) provides an exception, classifying city governance arrangements (what he calls *governing institutions*) in terms of the degree to which they are verti-cally or horizontally linked. In vertically linked governance arrangements, as in New York City, different networks at different scales overlap and are tied together by funding dependencies, dense networks of representative bodies, and historical patterns of reciprocity often reflecting a legacy of machine politics. In horizontally linked governance arrangements, as in Los Angeles, layered networks operate rather independently in a context of privatized pol-itics and dispersed political authority.

As he notes, nonprofit organizations enjoy a degree of autonomy in the free-wheeling horizontal arrangements characteristic of Los Angeles but op-erate in a fiscally precarious environment. As a result, identity-based groups act conservatively, avoiding turf challenges and overt competition with each other. In more vertical arrangements, such as in New York City, funding is stronger but tied to objectives that may not represent those of ethnic-based groups; incorporation in the dominant coalition comes at a price—potential cooptation and loss of representativeness. Incorporation into these arrange-ments, and the price paid, emerges as a more contemporary dimension of democratic inclusion.

"Thinking Federally"

Thinking federally (Elazar 1996) suggests the federal context influences the degree to which more local political incorporation is likely to mean greater equality for underrepresented groups in American cities. The expectation that greater democratic inclusion leads to greater social and political equal-ity can be thwarted by federalist arrangements. By implication, the rela-tionship of inclusion and equality varies under different types of federal arrangements.

Thinking of the U.S. system in comparative terms, as one type of federal arrangement,[11] puts U.S. federalism into the "inequality-inducing" rather than the "inequality-reducing" type of federal structures. Indeed, the United States is the outlier of inequality in exercises comparing different federal systems.[12] Stepan (1999) attributes this "inequality-inducing federalism" to the inability—leaving aside the question of political will—of the national government to make commitments to reduce inequalities for all citizens independent of their location. The "coming together" feature of U.S. federalism stresses "the equality of the states" rather than "the equality of citizens' living conditions" so that any national initiatives for equal provisions conflict with states' claim of federal intrusions into their areas of competence. Thus the political mechanisms and values embedded in the American federalist structure are likely to exacerbate the increasing inequalities associated with splintering urbanism. This is especially salient when local race relations are affected by national mandates (Lieberman 1998). The values entrenched in American federalism, therefore—along with the extensive range of veto opportunities, the absence of central authority, and now the declining federal role in community well-being—only exacerbate the local inequalities produced by splintering urbanism processes.[13]

ASSESSING APPROACHES TO LOCAL DEMOCRATIC INCLUSION

The major approaches to understanding local democratic inclusion include the conventional assumptions of the pluralist model, the more historically grounded argument of two-tiered pluralism, and the widely used model of political incorporation articulated by Browning, Marshall, and Tabb (1984, 1986) and applied by scholars to a wide range of cities (1990, 1997, 2002). These models are neither incorrect nor insensitive to changing contextual features. They may prove inadequate, however, in addressing how the splintering context of American cities—fractured local economies, competitiveness agendas, translocal identities, declining proximity, governance dilemmas, and an inequality-inducing federal system—alters the prospects for political incorporation.

Democratic Inclusion through Pluralist Competition for Power

Pluralist models of democratic inclusion presume formal, legal equality among individuals and groups; although not all groups have a voice in democratic processes, all groups have the potential to organize around their shared interests and to participate. The latent interests and uncertain potential for mobilization of unrepresented or underrepresented groups also may prompt those directly included in democratic processes to speak in their interest and compete for their support. Participation and representation are not likely in every arena but the dispersion of power and decision arenas makes access to some arenas more possible.

Democratic inclusion for unrepresented or underrepresented groups most often is seen as a question of mobilizing these groups for winning competitive elections, thereby directly representing their interests in formal decision-making bodies. Pluralist approaches view the potential for mobilization as contingent on resources internal to the group as well as the political opportunity structures and institutional arrangements creating incentives and disincentives for mobilization and electoral representation. These resources also presumably shape the odds of electoral success for any particular group.[14] There is clear evidence that representation of racial and ethnic minorities is

lower in cities with "reformed" political institutions where the threshold for inclusion is quite high.

In regime theory, the ability to get things done is an important aspect of power. Inclusion is a strategic factor, not necessarily dependent on group resources or mobilization. Power is contingent on the formation of governing regimes bringing together groups with access to critical resources. "Resource-rich" sectors such as business are attractive coalition prospects while, implicitly, resource-poor groups such as ethnic and racial minorities may be more problematic participants. They control few material resources; the typical use of selective incentives, or small opportunities (Stone 1989), to maintain coalitions among diverse interests may even exacerbate competition in multiethnic constituencies and destabilize coalitional arrangements. Ethnic, racial, and class cleavages may make these constituencies less attractive coalition members because of a lack of internal coherence. On the other hand, from a regime perspective, the influence wielded by racial and ethnic groups may be less a function of their internal resources than their control over resources and strategic knowledge essential for "getting things done" in their neighborhoods and relevant policy areas.

Pluralist models are often effective lenses for understanding the successes and failures of different groups in gaining a voice in subnational democratic processes. In Baltimore, a coalition of churches constructed an agenda of education issues and an organization to pursue that agenda—BUILD—that threatened to withhold votes from any candidate who refused to support the BUILD agenda for students of color (Orr 1999). In Los Angeles, Latinos have organized around community development issues for decades (Marquez 1993), more recently mobilizing around workplace issues as well (Dreier, Mollenkopf, and Swanstrom 2002). In addition, there is a significant increase in African American, Latino, and to a lesser extent, Asian, state and local elected officials across the United States (Geron and Lai 2001; Wong 2001, 2002). There is some evidence that candidates of color can bring out higher participation rates from minority groups but many, especially in mayoral races, depend on biracial coalitions (Stone 1989; Sonenshein 1994; Clarke and Saiz 2002) for electoral success. Whether this demands "deracialization" of political rhetoric and agendas is not clear (Reed 1995); once in office, however, most mayors of color are hemmed in by the same structural constraints and imperatives hampering any mayor—the need to bring in private investment and jobs in order to sustain tax revenues (Clarke and Saiz 2002) and to provide for public safety and order.

Heartening though such examples might be, it is difficult to generalize about the state of democratic inclusion through a pluralist lens. To trace the processes of group formation, mobilization, representation, and coalition or regime formation requires case studies of individual cities. Case studies are essential to understanding the processes of democratic inclusion but they can limit theory development because of the inconsistent standards used in assessing how successful different groups are in mobilizing and achieving their objectives (Sharp 2003). Toting up a democratic inclusion "score" from such disparate studies would be inappropriate.

Treating underrepresented racial and ethnic groups as "just another group" also is untenable, particularly as shifting demographics suggest a lag in the political system's responsiveness to the concerns of these groups and, indeed, as these group concerns become more distinctive and complex (Hochschild 2001). Furthermore, to the extent that passions, interests, and opinions stem from ethnic and racial identities rather than primarily material interests, our traditional understandings of pluralism and constitutional democracy are challenged (Hochschild 2003).

Most pluralist studies are forced to assume that lack of mobilization reflects a lack of shared interests; understandably, there is a focus on groups that have overcome the mobilization hurdle. But for many racial and ethnic groups, the inability to mobilize and gain representation cannot be attributed to the absence of shared interests or even sufficient resources (de la Garza et al. 1987; Kim 1999). Other barriers, such as citizenship status, discretionary time, organizational skills, and linguistic dilemmas may constrain participation (Bonilla et al. 1998; de la Garza et al. 1996; Staeheli and Clark 2003; Valle and Torres 2000). As preliminary results from the Pilot National Asian American Political Survey (NSF SES-9973435) indicate, these socioeconomic and linguistic inequalities can translate into partial and uneven political incorporation (Bonilla et al. 1998; Lien et al. 2001; Wong 2001).

In addition, pluralist models tend to slight the difficulties of organizing coordination and cooperation to promote agendas in a complex decision setting. As Stone (2002) and others underscore, cooperation is the exception rather than the rule in subnational politics. It requires trust and the ability to make commitments and follow through on them. This is a difficult burden for any group but especially trying for groups organized around contested identities of race and ethnicity. It also presumes a certain strategic capacity within and beyond local government. As political institutions splinter and the requisite actors necessary for any problem solving multiply, the ability to get things done becomes problematic. Even with trust and commitment, there must be processes and mechanisms in place to ensure that things do in fact get done.

Overall, as interest-based models of power, pluralist approaches view democratic inclusion in terms of organized groups and decision arenas. Politics and power are defined in terms of decisions and the inclusion of underrepresented groups in coalitions controlling these decision processes. This perspective not only slights political activities outside conventional arenas, it fails to account for the ideas that gain ground in cities and that shape local agendas before they ever reach the decision stage. These ideational factors can be crucial in determining the success of any group's efforts, independent of their mobilization and resources (e.g., Reed 1995). Stone (2002), for example, points out that the inclusion of African Americans in Atlanta, GA, Charlotte, NC, and other cities was contingent on linking their claims for justice to the economic success of the city. Arguing that Atlanta was "too busy to hate" reframed the race issue and linked it to an economic growth strategy. Similarly, the absence of a symbolic framework defining problems in ways that might bring together parents of color seems to hamper school reform in multi-ethnic cities (Chambers 2002; Sidney 2002).

Democratic Inclusion Limited by Two-Tiered Pluralism

The two-tiered pluralism model (Hero 1992) provides a more structural and institutional/historical outlook on minority politics (Hero 1998; cf. Lieberman 1998, 2002). The notion of two-tiered pluralism does not deny that pluralism, that is, "conventional" pluralism as described above, exists but argues that there are two tiers or "levels" of pluralism in American politics. Two-tiered pluralism describes a situation of simultaneous formal, legal equality along with actual practices in which tacit handicaps undercut equality for most members of minority groups. Even though individual members of minority groups may and do enjoy significant achievements and even though there are occasional successes for issues supported by minority groups, the different histories and circumstances of these groups interact with the political system in ways that limit their prospects for democratic inclusion (Hochschild 1995; Stone 1990; cf. King 2000; Smith and Feagin 1995, 5–9).

Two-tiered pluralism claims that pluralism exists in *form*, but not fully in *fact*, for groups whose "formative" or initial relationship within the United States was not entirely voluntary or consensual. Groups predominantly located within this second level, such as Latinos, African Americans, Native Americans, and Asians, have the formal rights of citizens. Indeed, they may be given special protection, being among the "protected classes" in a legal sense.[15] But two-tiered pluralism implies a marginal inclusion of minorities in most or all facets of the political process, a relatively pervasive phenomenon underscoring the subordinate status of minority groups (Hochschild 1995; cf. Smith and Feagin 1995).

The two-tiered pluralism approach puts pluralism into historical and social context. It provides an insightful means to understanding the limits on democratic inclusion imposed by historical circumstances political regulation and coercion targeting certain groups. Not only is it powerful theoretically and conducive to theory development about minority politics, it is amenable to empirical measurement and systematic comparison (see Hero 1992, 1998; Clarke et al. 2001). It also attends to inclusive citizenship and the limits of voting equality as a measure of democratic practice.

It is less effective, however, in explaining variations in democratic inclusion within underrepresented groups. Are all Asians, for example, in a similar situation in the second tier? Are all Latinos? If not, under what conditions do some parts of some groups such as Cuban Americans escape the second tier? The two-tiered pluralism model may be less effective in the face of escalating immigration and growing transnational identities. The two tiers themselves represent a society bounded within a nation state and with racial and ethnic identities constructed within these social parameters and constraints.

To the extent that immigrants no longer see themselves as irrevocably separated from their country of origin—and indeed may return regularly and remit payments to families left behind—they may now construct their identities in terms of dual societies. Their political attentions and shared interests may be more diffuse, not as a function of marginalization imposed by American political practices but as a conscious, nuanced strategy of constructing translocal identities.[16] Notably, by 1996, more Hispanics than blacks or whites agreed that groups should "maintain their distinct culture" rather than "adapt and blend into the larger society" (Hochschild 2003, 338). To both blacks and Latinos, political organizations based on race and ethnicity do not necessarily promote separatism (Hochschild 2003). These possibilities raise, of course, the larger question of agency. Although the virtue of the two-tiered pluralism model is its emphasis on history and structure, the links from these contextual dimensions to actual changes in democratic inclusion are less clear.

Democratic Inclusion Contingent on Local Political Incorporation

The conceptual framework for assessing political incorporation put forth by Browning, Marshall, and Tabb (1984, 1986, 1990, 1997, 2002) argues that the degree of political incorporation—the mobilization, representation, and incorporation of racial and ethnic groups into electoral decision-making bodies—drives policy responsiveness. Political incorporation is shaped by contextual variables or "preconditions" such as the growth of minority populations, population size and relative inequalities, a legacy of "demand–protest" activities, government structure, and the potential for coalition partners. Leadership is also a critical aspect in constructing coalitions and gaining greater incorporation (Sonenshein 1993).

"Descriptive representation" (Pitkin 1969)—having city council/mayoral positions held by members of the minority population—is a major dimension of the political incorporation model. To Browning, Marshall, and Tabb (1984), representational "parity" means having minority representation in approximate proportion to population numbers in the city as a whole. But political "incorporation" is more than representation: Incorporation measures the extent to which minorities are represented in "coalitions that dominate city policy-making on minority-related issues" (Browning, Marshall and Tabb 1984, 25, 18). Browning, Marshall and Tabb measure (1984) policy responsiveness to racial and ethnic groups through several indicators including contracting, grant allocations, city employment, membership on city boards and commissions, and other distributive, discretionary benefits. Their empirical findings indicate that different degrees of incorporation are associated with different levels of policy responsiveness on these measures.

Analyzing democratic inclusion in terms of political incorporation brings together historical and cultural contextual features in assessing minority representation and influence in local politics over time and across cities.[17] Analyses at three different time points (Browning, Marshall, and Tabb 1990, 1997, 2002) depict trends toward increasing multi-ethnicity in American cities, greater political incorporation of African Americans and Latinos, but constraints on further political incorporation stemming from contested identities among Latino and Asian groups in particular. These longitudinal analyses also chart the apparent decline of African American political incorporation in cities such as New York, Chicago, and Los Angeles where liberal biracial coalitions have been replaced by more conservative regimes. The combination of parity scores offering systematic measures of policy responsiveness and the more subjective assessments by each city "expert" of the degree of political incorporation of minority groups in different policy arenas details the patterns *and* processes of democratic inclusion.

Admirable though this project is, particularly the crucial emphasis on policy responsiveness, it tends to imply that greater incorporation of individual representatives means more influence and ability to alter distributive politics. These are important benefits for racial and ethnic groups (Stone 1989; McClain 1993) but not likely to affect the well-being of the community as a whole. So we are faced with the question of political incorporation—or democratic inclusion—for whose benefit?

It is likely that this model will have declining salience to the extent that it overlooks the growing role of nonelectoral and/or nonjurisdictional policy bodies. For example, political incorporation and representation in city-wide offices can pale in significance to the influence wielded by those controlling local schools. Latinos and blacks bring different experiences and preferences to school reform issues (Clarke et al. 2001) so the prospects for multi-ethnic coalitions and policy responsiveness are tenuous. Including parity scores and measures of political incorporation on nonelected and/or nonjurisdictional bodies is possible, but it blurs the meaning of political incorporation if these memberships are contingent on appointments rather than elections.

While the original emphases on biracial coalitions has expanded to reflect the diverse ethnic and racial constituencies in American cities, there is less attention to the distinctive participation and incorporation patterns across these groups (Marschall 2001). Given their demographics and settlement patterns, Latino elected officials are more likely to be elected from districts and in communities with sizeable Latino populations and to promote policies aimed at the Latino community. Asian American elected officials often are elected from non-Asian majority communities and districts; not surprisingly, these so-called non-ethnic representatives frame their agendas to address larger community issues (Geron and Lai 2001).

As in the two-tiered pluralism approach, the political incorporation model is weakened by its inability to contend with variations "within" racial and ethnic groups. Again, this could be addressed operationally but it may undermine the concept of political incorporation if the measures apply to increasingly small and possibly translocal communities. Furthermore, some analyses suggest that the political and cultural dimensions of African American and Latino identities preclude common, converging patterns (Browning, Marshall, and Tabb 2002). For example, the important differences in immigration experiences of Mexican Americans, Puerto Ricans, and Cuban Americans translate into significant political differences, undermining the prospects for a Hispanic voting bloc at the national level (de la Garza et al. 1992).

Such common identities may be less likely at the local level in policy arenas where competition for access to resources and power is strong.[18] Immigration has brought recent Latino and Asian immigrants into poorer neighborhoods, often pushing resident Latinos and Asians into historically black neighborhoods. In both instances, these newcomers appeared to be competing with black residents for jobs and housing. These frictions sparked riots in Los Angeles, Miami, Washington DC, and New York in the 1980s and early 1990s characterized by inter-ethnic conflict (Johnson et al., 1992; Jones-Correa 2000) rather than the stark racial violence of the 1960s.

To many of these new groups, political power in their communities seems to be controlled by other ethnic and racial groups. The previous struggles of African Americans especially contributed to political incorporation patterns and privileges that no longer correspond to their share of the population in many cities. To the extent that political incorporation is zero-sum (Jones-Correa 2001), the gains of these new underrepresented groups in formal political institutions could be at the expense of African Americans in many cities.

These contested political identities, complicated by class, cultural, and generational splits, make political mobilization and incorporation a complex matter. As Stone (2001) notes, Atlanta's biracial coalition functioned effectively on physical redevelopment and school desegregation issues but faltered in the face of changing economic and social conditions demanding different capacities and new forms of collaboration. Now, as city agendas evolve to include the working poor, low-performing schools, workforce development and livable wages, and lack of health care, as well as "morality" issues such as abortion and gay rights, these coalitions and distinctive models of political incorporation will be open to similar challenges.

As with other pluralist approaches, the focus on the decision stage rather than the pre-decision stage overlooks the ideational and institutional features contributing to democratic inclusion prospects: Institutions are present, but as arenas and playing fields for incorporation politics rather than as shaping those prospects. With the exception of local governmental structure, there is little sense of how institutions shape strategies and preferences nor is there recognition of the shifting local institutional landscape. In particular, there is little attention to the ways in which devolution complicates the incorporation process.[19]

As cities grapple with increasingly multi-ethnic and multi-racial populations, and with the politics of democratic inclusion that this entails, the factors identified in the mobilization/representation/incorporation framework (Browning, Marshall, and Tabb 1984) may prove to be necessary, if not sufficient, elements for understanding these new political alignments and agendas.

RETHINKING APPROACHES TO DEMOCRATIC INCLUSION

Incorporation and Inclusion

Although these approaches offer insights about democratic inclusion, several shortcomings are apparent. Most basically, there is a lack of precision in the use of the political incorporation concept. It is used to label a wide range of political activities, at different levels of analysis; furthermore, the causal mechanisms and processes contributing to political incorporation are often unspecified (Wong 2002). Nor do these approaches indicate how previous institutionalized linkages between earlier marginalized groups, such as African Americans, and the state shape and contribute to the difficulties in reaching new accords with new constituencies. As noted above, existing models of political incorporation are limited to the extent that they focus primarily on distributive politics, slight the growing role of nonelectoral and/or nonjurisdictional policy bodies, elide variations within racial and ethnic groups, retain a dominant–subordinate group orientation, and fail to encompass ideational and institutional features of local political settings. It is possible to tinker with extant models to bring in some of these concerns, although at some cost to the empirical utility and parsimony of current versions.

Political incorporation models presume a fixed institutional terrain as the object of political incorporation; in contrast, a focus on democratic inclusion recognizes that the different discourses, orientations, and political experiences that "the formerly excluded" bring to politics can transform political processes, institutions, and outcomes (Young 2000, 11). This more dynamic conceptualization of political incorporation processes suggests that democratic inclusion brings democratic transformations of local political arrangements. Future research strategies, therefore, must encompass analysis of the groups being incorporated, the institutions mediating and adapting to more inclusive processes, and the contextual features shaping these processes.

Three Challenges to Parsimony

Three aspects of this contemporary urban context undermine the prospects for parsimonious models in the face of complex, splintering contexts: (1) the political geography of democratic inclusion, (2) institutional attributes of nonelectoral governance arrangements, and (3) the discursive dimensions of democratic inclusion processes.

The Political Geography of Democratic Inclusion. Many scholars emphasize the need to direct attention to the subnational polities where political incorporation is most likely to occur and to be sensitive to the multiple layers of political power involved (Gerstle and Mollenkopf 2001; Jones-Correa 2001). It is clear that these experiences vary considerably over time and place so that the sites for political incorporation differ substantively and significantly. Latino and Asian immigration to ten metropolitan magnet areas in the 1990s—such as New York, Los Angeles, San Francisco, and Chicago—is now spilling over into labor markets in communities such as Seattle, Austin, Phoenix, Houston, Las Vegas, and Atlanta (Frey 1999). In twenty-five metropolitan areas, less than 60 percent of the population is now Anglo but in many other communities, Latinos and Asians continue to be small shares of the local population, despite extraordinary growth rates in the 1990s (Frey 1999). Political incorporation processes obviously will vary in these different local contexts as will the significance of time-related process such as the importance of length of residence and generational cycles (Wong 2002).

Political incorporation and democratic inclusion processes are multi-scale and complex. A more nuanced and differentiated understanding of these processes—a political geography of democratic inclusion—would analyze "the distribution of political power across geographic scales" (Agnew 2002, 6). Although the argument here is not that political incorporation now transcends scale completely, contemporary analyses must reach across geographic scales. Even though the locus may be urban or suburban or regional or state, it is increasingly inaccurate for the analysis to be limited to actors and political incorporation opportunities in these spatial arenas.[20] The increasing suburbanization of immigrant groups (Jones-Correa 1998) and of jobs and investment, for example, argues against the traditional urban focus of political incorporation models.

Institutional Attributes of Governance Arrangements. Given the problematic salience of electoral institutions and the emergence of governance arrangements with multiple actors, agendas, and decision rules, two institutional implications stand out: The local institutional landscape is denser, no longer primarily oriented to elections, and not necessarily state-centric; in addition, these diverse institutions are important for shaping preferences as well as mediating demands.

A splintering urban landscape does not imply that institutions are no longer relevant to democratic inclusion. Rather it suggests that more institutions are more important than traditional political incorporation models anticipate but that their relative importance is unknown, likely to vary by city and possibly by issue area, and likely to change over time. Representation and incorporation concepts assume a rather stable and consistent set of institutional arenas; they also traditionally focus on electoral mobilization and political incorporation aimed at making demands on the state. Many analyses of historical incorporation processes, for example, center on the roles of parties, unions, and political machines in mobilizing and incorporating urban newcomers. But parties are less significant today while community-based organizations, labor organizations, nonprofit organizations, religious institutions, and other non–party-based organizations offer different pathways to incorporation (Jones-Correa 1999; Wong 2002). And, of course, these institutional arrangements vary by community. What do we gain by abandoning this parsimonious model to deal with the untidy institutional landscapes in most cities today? And how might we go about reconstructing political incorporation models that can encompass these new institutional arrangements?

Historical institutionalist approaches emphasize the historical context in which institutions matter; this can include the types of broad economic and political changes noted here but historical institutionalism specifically highlights the iterative and dynamic effects of policy decisions at one point in time for choices possible at a later point (Rothstein and Steinmo 2002). In taking on this dynamic historical view, analyses of political incorporation would need to center on "critical junctures" for policy choices as well as the prospects for contingent but potentially path-dependent decisions (e.g., Lieberman 1998, 2002). These choices reflect—and institutionalize—coalitions of ideas and interests; as such, these coalitions contribute to the institutional resistance to change noted by many scholars (e.g., Jones-Correa 1998, 2000; Clarke 2001 et al). An historical institutional approach also extends the analysis from how institutions influence actors' strategies and present opportunities to promote or veto changes to the *ways* institutions shape preferences through social and cultural "logics" that essentially tell individuals what they "ought" to prefer in given situations and institutional settings (Clark et al. 2001, 9).

This promotes a move away from more structural, narrowly causal accounts of political incorporation to a more evolutionary analytic approach—unpacking historical patterns in order to understand the complex processes contributing to them. This does not mean abandoning any attempts at generalization but recognizing classes or clusters of patterns as amenable to analysis (e.g., Jonesth-Correa's (2001) classification of governing institutions as horizontal or vertical). It also encourages comparative analyses of political incorporation processes in cities sharing seemingly similar initial conditions and embarking on different incorporation paths (Lieberman 2002). Finally, it highlights the political conflicts likely when institutionally based coalitions of ideas and interests from previous generations—the racial politics linking African Americans and, in some cities, white ethnics and the state—face challenges from new constituencies.

The Discursive Dimensions of Democratic Inclusion Processes. Understanding political agency through political discourse allows us to construct an actor-generated sense of politics in place of the more "objectivist" knowledge based on aggregations of individual decisions and preferences. This is especially important in analyses of political incorporation, given the uncharted ways political identities are being constructed in American cities. Understanding how underrepresented groups construct their identities and characterize their situation is an essential step in analyzing inclusive citizenship (Sidney 2002; Hochschild 2003).

Analysis of the symbolic and discursive politics and policies in which democratic inclusion is embedded is also important. To many analysts, for example, the vaunted outreach by Presidential candidates in the 2000 election to Latino and Asian voters remained primarily symbolic and selective (Wong 2002). Looking more systematically at policy designs for new immigrants and underrepresented groups directs our attention to the framing of appropriate beneficiaries and the discourse used to justify allocations of benefits and costs. Schneider and Ingram (1997) emphasize how "policy affects the framing of problems and citizen identities through language, symbols, and discourse" (Ingram 2000, 3). Those controlling problem definitions and policy discourse may drive policy independent of the degree of political incorporation.

Policy designs also include "messages" about who is valued and who is a true citizen. To the extent that underrepresented groups receive different policy messages about the value of their participation and their "worthiness" to receive public benefits, their citizenship is degraded. This "degenerative" politics—fed by policies that treat different groups of citizens quite differently—represents "a policy failure as well as perversion of the democratic ideal of equal treatment" (Schneider and Ingram 1997; Ingram 2000). This notion of policy design reintroduces inclusive citizenship concepts to the analysis of political incorporation. In contrast, detaching citizenship from its larger political meaning can obscure the distinctive features of political incorporation processes at this point in time. By thinking about political incorporation in discursive terms, a stronger link between policy and democracy can be established by bringing together policy, identity, and citizenship.

Crafting New Research Strategies

From this discussion, and in light of other contributions to this volume, it is clear that analyses of democratic inclusion processes must move to the next stage. At a minimum, this requires consideration of the extent to which current conceptual frameworks are historically-specific and less useful in encompassing the changing conditions under which immigrants and other underrepresented groups seek a democratic voice. To the extent that we understand democratic inclusion as a transformative process, rather than the adjustment of newcomers to a fixed institutional setting, our future research strategies must encompass both group strategies and institutional rules and procedures. These are likely to vary across time and space: There will be many paths to political incorporation and many different sites of political incorporation. For researchers, the question now is how best to embrace these contingent and complex realities. To promote this discussion, this conclusion introduces two alternative research strategies for overcoming the shortcomings of existing models: thinking of democratic inclusion in terms of *local regimes of incorporation* or *local governance ecologies*.

One prospect for moving beyond singular models of political incorporation is to construct typological approaches that map the features of state institutions as well as group prospects for mobilization and participation. Thinking about *regimes of immigrant incorporation* is one possibility. Although initially developed at the national level to distinguish more individualist regimes—as in Great Britain—from more corporatist, group-oriented regimes, as in Sweden and the Netherlands, and more state-centered regimes as in France (Soysal 1994), similar configurations are evident at the subnational level. Regimes are distinguished by their coalitional features, with the expectation that institutions shape and constrain mobilization and participation activities. Inclusion in governing regimes would be the marker for incorporation rather than electoral representation; as noted above, the influence wielded by racial and ethnic groups may be less a function of their internal resources than their control over resources and strategic knowledge essential for "getting things done" in their neighborhoods and relevant policy areas. Inclusion in regimes of immigrant incorporation would reflect these strategic resources; with the regime focus on "getting things done," public institutions and distributive politics would remain central to the analysis but this more dynamic conceptualization of political incorporation processes would highlight transformations of local political arrangements.

Applying governance frameworks to political incorporation processes suggests another avenue, *governance ecologies*. By extending their scope to a range of public–private interactions and exchanges rather than limiting analysis to formal state institutions, governance approaches emphasize steering and coordination of a range of diverse actors (Pierre 2000). While these actors are not necessarily—or even likely—partners in coalitional regimes, their cooperation is essential to achieving mutual goals. Thinking in terms of *ecologies* rather than *regimes* captures the networked complexities of contemporary cities as well as the problematic roles of local government institutions. In contrast to the coherence, hierarchy, and intentionality implied by regime concepts, the emphasis is on the slippage and disorder inherent in the linkages of segmented groups operating with different, potentially conflicting, goals, agendas, ideologies, and incentives (Fong and Zdrazil 2003, 163). The notion of governance ecologies directs attention to the intermediaries linking—perhaps steering—the many arenas in which political incorporation occurs. Although not explicitly using these terms, Jones-Correa's (2000) work on the effects of vertical and horizontal linkages on political incorporation processes indicates the potential for thinking of governance ecologies.[21] These processes may be more central to inclusive citizenship than voting and participation although the prospects for incorporation in these more centrifugal, "post-institutional" (Pierre 2000, 243) governance arrangements requires further empirical research.

NOTES

1. In contrast to the contemporary setting, earlier struggles over political reforms took place in a period characterized by the expanding scale and scope of economic power and local political capacities. During this period of transition from a mercantile to an industrial economy, from small scale business to larger corporate organizations, other forces simultaneously also were pulling cities apart, from compact neighborhoods to early suburbs, and from relatively homogenous local cultures to more pluralistic ones. But the good city government rhetoric stressed consistency, standardization, and internal economies of scale to parallel similar features emerging in the economy. Reforms of political institutions created territorially cohesive—if socially diverse—at-large governing units. Given the historical legacy of separation of powers and checks and balances, there were limits on the extent to which city governments could mimic economic features; and not every city adopted, or wholly adopted, the reform agenda. But their increased scale and scope and representative political structures—whether reformed or un-reformed—meant that city governments were the obvious arena for underrepresented groups seeking access to material and political resources.

2. Referring to Dahl (1998).

3. For a more general analysis of local democratic processes as well as institutions, see Berry et al. (1993); also, Barber (1984).

4. This emphasis is especially salient in considering the provision of information technologies and the potential for creating technological ghettoes of ill-served consumers with little public voice or recourse.

5. John Dewey, for example, advocated the comprehensive development of public schooling to assist the nation in its integration of European immigrants. In his view, public schools were to be funded by the state and to be available to all youth living in the country. The "common school" envisioned by Horace Mann provided for a shared rather than selective enlightenment.

6. In 2001, the National Center for La Raza (NCLR), the largest national Hispanic advocacy organization, established a Charter School Development Initiative to assist Latino-serving community-based organizations in starting up new charters congruent with the educational needs of local Latino communities. Through planning, technical assistance, and implementation grants, NLCR hopes to support up to fifty new charter schools by 2005. In 2002, the Bill and Melinda Gates Foundation awarded NCLR $6.7 million for fifteen new charter schools to be established over a five-year period in California.

7. Most governance arguments are not linked to power or democratic inclusion concerns; they remain under-theorized and bolstered primarily by case studies of governance dilemmas in particular cities or clusters of cities (for exceptions, see DiGaetano and Klemanski, 1999; Stone 2001; Sellers, 2002; DiGaetano and Strom 2003). See the historical account of governance issues in Janet L. Abu-Lughod's *New York, Chicago, Los Angeles: America's Global Cities* (1999); also, see Stone (2002) and Pierre (2000).

8. Even with the rise of governance strategies, electoral institutions continue to mediate political incorporation in American cities. Indeed, current struggles in Baltimore to transform the multi-member city council districts to single-member districts speak to the significance of these institutional designs. The continuing evidence that there are greater numbers of blacks and Latinos in office in cities with district-based seats compared to those with at-large arrangements representation further bolsters these efforts. But, to the extent that city government and public authority is only one of many actors in local decision processes, the structures and mechanisms for political incorporation become elided. Even gaining representation and membership on elected and appointed bodies may be less salient if the key decisions are being made elsewhere—and by procedures crafted on a case-by-case basis.

9. Nonprofits often form their own policy networks and become political actors in diverse venues. Many Latino, Asian, and black organizations have pursued this path as well; it is not a matter of judging the effectiveness of nonprofits as policy tools but asking about the consequences of this trend for democratic inclusion.

10. There are other markers of this diffusion of public authority. It is amplified, for example, by the carving up of the city into special districts to govern certain parts of the city, such as Business Improvement Districts. The growing use of initiative procedures to circumvent elected government bodies at the state and local level is another feature of governance processes. Initiatives can be used by underrepresented groups to draw attention to salient issues but this is rare. The 1991 Children's Initiative (Proposition J) in San Francisco is an example of use of the initiative by political activists to support an issue that would benefit many underrepresented groups: It commits 2.5 percent of the property tax to services and programs promoting the well-being of those under eighteen years of age (Stone 2002). But this initiative came about through third-party allies rather than through political incorporation of minority interests. In many instances, these procedures are used to extend the power of waning elites or apprehensive voters/taxpayers by restricting benefits and protections for those not politically incorporated. The use of the initiative for "English Only" amendments and to abolish bilingual education programs in local school districts are recent examples.

11. In many studies of American federalism, there is a certain tyranny of scale—a reification of governmental units despite an argument that the analytic focus is on their interrelation. As a result, there is a tendency toward descriptive accounts reading off the current federalist situation from a spreadsheet of revenues, expenditures, and program initiatives. These clearly document the changing nature of federalism in the past two decades, as block grants shift power to the states and transfer payments to individuals replace national aid to cities. But these are arguably necessary but not sufficient elements in understanding the consequences of American federalism for democratic inclusion. Also, most American federalism studies are curiously nonspatial, uninformed by work in political geography or comparative federalism studies that might moderate some of the assertions about the consequences of federal structures. Most seriously, there is a tendency to explain federalism effects by referring to political and institutional fragmentation, a teleological argument at best.

12. On other measures of inequality, such as child poverty rates, elderly poverty, health care provisions, and Gini coefficients of economic inequality, the "coming together" federal systems such as the United States produce greater inequalities than the "holding together" federal structures such as Belgium, Germany, and Canada.

13. Of course, social change does occur in the U.S. federalist structure, in ways that reconfigure racial, ethnic, and gender relations at the state and local level. This is certainly the case with national civil rights legislation in the 1960s and 1970s, as well as affirmative action directives in the 1970s, and legislation supporting people with disabilities in the 1980s and 1990s. This raises the question of the conditions under which such changes occur as well as the obvious need to consider political incorporation prospects at these other levels.

14. The effectiveness of electoral representation is contingent on many factors, including the political incorporation of elected representatives in dominant coalitions and governing regimes (Browning, Marshall, and Tabb 1984, 1997, 2002; Stone 1989, 2002) and the strategic capacity of decision-making bodies. This coalitional perspective moves attention away from the assets of particular groups and draws attention to the conditions under which interests mobilize and coordinate their efforts. In *Politics in Black and White*, for example, Sonenshein (1993) emphasizes the importance of common interests, similar ideologies, and strong personal ties among leadership for successful coalition building. Regime theorists emphasize the linkages among groups as essential to policy responsiveness (Stone 1989; Henig et al 2001; Portz, Stein, and Jones 1999).

15. From the standpoint of two-tiered pluralism, however, the very need for "protection" or other "special" policies may be seen as indicating a flaw in pluralist processes. It suggests that the potential for mobilization and representation is not as even-handed and seamless as the pluralist model implies.

16. Although not allowed to return to Cuba, Cuban Americans may signify an early instance of this translocalism (Croucher 1997). The growing nationalism among some African Americans indicates another form of this dual sentiment, one that does not easily fit into conventional political behavior models (see Hochschild 2001). These examples suggest cohort effects for translocalism but also that these sentiments are not necessarily linked to recent historical experiences.

17. It is also amenable to analyses at different scales: Haynie's (2002) Political Incorporation Index for state legislators parallels Browning, Marshall, and Tabb's (1984) construct by tracing African Americans' numbers, leadership positions, party memberships, committee assignments and seniority in state legislatures.

18. An instrumentalist use of Hispanic identity can be used by some groups to strengthen their political standing, as Jones-Correa claims for Puerto Ricans in New York City.

19. In Denver, for example, there is little consensus on a Latino political agenda, much less one that would reflect the shared concerns of blacks and Latinos over poverty, affordable

housing, safety, health care and neighborhood well-being. And many salient issues seem beyond the control of local officials: Affirmative action is circumscribed by the courts, health care and welfare reform have devolved to state levels, local schools are independent of city officials, and senior-citizen pension programs are threatened at the national level (cf. Meier and Stewart 1991).

20. A critical stance to political incorporation processes is appropriate, given these assumptions. As Agnew (2002) sees it, boundaries, territory, place, and the state are key analytic concepts rather than "containers" for political action. And the focus on historical contingency rather than deterministic explanations means historical periodization sets limits on generalizations. These features resonate with the previous discussion of the growing translocal nature of local constituencies and identities and a rethinking of state-centric models of political incorporation (which also compels a more problematic take on the concepts of boundaries, place, and territory) through an emphasis on governance.

21. Long, 1958 is the seminal work on local ecologies. See also Fong and Zdrazil 2004.

REFERENCES

Abu-Lughod, Janet. 1999. *New York, Chicago, Los Angeles: America's Global Cities*. Minneapolis: University of Minnesota Press.

Agnew, John. 2002. *Making Political Geography*. New York: Oxford University Press.

Barber, Benjamin. 1984. *Strong Democracy: Participatory Politics for a New Age*. Berkeley: University of California Press.

Berry, Jeffrey M., Kent E. Portney, and Ken Thomson 1993. *The Rebirth of Urban Democracy*. Washington DC: The Brookings Institution.

Bluestone, Barry. 1995. "The Inequality Express." *The American Prospect*. 6. (Winter): 81–93.

Bonilla, Frank, Edwin Meléndez, Rebecca Morales, and Maria de los Angeles Torres, eds. 1998. *Borderless Borders: U.S. Latinos, Latin Americans, and the Paradox of Interdependence*. Philadelphia: Temple University Press.

Browning, Rufus P., Dale Rogers Marshall, and David H. Tabb. 1984. *Protest is Not Enough: The Struggle of Blacks and Hispanics for Equality in Urban Politics*. Berkeley: University of California Press.

———. 1986. "Black and Hispanic Power in City Politics: A Forum." *PS: Political Science & Politics*. 19 (Summer): 573–575.

———. 1990. *Racial Politics in American Cities*. New York: Longman.

———. 1997. *Racial Politics in American Cities*. 2nd ed. New York: Longman.

———. 2002. *Racial Politics in American Cities*. 3rd ed. New York: Longman.

Cairncross, Frances. 2001. *The Death of Distance*. Cambridge: Harvard Business School Press.

Chambers, Stefanie. 2002. "Urban Educational Reform and Minority Political Empowerment." *Political Science Quarterly* 117:643–665.

Clarke, Susan E. 2000. "Emerging Forms of Governance in the Context of Globalization." Background Paper prepared for the UN Centre for Human Settlements, Third Global Report on Human Settlements, July.

Clarke, Susan E., and Gary L. Gaile. 1998. *The Work of Cities*. Minneapolis: University of Minnesota Press.

Clarke, Susan E., Rodney E. Hero, Mara Sidney, Luis Fraga, and Bari Anhalt Erlichson, 2001. *The New Populism: The Multi-Ethnic Politics of Education Reform*. (manuscript under review)

Clarke, Susan E., and Rodney E. Hero. 2002. "Latinos, Blacks, and Multi-Ethnic Politics in Denver: Realigning Power and Influence in the Struggle for Equality." In *Racial Politics in American Cities*. 3rd ed, edited by Rufus Browning, Dale Rogers Marshall, and David Tabb, 310–330. New York: Longman.

Clarke, Susan E., and Martin Saiz. 2002. "From Waterhole to World City: Place Luck and Public Agendas in Denver." In *The Infrastructure of Urban Tourism*, edited by Dennis Judd and Alan Artibise, 168–201. New York: M. E. Sharpe.

Croucher, Sheila. 1997. *Imagining Miami*. Charlottesville: University Press of Virginia.

Cox, Kevin. 1997. "Governance, Urban Regime Analysis, and the Politics of Local Economic Development." In *Reconstructing Urban Regime Theory: Regulating Urban Politics in a Global Economy*, edited by Mickey Lauria, 99–121. Thousand Oaks, CA: Sage.

Dahl, Robert. 1998. *On Democracy*. New Haven, CT: Yale University Press.

de la Garza, Rodolfo O. ed. 1987. *Ignored Voices: Public Opinion Polls and the Latino Community*. Austin: Center for Mexican American Studies, University of Texas.

de la Garza, Rodolfo O., and Louis DeSipio, eds. 1996. *Ethnic Ironies: Latino Politics in the 1992 Elections*. Boulder, CO: Westview Press.

de la Garza, Rodolfo O., Louis Desipio, F. Chris Garcia, John Garcia, and Angelo Falcón. 1992. *Latino Voices: Mexican, Puerto Rican and Cuban Perspectives on American Politics*. Boulder, CO: Westview Press.

DiGaetano, Alan, and John Klemanski. 1999. *Power and City Governance: Comparative Perspectives on Urban Development*. Minneapolis: University of Minnesota Press.

DiGaetano, Alan, and Elizabeth Strom. 2003. "Comparative Urban Governance: An Integrated Approach." *Urban Affairs Review* 38(3): 356–395.

Dreier, Peter, John Mollenkopf, and Todd Swanstrom. 2002. *Place Matters: Metropolitics for the Twenty-First Century*. Lawrence: University Press of Kansas.

Elazar, Daniel J. 1996. "From Statism to Federalism: A Paradigm Shift." *International Political Science Review* 17:417–429.

Fong, Archon, and Scott Zdrazil. 2004. "Ecologies of Workforce Development in Milwaukee." In *Workforce Development Politics: Civic Capacity and Performance*, edited by Robert Giloth, 158–199. Pittsburgh: Temple University Press.

Frey, William H. 1999. "The United States Population: Where the New Immigrants Are." *U.S. Society & Values* (June). http/://usinfo.state.gov/journals/issv/0699.

Geron, Kim, and James S. Lai. 2001. "Transforming Ethnic Politics: A Comparative Analysis of Electoral Support for and Policy Priorities of Asian American and Latino Elected Officials." Presented at the American Political Science Association Annual Meeting, San Francisco, CA.

Gerstle Gary, and John H. Mollenkopf. 2001. *E Pluribus Unum*. New York: Russell Sage Foundation.

Graham, Stephen, and Simon Marvin. 2001. *Splintering Urbanism: Networked Infrastructures, Technological Mobilities and the Urban Condition*. New York and London: Routledge.

Harloe, Michael. 2001. "Social Justice and the City: The New "Liberal Formulation." *International Journal of Urban and Regional Research* 25:889–897.

Haynie, Kerry L. 2002. *African American Legislators in the American States*. New York: Columbia University Press.

Held, David. 1999. "The Transformation of Political Community: Rethinking Democracy in the Context of Globalization." In *Democracy's Edges*, edited by Ian Shapiro and Casiano Hacker-Cordsn, 84–111. Cambridge: Cambridge University Press.

Henig, Jeffrey R., Richard C. Hula, Marion Orr, and Desiree S. Pedescleaux. 2001. *The Color of School Reform: Race, Politics, and the Challenge of Urban Education*. Princeton: Princeton University Press.

Hero, Rodney E. 1992. *Latinos and the U.S. Political System: Two-tiered Pluralism.* Philadelphia: Temple University Press.

———. 1998. *Faces of Inequality: Social Diversity in American Politics.* London and New York: Oxford University Press.

Hochschild, Jennifer L. 1995. *Facing Up to the American Dream: Race, Class, and the Soul of the Nation.* Princeton, NJ: Princeton University Press.

———. 2001. "Pluralism, Identity Politics, and Coalitions: Toward Madisonian Constitutionalism." Presented at the American Political Science Association Annual Meeting, August, San Francisco, CA.

———. 2003. "The Possibilities for Democracy in America." In *The Making and Unmaking of Democracy*, edited by Theodore K. Rabb and Ezra N. Suleiman, 328–350. New York and London: Routledge.

Hula, Richard, and Cynthia Jackson-Elmoore. 2000. *Nonprofits in Urban America.* Westport, CT: Greenwood/Quorum Press.

Ingram, Helen. 2000. *Research Agenda for Public Policy and Democracy.* Irvine, CA: University of California at Irvine, Center for the Study of Democracy.

Jessop, Bob. 1998. "The Rise of Governance and the Risks of Failure." *International Social Science Journal* 155:29–45.

Johnson, James, C. Jones, W. C. Farrell, and M. L. Oliver. 1992. "The Los Angeles Rebellion of 1992: A Retrospective View." *Economic Development Quarterly* 6:356–372.

Jones-Correa, Michael. 1998. *Between Two Nations: The Political Predicament of Latinos in New York City.* Ithaca: Cornell University Press.

———. 2000. "Immigrants, Blacks, and Cities." In *Black Politics in America*, edited by Yvette Alex-Assensoh and Lawrence Hanks. Albany: New York University Press.

———. 2001. "Structural Shifts and Institutional Capacity: Possibilities for Ethnic Coorperation and Conflict in Urban Settings." In *Governing Cities* edited by Michael Jones-Correa, 183–209. New York: Russell Sage Foundation.

Katznelson, Ira. 1981. *City Trenches: Urban Politics and the Patterning of Class in the United States.* New York: Pantheon.

Kim, Claire Jean. 1999. "The Racial Triangulation of Asian Americans." *Politics and Society* 27(1): 105–138.

King, Desmond. 2000. *Making Americans.* Cambridge and London: Harvard University Press.

Lewis Mumford Center for Comparative Urban and Regional Research. 2001. "Metropolitan Racial and Ethnic Change—Census 2000." http://mumford1.dyndns.org/

Lieberman, Robert C. 1998. *Shifting the Color Line: Race and the American Welfare State.* Cambridge: Harvard University Press.

———. 2002. "Political Institutions and the Politics of Race in the Development of the Modern Welfare State." In *Restructuring the Welfare State*, edited by Bo Rothstein and Sven Steinmo, 102–128. New York: Palgrave Macmillan.

Lien, Pei-te, M. Margaret Conway, Taeku Lee, and Janelle Wong. 2001. "The Mosaic of Asian American Politics: Preliminary Results from the Five City Post-Election Survey." Presented at the Annual Meeting of the Midwest Political Science Association.

Lin, Jan. 1998. *Reconstructing Chinatown.* Minneapolis: University of Minnesota Press.

Long, Norton E. 1958. "The Local Community as an Ecology of Games." *American Journal of Sociology* 64:251–261.

Marquez, Benjamin. 1993. *LULAC: The Evolution of a Mexican American Political Organization.* Austin: University of Texas Press.

Marschall, Melissa J. 2001. "Does the Shoe Fit? Testing Models of Participation for African American and Latino Involvement in Local Politics." *Urban Affairs Review* 37:227–248.

Mayer, Margit. 1994. "Post-Fordist City Politics." In *Post-Fordism: A Reader*, edited by Ash Amin, 316–317. Oxford: Basil Blackwell.

———. 1995. "Urban Governance in the Post-Fordist City." In *Managing Cities: The New Urban Context*, edited by Patsy Healy, 231–249. Oxford: Basil Blackwell.

McClain, Paula D. 1993. "The Changing Dynamics of Urban Politics: Black and Hispanic Municipal Employment—Is There Competition?" *Journal of Politics* 55(2): 399–414.

Meier, Kenneth, and Joseph Stewart, Jr. 1991. *The Politics of Hispanic Education*. Albany: State University of New York Press.

Orr, Marion. 1999. *Black Social Capital*. Lawrence: University Press of Kansas.

Peterson, Paul. 1981. *City Limits*. Chicago: University of Chicago Press.

———. 1995. *The Price of Federalism*. Washington DC: The Brookings Institution.

Pierre, Jon. 2000. *Debating Governance: Authority, Steering, and Democracy*. Oxford: Oxford University Press.

Pitkin, Hannah. 1969. *The Concept of Representation. Berkeley*: University of California Press.

Portz, John, Lana Stein, and Robin Jones. 1999. *City Schools and City Politics: Institutions and Leadership in Boston, Pittsburgh, and St. Louis*. Lawrence: University Press of Kansas.

Reed, Adolph 1995. "Demobilization in the New Black Political Regime: Ideological Capitulation and Radical Failure in the Postsegregation Era." In *The Bubbling Cauldron: Race, Ethnicity, and the Urban Crisis*, edited by Michael Peter Smith and Joe R. Feagin, 182–208. Minneapolis: University of Minnesota Press.

Reich, Robert. 1991. *The Work of Nations*. New York: Basic Books.

Rhodes, R.A.W. 1996. "The New Governance: Governing Without Government." *Political Studies* 44:652–667.

Rosenau, James. 1992. *Governance Without Government*. Cambridge: Cambridge University Press.

Rothstein, Bo, and Sven Steinmo. 2002. "Restructuring Politics: Institutional Analysis and the Challenges of Modern Welfare States," In *Restructuring the Welfare State: Political Institutions and Policy Change*, edited by Bo Rothstein and Sven Steinmo, 1–19. New York: Palgrave Macmillan.

Schneider, Anne. L., and Helen Ingram. 1997. *Policy Design for Democracy*. Lawrence: University of Kansas Press.

Scott, Allan. 1992. "The Roepke Lecture in Economic Geography: The Collective Order of Flexible Production Agglomerations: Lessons for Local Economic Development Policy and Strategic Choice." *Economic Geography* 68:219–233.

Sellers, Jefferey. 2002. *Governing from Below: Urban Regions and the Global Economy*. Cambridge: Cambridge University Press.

Sharp, Elaine. 2003. "Political Participation in Cities." In *Cities, Politics, and Public Policy*, edited by John Pelissero. Washington DC: Congressional Quarterly Press.

Sidney, Mara S. 2002. "The Role of Ideas in Education Politics: Using Discourse Analysis to Understand Barriers to Reform in Multiethnic Cities." *Urban Affairs Review* 38: 253–279.

Smith, Michael Peter. 2001. *Translocal Urbanism: Locating Globalization*. Oxford, MA: Blackwell.

Smith, Michael P., and Joe R. Feagin., eds. 1995. *The Bubbling Cauldron*. Minneapolis: University of Minnesota Press.

Smith, S. R., and M. Lipsky. 1993. *Nonprofits for Hire: The Welfare State in the Age of Contracting*. Cambridge: Harvard University Press.

Sonenshein, Raphael. 1994. *Politics in Black and White*. Princeton: Princeton University Press.

Sousa, David J. 2002. "Converging on Competitiveness: Garbage Cans and the Global Economy." *Government and Policy* 20:1–18.

Soysal, Yasemin Nuhoglu. 1994. *Limits of Citizenship: Migrants and Postnational Membership in Europe*. Chicago: University of Chicago Press.

Staeheli, Lynn, and Susan E. Clarke. 2003. "The New Politics of Work and Time." *Urban Geography* 24:103–126.

Stepan, Alferd. 1999. "Federalism and Democracy: Beyond the U.S. Model." *Journal of Democracy* 10:19–34.

Stoker, Gerry. 1998. "Governance as Theory: Five Propositions." *International Social Science Journal* 155:17–28.

Stone, Clarence. 1989. *Regime Politics: Governing Atlanta, 1946–1988*. Lawrence: University Press of Kansas.

———. 1990. "Race and Regime in Atlanta." In *Racial Politics in American Cities*, edited by Rufus Browning, Dale Rogers Marshall, and David Tabb, 125–139. New York: Longman.

———. 2001. "The Atlanta Experience Re-examined: The link between Agenda and Regime Change." *International Journal of Urban and Regional Research* 25:20–34.

———. 2003. "Power and Governance in American Cities." In *Cities, Politics, and Public Policy*, edited by John Pelissero, 126–147. Washington DC: Congressional Quarterly Press.

Stone, Clarence, Jeffrey Henig, Bryan Jones, and Carol Pierannunzi. 2001. *Building Civic Capacity: The Politics of Reforming Urban Schools*. Lawrence: University Press of Kansas.

Suleiman, Ezra N. 2003. "Dilemmas of Democracy in the European Union." In *The Making and Unmaking of Democracy*, edited by Theodore K. Rabb and Ezra N. Suleiman, 134–158. New York and London: Routledge.

Suro, Roberto. 2002. "Latino Growth in Metropolitan American: Changing Patterns, New Locations." Washington DC: Brookings Institution, Center on Urban and Metropolitan Policy and the Pew Hispanic Center.

Valle, Victor M., and Rodolfo D. Torres. 2000. *Latino Metropolis*. Minneapolis: University of Minnesota Press.

Wilson, William Julius. 1997. *When Work Disappears: The World of the New Urban Poor*. New York: Vintage Books.

Wong, Janelle S. 2001. "Political Participation among Asian Americans: Mobilization or Selective Recruitment?" Presented at the Annual Meeting of the American Political Science Association, San Francisco.

———. 2002. "Thinking About Immigrant Political Incorporation." Workshop on Immigrant Incorporation, Mobilization, and Participation, Syracuse, NY, December 6: 1–3.

Yates, Douglas. 1977. *The Ungovernable City*. Cambridge: MIT Press.

Young, Iris Marion. 2000. *Inclusion and Democracy*. London: Oxford University Press.

KENNETH J. MEIER

April 17

11 School Boards and the Politics of Education Policy

Downstream Consequences of Structure

SCHOOL BOARDS ARE NEGLECTED INSTITUTIONS in the study of democracy, representation, and minority empowerment. Such neglect is unfortunate because education is a key policy forum that can produce positive externalities in other policy areas, in other political jurisdictions, and for other political institutions (Carnevale 1999). Education systems are crucial to the politics of democratic inclusion for two reasons. First, the most obvious is that education provides the skills and knowledge that are used by citizens to participate in the democratic process. The nature of education's contribution in this regard is so obvious that some measure of education is virtually mandatory in any study of political participation. Second, somewhat less obvious is the impact of the education process itself on democratic inclusion. Similar to all other processes, education provides greater benefits to some individuals than it does to others. Just as policy scholars accept that the meaning of a high school diploma varies a great deal from state to state and school to school, education not only improves the prospects for democratic inclusion more for some students than others; it might actually retard prospects for some.

The goal of this chapter is to sketch out some new research ideas based on what we currently know or what might be implied from a close look at education politics. The current state of scholarship will be referenced but not discussed in great detail; after all, the existing literature is fairly small and can be read in its entirety in a couple of days. Rather, this chapter identifies some key concepts and reasons out the implications of these concepts for democratic inclusion, minority representation, and empowerment. The chapter will deal with school boards, but the arguments here might have implications for city councils and other local governing structures. They also might be applicable in general terms to politics at the state level or at the national level, but those possibilities will not be discussed. The chapter will also limit its discussion to African Americans and Latinos only.

EDUCATION POLICY AND DEMOCRATIC INCLUSION

Politics is the determination of who gets what, when, and how (Lasswell 1958). The answers to these core questions depend on who is permitted to participate in the political process and what resources those citizens bring to the process. Democratic inclusion in my mind is the openness of the political system to all citizens, regardless of race, ethnicity, gender, economic disadvantage, or other ascriptive characteristics. The relationship between education and democratic inclusion is framed by two contradictory perspectives. The American ideal, as one, places great emphasis on education as the path to upward mobility, the equalizer that permits all individuals to participate in politics and economics on an equal basis. If anything, the American ideal views education as a solution to the inequities of democratic inclusion. The countervailing frame is best expressed by Marxists who contend that the purpose of education is to reinforce political biases, to structure education so that differences between groups widen rather than narrow (Bowles and Gintis 1976).

In reality, the American education system fits somewhere between the American ideal and the Marxist view. Just like most other policies, education has redistributive consequences; it benefits some students and prepares them to be democratic citizens more than it benefits others. My work has been concerned with the racial and ethnic correlates of a variety of educational practices that are widespread in the American educational systems (grouping, tracking, and discipline; see Meier, Stewart, and England 1989; Meier and Stewart 1991). The education system has established a set of institutional practices to group and sort children and then to design specialized curricula for them. At the extremes this includes sorting students into a variety of special education classifications or into various honors or college prep options. But even within the broad middle range of students, ability grouping is frequently used to sort students into homogeneous groups of "robins, bluebirds, and magpies." Ability grouping eventually becomes tracking with some students targeted for vocations and others for higher education. Decisions about grouping and tracking are done via a set of established institutional rules based on testing, other "objective" criteria, and subjective assessments. Studies consistently find that minorities are assigned in disproportionate numbers to special education, lower ability groups, and vocational tracks, and at the same time are less likely to gain access to advanced classes, advanced placement classes, gifted programs, and college prep tracks. The quality of education varies dramatically across these groups with little evidence that tracking into lower level groups provides any benefits for students. In short, this sorting increases inequities rather than eliminating them. Because the processes that generate racial and ethnic disparities in the student population are institutionalized in rules and standard operating procedures, school systems can discriminate without ever being conscious of doing so. Teachers and administrators apply what are accepted (albeit not uncontroversial) educational practices, and the result is unequal access to educational opportunities.

The sorting process in grouping and tracking also occurs in terms of discipline. Minority students are more likely to be disciplined, suspended, expelled, and in states that permit it, corporally punished than Anglo students. High rates of discipline in turn are associated with a greater probability of dropping out and a lower probability of graduating from high school or going on for additional education. Most striking, disparities in discipline are strongly correlated with disparities in grouping and tracking. Although the issue has not been examined to the same degree, there is also some evidence that ability grouping decisions are subsequently reflected in the high stakes standardized test scores that are now common in many states (Meier, Wrinkle, et al. 2001).

The racial and ethnic disparities in access to quality education has been documented by numerous scholars, the contribution of my colleagues and I is to directly link these outcomes, outcomes that cannot but affect future democratic inclusion, to politics and the distribution of political power (Meier and Stewart 1991; Meier, Stewart, and England 1989). We present evidence that both discriminatory electoral structures (at-large elections) and differences in political resources affect the ability of minority candidates to be elected to school board seats. We then demonstrate strong correlations between minority access to school board seats and the subsequent hiring of more minority administrators and minority teachers. Finally, minority teachers are associated with fewer negative consequences for minority students across a wide range of educational indicators (see Meier and Juewke 2003). In short, democratic inclusion, the ability of minorities to gain access to political power, is positively associated with positive consequences for minority students. Although we have not gone on to demonstrate the relationship, it is quite clear that greater access to quality education at time one should then affect democratic inclusion at time two.

The literature on democratic inclusion in schools and school district politics differs from much of the other literature on democratic inclusion in that it is consciously focused on policy outputs and policy outcomes and it pays more attention to bureaucratic politics and the overall governance system rather than just elected officials. Perhaps for these reasons, it is less likely to be cited by other students of democratic inclusion. The remainder of this chapter suggests some ways that the relatively unique focus on this literature might be useful to scholars of democratic inclusion in different research traditions. Seven issues will be discussed: institutional size, majoritarian structures, relationships among representatives, the case of minorities as majorities, the influence of exogenous actors, the relationship of social diversity to educational policy, and the feedback loop from politics and policy to citizens.

INSTITUTIONAL SIZE

Local governing bodies are almost always smaller than state or federal governing bodies. Although the size of school boards and city councils varies from city to city, 96.6 percent of school boards have nine or fewer members (40.8 percent have seven and 37.2 percent have only five).[1] The size of the school board has consequences for representation for both the representatives and the represented.

For representatives, variations in group size can change the dynamics of interaction. The structural differences between the U.S. House of Representatives with its more elaborate rules and procedures and the more free-wheeling Senate could be linked to size and the need to conduct business efficiently

(Congressional Quarterly 1993). Local governing bodies, because they are dramatically smaller, change the nature of interrepresentative relationships; small group dynamics assert patterns with each representative interacting more frequently with each of the other representatives. Frequency of inter-action in repeat games means that personal relationships are more likely to intervene and communication is more likely to be face to face.

One consequence of this smaller size might well be a solution to the collective representation dilemma. Studies of minority representation consistently find that minority representatives are likely to vote consistent with their constituents' interests and thus different from non-minority representatives (Bullock and MacManus 1981; Hero and Tolbert 1995; Whitby 1997; Bratton and Haynie 1999; Lublin 1999, 69). These dyadic representation impacts, however, are generally washed out at the collective level for state and national legislatures (Nelson 1991; Swain 1995; Cameron, Epstein, and O'Halloran 1996; Lublin 1999) so that an increase in minority representatives is not associated with an increase in policies/votes in favor of minority positions (see Weisberg 1978 on collective versus dyadic representation). The leading reason proposed for this phenomenon is the balancing of redistricting needs (Cameron, Epstein, and O'Halloran 1996; Epstein and O'Halloran 1999; Lublin 1999; Lublin and Voss 2000). To create districts more likely to send minorities to Congress means leaving the remainder of the districts less minority and more conservative, and conservative representatives from these other districts are likely to counterbalance the liberal policy orientation of the minority representatives.

For school districts, however, collective representation has been found in three separate national studies for Latinos (Fraga, Meier, and England 1986; Meier and Stewart 1991; Meier, Martinez-Ebers, and Leal 2002b) and two for African Americans (Meier and England 1984; Meier, Stewart, and England 1989). The smaller size of school districts' governing boards likely has much to do with this greater collective representation for two reasons (consider these hypotheses). First, the greater interpersonal interaction is more likely to facilitate log rolling on a wide variety of issues.[2] Repeat games allow for building trust among the board members, and trust can be used to overcome differences in policy positions or constituencies. Second, each board member is a far more significant piece of a majority than is a single member of Congress. With 435 members, some members of Congress can be ignored with few costs to building a winning coalition. With five members, any individual school board member needs to convince only two other individuals to become a majority.

MAJORITARIAN STRUCTURES

Government reform often includes the establishment of majoritarian structures (at-large elections, the initiative) or structures that have similar biases in terms of social class (nonpartisan elections, elections at odd times of the year, etc). The early twentieth-century education reforms (as well as the urban reforms) were designed to move control to centralized, majoritarian structures that were then augmented by professional managers (Tyack 1974). This section discusses the traditional structure debate involving school boards (at-large versus single-member district elections) and also a new structural reform, the centralization of control in the hands of a single elected official such as a mayor.

At one time the issue of single-member districts versus at-large elections was a hotly contested issue at the local level (MacManus 1978; Robinson and Dye 1978; Taebel 1978; Welch and Karnig 1978; Engstrom and McDonald 1981). The logic of single-member districts is that they permit minorities who are spatially compact to elect a member to a board with a much smaller percentage of the overall population. Smaller electoral jurisdictions also lower the resource cost of running for election and winning. Interpersonal contact becomes important in smaller jurisdictions, and that contact can substitute for more expensive media-based campaigns.[3] Both arguments imply that minorities will be at less of a disadvantage in single-member district systems.

Studies of this electoral structure generally disappeared from the political science literature in about 1990 with the publication of Welch's (1990) work that found no relationship between structures and minority representation for city councils (but see Zax 1990; Bezdek, Billeaux, and Huerta 2000). That lacuna is unfortunate for several reasons. First, most large cities with a sufficient minority population to elect a member to the city council had already been forced through litigation to modify at-large election systems. Most school districts, however, had not been forced to change; and the overwhelming proportion remained at-large election systems. In 2002 60.7 percent of school districts with more than 5,000 students used at-large elections for all of their members; only 26.7 percent used single-member district elections for all their members (the remainder used a mixed system with some board members elected at-large and others by ward or had an appointed board; Meier, Martinez-Ebers, and Leal 2002a). Second, most of the studies were done with relatively small samples and thus statistically significant findings were hard to achieve.[4] Recent work with larger samples (see below), however, continues to demonstrate the bias of at-large elections. Third, at-large elections are only one variation of majoritarian structures. Electoral structures come in a wide variety of forms that fit along a continuum from pure at-large systems to pure ward systems. In some cases, the electoral systems themselves are mixed—x members are elected from single-member districts and y members from at-large. In other cases, such as in San Diego, the process is mixed; school board members there run in single-member districts in a primary, and the top two candidates then face off in an at-large election (in an election by position that the entire school district votes on).

Recent large sample studies of city councils and schools demonstrate that at-large systems continue to disadvantage minorities. Meier, Martinez-Ebers, and Leal (2002b) in a study of 1,751 school districts with more than 5,000 students (96 percent of the total districts of this size were included in their sample) found that at-large elections significantly reduced Latino representation on the school board. Meier, Juenke, et al. (2003), examining more than nine hundred school districts in Texas where Latinos or African Americans were not a majority, found a similar negative impact for both groups. Both recent studies are consistent with Austin's (1998) finding for blacks in Southern cities; however, in contrast he found no impact on either Northeastern cities or on school boards in either region. Austin also investigated the certainty of representation given a specific percentage of the population. He found that district elections made the transformation from population to election with far more certainty (that is, the error for the estimated coefficients is smaller) than did at-large systems.

The impact of a variety of other structural forms merits extended study (see Engstrom 1994). Among the key variables are partisan elections, elections held during the normal November electoral cycle, at-large elections that elect individuals by position (e.g., seat A, seat B) rather than purely at-large, and hybrid systems such as San Diego or the Sisseton Sioux (Engstrom and Barrilleaux 1991). We know little about the electoral consequences of these other structures. Austin's (1998) work suggests that partisanship can overcome the electoral disadvantages that African American candidates have in at-large systems, implying that political parties seek to build an overall electoral coalition and thus mitigate some of the structural biases. At the same time, the history of political parties in regard to both African Americans and Latinos has been an initial resistance to incorporation of minorities often forcing them into radical third parties. Only after minorities gained sufficient political strength to force themselves into mainstream parties in large numbers have parties been responsive to the incorporation of minorities into political coalitions (see Meier and Stewart 1991, chapter 2).

A second generation of electoral structure studies is starting to focus on the impact these structures have on how the representatives themselves act. Logic suggests that a minority elected in an at-large system is likely to be different from a minority elected in a single-member district system. In the former case, the candidate would have to appeal to a city-wide majority and thus be less likely to have strong ties to the minority community. Nonpartisan slating groups, for example, were once used by majorities to select the "right" type of minority representatives in many cities (Fraga 1984). The Polinard et al. (1994) in-depth study of ten Texas cities and their school districts after a change to single-member districts showed that minority members were more likely to come from minority neighborhoods than did the previously elected at-large officials who were also minorities.

Indeed the logic of the early twentieth century urban reform movement was that at-large elections would break down the ties to neighborhoods and have representatives act on behalf of the entire city. This suggests that how a representative is elected should affect how hard the representative pushes minority interests. Only three studies have examined this election structure and subsequent representative behavior linkage. Meier, Martinez-Ebers, et al. (2003) with a national sample of school districts show that Latinos elected from single-member districts are associated with more Latino school board administrators and more Latino teachers than are Latino members elected at-large. Meier, Juenke, et al. (2003) in a similar study in Texas found exactly the same results for both Latinos and blacks.[5] Meier, Martinez-Ebers, et al. (2003) go one step further and examine the representational characteristic of appointed board members (appointed board members exist in dependent school districts). Although appointed school board members are highly representative in terms of the demographics of the city electorate, they have virtually no representational impact. In fact, Latino appointed board members are negatively associated with the proportion of Latino administrators and Latino teachers. Such a finding implies that appointed board members act as representatives of the mayor rather than the citizens. The third study, Austin (1998), uses a set of six carefully selected cities to examine behavior on city councils. He finds that district elections keep racial issues on the legislative agenda. Both at-large and mixed electoral systems in contrast downplay race in day-to-day decision making. Austin also finds that partisan elections contribute to biracial coalitions, primarily via the Democratic Party.

Robinson (2002) proposes that rethinking what representation means might lead us to additional findings on representation. Robinson argues that representation is a process, and as a result, might change how things are done rather than the actual outputs of a political jurisdiction. He demonstrates in the area of bilingual education that having Latino members on a school board changes the relationship between other key variables and the hiring of bilingual education teachers. The logic of his analysis suggests that we should systematically compare jurisdictions with representation and without representation on how they transform inputs into outputs. In particular, he finds that representation affects the relationship of minority enrollments to bilingual teachers in some interesting ways.

Except for Robinson (2002), these second-generation representation studies have only examined the patronage side of policy, the appointment of minorities to administrative and teaching positions. While minority administrators and especially teachers have significant impacts on policies that benefit minority students on everything from academic tracking, discipline, and attendance to standardized test scores and potential readiness for higher education (Meier, Stewart, and England 1989; Meier and Stewart 1991; Meier, Wrinkle and Polinard 1999; Meier, Eller, et al. 2001), the topic of elected representatives' direct policy impact (as opposed to indirect through bureaucratic means) remains to be investigated.

Much of the work on policy impact and the bureaucracy appears under the rubric of the theory of representative bureaucracy.[6] A fair amount of that literature assesses the impact of bureaucratic representation and does not consider any influence from electoral institutions (see Hindera 1993a; Hindera 1993b; Selden 1997). The studies have only found this influence in three policy areas—Equal Employment Opportunity Commission (EEOC) employment discrimination cases, rural housing loans by the Department of Agriculture district offices, and school districts. The research possibilities in other policy areas particularly at the local level appear limitless. As an illustration of the potential, until Keiser et al. (2002), no one had found gender composition of a bureaucracy mattered in terms of public policies for women.[7] The theory presented in that study predicted that gender representation would also be found in a variety of other situations. Empirical studies since then have confirmed gender representation in child support collections (Wilkins and Keiser 2001), the processing of sexual assault cases (Nicholson-Crotty and Meier 2002), and the disposition of cases by the EEOC for both sex discrimination and other charges (Meier et al. 2002). Because the theory in Keiser et al. (2002) is presented as a general theory of representation in bureaucracy, it implies that other cases of racial and ethnic representation should occur in a wide variety of public policy areas where bureaucrats exercise discretion on racially salient issues. That field of study is wide open, whether at the local, state, or federal level.

One lesson of this set of bureaucracy studies is that the bureaucracy can act as a representative institution and in the process affect the empowerment of minorities. Politics does not stop at the point in a process when it moves from an electoral institution to an administrative one. Bureaucracies, in fact, have some major advantages compared to electoral institutions when it comes to influencing policy, including their extended time frame and specialized expertise. Bureaucracies, however, can also be a serious obstacle to minority communities as they seek the benefits of democratic inclusion as pre-1965 voter registrars demonstrated in the South and as the Los Angeles Police Department continues to illustrate. The key is quite clearly the values held by bureaucrats; to the extent that bureaucracies are open to disadvantaged individuals and groups, we should expect bureaucracy to play a positive role. As Weber concisely noted, bureaucracy is a power instrument of the first order—for the one who controls the bureaucracy.

STRUCTURE AND THE RELATIONSHIP AMONG REPRESENTATIVES

So far, the findings that indicate that the quality of representation is related to structure apply to only a handful of domains. One might speculate that type of selection would affect a full range of relationships either among the representatives or between representatives and constituents. In a single-member district system with strong constituent ties and a narrower range of constituents per district, one would expect greater conflict on the school board and more issues with the racial and ethnic dimensions brought to the forefront (see Austin 1998). Incorporating a greater range of values in a legislative system has both advantages and disadvantages.

On the advantage side, the politics of race is out in the open and taking place in a visible forum. In Madisonian terms, the narrow interests of one representative could be used to check the narrow interests of another. The logic suggests that collective representation would be enhanced because any individual citizen would be more likely to find a representative advocating his or her interest. On the disadvantage side, the advocates of more centralized control of school boards contend that these same characteristics are the causes of stalemate and a preoccupation with pork-barrel types of issues (see Henig and Rich 2004). Representatives fixated on bringing benefits back to the district are representatives less likely to be focused on issues of a more general appeal. Given the logic that supports either side on this question, what is clearly needed are studies of how representatives act and whether or not such behaviors can be linked to structural factors. In short, we need studies that examine whether active representation always benefits constituents and studies that probe the progressive-era argument that representing broad general interests produces the best policy results.

Several other representative-related issues could also be linked to structure. Does election from a single-member district system affect the legislative and political skills of the representative? Are such representatives more or less likely to be able to build coalitions across racial and ethnic groups on the school board? Does it affect the representative's ability to build coalitions *across jurisdictions*, that is, to work with key state legislators or federal officials on issues of common interest? How does the tradeoff between close constituency ties in single-member districts and the more visible position of an at-large representative affect the political upward mobility of the representative? Is one type of representative more likely to run for higher office?

The relationships between constituents and representatives should also be transformed by how the representatives are selected. At-large representatives have more constituents and thus the importance of any single constituent is less. Responsiveness to individual constituents, therefore, is likely to be lower. Such behavior could affect a wide range of political behavior on the part of the constituent, everything from turnout in school board elections, to more active participation such as direct contact, campaign contributions, actively working for a candidate, and so forth (see Gay 2002 on contacting one's member of Congress and her contradictory findings on turnout, Gay 2001; see also Barreto, Segura, and Woods 2004). A substantial literature demonstrates that context affects political participation (see Leighley 2001 and the references therein). Part of that context is clearly how the representative responds to the citizen. To the degree that electoral structure affects the representative's behavior, we would also expect electoral structure to have an indirect influence on constituent political behavior.

Electoral structure might also have a direct impact on the context of political participation. A single-member district system implies more frequent within-race contacts aimed at political mobilization. Leighley (2001) demonstrates that an increase in contacts generates greater participation; the implication is that participation should increase in locations with ward-based single-member districts.

WHEN MINORITIES RULE

The structural discussions here have assumed that ethnic minorities constitute a minority of the population. In numerous cities and school districts either African Americans or Latinos constitute a majority, and in such cases the structural biases should work in their favor. Despite the growth in such cases, no studies explicitly examine majority–minority jurisdictions and the impact structure has in these jurisdictions. Theoretically, the structural biases of electoral systems should have the same impact on Anglos when they are a minority of the population as they do when African Americans or Latinos are a numerical minority. In addition to the questions raised above, the majority–minority case raises two additional interesting questions.

First, particularly with school districts, what does constituting a majority mean? Given the differences in family sizes and white flight to private schools, the composition of students will almost always be more minority than the population, especially the voting-age population. Because citizens are less likely to vote when they do not have a direct stake in the issue, in this case children in public schools, the actual electorate might have larger percentages of minorities in a school district election than the population. The bias in this direction is countered by the generally lower levels of turnout for minority populations (Leighley 2001).

A relatively interesting research agenda could address this question. Comparing exit polls to population figures, for example, would provide estimates of the differences between voting-age population and the actual electorate (something that has not been done in school board elections and probably also not done for city council elections).[8] The other way to assess this question with aggregate data would be to use multiple estimates of the population base (voting age population, population adjusted for likely voting, population with children in schools, etc.) to provide different possible views of the translation of population into electoral results. In regard to Latino voters, time of residence appears to be extremely important; population figures for 1990, for example, predict Latino school board representation in 2000 better than do 2000 population figures (Meier, Martinez-Ebers, and Leal 2002a).

Second, what is the impact of majority–minority jurisdictions on the relationships among ethnic minorities? A cottage industry has developed on the question of cooperation versus conflict among ethnic minorities with several studies on both sides of the issue (Browning, Marshall, and Tabb 1984; McClain and Karnig 1990; Meier and Stewart 1991; McClain 1993; McClain and Tauber 1998). Logically, having an absolute majority changes the incentives for any ethnic group to seek a rainbow coalition. Whether they do or not, however, is a topic that has not received any empirical attention.

EXOGENOUS ACTORS

The structure of American politics dictates that local governments, both cities and school districts, are forced to interact with other units of government. Neither school districts nor cities raise all of their own funds (although there are exceptions to this rule in terms of some wealthy school districts), and with outside funds often comes efforts to restrict local action. Three other sets of governmental actors impinge on the politics of local school districts—cities, states, and the federal government. A set of concentric circles of politics surrounds education policy with school district politics at the inner circle, urban politics at the next circle, state politics outside urban politics, and federal politics at the outer circle. To correct the aphorism of Everett Dirksen, "All [school] politics is local, if you can limit the scope of the conflict."

Federal government politics and the possibility of federal intervention either via the Voting Rights Act or through school desegregation cases were at one time a dominant consideration in school district politics. On the desegregation side, more and more school districts are being declared unitary and thus free from court orders to desegregate. This trend reflects the changing racial composition of major urban schools (that is, the decline in the number of Anglo students) and the lack of effective policy instruments to overcome segregation that crosses school district boundaries. The trend also reflects the shift in federal government priorities from equity to quality (or in the words of some cynics, to the triumph of test scores). Federal pressures are now more likely to focus on the state level and to pressure states to force school districts to raise test scores. To the extent that equity concerns are expressed in such pressures, they are expressed in test score differentials. While there remain residual federal government programs that concern equity (e.g., bilingual education), in effect the federal government has ceased to be an effective ally for minorities engaged in school politics.

In terms of voting rights cases, we are faced with another major research gap. I could find no studies on the impact of school district voting rights cases published in the last decade. At the present time, I also suspect that being under a federal court order to desegregate matters little because most of those cases were triggered by physical segregation within a district (that is, the concentration of minorities in one set of schools and Anglos in others). Given the unwillingness to act across district boundaries in most cases, the paucity of Anglos who attend schools in major urban systems, and a general feeling that all this busing does not benefit the students, I surmise that there is little federal impact here but could be convinced otherwise.

The federal influence on democratic inclusion, therefore, has changed dramatically. At one time, through school desegregation pressure or via the Voting Rights Act, the federal government provided additional pressure in support of the democratic inclusion of minorities. At the present time, federal pressure via either policy actions is not only unlikely, but the federal government's priorities have changed to stress policy actions (opposition to affirmative action, high stakes standardized testing; see below) that are inimical to greater democratic inclusion of minorities.

In contrast to the federal government, the role of state governments in school politics has increased dramatically. In part this reflects the increase in state aid (Wong 1999, 46) growing from 38 percent of the total in 1959 to 50 percent in 1996. Seventeen states are under court order from their state supreme courts to equalize educational funding within their respective states (Evans, Murray, and Schwab 1998); the federal government, however, has avoided this issue (see *San Antonio v. Rodriguez* 1974). The essence of these cases is that reliance on local property taxes to fund education results in unequal access to educational opportunities based on where students live. Because minorities tend to reside in districts with less property wealth, redistributive legislation has generally benefited minority students (Murray, Evans, and Schwab 1998).

Accompanying the rise in state funds has been the increased salience of issues of accountability and performance. In policy terms, standards have been raised, and state systems seek to hold local school districts accountable for their actions. This has two ramifications for minorities and educational politics in terms of representation and democratic inclusion. First, local politicians have lost agenda control. Local policy discretion has declined as state governments have increased the level of regulation focused on accountability. While membership on the local school board remains important, equally important is who sits in the state legislature or the governor's chair. Politics now determines who negotiates with whom, when, and how. The ramifications of the differences in minority representation at local versus state levels should be obvious. Second, state governments have become more likely to intervene directly in the business of the local school district by taking over the school system and operating it directly. Such actions are permitted in twenty-six states and have occurred in eleven states plus the District of Columbia.[9] The ability of state governments to take over school districts raises some interesting questions about the nature of democracy. That such efforts generally involve an Anglo majority jurisdiction taking control over a minority-run jurisdiction raises additional questions in regard to the politics of race, ethnicity, and democratic inclusion.

Less severe than an outright takeover has been the willingness of states to intervene structurally in major urban school systems. Generally, such efforts involve giving more authority to the city mayor. In dependent school systems, the school district is a unit of city government, and its board is appointed by other politicians rather than elected. Dependent school systems also do not generally have independent taxing authority. Although each mayoral takeover is somewhat unique, they generally give the mayor authority to appoint the school board, appoint the chief operating officer (the superintendent) and subordinate officers, and to set the budget (Henig and Rich 2004). Mayoral control is, of course, a pure majoritarian structure with a single elected official controlling the entire system. Representation, particularly school board representation, takes on a different meaning in such systems. School board representatives tend to mirror the demographic composition of the population exceptionally well. At the same time, board members represent the mayor and are likely to be quite unified in their views of education policy. Mayoral systems concentrate the political representation function in a single office. If the mayor cares about minority concerns, then minorities could have an advantage in mayor-centric reforms. If minorities are not a key part of the mayor's coalition—and many times they are not—then minority interests are likely to be ignored.

SOCIAL DIVERSITY AND SCHOOL BOARD POLICY

A relatively undeveloped agenda in the study of race and education is the use of school district data to test theories developed for other political jurisdictions. Current education data sets have the advantage of a large range of policy indicators, both outputs and outcomes that can be directly linked to issues of racial and ethnic equity. Linking racial representation in state legislatures to the normal array of public policy measures often requires some fairly elaborate justification to link minority interests to such items as greater spending on health care. These linkages, although correct, are neither as direct nor as obvious as they could be, and that could attenuate the representation linkage. Such measures as African American dropout rates or Latino test scores, in contrast, are closely tied to the interests of the minority community.

One promising area for additional theory testing is Hero's social diversity hypotheses. Hero (1998) argues that various combinations of minorities, white ethnics (i.e., southern and eastern Europeans), and whites (i.e., northern Europeans) generate three distinct racial environments: homogeneous, heterogeneous, and bifurcated. These combinations are then used to predict which groups are most likely to benefit from public policy decisions. Although Hero (1998) developed his theory for state-level politics, he tests part of it using sub-state units of analysis. A national sample of school districts could provide an additional theoretical test that, because of the clustering of school districts, might permit a separation of social diversity from the broader concept of political culture. School districts with the same political culture or located in jurisdictions with a uniform political culture could well have a great deal of variance in terms of social diversity. Using this difference could separate the impact of social diversity from that of political culture. Extending Hero's theory, an additional fruitful topic might be whether or not social diversity interacts with representation and produces more effective representatives in some situations than it does in others.[10]

EXAMINING THE FEEDBACK LOOP

Virtually every view of politics and policy includes a feedback loop. The purpose of public policy, after all, is to change the behavior of individuals in some way. Education policy has always been even more focused on changing individual behavior given its goal of producing effective democratic citizens. Even as the content of this goal has changed over time (current anti-immigrant policies, if one can believe it, are actually less intrusive than those in the 1920s), much of the purpose of education involves political socialization of citizens.

A long-expressed policy goal of education is to teach democratic values, including tolerance and support for the rights of political minorities. The existing research, however, shows that public schools (or private schools for that matter) are not very good at instilling such values (Godwin, Ausbrooks, and Martinez 2001; Godwin and Kemerer 2002). If school systems vary in this ability—and they likely do given that they vary on almost everything else—then this variance has some long-term ramifications for political behavior both electoral and nonelectoral. The inability to teach democratic values coupled with the patterns of institutionalized discrimination often found in school systems (Meier, Stewart, and England 1989; Meier and Stewart 1991) implies that overall the education system limits greater democratic inclusion rather than encourages it.

Following a similar line of logic, some scholars contend that the current national emphasis on high-stakes testing has shifted schools to an emphasis on a set of values favored by economists (i.e., training for jobs, efficiency as an evaluation criterion, etc.; see McNeil 2000) and away from the values linked to democracy. An extensive literature, however, has found that educational outputs—that is, test scores—are rarely related to future behavior, be it greater job earnings, increased political behavior, or less socially desirable behavior such as crime. In contrast, the inputs to education, such factors as expenditures per student and class size, are consistently correlated with these same factors (see Smith 2003 and the references cited therein). The Bush Administration's educational policy, thus, creates a natural experiment in regard to the influence of education and its goals on individual behavior. Since several states adopted the Bush reforms many years before they became federal policy, some of the effects of such policies might already be visible in some states.

School choice policies might also provide another route for studying minority empowerment. The impact of public school choice on building political capital is well documented by Schneider, Teske, and Marschall (2000). What remains to be studied are the far more extensive types of quasi-public service networks put together by the growing number of charter schools. As an illustration, the Tejano Center in Houston not only operates a charter school for disadvantaged students, but also runs a housing assistance program (for home ownership), a job training center, a day care center, and has links with private organizations that teach English as well as skills for surviving in the modern world of government bureaucracy. These charter networks resemble somewhat the set of private Latino self-help organizations that have sprouted in most major cities in the United States (see Stone 1998). Hybrid forms of social and education services like this can have far more effect on individual behavior and democratic inclusion than can government organizations that often face restrictions on how extensively they can intervene in a family's life.

Studying the policy feedback loop and its impact on democracy, representation, and democratic inclusion should not be limited to just education policy. A wide variety of other policies also subtly and not so subtly influence the American polity. The long-run impact, for example, of the current war on drugs is a fruitful area of study to determine the extent that effort affected turnout by disenfranchising large percentages of young, minority males (Brown-Dean 2003), how much the corruption and violation of individual rights spawned by the war may have affected citizens' trust in government, and how government policies linked to the war such as denial of other government benefits might have limited building social capital in minority communities.

CONCLUSION

This meandering chapter on school districts and politics addresses a variety of issues. What are the implications of this discussion and research agenda for our understanding of contemporary American democracy? First, in the study of democratic inclusion, representation, and minority empowerment, a policy focus is often useful. Policy congruence with constituent interests after all is one, albeit not the only, definition of representation. Democratic inclusion means not just who votes or who is elected but also who benefits from government action. Studies need to go beyond elections and examine the full range of governance processes. Second, in politics, structure matters. It is not the dominant influence, but it does shape the relationships between representatives and their constituents and among representatives. Third, bureaucracy should not be ignored in studies of democracy and representation. The influence of structure continues beyond elections to affect policy and even future democratic inclusion. Bureaucracies have the ability to penetrate deeply into citizens' lives in a large number of areas. Given their reach and given their ability to represent, bureaucracies might even be the most important political institution for fostering democratic inclusion. Bureaucracies, however, can both facilitate and retard democratic inclusion; bureaucratic values, as a result, become crucial in the process. Fourth, issues in this area, unlike the organization of the discipline, are all interlinked. They involve questions of political behavior, questions about political institutions, and questions about public policy. Studies in this area, as a result, are likely to be more involved and more difficult to design and implement than studies in other, less interesting, areas of political science.

NOTES

Acknowledgments. I would like to thank Chris Owen and Nick Theobald for research assistance and Texas A&M's Project for Equity, Representation and Governance group for helpful comments.

1. These figures are from the data base of the National Latino Education Study (Meier, Martinez-Ebers, and Leal 2002a). That study includes 96 percent of all school districts in the United States with more than 5,000 students.

2. This is not to say that rigid coalitions along racial lines do not exist in some school boards. My impression is that voting on school boards is more fluid than voting in legislatures or Congress.

3. The relationship between size and representation could well be nonlinear. Meier, Polinard and Wrinkle (2000) argue that in small enough jurisdictions the Anglo economic structure can coerce potential Latino candidates so that they are unlikely to run for office. In support of this argument, they present evidence that the effectiveness of Latino representation declines in smaller school districts.

4. Students of electoral structure have to gather their own data and thus samples are smaller. Imagine the problems this would create for the study of voting behavior.

5. Austin (1998) finds no impact of electoral structure on the hiring of African American teachers, but he uses a different specification which interacts both population by electoral structure and representation by electoral structure. This specification generates a great deal of co-linearity and may be the reason why his representative coefficients are insignificant.

6. Bureaucracy is part of the democratic governance process and thus I view how the bureaucracy responds and makes decisions as a fundamental element in any notion of democratic inclusion.

7. Keiser et al. (2002) was originally presented at the 2000 meeting of the American Political Science Association thus explaining why a 2002 publication could spawn an extended research agenda.

8. My source for claiming this has not been done is Robert Stein who spends far more time than I do studying local elections.

9. Educational Commission of the States, *Rewards and Sanctions for School Districts and Schools*. http://www.ecs.org/ecsmain.asp?page=/html/issues.asp?am=1. Accessed July 20, 2002. I have added Philadelphia to their list.

10. A related topic is dealing with the heterogeneity of the Latino population (de la Garza et al. 1992). Other than assessments of differences between the three largest groups, little has been done with the general concept of Latino diversity. One hypothesis is that such diversity matters only in terms of intra-Latino politics; another might be that diversity makes the delivery of an electoral or a governing coalition more difficult.

REFERENCES

Austin, Rory A. 1998. "Testing the Impact of Electoral Structures on Minority Office-Holding and Policy Representation." PhD diss., University of Rochester, NY.

Barreto, Matt A., Gary M. Segura, and Nathan D. Woods. 2004. "The Mobilizing Effect of Majority–Minority Districts on Latino Turnout." *American Political Science Review* 98 (March): 1–11.

Bezdek, Robert, David Billeaux, and Juan Carlos Huerta. 2000. "Latinos, At-Large Elections, and Political Change: Evidence from the 'Transition Zone.' " *Social Science Quarterly* 81:207–225.

Bowles, Samuel, and Herbert Gintis. 1976. *Schooling in Capitalist America*. New York: Basic Books.

Bratton, Kathleen A., and Kerry L. Haynie. 1999. "Agenda Setting and Legislative Success in State Legislatures: The Effects of Gender and Race." *Journal of Politics* 61:658–679.

Brown-Dean, Khalilah L. 2003. "One Lens, Multiple Views: Felony Disenfranchisement Laws and Black Political (In)Equality." PhD diss., Ohio State University.

Browning, Rufus P., Dale Rodgers Marshall, and David H. Tabb. 1984. *Protest is Not Enough*. Berkeley: University of California Press.

Bullock, Charles S., and Susan A. MacManus. 1981. "Policy Responsiveness to the Black Electorate." *American Politics Quarterly* 9:357–368.

Cameron, Charles, David Epstein, and Sharyn O'Halloran. 1996. "Do Majority–Minority Districts Maximize Substantive Black Representation in Congress?" *American Political Science Review* 90 (December): 794–812.

Carnevale, Anthony. 1999. *Education=Success: Empowering Hispanic Youth and Adults*. Princeton: Educational Testing Service.

Congressional Quarterly, Inc. 1993. *Congress A to Z: A Ready Reference Encyclopedia*. 2nd ed. Washington, DC: Congressional Quarterly.

de la Garza, Rodolfo O., Louis DeSipio, F. Chris Garcia, John Garcia, and Angelo Falcon. 1992. *Latino Voices: Mexican, Puerto Rican and Cuban Perspectives on American Politics*. Boulder, CO: Westview Press.

Engstrom, Richard L. 1994. "The Voting Rights Act: Disfranchisement, Dilution, and Alternative Election Systems." *PS: Politics & Political Science* 27 (December): 685–688.

Engstrom, Richard L., and Charles J. Barrilleaux. 1991. "Native Americans and Cumulative Voting: The Sisseton-Wahpeton Sioux." *Social Science Quarterly* 72 (June): 388–393.

Engstrom, Richard L., and Michael McDonald. 1981. "The Election of Blacks to City Councils." *American Political Science Review* 75:344–354.

Epstein, David, and Sharyn O'Halloran. 1999. "Measuring the Electoral and Policy Impact of Majority–Minority Voting Districts." *American Journal of Political Science* 43(April): 367–395.

Evans, William N., Shelia E. Murray, and Robert M. Schwab. 1997. "Schoolhouses, Court-houses, and Statehouses after *Serano*." *Journal of Policy Analysis and Management* 16(Winter), 10–31.

Fraga, Luis R. 1984. "Nonpartisan Slating Groups: The Role of "Reformed" Parties in City Electoral Politics." PhD diss., Rice University.

Fraga, Luis R., Kenneth J. Meier, and Robert E. England. 1986. "Hispanic Americans and Educational Policy: Limits to Equal Access." *Journal of Politics* 48:850–376.

Gay, Claudine. 2001. "The Effect of Black Congressional Representation on Political Par-ticipation." *American Political Science Review* 95 (September): 589–602.

———. 2002. "Spirals of Trust? The Effect of Descriptive Representation on the Relation-ship between Citizens and Their Government." *American Journal of Political Science* 46(October): 717–732.

Godwin, Kenneth, and Frank Kemerer. 2002. *School Choice Tradeoffs: Liberty, Equity, and Diversity*. Austin: University of Texas Press.

Godwin, Kenneth, Carrie Ausbrooks, and Valerie Martinez. 2001. "Teaching Tolerance in Public and Private Schools." *Phi Delta Kappan* (March): 542–546.

Henig, Jeffery R., and Wilbur C. Rich. 2004. *Mayors in the Middle: Politics, Race, and the Mayor-Centric Approach to Urban Schools*. Princeton: Princeton University Press.

Hero, Rodney E. 1998. *Faces of Inequality: Social Diversity in American Politics*. New York: Oxford University Press.

Hero, Rodney E., and Carolyn J. Tolbert. 1995. "Latinos and Substantive Representation in the U.S. House of Representatives." *American Journal of Political Science* 39:640–652.

Hindera, John J. 1993a. "Representative Bureaucracy: Imprimis Evidence of Active Repre-sentation in the EEOC District Offices." *Social Science Quarterly* 74 (March): 95–108.

———. 1993b. "Representative Bureaucracy: Further Evidence of Active Representation in the EEOC District Offices." *Journal of Public Administration Research and Theory* 3:415–429.

Keiser, Lael R., Vicky M. Wilkins, Kenneth J. Meier, and Catherine Holland. 2002. "Lip-stick and Logarithms: Gender, Identity, Institutional Context and Representative Bu-reaucracy." *American Political Science Review* 96 (September): 553–564.

Lasswell, Harold. D. 1958. *Politics: Who Gets What, When and How*. New York: Meridian Books.

Leighley, Jan E. 2001. *Strength in Numbers? The Political Mobilization of Racial and Ethnic Minorities*. Princeton: Princeton University Press.

Lublin, David. 1999. "Racial Redistricting and African-American Representation." *Ameri-can Political Science Review* 93:183–187.

Lublin, David, and D. Stephen Voss. 2000. "Racial Redistricting and Realignment in South-ern State Legislatures." *American Journal of Political Science* 44 (October): 792–810.

MacManus, Susan. 1978. "City Council Election Procedures and Minority Representation." *Social Science Quarterly* 59:153–161.

McClain, Paula D. 1993. "The Changing Dynamics of Urban Politics: Black and Hispanic Municipal Employment: Is There Competition?" *Journal of Politics* 55:399–414.

McClain, Paula D., and Albert Karnig. 1990. "Black and Hispanic Socioeconomic and Political Competition." *American Political Science Review* 84:535–545.

McClain, Paula D., and Steven C. Tauber. 1998. "Black and Latino Socioeconomic and Political Competition: Has a Decade Made a Difference?" *American Politics Quarterly* 26:237–252.

McNeil, Linda M. 2000. *Contradictions of School Reform: Educational Costs of Standardized Testing*. New York: Routledge.

Meier, Kenneth J., and Robert E. England. 1984. "Black Representation and Educational Policy: Are They Related?" *American Political Science Review* 78 (June): 392–403.

Meier, Kenneth J., and Eric Gonzalez Juenke. 2003. "Electoral Structure and the Quality of Representation: The Policy Consequences of School Board Elections." Paper presented at the Harvard Conference on "School Boards: Politics and Elections," October 16–17, Boston.

Meier, Kenneth J., and Joseph Stewart, Jr. 1991. *The Politics of Hispanic Education. Albany*: State University of New York Press.

Meier, Kenneth J., Valerie Martinez-Ebers, and David Leal. 2002a. The National Latino Education Study. Unpublished Data. College Station, TX.

Meier, Kenneth J., Valerie Martinez-Ebers, and David Leal. 2002b. "The Politics of Latino Education: The Biases of At-Large Elections" Paper presented at the annual meeting of the Western Political Science Association, Long Beach, CA.

Meier, Kenneth J., J.L. Polinard, and Robert D. Wrinkle. 2000. "Micheal Giles and Mancur Olson Meet Vincent Ostrom: Jurisdiction Size and Latino Representation." *Social Science Quarterly* 81 (March): 123–135

Meier, Kenneth J., Joseph Stewart, Jr., and Robert E. England. 1989. *Race, Class and Education: The Politics of Second Generation Discrimination*. Madison: University of Wisconsin Press.

Meier, Kenneth J., Robert D. Wrinkle, and J.L. Polinard. 1999. "Representative Bureaucracy and Distributional Equity: Addressing the Hard Question." *Journal of Politics* 61:1025–1039.

Meier, Kenneth J., Warren S. Eller, Robert D. Wrinkle, and J.L. Polinard. 2001. "Zen and the Art of Policy Analysis: A Reply to Nielsen and Wolf." *Journal of Politics* 63:616–629.

Meier, Kenneth J., Eric Gonzales Juenke, Robert D. Wrinkle, and J.L. Polinard. 2003. "Structural Choices and Representational Biases." Paper presented at the annual meeting of the Midwest Political Science Association, Chicago.

Meier, Kenneth J., Lael R. Keiser, Jill Nicholson-Crotty, and Vicky M. Wilkins. 2002a. "Sex, Gender, and the EEOC: The Evolution of Representation." Unpublished paper, Texas A&M University.

Meier, Kenneth J., Valerie Martinez-Ebers, David Leal, and Eric Juenke. 2003. "Political Structure and Representatives Effectiveness: The Case of Latino School Board Members." Paper presented at the annual meeting of the Western Political Science Association Portland, OR.

Meier, Kenneth J., Robert D. Wrinkle, Scott Robinson, and J.L. Polinard. 2001. "Path Dependence and Organizational Performance: Representative Bureaucracy, Prior Decisions, and Academic Outcomes." Paper presented at the 59th Annual Meeting of the Midwest Political Science Association, Chicago.

Nelson, Albert J. 1991. *Emerging Influentials in State Legislatures*. New York: Praeger.

Nicholson-Crotty, Jill, and Kenneth J. Meier. 2002. "Gender, Representative Bureaucracy, and Law Enforcement: The Case of Sexual Assault." Paper presented at the annual meeting of the American Political Science Association, Boston.

Polinard, J.L., Robert D. Wrinkle, Tomas Longoria, and Joseph Binder. 1994. *Electoral Structure and Urban Politics*. Armonk, NY: M. E. Sharpe.

Robinson, Scott E. 2002. "Rules, Roles, and Minority Representation: The Dynamics of Budgeting for Bilingual Education in Texas." *State Politics and Policy Quarterly* 2 (Spring): 52–65.

Robinson, Theodore P., and Thomas R. Dye. 1978. "Reformism and Black Representation on City Councils." *Social Science Quarterly* 59:133–141.

San Antorio v. Rodriguez 411 U.S. 1 (1974).

Schneider, Mark, Paul Teske, and Melissa Marschall. 2000. *Choosing Schools: Consumer Choice and the Quality of American Schools*. Princeton: Princeton University Press.

Selden, Sally C. 1997. *The Promise of Representative Bureaucracy*. Armonk, NY: M. E. Sharpe.

Smith, Kevin B. 2003. *The Ideology of Education: The Commonwealth, The Market, and America's Schools*. Albany, NY: SUNY Press.

Stone, Clarence N. 1998. *Changing Urban Education*. Lawrence: University Press of Kansas.

Swain, Carol. 1995. *Black Faces, Black Interest*. Cambridge, MA: Harvard University Press.

Taebel, Delbert. 1978. "Minority Representation on City Councils." *Social Science Quarterly* 59:142–152.

Tyack, David. 1974. *The One Best System*. Cambridge, MA: Harvard University Press.

Weber, May, 1946. *From Max Weber: Essays in Sociology*. H. H. Gerth & C. Wright Mills, Trans. New York: Oxford University Press.

Weisberg, Robert. 1978. "Collective vs. Dyadic Representation in Congress." *American Political Science Review* 72:535–547.

Welch, Susan. 1990. "The Impact of At-Large Elections on the Representation of Blacks and Hispanics." *Journal of Politics* 52:1050–1076.

Welch, Susan, and Albert Karnig. 1978. "Representation and Blacks on Big City School Boards." *Social Science Quarterly* 59:162–72.

Whitby, Kenny. 1997. *The Color of Representation: Congressional Behavior and Black Interests*. Ann Arbor: University of Michigan Press.

Wilkins, Vicky M., and Lael R. Keiser. 2001. "Linking Passive and Active Representation by Gender: The Case of Child Support Agencies." Paper presented at the Sixth National Public Management Research Conference, Bloomington, IN.

Wong, Kenneth K. 1999. *Funding Public Schools: Politics and Policies*. Lawrence: University Press of Kansas.

Zax, Jeffrey. 1990. "Election Methods and Black and Hispanic City Council Membership." *Social Science Quarterly* 71:340–355.

12   A Tangled Legacy

Federal Courts and Struggles
for Democratic Inclusion

ANY EFFORT TO UNDERSTAND THE CONTRIBUTIONS of U.S. federal courts to the politics of democratic inclusion must confront a host of vital, thorny, and provocative issues. In addressing these issues, we orient our analysis to the perspectives of marginalized groups who might be seeking increased voice, standing, power, and position in American society. In short, our basic questions are: What have excluded, exploited, or subaltern groups in the United States realistically obtained from the federal courts in their struggles for increased position? What might this legacy suggest for groups that continue to be denied full participation and status in American government and civil society?

Generally, we argue, that far from being the crucial and independent forces for democratic inclusion that late twentieth century observers have suggested, federal courts rarely have strayed far from the prevailing ideological and policy orientations of mainstream politics. However, this position alone is too simple; it proclaims both too much and too little. Historical analysis confirms that the courts are rarely either just passive followers or instruments of other institutions and groups; rather, by both their actions and inactions, courts often contribute to and participate in the construction of prevailing agendas. Indeed, courts perform a myriad of varying, often unique, and sometimes even dramatic roles in the development and working out of policy politics, if only occasionally in ways that increase the democratic character of the polity. Courts variously help to define and refine, expand and limit, enforce and undo, amplify and mute, challenge and legitimate policies and visions negotiated in other political domains. Litigation and related legal mobilization tactics thus often are important and productive fronts on which to wage struggle, even if courts are fickle allies and rarely capable of single-handedly effecting positive change.

Thus, the underlying theme of our analysis, which owes much to "new institutionalist" scholarship, is that courts must be understood in terms of the larger political context in which they are situated at any historical moment. This emphasis on context implies attention both to other national state actors and to organized social groups who lobby through the litigation process and other political channels. Hence our title underlining the "tangled" legacy of U.S. federal courts, which is at once complex, elusive, constrained, and inevitably intertwined with other strands of politics.

We organize our inquiry regarding this knotted institutional history into six analytical sections following this introduction. The first part will generally discuss how mainstream assumptions about judicial independence are highly misleading and require subtle reconceptualization to understand the unique politics of courts. The next four sections will take up two central questions about courts and the politics of democratic inclusion. Two sections (the second and third) will address the question of when courts are and are not most likely to act in ways that advance the causes of unjustly excluded groups and interests. The two following sections (fourth and fifth) will then briefly address the conditions under which such judicial action for subaltern groups is most and least likely to be effective. Each set of questions in turn will be addressed by examining relations of courts to other state actors (second and fourth), followed by relations of the courts to social groups pressuring from "below" (third and fifth). The final section will summarize our larger argument and propose some thoughts for future research. Throughout this discussion, we will cite a host of historical examples and scholarly works regarding struggles of many subaltern groups before the courts, although we will try to sustain some continuity by focusing on racial politics in each section. Due to space constraints, we focus primarily on the U.S. Supreme Court, although we do extend some attention to other federal courts and our analysis is intended to be applicable to the politics of federal courts generally.

Challenging the Enduring Myth of Judicial Independence

Judicial scholars have not established any clear consensus on the question of whether the courts can contribute to democratic inclusion. Part of the reason for the current lack of consensus is a split between traditional scholars who portray judges as powerful and independent policy makers and recent work by an eclectic group of new institutionalist scholars who challenge conventional assumptions about judicial independence. To make progress toward a better theoretical understanding of the capacities of courts to advance democratic inclusion, this section uses some insights from recent research by new institutionalist scholars to challenge common assumptions about judicial power and independence. Such a rebuke of the judicial independence thesis may at first seem to suggest that judges lack power and are thus unable to advance (or hinder) goals of democratic inclusion. However, the challenges developed here draw attention to some important but overlooked features of institutional interaction that can create opportunities for judges to advance democratic inclusion.

The Assumption of Judicial Independence

Much of the academic literature on the policy-making authority of American courts portrays judges as powerful and independent actors within a system of separate powers. For the past several decades, the basic institutional story about the courts among legal academics has been that judicial independence threatens democratic accountability. Writing in the aftermath of some allegedly activist Warren Court decisions, Alexander Bickel declared in 1962 that that the power of unelected federal judges to reverse policy decisions made by elected officials was "deviant" and a "counter-majoritarian" force. That claim inspired (or perhaps, damned) a generation of constitutional scholars to conduct an ultimately futile quest to discover interpretive principles that could somehow constrain judicial power and thus reconcile with majoritarian democracy the authority of judges to strike down laws (for overviews, see Shapiro 1983; Kalman 1996).

The scholars participating in this legal-interpretive project have analyzed and evaluated the justifications offered in judicial opinions, but they have typically paid less attention to how well rulings made by judges are implemented by actors in other branches. They instead assume, and thus worry, that judges exercise the power of judicial review at will and that, except in extraordinary circumstances, actors in other branches have little choice but to comply with court rulings. Bickel (1962), for example, identified the finality of Supreme Court decisions as their most troublesome feature. Other legal scholars responded to *Brown v. Board of Education* by fretting openly about the possibility that the style of reasoning used by the Court left judges free to hijack democratic processes (e.g., Wechsler 1959). To reach such conclusions, however, scholars had to take for granted such problematic notions as the idea that the South Carolina state legislature of 1954 was a democratic institution. Few legal scholars tempered their hand-wringing with the observation that *Brown* had little immediate effect on the policies implemented by defiant "elected" officials in the segregated South. The flood of books and articles advocating competing interpretive theories as constraints on judicial power has lately become a trickle, in part because skeptical scholars raised doubts about the capacity of legal doctrines and interpretive methods to constrain judges or to provide objective standards. Nevertheless, the basic concerns that prompted the quest continue to animate scholarly work on the courts and much of the public political discourse on judicial power.

A second, otherwise very different, group of scholars—political scientists in the judicial behavior tradition—has also offered accounts that portray judges as powerful and independent policy makers. These scholars have coded large numbers of Supreme Court cases on a simple ideological scale and observed correlations between the attitudes of individual judges and the votes judges cast in cases. Based on those correlations, behaviorists conclude confidently that justices vote according to their own personal attitudes toward policy, not according to independent legal rules found in legal texts or precedent (Segal and Spaeth 1993; Baum 1997). Although behaviorists self-identify as sharp critics of interpretive theorists in the legal academy, their account of the institutional foundations of judicial power is strikingly similar. Scholars in both camps explain the development of judicial power by recounting the legend of *Marbury v. Madison* (1803). They assume that judicial review has been a fixed and largely uncontested power ever since. They explain the persistence of judicial power and independence primarily in terms of fixed features of the constitutional design, for example, the guarantee of appointment and life tenure in Article III.

Independent Courts and Democratic Inclusion

If the legal and behavioral scholars are correct in their portrayal of judges as wielding power that is largely independent, what conclusions emerge regarding the courts as vehicles for promoting democratic inclusion? The independent power found by both groups of scholars suggests that if judges were inclined to advance democratic inclusion, they would have the capacity to do so. But should advocates for causes related to democratic inclusion expect judges to be so inclined?

The work of behaviorist political scientists suggests a straightforward approach to answering to such questions. If the behaviorists are right, one need only count the number of judges on the Supreme Court who favor a particular inclusion-related goal to determine whether the courts will act to advance that goal. While this approach is admirable for its elegance, it does not provide much help in explaining the significant variations over time in judicial support for goals related to democratic inclusion, or in predicting whether independent judges will favor such goals in the future.

In contrast, the account offered by legal-interpretive scholars seems at first to lead to a more optimistic conclusion. Much of the academic literature on interpretive legal theory was produced in response to the Warren Court. Liberal scholars working within this tradition applauded those decisions and attempted to justify judicial efforts to protect minorities from majority tyranny and to improve representative processes (e.g., Ely 1980). Recently however, scholars have begun to confront the fact that the Court for well more than a decade has been controlled by conservative judicial activists. The Warren Court seems finally to be losing its grip on the scholarly imagination (Kalman 1996; Keck 2004; Tushnet; 2005). The Rehnquist Court has occasionally done such Warren-Court-style, vaguely inclusionary things as voiding the convictions of apparently dangerous criminals (*United States v. Lopez* 1995; *RAV v. St. Paul* 1992) and finding new rights and immunities in the penumbras of constitutional amendments (*Board of Trustees v. Garrett* 2001). However, the most important Rehnquist Court contributions to constitutional jurisprudence have come in a growing body of cases where the Court has prevented legislative majorities from taking steps to protect the rights of marginalized groups (e.g., *City of Boerne v. Florez* 1997, religious minorities; *United State v. Morrison* 2000, women's rights). This recent behavior matches the broader pattern that emerges in American history: The Supreme Court has much more often been more conservative than the other branches than it has been more liberal.

Judicial Power and Political Context: Opportunities for Democratic Inclusion

During the past decade, an alternative account of judicial power has begun to emerge in the work of political scientists who have paid more attention to the institutional context in which judges make decisions. This group includes historically oriented scholars who use detailed case studies of particular historic moments to illustrate how institutional and political context affects the capacity of judges to influence policy development (e.g., Graber 1993, 1998, 1999; Gillman 1999, 2002; Whittington 1999), as well as rational choice scholars who make more abstract and ahistorical claims about the complicated effects of institutional context on judicial behavior (e.g., Maltzman, Spriggs, and Wahlbeck 1999; Martin 2001; Rogers 2001). This work seems to be moving toward a new paradigm for understanding judicial power and capacities, one that poses a serious challenge to some of the core assumptions about judicial power at the foundation of much legal and behaviorist scholarship.

To understand how new institutionalists' insights might lead to a better understanding of the ability of the courts to advance democratic inclusion, this section articulates and challenges the foundational assumptions about judicial power and its relationship to democratic processes. Once the problematic assumptions are laid bare, it is possible in the next section to illustrate some scenarios in which judges will have opportunities to advance democratic inclusion.

From Conflict to Cooperation

In conventional accounts, the capacity of judges to advance particular causes (be it democratic inclusion or something else) is measured by looking for cases where judges successfully take action that conflicts with the expressed preferences of elected officials in other branches. Judicial power is most visible in cases where overt conflicts between judges and legislators result in outcomes where the position announced by judges triumphs. Recent scholarship has shown, however, that other important aspects of judicial power can be uncovered after envisioning relations between judges and legislators as potentially cooperative rather than conflicting. Such scholarship has identified a wide variety of ways in which judges can serve the interest of elected officials, even in cases where judges reverse the outcome officially chosen in other branches. For example, studies of judicial deference to the courts by Mark Graber (1993) and George Lovell (1994, 2003) show how apparent judicial reversals can be the result of rigged confrontation where judges serve the interests of elected officials by shielding them from the political consequences of difficult choices. Legislators also routinely empower judges to decide policy issues by making compromises that create ambiguous statutory language that judges are later called upon to interpret (Lovell 2003). Another possibility, discussed by James R. Rogers (2001), is that legislators maintain judges as rival sources of power because judges have informational advantages that make them useful agents for helping to advance congressional policy goals.

The more collaborative aspects of inter-branch interaction are harder to identify because cooperation can be covert or inadvertent. Legislators are not likely to brag openly when they try to avoid accountability by shifting responsibility to unelected officials in another branch, and judges may not always realize that legislators are deliberately deferring to the courts. Nevertheless, the possibility of such cooperation means that an exclusive focus on overt conflicts among the branches produces a systematically distorted account of the effect of judges on democratic processes.

Toward a Dynamic, Contingent Conception of Judicial Power

It is also important for scholars to move away from thinking of judicial capacity to advance democratic inclusion as the result of fixed institutional powers over which actors in other branches have little control or influence. While conventional scholars have emphasized fixed constitutional guarantees like appointment and life tenure as sources of judicial power, recent historical work has shown how changes in political and institutional context have altered judicial capacities over time (Graber 1998; Whittington 1999; Powe 2000; Gillman 2002). For example, in a series of recent articles, Mark Graber (1998, 1999) has debunked both the myth that *Marbury* was the first exercise of the power of judicial review and the myth that *Marbury* forever settled the question of judicial use of that power. Graber shows instead that the Supreme Court's powers developed more gradually during the course of the nineteenth century, and only because of the ability of judges to serve important political constituencies in a fractured government.

Such scholarship draws attention to the often-overlooked fact that the institutional capacities of courts are structured almost entirely by revocable decisions made by actors in other branches. The judicial monster so feared for its power to thwart democracy is almost entirely the creation of elected officials. The Constitution leaves it to Congress to create and staff almost all federal judicial positions, gives Congress plenary power to eliminate judgeships on death or retirement, and invites Congress to alter the jurisdiction of the courts. The broad pattern cast by the choices legislators have made regarding the duties of judges presents a stark challenge to the view of courts as independent rivals: The pattern seems indisputably to be one where legislators have gradually given judges more rather than less power to influence policies. For example, legislators have increased the power of the Supreme Court by gradually making it easier for the justices to control the Court's agenda (Perry 1991) and have dramatically expanded opportunities for policy making by creating important judicial oversight powers in the administrative state (McCann 1986). Such deliberate choices show that, even though legislators may sometimes disagree with judicial decisions, they also have important reasons to value maintenance of the courts as a separate source of institutional power.

Rethinking the Counter-Majoritarian Assumption

The final important step toward rethinking the courts and democratic inclusion is to question the assumption that the most important difference between the courts and other branches is that the courts are undemocratic and thus unresponsive while the other branches are democratic and majoritarian (Peretti 1999). While it is undeniable that the lack of direct electoral controls on judges is important to understanding judicial power, the sharp dichotomy between "democratic" branches and the "counter-majoritarian" courts obscures numerous institutional mechanisms that facilitate accountability in the American constitutional system. The dichotomy leads scholars to focus on judges' independence from direct electoral controls as the sole source of a special judicial capacity to protect "minorities" from the wishes of the "majorities" who control electoral contexts. Such a focus is too crude to capture the complexity of judicial opportunity structures.

The first, most elemental problem with such a conceptualization is that the obstacles that excluded groups encounter in the elected branches is never simply that they are a numeric minority. To see this, one need only to observe that there are many groups in the United States that are numeric minorities but nevertheless manage to protect their interests very well through electoral processes, often at the expense of majorities. Consider, for example, the following minority groups: persons whose wealth is sufficient to subject them to estate taxes, medical doctors, and NRA members. Conversely, many numeric majorities—for example, wage-laborers, net-debtors, and women—seem to be systematically disadvantaged in electoral outcomes.

The reasons some minorities are able to protect their interests better than others are complex, but the basic starting point for any explanation is that the United States constitutional system is not, in *any* of its component parts, majoritarian. In the legislative branch, for example, Senate seats are grotesquely malapportioned and House elections are shaped by political districting and apportionment processes that make the overwhelming majority of seats "safe." Constraints and biases associated with elections are compounded by internal decision-making processes that give minorities in each chamber numerous veto points. The importance of these non-majoritarian features for processes of democratic inclusion should not be underestimated. For example, NAACP efforts to pass federal anti-lynching legislation during the first half of the twentieth century failed despite the fact that majorities in Congress supported such legislation. The failure had much more to do with the Senate filibuster and other avenues of minority obstruction than it had to do with the fact that African Americans were a numeric minority and excluded from voting in much of the country (Zangrando 1980).

Second, while it is true that constitutional guarantees ensure that federal judges serve for life without facing election or diminution in salary, those guarantees do not explain why judges have remained powerful and capable of influencing public policies. Many college professors have effective guarantees of life tenure without salary reduction, but they find themselves unable to engage in any binding counter-majoritarian policy making. Judges influence policy only because of the continued solicitude of actors in other branches. Elected officials have numerous weapons for controlling or reversing decisions made by judges. Congress regularly overturns Supreme Court statutory decisions by simply passing new statutes (Eskridge 1991). Moreover, the Constitution explicitly invites Congress to alter the jurisdiction of federal courts—a power used more often, more recently, and to greater consequence than scholars have realized (Lovell 2003). These and other institutional mechanisms for controlling courts mean that even unelected judges are subject to substantial, albeit indirect, forms of democratic control.

A final observation is that the most important dilemma of democratic accountability may not be that the outcomes announced by judges cannot be altered through voter participation in electoral processes. Rather, the problem

may be that having decisions announced by judges (rather than other officials) can distort the way publics respond to the decision. As noted previously, Graber's (1993) and Lovell's (2003) studies of legislative deference to
the courts show that political actors sometimes allow judges to make policy as a means of shielding themselves from the political consequences of
making difficult decisions. A more general source of distortion, identified
by many critical legal studies (see McCann 1999) and critical race scholars
(e.g., Spann 1993), comes from the ideological dimension of judicial decision making. Popular images of judges as impartial arbiters may mean that
people may blandly accept a policy outcome announced in a court decision as
final even though they would protest vigorously if the president or congress
had announced the same outcome (Brigham 1987). When placed alongside
Graber's suggestion that political actors will shift particularly contentious
issues to the courts, such observations reveal that the real problem with judicial power is not a lack of electoral accountability. Rather, the problem is that
the availability of judges as alternative locations of power and responsibility
makes it much more difficult for citizens to hold elected officials accountable
for their choices.

WHEN DO COURTS ADVANCE DEMOCRATIC INCLUSION?

Alternative Scenarios of State Interdependence

The preceding observations suggest that scholars could better understand the
ability of judges to advance democratic inclusion by focusing on circumstances where it serves the interest of political actors in other branches to
allow judges to resolve policy controversies related to democratic inclusion.
Scholars need to pay more attention to the ways interdependency shapes
the interaction of governmental branches, the ways that each branch helps
to shape the capacity of other branches to affect outcomes of inter-branch
processes, and the ways complex institutional processes together effect democratic accountability. To illustrate the potential relevance of such institutional
factors, we provide examples of three scenarios in which judges could have
the opportunity to facilitate inclusion. These examples are just a starting
point, and they are not meant to provide an exhaustive list of possibilities or
even exclusive categories.

Scenario One: Courts Are Empowered by Paralysis of Other Institutions. Judges
may be in a position to resolve a pressing policy issue because institutional
features of other branches make it impossible for them to deal with the issue
directly. For example, the other branches may be stalemated and thus unable
to act decisively on a pressing issue. Such stalemates are particularly likely to
occur in the American political system because decision-making processes
are structured with numerous veto points that allow organized minorities to
obstruct outcomes. Such stalemates will likely make judges more willing
to act aggressively to shape policy outcomes because exercises of judicial
power are more likely to survive threats of retaliation when actors in other
branches are divided.

Consider, for example, the line of Warren Court decisions advancing civil rights of African Americans. The fact that the Court issued its landmark decision in *Brown* a decade before Congress enacted the landmark Civil Rights Act of 1964 does not mean that the Court was acting contrary to the wishes of majorities of elected federal officials. Nor does it mean that the Court was able to advance democratic inclusion solely because judges did not have to face election. Congress would have acted more aggressively to protect civil rights long before 1964 had it not been for the Senate filibuster, which allowed a small group of Senators representing an even smaller percentage of the national population to block civil rights reforms. The decision issued by the Court easily survived various attempts in Congress to overturn it because desegregation had the strong support of important elites in both parties and in both the executive and legislative branch (Dudziak 2000; Murphy 1962).

The fact that the Court's ability to influence outcomes depended on the passive assent of important political actors in other branches can be seen by looking at what happened when the drive for school desegregation moved north of the Mason-Dixon Line. At that point, the political pressures on the court began to come from across more regions of the country, and the Court quickly backed down from some of the most promising principles of equal rights suggested in Warren's original ruling in *Brown* (Patterson 2001).

Scenario Two: Other Institutional Actors Leave the Details to Courts. This category can overlap with the first, but it can also be distinct in cases involving technical policy issues that are of low salience to organized constituencies. Congress routinely passes regulatory statutes without fully resolving many pertinent questions about substantive rules and categories. Legislators have also created an administrative process through which bureaucrats in regulatory agencies and judges on appellate courts together resolve such questions. The potential for the resulting judicial decisions to affect processes of democratic inclusion can be seen in the recent line of Supreme Court interpretive decisions on the meaning of the Americans with Disabilities Act of 1990. The statute itself fails to define the key terms that express what counts as a "disability." Thus, the Supreme Court has had to resolve such questions as whether persons who are HIV positive, nearsighted pilots, hypertensive UPS drivers, or pro-golfer Casey Martin are covered by the act. Each of these issues was left unresolved in the text of the statute. While some of these unresolved issues were discussed extensively in Congress and thus perhaps best fit our first scenario (e.g., HIV), others were surely issues that legislators did not think about at the time they drafted the statute. Of course, if enough legislators decide that they do care about the issue, they can reverse the courts' decisions.

Scenario Three: Other Branches Delegate to Courts. In the first two scenarios, the presumption is that judges influence outcomes because a substantial number of legislators care less about which resolution the judges choose than they care that judges assume responsibility for making the decision. In other cases, legislators may grant courts discretion to resolve a particularly policy issue only because they expect the courts to rule in a particular way. This may happen in cases where legislators prefer that one side win a deep conflict between powerful and badly divided constituencies. Cases fitting this scenario are more likely to involve divisive, high-salience issues. For example, despite the fact that judges were notoriously hostile to labor organizations during the first third of the twentieth century, Congress passed several "reform" statutes with deliberate ambiguities that gave judges discretion to shape labor policy (Lovell 2003). The anti-labor judicial rulings that resulted have been interpreted by many scholars as counter-majoritarian rejections of democratic reforms. However, many elected legislators happily anticipated such judicial rulings when they created the ambiguous laws. The labor example suggests that cases fitting the third scenario are more likely to involve judges hindering democratic inclusion than facilitating it. However, there may also be cases where legislators covertly empower the courts to empower the weak. Arguably, the sometimes unpopular criminal justice decisions of the Warren Court advanced the long-term goals of elected officials by forcing reforms that ultimately made the criminal justice system a more effective and reliable means of social control.

The three scenarios just outlined are not an exhaustive list. Additional possibilities could be developed and distinguished by paying attention to variations on some of the factors that distinguish the ones just offered. These include: (1) the level of agreement or conflict about policy choices among and within the other branches of government, (2) the way the issues in question cut across political alignments that are important or enduring at the time of the decision, and (3) the salience of the issues that the courts resolve. The important point is that the logic of judicial action advancing inclusionary goals has to be understood as growing out of complicated institutional processes. Activists cannot make strategic decisions about whether or not to pursue litigation strategies by looking only at the individual preferences or ideological proclivities of sitting judges or by noting the ability of judges to win overt conflicts with other branches. Strategic actors must also look at how the broader political context structures the opportunities judges have to influence outcomes.

Bottom-Up Legal Mobilization

The interrelationships between courts and other state institutional actors outlined above can be usefully understood in terms of changing "opportunity structures" for judicial action (McCann 1994). Such opportunity structures vary as nonjudicial institutional actors alternately defer to, delegate, invite, deter, or discourage certain types of judicial action. Most often the political context is highly complex, with multiple institutional actors pushing or pulling in different, cross-cutting ways, although sometimes the space and/or incentives for judges to act on certain issues shapes up in fairly clear ways. The political context of judicial action is yet further complicated, moreover, by a second set of forces: organized social groups who push from below through what often is labeled *legal mobilization* politics. Legal mobilization politics generally refers to the process by which individuals and non-state groups advance claims for their legal rights and utilize legal tactics, like litigation, to defend or develop those rights (Zemans 1981; McCann 1994; Epp 1998).

Scholars who focus on legal mobilization politics tend to emphasize that successful judicial action on behalf of rights—including for minorities and marginalized citizens—requires more than a constitutional structure of rights, a cultural predisposition toward recognizing citizen rights, activist judges personally committed to rights-based agendas, and accompanying pressures, invitations, or deference from other political branches. In addition, judicial action depends on well-funded, strategically savvy, and persistent litigation campaigns that, like lobbying, create pressure for rights-based causes. Charles Epp's (1998) important book, *The Rights Revolution*, underlines in particular what he calls the "support structure" of rights advocates and resources that represent a necessary, if not sufficient, condition for inclusionary rights-based policy action by courts. The support structure includes: (1) bands of committed lawyers, who often are called "cause lawyers" when joined to egalitarian causes (Sarat and Scheingold 1998); (2) public interest organizations and nongovernmental associations, such as the NAACP, WLDF, ACLU, unions, and the like; (3) financial resources; and (4) willing litigants. A key point at stake is that most rights-oriented social reform litigation is not conducted by a solitary plaintiff or attorney with little experience in court, what Marc Galanter (1974) has called the "one shotter." Instead, success in legal mobilization is far more likely among groups of "repeat players" who have long-term interests, possess ample resources to advance those interests, and develop experience and power through sustained legal advocacy on related issues.

Not the least of the resources that such advocates often mobilize on behalf of disadvantaged groups is compelling legal argument, which itself often creates pressures and opportunities for democratic doctrinal change in the courts (Epstein and Kobylka 1992). After all, legal language provides important resources by which actors frame claims, define problems, articulate aspirations, and try to persuade authorities—judges as well as legislators, bureaucrats, and so forth—to articulate new policies and principles. One fundamental role of courts, of course, is to place boundaries and constraints on the terms of legitimate political argument and sensible political claims. Judges "police" the terms of legitimate political discourse, "killing" off myriad socially generated visions of justice while validating others as legally plausible and authoritative (Cover 1983). But it is critical to recognize that the languages and logics of courts are indeterminate, which means that advocates of social justice and democratic inclusion can construct possibilities and plausible claims from judicial actions that judges never intended. Indeed, it is the creative, unintended openings for social justice articulated, whether intentionally or unintentionally, by judges over time that have provided one of the richest and most important dynamics to propelling progressive change. What thus is crucial for our concerns in this chapter is that advocates of rights for excluded or exploited minority groups sometimes effect change by moving streams of cases advancing new legal visions of justice and democracy through the long haul of court processes.

A number of studies have demonstrated that compelling legal argument or the mobilization of legal discourse by litigants can make a big difference to the prospects for success in court (Epstein and Kolbylka 1992). For example, Epp (1998) convincingly evidences his argument through a cross-national comparative study regarding the character of "revolutions" for women's rights and the rights of suspected criminals. He points out, in the U.S. case, for example, that the allegedly liberal Warren Court rejected the only women's rights claim it heard, while the more conservative Burger Court undertook a "momentous intervention into highly contentious issues" affecting women, including equal treatment, equal pay, and abortion (52). While many factors contributed to this outcome, Epp shows that it was the rise of well-funded, politically and legally savvy women's rights organization—the Legal Defense and Education Fund of NOW, the Women's Legal Defense Fund, the Women's Rights Project of the ACLU—who flooded lower federal courts with test-case litigation that best accounts for the redefined judicial agenda. Following the model of NAACP litigation and Warren Court doctrinal logic on race-based civil rights, women's rights advocates challenged courts throughout the land to respond in various ways, creating a patchwork of uncertain and often contradictory rulings, eventually demanding higher review and more coherent doctrine. As such, legions of well-funded organizations and cause lawyers "propelled new rights issues onto the Supreme Court's agenda," providing incentive, pressure, opportunity, and even legitimating cover for action on women's issues (69).

Such direct mobilization of legal pressure from the "bottom up" often involves alliances between state- and privately-funded public interest advocates, of course. Perhaps the most dramatic example of this was the coalition of progressive Legal Services attorneys, who were funded by the Office of Equal Opportunity but acted relatively independently under the umbrella of local Community Action Agencies and non-state advocates for the poor such as the National Welfare Rights Organization. As Susan Lawrence (1990) demonstrated in a masterful study, a massive outpouring of litigation on behalf of the poor dramatically shaped the policy agenda of federal courts, especially that of the Supreme Court, in the 1960s and 1970s. LSP attorneys initiated 164 cases; of these, 118 were accepted and 80 received plenary consideration by the justices, representing about 7 percent of all Court-written opinions in a nine-year period. While actual advances for the poor were restricted primarily to procedural issues, the capacity of litigation campaigns to set the agenda and shape policy making by federal judges was noteworthy.

Both Lawrence (1990) and Epp (1998) underline in their analyses that legal mobilization politics also typically involves indirect efforts to generate judicial responses favorable to inclusionary policies. In short, most legal mobilization campaigns seek to generate or to build on extra-judicial pressures for democratic reform through tactics aimed at the media, elected officials, and other policy makers. In this way, rights activists' litigation tactics are often paralleled by efforts to mobilize other state actors and the public, creating a favorable environment of exogenous pressures and opportunities encouraging favorable judicial action. This effort to link multiple advocacy tactics, where lawsuits are used to influence relevant audiences beyond the courts and vice versa, is well demonstrated in McCann's (1994) analysis of wage equity politics in the 1970s and 1980s. His study illustrates how unions, women's groups, and lawyers used grassroots demonstrations, legislative lobbying campaigns, and media stories to create a context in which both federal and local judges felt pressure to act on cases of unequal pay to workers concentrated in "women's jobs."

The same dynamic was again very much at play in perhaps the most dramatically inclusionary decision of the Supreme Court, *Brown v. Board of Education*. The international pressures of Cold War ideological battles led to increased concern among federal officials in the foreign policy establishment and Department of Justice about the need to address racial segregation, lynching, and police brutality in the South. Fearing a potential backlash against Democratic Party members that federal civil rights legislation might provoke, the Truman administration looked to the judiciary for action challenging officially sanctioned practices of American apartheid. The dedicated attorneys in the Civil Rights Division of the Justice Department thus conducted a small number of test prosecutions under some of the long dormant statutes, but technical problems related to the wording of those scattered provisions resulted in a mixed set of divided rulings from the Supreme Court that sent only muddled signals about the Court's position. While not directly successful, this activity among federal officials created new opportunities, resources, and hopes for black leaders, including private lawyers and legal strategists for the NAACP, to lobby for desegregation directly in the federal courts as well as in the mass media, among legislators, and before the court of public opinion (see Dudziak 2000). The result was to contribute at once from both below and above, through litigation and other political tactics, to a more hospitable context in which federal courts, including newly appointed judges, might respond with progressive democratic action. This example thus well illustrates the unique combination of many factors—sustained litigation by well-funded, skilled lawyers; multi-dimensional political campaigns pressuring elected officials, policy makers, the media, and general public for inclusionary policies; new judicial appointments; and either delegation or deferral of initiative to the courts by other key political players—that most often are necessary for the courts to contribute to democratic or egalitarian politics. Sometimes courts do act independently, as with prison reform in the 1970s, but even then action depended on deference from other political players and support or cooperation of middle-level corrections officials around the nation (Feeley and Rubin 1998).

Of course, litigation by organized interests and repeat players more often in our history has neutralized legal mobilization by progressive activists committed to inclusionary democratic goals, reversed prior egalitarian advances, and produced outcomes supportive of more exclusionary or hierarchical relationships in society. After all, the primary work of courts in the first 150 years of our history involved structuring the terms of capitalist market relations outside the South, which often favored developers over subsistence owners, large over small capital, and employers over workers. Indeed, federal courts responded to both corporate litigation and legislative deferrals of authority in thwarting organized labor for decades prior to the 1930s, thus freeing big business to construct modern economic and social relations in hierarchical corporate terms (Lovell 2003). This legacy continues today, as shown by Richard Brisbin's (2002) powerful account of how mine workers were violently crushed by a combination of judicial rulings and other government actions supporting corporate owners.

Moreover, many of the most important democratic advances on civil rights and liberties in the period during and following the Warren Court were halted, neutralized, and even rolled back through legal counter-mobilization by conservative groups, buttressed in no small part by their influence in electoral politics and public agenda setting. While southern segregationists were momentarily thwarted by the combined pressures of the Cold War on elected officials and a brilliant litigation campaign by NAACP lawyers, the former allied with a variety of conservative forces to redefine the agenda from the 1960s until today. Conservatives mimicked the earlier tactics of liberals by initiating sustained litigation campaigns waged by well-funded legal advocacy groups, working at elite levels to appoint more conservative judges, and reshaping the entire political environment of judicial policy making (Klinkner and Smith 1999). By the 1990s, earlier faith in the courts as venues of more inclusionary, egalitarian reform—for racial minorities, the poor, women, workers, and like—had all but faded away (Rosenberg 1991; Keck 2004).

Once again, what courts do is largely shaped by both the capacities of litigants and pressures or opportunities posed by other powerful players in elite politics. Federal courts generally have shifted toward more democratic directions only in rare moments of favorable political circumstances, which often have been followed by long periods of retrenchment (Klinkner and Smith 1999). As such, courts have typically mirrored the tendency of mainstream politics to uphold more than challenge the prevailing hierarchical class, racial, ethnic, gender, sexual, and religious order, thereby limiting democratic possibilities in the United States.

DO COURTS MATTER?

Judicial Capacity and State Power

Even in those relatively rare moments when courts act on behalf of inclusionary, democratic goals, are courts capable of making a difference, of generating significant change? Judicial action that has little behavioral impact is at best symbolic politics, at worst a diversion of hopes and energies from activists who invest in such venues (Scheingold 1974). Our overview of this issue parallels the discussion above. We argue that courts can have substantial impact, but their capacity for influence is highly contingent on their political context, including especially the interests, inclinations, and actions of other institutional players in both the state and society. In short, many of the factors that figure prominently in facilitating progressive judicial rulings also affect the court's capacity to render its will as an effective force for change.

One obvious place to begin such an inquiry is the scholarly literature addressing the capacities of courts to implement and enforce their rulings (McCann 1986; Rosenberg 1991). There are many components to the argument that courts lack substantial institutional power, and they can only be briefly listed here. For one thing, courts lack the basic tools and resources that other state institutions utilize to effect their will. As Alexander Hamilton pointed out in *Federalist #78*, the judiciary "has no influence over either the sword or the purse; no direction either of the strength or the wealth of the society; and can take no active resolution whatever. It may truly be said to have neither FORCE nor WILL, but merely judgment; and must ultimately depend on the aid of the executive arm even for the efficacy of its judgments" (1961, 465). The fact that the courts lack control over money and military or police is why the judiciary has long been considered "the least dangerous branch" (see Bickel 1962). In short, courts, more than any other branch, must rely on the voluntary cooperation, assistance, and enforcement powers of other governmental agents. As such, the directives of judicial majorities are always contingent, and easily undone by the evasions and resistances of others on which judges depend. This is important especially when one considers the dynamics of "symbolic politics" common to policy areas concerning the poor, minorities, women, and the like. In short, elected officials can reap the symbolic benefits of government action on issues affecting marginalized populations while suffering few electoral costs for foot dragging or even stonewalling on issues of judicially constructed rights implementation.

Courts, skeptics point out, are at a dramatic institutional disadvantage with regard to policy implementation in other subtle ways. For one thing, the judicial process is a largely reactive and piecemeal process; courts cannot choose when to act, and must wait for ripe cases to emerge, thus inhibiting the type of continuous supervisory oversight and policy adjustment that bureaucratic agencies wield in implementation politics. Likewise, it is often argued that the judicial process renders judges more oriented to abstract principles than to pragmatic outcomes and to specific remedies for litigants rather than to comprehensive social policies, thus further undermining their capacities for effective social engineering. Moreover, it is often noted that judges generally lack the type of detailed expertise about complex policy matters necessary to incremental problem solving in policy administration. All in all, courts seem to be institutionally ill-suited for policy development and too dependent on other state actors to achieve effective policy implementation.

These weaknesses have been evidenced by many scholarly studies. Dolbeare and Hammond (1971) long ago substantiated, for example, that local officials resisted Supreme Court school prayer decisions through a variety of practices, thus reducing compliance with court rulings dramatically. Gerald Rosenberg (1991) further provides evidence that the landmark desegregation ruling in *Brown* had "virtually no direct impact on discrimination" in multiple venues—schools, voting, transportation, public accommodations—prior to the mid-1960s, despite the mythology that developed around the Supreme Court decisions. The reason, he argues, is that judicial antidiscrimination rulings had at best modest support from either other federal elites or the broader culture, while opposition in the South was intense. In short, the Court found itself alone, vainly spitting into the winds of Southern opposition and northern indifference. By the mid-1960s, after the passage of the 1964 Civil Rights Act, federal support for civil rights accelerated, thus providing the necessary implementation pressures and resources that courts alone lacked. "Courageous and praiseworthy decisions were rendered, and nothing changed. Only when Congress and the executive branch acted in tandem with the courts did change occur in these fields. In terms of judicial effects, then, *Brown* and its progeny stand for the proposition that courts are impotent to produce significant social reform" (71). Rosenberg goes on to find similarly unimpressive results of court actions for rights to abortion, equal protection for women, and rights of suspected criminals.

This argument about judicial powerlessness is important, but it has also been vigorously contested. Other scholars have responded: that all branches of government are interdependent and alone can accomplish little; that judicial appointments empower as well as constrain judges to act boldly; that the "constrained court" model of reactive, generalist, principle-bound judges reflects more a mythical civics text image than empirical realities where courts actively make policy, implement remedies and social reconstruction, consult experts, and rely on mechanisms such as "special masters" for effective incremental implementation; and that institutional critics too often dismiss the unique constitutive or moral authority of courts (Brigham 1987). Indeed, Feeley and Rubin's (1998) study of judicially led prison reform in the 1970s demonstrates that judges are policy makers who initiate and implement policy with stunning effectiveness that sometimes even exceeds the capacities of bureaucrats. As such, federal courts are very much a vital, if unique, part of the modern administrative state. "Courts are policy makers, as well as fact-finders and interpreters. While certain disadvantages attend their efforts in this capacity, the courts have certain strengths as well, and are fully able to function in this dominant mode of modern governmental action" (388).

Similarly nuanced understandings of the court have informed contrary readings of the civil rights legacy. Once we recognize that the very action of the Supreme Court in *Brown* was variously encouraged, permitted, or deferred by other powerful policy elites in federal government, Rosenberg's (1991) argument becomes problematic. Far from boldly staking out an independent terrain, the Court acted in ways that the foreign policy establishment and Department of Justice officials in the executive branch as well as many legislators welcomed. The impact of *Brown* was similarly shaped by this connection to other federal policy makers. After all, two successive Presidents in the decade after *Brown* called out the National Guard to override Southern resistance and implement desegregation rulings. The 1964 Civil Rights Act, moreover, was hardly an independently conceived action, but was largely a product of growing consensus among legislators that desegregation now was palatable, and even popular, in the national electorate. There are many reasons for this development of consensus, but most analysts agree that the televised expressions of ugly, irrational white violence against nonviolent black protestors demanding their newly won rights, often proudly displaying the Supreme Court's imprimatur in *Brown*, were critical (see McAdam 1982). There can be no doubt that the courts relied on assistance from other branches of government in enforcing desegregation and other anti-discrimination rulings, nor that the Civil Rights Act provided critical legislative leverage and expanded reach to the earlier rulings. But it is equally true that the courts were a critical part of a complex policy process, which would have turned out rather differently had the courts not acted or acted differently.

The *Brown* example raises a further general point. As noted above, the constitutive power of prevailing judicial language and logics often matters as much as their more narrowly instrumental implications. In the rare moments when courts act on inclusionary principles, they authorize various categories, prescriptions, predictions, justifications, visions, and rationalities of action through which social life is imagined and by which citizens understand, transact, and reconstruct social relations. Courts thus add a unique normative component to political discourse that, when mobilized by social groups and political activists, sometimes can transform favorably the policy agenda and terms of political contests. Judicial constructions of law can and do constrain actors but, because indeterminate, they also can provide flexible resources for the ongoing redefinition of entitlement claims, articulation of aspirations, and endeavors to reconstitute social relations at various levels. As Brigham (1987) argues, "By interpreting the authoritative concepts governing politics, the courts exert their greatest influence. By refining the language of politics they contribute to the association of what is possible with the authority of the state" (196). The power of courts thus turns in part on their capacity to articulate compelling reasons and persuasive logics supporting their positions.

The constitutive and interactive dimensions of the federal courts have been evidenced with regard to issues concerning subaltern groups—racial minorities, workers, the welfare poor, and women. The fact that courts most often act in a context of deference or delegation from other policy elites means that supporting actions from those elites amplifying court authority often follow. When courts act alone, against other branches of government, it stands to reason that effective policy implementation will be undermined. When courts act on issues about which other elites care little, judges have demonstrated considerable capacity for influence, such as on prison reform. Other times, judicial articulations actually alter the terms of debate and the perceptions of key actors, as did court rulings for a time in the 1970s that redefined welfare as an entitlement rather than as charity (Lawrence 1990; Bussiere 1997). At yet other times, "symbolic politics" prevails. Legislators and Presidents may publicly scorn some court rulings, such as rulings on flag burning or due process limits on police or immigration officials' discretion, while supporting them privately. Moreover, as we shall see below, even intentionally symbolic rulings by courts and support for them by other elites sometimes can snowball, unintentionally, into transformative politics, once other advocates become involved, take seriously the promises at stake, and mobilize law through various means. Again, it is very difficult to generalize about the potential capacity of courts to initiate and play a role in significant social change without analyzing the entire political context.

The Politics of Legal Mobilization

Perhaps the most important contribution of legal mobilization scholarship has been in expanding our understandings about how litigation and judicial action can sometimes shape the terms of social relations and contestation among citizens in society. In short, how and how much court actions matter depends in large part on how variously situated groups—individual or class plaintiffs, targeted defendants, other affected social groups, the mass media, the general public—respond to, and act on, legal signals from the courts (see Canon and Johnson 1984; McCann 1993). In this way, legal mobilization frameworks tend to expand the relevant purview of judicial impact analysis beyond mere court rulings to the broader social manifestations of litigation, legal rights advocacy, and political struggle among these various groupings.

Socio-legal scholars have demonstrated that mobilization of legal norms, principles, and threats often occurs in varying ways at different moments, or stages, of both individual and group (McCann 1994) struggles. For example, social and political actors can aspire to provide meaningful expression to judicial logics through: (1) the very framing of rights claims for the prevention, reconstruction, or redress of harmful practices; (2) the organization of resources (enlisting a lawyer, mobilizing a support group, cultivating allies) to advance claims; and (3) the development of mobilization strategies to utilize these resources effectively in contests for power. Again, the availability of what Epp (1998) calls "support structures" can be as important to effective implementation as to the initial efforts to elicit favorable rulings expanding citizen rights themselves.

McCann's (1994) research on the legal mobilization strategies of unionized women to achieve equitable wages during the 1970s and 1980s provides a detailed picture of how social movements can mobilize and magnify judicial influence in political struggles for marginalized groups. He demonstrates that the very idea of pay equity as a reform cause was consciously shaped in response to both specific rulings by federal courts signaling opportunities for further claims and by the general legal frame of "antidiscrimination" that had come to structure political debates over race and gender-based inequality in American society. Federal courts—and especially the Supreme Court in the key cases—thus not only shaped the conscious formulation of particular goals and tactics of the movement, but they generated the very normative and conceptual framework within which the movement was imagined. As the movement developed, litigation was utilized to publicize reform claims, to mobilize active grassroots constituencies, to leverage bargaining power with employers, and to pressure for effective reform implementation. These legal tactics varied in their effectiveness in different locations of strategic interaction. But even where wage gains were modest, McCann's study shows, the legacy of legal action shaped and reshaped the political identities of individual actors and the institutional context in which they acted: "Legal rights became increasingly meaningful both as a general moral discourse and as a strategic resource for ongoing challenges to status quo power relations" (281). In short, while courts did not directly generate social change, political action in the shadow of lawsuits in federal (and state) courts contributed in important ways to reproducing and transforming the intersubjective legal terrain of interaction in many female-intensive workplaces around the nation.

Much the same type of judicial influence—at once enabling and delimiting the terms of political challenge—was evident in the civil rights movement. On the one hand, *Brown* was constructed in ways that proved empowering to many black leaders. First, it raised Southern blacks' hopes less by moral inspiration than by "demonstrating that the Southern white power structure was vulnerable at some points" (Morris 1984, 32, 34) and providing scarce practical resources for defiant action. This was especially important, as NAACP local activists "were the leaders who spearheaded the resistance of the black community" (McAdam 1982, 108).

Second, the increasing "pressure on the Southern white power structure to abolish racial domination" led to a massive, highly visible attack—including legal assaults as well as violent intimidation—on the NAACP itself. These reactions in turn forced a split between local, church affiliated NAACP leaders urging more radical forms of protest action and the bureaucratic, legally oriented national organization. The result was a marked increase in both the momentum of the grassroots protest campaign among Southern blacks generally and frustration about the effectiveness of legal tactics alone: "The two approaches—legal action and mass protest—entered into a turbulent but workable marriage" (Morris 1984, 39).

Brown not only created strategic opportunities and leverage for further collective action discussed previously, but it also consolidated the liberal, legalistic, civil "rights" logic of anti-discrimination at the heart of the civil rights movement. And this basic legal logic continued to prevail even as movement tactics gravitated toward grassroots nonviolent protest and demands for more radical social agendas were voiced. This experience with legally oriented rights claims before the federal courts has left an enduring legacy—one entailing both transformation and constraint—in the African American community and the nation overall. As Kimberle Crenshaw (1988) has argued, "Anti-discrimination law represents an ongoing ideological struggle in which the occasional winners harness the moral, coercive, and consensual power of law" (1335).

Many other examples could be cited from studies of individual and small-scale social interactions as well as of social movement struggles. Indeed, many of the most salient public issues surrounding the politics of democratic inclusion—discrimination against women, ethnic and racial minorities, gays and lesbians; rights to speech and association by dissenting activists; immigration procedures and rights of immigrants; voting rights; school finance; union rights to organize and bargain collectively; and the like—have been understood and contested in distinctly legal terms delineated by the federal courts over time. Moreover, studies confirm that many marginalized individuals often breathe life into legal principles through legal mobilization practices in ordinary life (Zemans 1983), while yet others can both expand

and challenge law's reach through acts of resistance. It would be a gross over-statement to contend that courts essentially determined these relationships. But it surely is true that judicially authorized logics have provided resources that sometimes can be mobilized by advocates with varying degrees of success. In fact, the rise of the inclusionary politics of rights that characterized the mid-twentieth century America owes greatly to changes in the Court's basic jurisprudential practices.

This said, it is important to recognize that legal mobilization efforts have proved a highly contingent and limited strategy for democratic social change. For one thing, we have noted repeatedly that federal courts have only occasionally articulated opinions, logics, and principles supporting highly inclusive, progressive conceptions of democratic social relations. And even many of those rulings often characterized as "progressive" have been moderate alternatives to more far-reaching egalitarian logics voiced by subaltern groups. Moreover, successful mobilization of progressive legal principles in reconstituting social power relations typically turns on capacities of social groups to mobilize considerable organizational, financial, and technical resources—resources that often far exceed their capacity. McCann's (1994) study, for instance, documents how committed unions, women's groups, lawyers, and leaders among women workers were vital elements in the legal mobilization efforts around pay equity, and even then the gains of that movement were short lived and modest. And many volumes have demonstrated the limited advances court rulings have provided to marginalized, stigmatized, and disadvantaged citizens in our society.

In sum, while we differ with Rosenberg (1991) in many ways, we find his general thesis that litigation for democratic change is a "hollow hope" overstates the point by only a small bit. It is hard to dispute that the most promising possibilities for democratic reconstruction through legal mobilization often remain unrealized possibilities, mere "symbolic" odes to democratic life that support hypocritical complacency by the haves, disenchantment or resignation by the have nots, and thus the status quo for all (see Scheingold 1974).

CONCLUSION

Our conclusion returns us to our original questions. What have excluded, exploited, or subaltern groups in the United States realistically obtained from the federal courts in their struggles for increased position? An informed, frank answer cannot be inspiring or encouraging. Courts have at times acted on behalf of the dispossessed, marginalized, subaltern, and disadvantaged. But these moments have been relatively rare and far between. When courts have made rulings that have advanced democratic inclusion, as in the 1950s and 1960s, it has been largely because the larger political context was supportive, key state actors deferred or delegated policy-making initiative to courts, and creative litigation campaigns for expanded civil rights and civil liberties provided pressures and opportunities for progressive judicial action. For the most part, the courts instead have followed mainstream political currents and been attentive to the security of prevailing social interests.[1] Indeed, the most fundamental role of the courts for most of our history has been securing property rights, contracts, and commercial "liberty" from democratic control. The courts were thus critical to the evolution of a vibrant corporate capitalist regime characterized by radical inequalities of wealth and power. Courts were never important allies in challenging the institutions of slavery in the nineteenth century, the prerogatives of corporations in the fifty years spanning the turn of the century, or the institutionalized prerogatives of patriarchy until recent decades. As we have suggested, it would be misleading, to single out the courts as blameworthy for the unequal conditions of slaves, Native Americans, women, or exploited workers; courts were part of a larger political complex in these matters. But courts only rarely have demonstrated the independent voice for inclusionary democracy that so many observers have associated—too simplistically, we think—with events in the mid-twentieth century.

This legacy of judicial practice warrants skepticism and wariness, to be sure, but not necessarily cynicism nor resignation about the value of litigation for civil rights, civil liberties, and egalitarian change. If Klinkner and Smith (1999) are correct that progressive, inclusionary reform occurs only episodically in short bursts, then activists and allies for the disadvantaged would do well to identify and even anticipate expanding opportunities for mobilization. Because courts sometimes can and do play a role in advancing the interests or opportunities of marginalized citizens, it is quite worthwhile to scrutinize continuously the political context for features that we have described as favorable to effective progressive action. Groups of citizens that traditionally have been excluded from power probably would do best to focus organizing efforts through other political means—political parties and other electorally oriented groupings, interest groups to pressure legislatures, grassroots social movements, and the like. But these investments should not dismiss or overlook appeals to courts through litigation. Indeed, effective political action usually entails working simultaneously on multiple political fronts. The cultivation of political influence in legislatures, in elections, in the mass media, and in courtrooms can be quite complementary, while gaining success in one venue alone threatens veto or defeat in other realms. That simply is how our multiple access-point, multiple veto political system works. In this enterprise of seeking to understand the contextual complexities of the larger political system in which courts are embedded, we find the recent outpouring of historical institutionalist scholarship to be invaluable.[2] The past rarely provides clear guidance to reading contemporary complexities, but it at least alerts us that politics is complicated and renders us far more sophisticated and realistic in our efforts to advance democracy and welfare for all.

NOTES

1. As Scheingold (1974) notes, courts—as well as the rights doctrines they articulate—"do cut both ways—serving at some times and under some circumstances to reinforce privilege and at other times to provide the cutting edge of (democratic) change" (76).

2. For examples of progressively oriented historical institutionalist scholarship on courts, see: Graber (1993); Klinkner and Smith (1999); Clayton and Gillman (1999); Lovell (2003).

REFERENCES

Baum, Lawrence. 1997. *The Puzzle of Judicial Behavior*. Ann Arbor: University of Michigan Press.

Bickel, Alexander M. 1962. *The Least Dangerous Branch: The Supreme Court at the Bar of Politics*. New York: Bobbs-Merrill.

Brigham, John. 1987. *The Cult of the Court*. Philadelphia: Temple University Press.

———. 1997. *The Constitution of Interests: Beyond the Politics of Rights*. New York: New York University Press.

Brisbin, Richard A., Jr. 2002. *A Strike Like No Other Strike: Law and Resistance During the Pittston Coal Strike of 1989–1990*. Baltimore: Johns Hopkins University Press.

Bussiere, Elizabeth. 1997. *(Dis)Entitling the Poor: The Warren Court, Welfare Rights, and the American Political Tradition*. University Park: Pennsylvania State University Press.

Canon, Bradley C., and Charles A. Johnson. 1984. *Judicial Policies: Implementation and Impact*. Washington, D.C.: Congressional Quarterly Press.

Clayton, Cornell W., and Howard Gillman, eds. 1999. *Supreme Court Decision-Making: New Institutionalist Approaches*. Chicago: University of Chicago Press.

Cover, Robert. 1983. "The Supreme Court, 1982 Term. Foreword: Nomos and Narrative." *Harvard Law Review* 97:4.

Crenshaw, Kimberle Williams. 1988. "Race, Reform, and Retrenchment: Transformation and Legitimation in Antidiscrimination Law." *Harvard Law Review* 101:1331.

Dolbeare, Kenneth, and Phillip E. Hammond. 1971. *The School Prayer Decisions: From Court Policy to Local Practice*. Chicago: University of Chicago Press.

Dudziak, Mary L. 2000. *Cold War, Civil Rights: Race and the Image of American Democracy*. Princeton: Princeton University Press.

Ely, John Hart. 1980. *Democracy and Distrust*. Cambridge: Harvard University Press.

Epp, Charles. 1998. *The Rights Revolution: Lawyers, Activists, and Supreme Courts in Comparative Perspective*. Chicago: University of Chicago Press.

Epstein, Lee, and Joseph Kobylka. 1992. *The Supreme Court and Legal Change*. Chapel Hill: University of North Carolina Press.

Eskridge, William N., Jr. 1991. "Overriding Supreme Court Statutory Interpretation Decisions." *Yale Law Journal* 101:331.

Feeley, Malcolm M., and Edward L. Rubin. 1998. *Judicial Policy Making and the Modern State: How the Courts Reformed America's Prisons*. Cambridge: Cambridge University Press.

Galanter, Marc. 1974. "Why the 'Haves' Come Out Ahead: Speculations on the Limits of Legal Change." *Law & Society Review*. 8:95–160

Gillman, Howard. 1995. "Judicial Behavioralism's Problematic Jurisprudence: Post-Postivist Legal Theory and Social Science Investigations of the Legal Model." Unpublished paper for annual meeting of the American Political Science Association, Chicago.

———. 1997. "The New Institutionalism, Part I: More and Less Than Strategy: Some Advantages to Interpretive Institutionalism in the Analysis of Judicial Politics." *Law and Courts* 7:6.

———. 1999. "The Court as an Idea, Not a Building (or a Game): Interpretive Institutionalism and the Analysis of Supreme Court Decision-Making." In *Supreme Court Decision-Making: New Institutionalist Approaches*, edited by Cornell Clayton and Howard Gillman, ch. 3 pp. 65–87. Chicago: University of Chicago Press.

———. 2001. "What's Law Got to Do with It? Judicial Behavioralists Test the 'Legal Model' of Judicial Decision Making." *Review of Majority Rule or Minority Will: Adherence to Precedent on the U.S. Supreme Court*, by Harold J. Spaeth and Jeffrey A. Segal. *Law and Social Inquiry* 26:465–504.

———. 2002. "How Political Parties Can Use the Courts to Advance Their Agendas: Federal Courts in the United States, 1875–1891." *American Political Science Review* 96:511–524.

Gillman, Howard, and Cornell Clayton, eds. 1999. *The Supreme Court in American Politics: New Institutionalist Approaches*. Lawrence: University of Kansas Press.

Graber, Mark A. 1993. "The Nonmajoritarian Difficulty: Legislative Deference to the Judiciary." *Studies in American Political Development* 7:35–73.

———. 1998. "Establishing Judicial Review? *Schooner Peggy* and the Early Marshall Court." *Political Research Quarterly* 51:7–25.

———. 1999. "The Problematic Establishment of Judicial Review." In *The Supreme Court in American Politics: New Institutionalist Interpretations*, edited by Howard Gillman and Cornell Clayton, 28–42. Lawrence: University of Kansas Press.

Kalman, Laura. 1996. *The Strange Career of Legal Liberalism*. New Haven: Yale University Press.

Keck, Thomas M. 2004. *The Most Activist Supreme Court in History: The Road to Modern Judicial Conservatism*. Chicago: University of Chicago Press.

Klinkner, Philip A., with Rogers M. Smith. 1999. *The Unsteady March: The Rise and Decline of Racial Equality in America*. Chicago: University of Chicago Press.

Lawrence, Susan E. 1990. *The Poor in Court: The Legal Services Program and Supreme Court Decision Making*. Princeton: Princeton University Press.

Lovell, George. 1994. "The Ambiguities of Labor's Legislative Reforms in New York State in the Late Nineteenth Century." *Studies in American Political Development* 8:81–102.

———. 2003. *Legislative Deferrals: Statutory Ambiguity, Judicial Power, and American Democracy*. New York: Cambridge University Press.

McAdam, Doug. 1982. *Political Process and the Development of Black Insurgency, 1930–1970*. Chicago: University of Chicago Press.

McCann, Michael W. 1986. *Taking Reform Seriously: Perspectives on Public Interest Liberalism*. Ithaca: Cornell University Press.

———. 1993. "Reform Litigation on Trial." *Law and Social Inquiry* 18:1101.

———. 1994. *Rights at Work: Pay Equity Reform and the Politics of Legal Mobilization*. Chicago: University of Chicago Press.

———. 1999. "How the Supreme Court Matters in American Politics: New Institutionalist Perspectives." In *The Supreme Court in American Politics: New Institutionalist Interpretations*, edited by Howard Gillman and Cornell Clayton, 63–97. Lawrence: University Press of Kansas.

Maltzman, Forrest, James F. Spriggs II, and Paul J. Wahlbeck. 1999. "Strategy and Judicial Choice: New Institutionalist Approaches to Supreme Court Decision-Making." In *Supreme Court Decision-Making: New Institutionalist Approaches*, edited by Cornell W. Clayton and Howard Gillman, 43–63. Chicago: University of Chicago Press.

Martin, Andrew D. 2001. "Congressional Decision Making and the Separation of Powers." *American Political Science Review* 95:361–378.

Morris, Aldon. 1984. *The Origins of the Civil Rights Movement*. New York: Free Press.

Murphy, Walter F. 1962. *Congress and the Court*. Chicago: University of Chicago Press.

Novkov, Julie. 2001. *Constituting Workers, Protecting Women: Gender, Law, and Labor in the Progressive Era and New Deal Years*. Ann Arbor: University of Michigan Press.

Patterson, James T. 2001. *Brown v. Board of Education: A Civil Rights Milestone and Its Troubled Legacy*. New York: Oxford University Press.

Peretti, Terri Jennings. 1999. *In Defense of a Political Court*. Princeton: Princeton University Press.

Perry, H. W., Jr.. 1991. *Deciding to Decide: Agenda Setting in the United States Supreme Court*. Cambridge: Harvard University Press.

Powe, Lucas. 2000. *The Warren Court and American Politics*. Cambridge: Harvard University Press.

Rogers, James R. 2001. "Information and Judicial Review: A Signaling Game of Legislative-Judicial Interaction." *American Journal of Political Science* 45:84–99.

Rosenberg, Gerald. 1991. *The Hollow Hope: Can Courts Bring About Social Change?* Chicago: Chicago University Press.

Sarat, Austin, and Stuart Scheingold. 1998. *Cause Lawyering: Political Commitments and Professional Responsibilities*. New York: Oxford University Press.

Scheingold, Stuart A. 1974. *The Politics of Rights: Lawyers, Public Policy, and Political Change*. New Haven: Yale University Press.

———. 1989. "Constitutional Rights and Social Change." In *Judging the Constitution*, edited by Michael W. McCann and Gerald L. Houseman, 73–91. Glenview, IL: Scott, Foresman/Little, Brown.

Segal, Jeffrey A., and Harold J. Spaeth. 1993. *The Supreme Court and the Attitudinal Model*. New York: Cambridge University Press.

Shapiro, Martin M. 1983. "Fathers and Sons: The Courts, the Commentators, and the Search for Values." In *The Burger Court: The Counter-Revolution That Wasn't*, edited by Vincent Blasi, 218–33. New Haven: Yale University Press.

Spann, Girardieau A. 1993. *Race Against the Court: The Supreme Court and Minorities in Contemporary America*. New York: State University of New York Press.

Tushnet, Mark 1987. *The NAACP's Legal Strategy against Segregated Education, 1925–1952*. Chapel Hill: University of North Carolina Press.

Tushnet, Mark. 2005. *A Court Divided: The Rehnquist Court and the Future of Consititutional Law*. New York: W. W. Norton & Co.

Wechsler, Herbert. 1959. "Toward Neutral Principles of Constitutional Law." *Harvard Law Review* 73:1–35.

Whittington, Keith A. 1999. *Constitutional Construction: Divided Powers and Constitutional Meaning. Cambridge*: Harvard University Press.

Zangrando, Robert L. 1980. *The NAACP Crusade against Lynching, 1909–1950*. Philadelphia: Temple University Press.

Zemans, Frances Kahn. 1983. "Legal Mobilization: The Neglected Role of the Law in the Political System." *American Political Science Association* 77:690.

DAVID T. CANON

13 The Representation of Racial Interests in the U.S. Congress

A CENTRAL CHALLENGE FOR representative democracy is to provide a voice for minority interests in a system dominated by majority votes. Any democracy's legitimacy and stability depends, in part, on its ability to accomplish that difficult aim. The founders' institutional solution of the separation of powers within and across levels of government, in addition to the great size of the republic, provided multiple access points for various interests and some assurance that no single interest would dominate government for extended periods. Hailed by generations of pluralists within political science, this competitive political process was thought to produce optimal results.[1] Majority tyranny was to be prevented by a pluralist politics characterized by overlapping memberships, cross-cutting cleavages, and responsiveness to intense preferences—a republic where "minorities ruled," to use Robert Dahl's famous phrase (1956, 124–151).

However, for at least forty years, scholars and politicians have recognized that this system does not equally encompass the democratic inclusion of racial and ethnic minorities (see McClain and Garcia 1993, for a review of research on this topic). The most distinct break from the pluralist tradition came with the publication of Stokley Carmichael and Charles V. Hamilton's *Black Power: The Politics of Liberation in America* (1967). They argued that blacks needed to control their own political organizations and that coalitions with whites would not be productive. This black separatist perspective lives today in the Nation of Islam and other black nationalist groups.

The political strategy most commonly used within the civil rights movement today to address the gap between the representation of majority and minority interests has been what Lani Guinier (1991a) calls the "black electoral success strategy," which was intended not only to mobilize more blacks to vote but to enhance political representation of their interests (1081–1134). The most recent step in pursuit of this strategy was the creation of fifteen new black-majority and ten Hispanic-majority districts in 1992 (Lublin 1997b, 23). Many of these districts were ruled unconstitutional in the line of cases that followed the landmark ruling in *Shaw v. Reno* (1993) and at least eleven of them were redrawn in the 1990s (several of them went through multiple iterations). However, the extent to which race may be used in redistricting and the role the racial redistricting plays in the representation of minority interests in legislatures remain open questions.

This chapter examines the empirical, normative, and legal dimensions of this topic: How *are* minority interests represented (the empirical literature on representation), how *should* representation be provided to minorities within a majority rule system (the normative literature), and how *can* representation be provided (the legal literature). There is surprisingly little cross-fertilization across these subfields within American politics; thus one of the goals of this chapter is to point out the common themes that cut across subfield lines within American politics. Another theme of this chapter is to examine the impact of electoral institutions, such as the creation of black-majority districts, on racial representation and the politics of democratic inclusion. I conclude by offering suggestions for future research.

ARE MINORITY INTERESTS REPRESENTED IN LEGISLATURES?

Part III of this volume poses the central question: to what extent does representation and governance reflect democratic inclusion? Two basic approaches have been used to examine this question in the context of the representation of minority interests in Congress: descriptive and substantive representation. First I examine these concepts, next I review the empirical literature on the subject, and I close the section with my alternative perspective.

Descriptive Representation

A first set of concerns is rooted in the politician's side of the relationship. Does the member of Congress "look like" his or her constituency? Is the member black or white, male or female, Catholic or Protestant? There are three positions on the value of descriptive representation. The first argues that there is a distinct value in having role models and notes the benefits that come from the simple act of being represented by someone who shares something as fundamental as skin color. For example, Davidson and Grofman (1994) quote Tom McCain, one of the first black office holders in South Carolina, "There's an inherent value in office holding that goes far beyond picking up the garbage. A race of people who are excluded from public office will always be second class citizens." (16). The intangibles of descriptive representation and the role models that help create greater trust in the system are important. Thernstrom (1987), a critic of black-majority districts, sees the advantages of having racially diverse political bodies. She says:

> Whether on a city council, on a county commission, or in the state legislature, blacks inhibit the expression of prejudice, act as spokesmen for black interests, dispense patronage, and often facilitate the discussion of topics (such as black crime) that whites are reluctant to raise. That is, governing bodies function differently when they are racially mixed, particularly where blacks are new to politics and where racially insensitive language and discrimination in the provision of services are long-established political habits. (239)

Jane Mansbridge (1996) argues that descriptive representation is valuable when "communication between constituents and representatives is impaired by distrust," when "important substantive interests of a descriptive group are relatively uncrystallized," or when a group is "disadvantaged and dispersed" (1, quoted in Bianco 1997, 1). William Bianco (1997) models these scenarios in an evaluation game and concludes that if the constituents have relatively homogeneous interests, "constituents are more likely to trust a representative who shares their demographics compared to one who does not, and such trust will increase the chances that the representative's behavior is consistent with constituent interests" (6). However trust and responsiveness will not prevail if constituent interests are heterogeneous (9).

The other two positions argue that descriptive representation by itself is not useful unless it is linked to substantive representation; the left-of-center perspective argues that having "black faces in high places" may come at too high a price. Robert C. Smith (1990) says, "Like the transformation of black music, it will be a hollow victory if in order to achieve equitable descriptive-symbolic representation blacks are required to sacrifice their substantive policy agendas. The new black politician would then be a shell of himself, more like a Prince or Michael Jackson than a B.B. King or Bobby Bland" (161; Jones 1985 and Pinderhughes 1987, xix, make similar arguments). The right-of-center perspective recognizes the value of descriptive representation in some limited contexts, but argues that whites can adequately represent black interests and that descriptive representation comes at a price (which is the loss of white Democrats in legislative districts that surround minority–majority districts; see NAACP 1994; Engstrom 1995; Hill 1995; Swain 1995, 78–83; Lublin 1997b, 111–114 for various estimates of the extent of Democratic losses).

Anne Phillips (1995) makes the case that empirical research has focused almost exclusively on representation of *ideas* (substantive) rather than *presence* (descriptive). While substantive representation receives a disproportionate share of attention, there are many studies that focus on descriptive representation. These works either describe how the presence of blacks in Congress has grown in the past century (Clay 1993, appendix A and B) or provide explanations for how blacks get elected (Grofman and Handley 1989; Grofman, Griffin, and Glazer 1992; Handley and Grofman 1994; Cameron, Epstein, and O'Halloran 1996, 803–805; Lublin1997a, chapter 3). All of this work concludes that a greater percentage of black voters are needed to elect a black member in the South than in the non-South. Also, when a district is more than 40 percent black, there is almost no chance that a Republican would be elected (Camerson, Epstein, and O'Halloran, 1996, 805). Grofman and Handley (1989) and Handley and Grofman (1994) make the strongest statement by claiming that black-majority districts are nearly a *necessary condition* to elect blacks to office.

Descriptive representation is also important because the political world has recently shown a much greater sensitivity to having leaders who "look like America." President Clinton's well-publicized efforts to appoint a diverse cabinet brought more attention to the importance of descriptive representation, and George W. Bush has actively campaigned for the Latino vote while stressing the importance of the Republicans' "Big Tent." Congress watchers, such as *Congressional Quarterly* and *National Journal* also mention the racial, gender, and even occupational composition of every new Congress, and every Congress textbook dutifully mentions the similar sets of demographic figures.

Substantive Representation

Substantive representation moves beyond appearances to specify *how* the member serves constituents' interests. Two models go back to at least the time of Edmund Burke: (1) the trustee who represents constituents' interests from a distance, weighing a variety of national, collective, local, and moral concerns; and (2) the delegate who has a simple mandate to carry out the direct desires of the voters. Hannah Pitkin (1967) advanced the discussion by combining both approaches. She says, "Representation here means acting in the interest of the represented, in a manner responsive to them. The representative must act independently; his action must involve discretion and judgement; he must be the one who acts...." [Pitkin 1967, 209–210, quoted in Jewell 1983, 304].

This characterization of the representative–represented relationship raises a host of empirical questions. How much do voters monitor their representatives' behavior? To what degree do representational linkages work if voters are not paying attention? The most demanding theory of representation, known as *policy responsiveness,* requires that voters express basic policy preferences, representatives respond to those desires, and then voters monitor and assess the politician's behavior (Miller and Stokes 1963). Other scholars paint a more subtle picture. John Kingdon (1989), among others, demonstrates that members of Congress behave *as if* voters are paying attention, even when constituents may be inattentive. Clausen (1973) argues that the representational linkages will vary depending on the electoral context and constituents' issue attentiveness. Douglas Arnold (1990) noted the importance of the "potential preferences of inattentive publics" that could be aroused by a well-funded challenger, so members may be held accountable by *anticipating* what constituents would want *if they were fully informed* (68–71). Bianco (1994) points out that one important dimension of representation is the trust that members of Congress develop under varying circumstances. In this view, constituents do not have to engage in constant monitoring if they are convinced that the member will "do the right thing."

Incorporating the component of race while applying the above basic components of representation adds a layer of complexity. At the constituency level, the district's racial composition district intersects with Fenno's (1978) concentric circles. Within the district, reelection, and primary constituencies (and to some extent the personal constituency, depending on the politician), race overlays a complex set of relationships that vary from district to district. Black constituents have distinct needs and interests that differ from the white constituency (Swain 1993, 7–10; Canon 1999a, 22–26). For example, blacks are disproportionately affected by problems such as crime, drugs, poverty, discrimination, and poor health. Politicians representing districts comprised of a substantial African American population differ from each other in their responsiveness to the needs and interests of these constituents. Some members of Congress focus on one race within their reelection constituency; others give attention to both races within one party; and others may focus on a single race at the district level. These patterns of representation obviously vary across issues. Most issues addressed in Congress do not have any direct racial content. But some are centrally concerned with race—and another substantial portion may or may not concern race depending on the member's framing of the issue (Canon 1999a, chapter 4).

Yet another layer of complexity that must be factored in is a district's homogeneity or heterogeneity. As Morris Fiorina (1974) argued twenty-five years ago, heterogeneous districts are more difficult to represent. This is especially true in districts such as John Conyers' district in Detroit that encompasses both very poor urban areas and relatively wealthy suburbs. Another district variable that is important for inner-city northern districts is the relative electoral safety of those seats. As Swain notes, these members have much more leeway than members from more marginal districts (1993, chapter 3).

The Supply-Side Theory of Representation and the Politics of Difference and Commonality

The debate over the nature of representation provided by new black-majority districts presents yet another aspect of racial representation. The common assumption, from both supporters and critics of the districts, is that they were created to represent black interests and to empower blacks. This "blacks must represent blacks" or "politics of difference" school of thought lies at the heart of racial redistricting. In the majority opinion in *Shaw v. Reno*, Sandra Day O'Connor states that "When a district obviously is created solely to effectuate the perceived common interests of one racial group, elected officials are more likely to believe that their primary obligation is to represent only the members of that group, rather than their constituency as a whole" (113 S.Ct. 2816 [1993], 2827). According to the Court, this leads to the inescapable conclusion that white voters will not be adequately represented in black-majority districts.

My work challenges Justice O'Connor's position by showing that the process of candidate emergence and political campaigning exerts a powerful influence on representation in black-majority districts. I challenge the prevailing notion that there are monolithic black interests that could produce *a* "representative of their choice" in most districts. Instead, factions within the African American community produce candidates with different ideological backgrounds and different visions of the representation of racial interests. One significant effect of this ideological diversity among black candidates is having ideological diversity in the pool of black candidates gives a centrist coalition the power to elect candidates of their choice, which would be the candidate who practices a politics of commonality. (Canon, Schousen, and Sellers 1996; Canon 1999a).

This "supply-side" theory of redistricting provides a new understanding of the electoral sources of representation in the new black districts. The traditional "demand-side" perspective of redistricting focuses on voters and elections, addressing such topics as incumbency safety, partisan bias, racial block voting, political geography and demographics, vote dilution, and runoff primaries. In contrast, the supply-side perspective examines how individual politicians respond to the changing electoral context imposed by new district lines and how, in turn, their decisions shape the electoral choices and outcomes in a given district. Rather than simply assuming that goals for minority representation translate into a specific configuration of district lines and predictable consequences, the supply-side perspective cautions that all outcomes depend on the calculations of potential candidates.

The supply-side argument also contradicts the common view that black-majority districts are rooted in the politics of difference. The supply-side effects of racial redistricting show that many African American politicians elected in the new districts embody the politics of commonality rather than the politics of difference. Furthermore, even those who *campaign* by appealing only to black voters do, in fact, spend a substantial proportion of their time in Congress representing the interests of white and black voters alike. This is a story of unintended consequences: the Madisonian-style institutional engineering that attempted to implement a politics of difference was trumped by individuals operating as sovereign actors within the broader Madisonian system that is based on the politics of commonality. I argue that this outcome should be encouraged in a political system that continues to cope with racial fear, animosity, and discrimination.

Measuring Racial Representation

Many of these complexities of race and representation have yet to be examined in the popular and academic literature on the topic, especially as they are applied to the new black-majority districts created in 1992. However, a rapidly growing literature is beginning to take up the challenge. Most of this research does not directly address the linkages between redistricting and representation, but is concerned with the broader questions of democratic inclusion and how minority interests are represented in Congress. This is a necessary first step. If blacks do not represent black interests any differently than do whites, then the normative and political arguments in favor of black-majority districts disappear.

The empirical literature on racial representation examines a broad range of topics: the extent to which African Americans in the House have achieved influence within the institution (Levy and Stoudinger 1978; Loomis 1981; Canon 1995; Cobb and Jenkins 1996; Singh 1998), responsiveness of members to characteristics of their constituency, with a focus on the percentage of black voters (Combs, Hibbing, and Welch 1984; Welch and Hibbing 1984; Nye and Bullock 1992; Swain 1993; Lublin 1997b), the ideological orientation and cohesiveness of the Congressional Black Caucus (CBC; Smith 1981; Swain 1993; Walton 1995; Menifield 1996; Pinney and Serra 2002), role orientations of members of the CBC (Johnson and Secret 1996), the development and institutionalization of the CBC (Levy and Stoudinger 1976, 1978; Clay 1993), and the impact of the new minority–majority districts on racial representation (Overby and Cosgrove 1996; Lublin 1997b; Canon 1999a). This literature uses a range of research methods: case studies based largely on interviews, observation, or first-hand accounts (Clay

1993; Swain 1993, Singh 1998,); quantitative analysis of roll-call behavior linked to district characteristics, such as percentage of black voters (Cameron, Epstein, and O'Halloran 1996; Menifield 1996; Overby and Cosgrove 1996; Lublin 1997b); and analysis of congressional behavior that goes beyond roll-call voting (Canon 1995, 1999a; Cobb and Jenkins 1996; DiLorenzo 1997). First, I briefly review some of the earlier work on the topic.

Early work on racial representation focused on urban politics, which is where African Americans first achieved significant political power. Blacks in Congress had almost no power, so they were largely ignored by scholars (of 350 citations in McClain and Garcia's [1993] extensive review of the minority politics literature, only seven concerned African Americans in Congress). This lack of attention may also be attributed to the perception that the CBC was weak and ineffective during its first twenty years (see Swain 1993, 37–39, for a review of various studies that make this argument).

Subsequent work has demonstrated that the CBC has played a more prominent role in Congress since 1993 when its numbers increased by 50 percent. Canon (1995) shows that the CBC played a pivotal role in nine of the sixteen key votes identified by *Congressional Quarterly* in the first session of the 103rd Congress; increased their presence on most committees, especially constituency committees on which they were underrepresented before 1993; held three full committee chairs and sixteen subcommittee chairs; and played a larger role in the whip system (see Singh 1998, chapter 7, for similar evidence). Singh points out that the Republican takeover of Congress forced the CBC back into their more confrontational role; he also sees the increased diversity within the CBC as a source of weakness rather than strength (202). Cobb and Jenkins (1996) show that the CBC proved a powerful voice for black interests within the House by introducing a disproportionate share of the legislation that offered symbolic benefits and direct and indirect economic and social benefits for blacks.

Other scholars have shifted focus from the internal political clout of the CBC to the responsiveness of members of Congress to their black constituents. Carol Swain (1993) employs participant observation, detailed case studies of thirteen districts, and quantitative analysis of roll-call voting in her analysis of racial representation in Congress. Her central conclusion is that blacks and white Democrats both do a good job of representing black interests. Swain argues that creating black-majority districts is a self-limiting strategy (due to the relatively few numbers of such districts that could be drawn) and that blacks are better off entering biracial coalitions with whites to elect more blacks and counting on whites to represent their interests.

Other authors have tackled the responsiveness issue by examining roll-call data and interest groups ratings. Five hypotheses concerning the patterns of responsiveness are suggested in the literature. V.O. Key's (1949) *racial threat* or *polarization* hypothesis was based on the observation that Southern Democrats in the "black belt" regions "have the deepest and most immediate concern about the maintenance of white supremacy" (5; also see Jewell 1967, 34). Thus representatives from districts with the highest percentage of black voters would be least supportive of black interests. William Keech (1986) modified this hypothesis to suggest that the majority would not be responsive to relatively small concentrations of black voters, but responsiveness would increase up to some critical level (around 30 percent), at which point the racial threat hypothesis would again became relevant. However, at the highest levels of black population, where blacks could be elected (a situation that was not possible in the pre–Voting Rights Act [VRA] era that Key was writing about), responsiveness would again increase. The third hypothesis posits a straight linear relationship of responsiveness (what Cameron, Epstein, and O'Halloran [1996] call the *influence* hypothesis). Fourth, several versions of threshold models have been suggested to capture the low levels of responsiveness at the lowest level of black population and the diminishing returns at the higher levels. Finally, the *color blind* hypothesis holds that race does not matter, and instead factors like party, region, and percent urban will determine the roll-call behavior of members of Congress.

Black (1978) finds support for Key's threat hypothesis in the pre-VRA era, but after blacks gained the right to vote in the South the data support Keech's (1986) curvilinear hypothesis. Bullock and MacManus (1981) also support this hypothesis, finding that representatives with districts that are more than 30 percent black are least supportive of black interests. Bullock (1981, 1985) finds a bimodal distribution with the most liberal members appearing in the 6 percent to 20 percent and 26 percent to 30 percent black ranges. Combs, Hibbing and Welch (1984) attempt to sort out these conflicting findings and show that the influence hypothesis holds in non-Southern districts (representatives become more liberal in the roll-call voting, as measured by Conservative Coalition scores, as the proportions of blacks in their districts increase). Southern Democrats were responsive to blacks only if there was a substantial urban population; in the rural south, Key's threat hypothesis still holds (432–433). Whitby and Gilliam (1991) and Nye and Bullock (1992) both report that Southern Democrats have become more supportive of the civil rights agenda since the 1960s. Both find that some remnants of the "old South" remain: Nye and Bullock find that the "deep South" states are still somewhat more conservative than the other southern states (92–93; though the differences are less pronounced than in the 1960s) and Whitby and Gilliam (1991) find that older cohorts of southern Democrats (elected in the 1960s and before) have been slower to change their roll-call voting habits than more-recently elected southern Democrats (514). However, both studies conclude that southern Democrats are responsive to the proportion of blacks in their districts; the higher the percentage of blacks, the greater the support for the civil rights agenda (thus lending support for the influence hypothesis). These findings are also consistent with David Rohde's (1991) evidence that Southern Democrats moved much closer to their non-Southern counterparts on roll-call voting in the 1980s. Differences in the party unity of southern Democrats and northern Democrats shrunk from 43 points in 1970 to 14 points in 1988 (56).

Whitby finds some evidence for the color blind hypothesis—the percent black in the district was a significant predictor of neither Leadership Conference on Civil Rights (LCCR) scores of Southern members of Congress between 1969 and 1982 nor a range of roll-call rating from 1983 to 1984 (1985, 1987, respectively). However, in two Congresses, the 91st and 93rd, there is support for the racial threat hypothesis. When the deep Southern states are separated, Whitby's findings are similar to Black's (1978): from the 91st through 94th Congresses, the coefficient on percent black is negative (one is significant); from the 95th through the 97th the coefficients are positive (and two nearly reach significance). Whitby's most important finding is that the interaction of percent black and percent urban is highly significant in both the South and deep South models (1985, 511, 515). As noted above, Swain (1993, 16) also supports the color blind hypothesis, but studies of roll-call voting in the 1990s show that this pattern no longer holds.

The most recent work on responsiveness examines the impact of black-majority districts on racial representation. These studies test the influence and threshold hypotheses. Overby and Cosgrove (1996) conclude that the loss of black constituents in white southern Democrats' districts made members less responsive to black interests after the 1992 round of redistricting. They also find that Republicans were not noticeably affected by the change in racial composition of their districts. They conclude that there may be a tradeoff between descriptive representation and substantive representation: By creating black-majority districts, there may be more blacks in Congress, but overall, black interests may be hurt (which supports Swain's position). This finding is consistent with Rohde's (1991) warning that creating black-majority districts in the South would "not only weaken other Democrats but would also mitigate the liberalizing effects of Black enfranchisement in the South" (210, note 10). However, Overby and Cosgrove (1996) point out that the actual consequences were relatively small as white Democrats were protected through "creative cartography" (549).

Cameron, Epstein, and O'Halloran (1996) reach a similar conclusion with a somewhat more sophisticated research design that models both the electoral and representational effects of the percent black constituents. They find strong support for the threshold hypothesis and conclude that the representation of black interests (as measured by LCCR support scores) would be maximized by creating as many 47 percent black districts as possible in the South and equally distributing blacks in non-Southern districts (808). Such a strategy could produce sixty sympathetic white Democrats, but no black incumbents. Of course this distribution would be impossible, given actual concentrations of black population, but this outcome would be preferable, they argue, to the distribution of black voters in the 1992 districts in which only six districts were between 40 percent and 50 percent black and thirty-two were black majority. David Lublin (1997b) finds a threshold at 40 percent black population—above that level there are diminishing returns for substantive representation of black interests. Lublin also finds that southern Democrats are more responsive to percentage of black population than northern Democrats (both above and below the 40 percent threshold), and below the 40 percent threshold, Republicans are actually more responsive than Democrats (table 5.3).[2]

Lublin places more emphasis on the value of descriptive representation than does Swain or Cameron, Epstein, and O'Halloran (1996), which leads him to recommend a balanced approach where as many 40 percent to 55 percent black districts as possible are drawn (55 percent to ensure that as many blacks are elected as possible—anything more than 55 percent is wasted according to Lublin; 40 percent to ensure maximum responsiveness from white representatives [102]). Grofman, Griffin, and Glazer (1992, 375) reached a similar compromise position, noting that if descriptive representation is the goal, then a maximum number of black-majority districts should be created, but if the goal is to elect liberal Democrats without regard to race, then districts with 20 percent to 30 percent blacks would be ideal (a substantially lower threshold than Lublin recommends).

Charles Bullock (1995) counters these findings with his analysis of roll-call voting in the 102nd and first session of the 103rd Congress. He concludes, "No evidence was found to support the hypothesis that White Democrats were moving away from civil rights (after the 1992 redistricting). With the Black vote a bulwark for Democrats, many are unwilling to vie with Republicans for White support by using opposition to civil rights as a lure" (154). Bullock finds that southern blacks are far more responsive to changes in levels of black population than are southern whites (151). Hill (1996) also challenges the conclusion that black-majority districts hurt overall support for black interests in Congress. She finds that the twenty-two members who lost at least 10 percent of the black district population actually became slightly *more* supportive of the LCCR's agenda (12–13).

Another body of work focuses on the internal dynamics of the CBC—its level of cohesion (Levy and Stoudinger 1978; Walton 1995; Pinney and Serra 2002) and the sources of cues (Levy and Stoudinger 1976; Menifield 1996; Pinney and Serra 2002). This work reveals that the CBC is a very cohesive group (as measured by the standard deviation of their Americans for Democratic Action [ADA] scores) that becomes even more cohesive in response to presidential agendas that are adverse to its interests (Pinney and Serra 2002). They are extremely liberal as a group, but the younger generation of members is introducing more diversity (Walton 1995, 15–16). Menifield (1996) examines a series of key votes on foreign, economic, and social policy to determine the relative influence of the CBC, the Hispanic Caucus, and the Women's Caucus. The CBC provided the strongest cues (they had a significant impact on twelve of the twenty key votes he examined compared to nine of twenty for the Hispanic Caucus and two of twenty for the Women's Caucus; 24–41). While this body of work makes a useful contribution to the literature, more explicit linkages need to be made to policy and broader questions of representation. Ideology and cohesion are not important for their own sake, but in terms of how they affect the ability of various groups within Congress to meet their goals and serve their constituents.

All of the literature cited above on responsiveness, cohesion, and ideology share one common problem: an exclusive use of roll-call votes to measure congressional behavior. The standard approach regresses district-level characteristics on various interest group ratings such as ADA, LCCR, or COPE (Committee on Political Education), or Poole and Rosenthal's NOMINATE scores. This practice can largely be explained by the "law of available data."

Roll-call data, especially interest group ratings, are readily available and easily analyzed, but are not accurate measures of a member's overall behavior in Congress because of the "censored sample problem" (King 1989, 208–213). Assume a range of activities in support of black interests on a continuum from 0 to 100, with one extreme of the scale (0) anchored by Sen. Jesse Helms (R–NC) and his opposition to almost anything that would be of interest to the black community and the other (100) by Rep. John Conyers (D–MI) and his slavery reparations bill that he introduces every session. On this 0 to 100 scale, only the middle range of concerns ever makes it to a roll-call vote. The more extreme positions on either side are weeded out in the legislative process or are reflected in different aspects of the process such as speeches on the floor of the House or constituency service. A statistical analysis based on this censored sample (in effect, the two tails of the distribution are chopped off) yields biased parameter estimates. In other words, one can say very little about the extent of black representation based on roll-call votes or the interest group support scores that are based on roll-call votes (Hall and Wayman 1990, 801; Hall 1996; and DiLorenzo 1997, 1742–1743, make similar arguments in different contexts).

Furthermore, general ideological ratings are not an especially good measure of black interests because most of the issues they include in their measure of support are not of central importance to the African American community. Even LCCR scores, which are supposed to be the most closely related to race, do not reflect a racial agenda. Only one of the fourteen votes used to derive the LCCR support scores for the 103rd Congress—the Racial Justice Act—is explicitly related to black interests. On two other votes the LCCR's position was opposed by a majority of blacks (school choice and abortion). ADA votes reflect a similar absence of racial content; of the thirty-nine roll calls used by the ADA in the 103rd Congress, one was directly related to race (the Racial Justice Act) and four implicitly involved race (DC statehood, the CBC budget vote, the death penalty, and U.S. policy toward Haiti; Canon 1999a, chapters 1 and 4). The standard practice of regressing ADA, LCCR, COPE, or NOMINATE scores on district characteristics such as percent black, percent urban, and income, is difficult to justify as a reasonable approach for measuring racial representation.

Some recent work attempts to overcome this problem by employing a broader range of measures of congressional behavior. Cobb and Jenkins (1996) and Vincent DiLorenzo (1997) both examine sponsorship of legislation that is of interest to black constituents, arguing that this alternative measure of legislative behavior is a good indicator of the intensity of commitment to black interests. My research on racial representation in Congress examines sponsorship and co-sponsorship of legislation, speeches on the floor of the house, amendments offered, committee assignments, leadership positions, constituency newsletters, the location of district office, the racial composition of the staff, and newspaper coverage of members (in addition to roll-call voting) in all districts that were at least 25 percent black in the 103rd Congress. I conclude that black members of Congress do a better job of representing a balance of racial interests than do white members and that there are important differences in the representational styles of members of the CBC. Some are explicitly biracial in their politics, while others continue to practice a "politics of difference" (Canon 1999a, chapters 4 and 5).

This recent research looking at a broader range of legislative behavior demonstrates that the race of the member matters. These findings contradict the research by Swain (1993), Cameron, Epstein, and O'Halloran (1996), Thernstrom and Thernstrom (1997, chapter 16) and others who are more inclined to the color blind approach to racial representation.

There is relatively little research on the substantive representation of black interests in state legislatures (most of the work, which was cited above, concerns descriptive representation). Mary Herring's excellent analysis of state senate roll-call voting in Louisiana, Georgia, and Alabama between 1979 and 1981 on redistributive, racial, and "rights" issues finds that white state senators are not as responsive to black constituents as are black state senators (1990, 749). Kerry Haynie (2001) examines a broad range of political behavior, including committee assignments, bill introduction, and success in passing legislation. His index of political incorporation is a useful tool for charting the gains made by black state legislators. Not only did the index have intuitive appeal, but it also had some success in explaining variation in policy outcomes, especially in the area of health care and education expenditures. Haynie also finds that despite the gains made by blacks in electoral and legislative politics, black legislators are perceived as being less effective than whites by lobbyists, members of the press, and fellow legislators (controlling for relevant institutional and personal variables). These themes are also explored in an article in which Haynie and Kathleen Bratton examined the legislative success of both African Americans and women in six state legislatures. The strongest aspect of this article is that it moves beyond the typical focus on roll-call voting to examine bill sponsorship and success in passing legislation. They conclude that while women are as successful as men in passing legislation, blacks are less successful than whites in three of the six states they examine (Bratton and Haynie 1998).

Pursuing a different angle in the state politics literature, Rodney Hero (2000) argues that our system is characterized by "two-tiered pluralism," in which "substantive democracy has not been attained by racial/ethnic minorities" despite the achievement of procedural democracy (3). He systematically demonstrates that V.O. Key's (1949) insights about the importance of racial politics for understanding state politics hold with a vengeance in modern U.S. politics, and *not only* in the South. Hero argues that the racial and ethnic diversity of the states, along with other contextual variables, are critical for understanding state political institutions and policies.

SHOULD MINORITIES RECEIVE SPECIAL CONSIDERATION?

While strong evidence exists that our legislative institutions reflect democratic inclusion on several levels, important normative questions remain concerning how minority interests *should* be represented in Congress. Can white politicians adequately represent minority interests? Should racial minorities have congressional districts explicitly drawn to maximize their political power, even if it requires tortuous district lines? Once the districts are created, should black representatives focus their attention on black constituents, or attempt to represent the entire district? What does the creation of minority–majority districts mean for the quality of democracy? What impact do they have on the nature of representation, accountability, legitimacy, and equality?

One basis for answering these questions is found in the debate in the minority politics and women's studies literatures concerning the "politics of difference" versus the "politics of commonality" (Gilligan 1982; MacKinnon 1987; Eisenstein 1988; Young 1990; Connoly 1991) and the broader literature on community, identity, and democracy (Beitz 1989; Gates 1992; Taylor 1992; Kymlicka 1995; Phillips 1995; Gutmann and Thompson 1996). I cannot do justice to the complexity and scope of the normative literature on these topics,[3] but I will briefly outline its contours.

The literature on identity, community, and democracy helps sort out the general principles that should govern the relationships among groups and between politicians and constituents. Stated in general terms, the racial politics questions posed above look like this: Should government treat everyone as individuals or recognize group differences? If group differences are recognized, what are the proper mechanisms for ensuring fair representation? Should group differences be confined to the private sphere and only tolerated in the public sphere within a broader Madisonian system of majority rule (Rawls 1971) or should identity politics be embraced, recognizing that permanent majorities may be tyrannical (Guinier 1994)?

These questions reveal the central fault lines in current democratic theory. There are myriad combinations across dueling dualisms: Does the ideal democracy place more emphasis on individualism or identity, community or liberty, rights or responsibility (for citizens), accountability or autonomy (for politicians), authenticity or assimilation, equality of opportunity or outcomes? There are no obvious groupings across all these dimensions that can be captured in a single belief system or theory, nor could consistent choices across pairs be made by those who seek racial justice and equality.

Political liberalism favors individualism, liberty, rights, assimilation, and equality of opportunity across the pairs outlined above; however, there is a great deal of variation among political liberals. In general, political liberalism attempts to downplay, or even avoid, difference while emphasizing shared values, consensus, and tolerance (Rawls 1971). However, unlike American national identity, there is room for cultural and racial differences within Rawlsian liberalism (Dworkin 1989, 499–504; Kymlicka 1995). Kymlicka attempts to resolve the tension between liberalism and group rights by arguing for a "societal culture" that allows individuals to express their political and cultural identities.

Communitarians focus on shared meanings and values, the common good, and consensus that bonds communities together. Difference is not easily incorporated into a theory that focuses on unity and common experiences, but Michael Sandel (1982) and other communitarians argue that "outsiders" can fit in by expanding shared meanings to encompass new experiences. Charles

Taylor (1992) makes additional room for difference in his "politics of recognition" by balancing procedural liberalism with the distinctive interests of racial or ethnic groups (French Canadians are of special interest to Taylor). Through their interest in shared values, communitarians share a link with advocates of American national identity, but communitarians tend to focus on smaller political units than the nation. Some communitarians also overlap with deliberative democrats in arguing that shared meanings and values are open to a variety of perspectives and may be shaped through discussion and debate (Downing and Thigpen 1986). In general, the balance that communitarians maintain between commonality and difference is likely to be unsatisfactory to both sides. Advocates of commonality would see too much emphasis on recognition and incorporation of difference, while difference theorists (or liberals for that matter) are concerned about the exclusive practices implied by dominant shared values.

Deliberative democrats do not fare much better in resolving these tensions, but they provide a strong normative argument in favor of minority representation in Congress. Advocates of deliberative democracy argue that deliberation itself is an important component of representation. How members vote on roll calls may be important, but the words they speak are equally important. Speeches can change debates, agendas, and even preferences. After outlining the versions of deliberative democracy as discursive (Drysek 1990), communicative (Young 1994), civic republicanism (Sunstein 1993), and strong democracy (Barber 1984), Anne Phillips (1995) argues that all versions share a criticism of interest-based democracy and the common view "that political engagement can change initial statements of preference and interest" (149). While I part company with deliberative democrats in their critique of interest-based democracy, I see great value in their focus on deliberation, participation, and agendas and how minority voices can contribute to the richness of this debate.

Kathryn Abrams (1988) was one of the first to make the connection between deliberative democracy and minority districting. She recommends creating the maximum number of districts that have a relatively even split between majority and minority voters, arguing that different races will be more likely to understand each other if the opportunities for cooperation across difference are promoted by racially conscious districting (477). Phillips (1995) is less convinced, arguing that there is a logical inconsistency between group representation and deliberative democracy, at least in its more extreme "difference" or essentialist manifestations, in that true deliberation requires movement from initial positions; if a politician is held on a short group identity leash, there is no room for cooperation and compromise (154–156).

Gutmann and Thompson (1996) provide a compelling account of how the politics of presence shook up the status quo in the U.S. Senate when Carol Mosely Braun (D–IL) successfully challenged the Daughters of the Confederacy's renewal of their patent on the Confederate Flag insignia (1993). The measure was about to sail through as a non-controversial non-germane amendment that had been attached by Jesse Helms (R–NC) and Strom Thurmond (R–SC). Braun, the only African American in the Senate, was outraged.

Her passion carried the day as twenty-seven senators switched their votes on the amendment which was defeated by a 75 to 25 vote (Gutmann and Thompson 1996, 135). It is quite likely that the amendment would have not been questioned had Braun had not been in the Senate. Students of Congress are increasingly enamored of deliberative democracy. Prominent scholars such as Lawrence Dodd, Steven Smith, Tom Mann and Norman Ornstein, and Joseph Bessette have all called for a greater role for deliberation within the institution as a way to improve the policy-making process and enhance the public's understanding of the institution. The quality of that debate would certainly be improved by enlarging its scope.

Difference theorists are concerned that all the talk advocated by deliberative democrats will simply serve to obscure the real issues of power differentials, permanent exclusion, and coercion. "It also can become a rhetorical substitute for the concrete action needed to reach racial equality and social justice" (Streich 1997, 24, citing Gates 1992). While some difference theorists, such as Iris Young (1990), advocate dialogue across differences, "essentialist" or radical difference theorists doubt our ability to meaningful communicate across the racial divide.

In summary, political liberals would prefer to ignore racial differences, but also tolerate them and in some cases accept them as part of a multicultural society (Kymlicka 1995). Advocates of American national identity are even less tolerant of difference while difference theorists are critical of the homogenizing assumptions made by communitarian and liberal theorists who emphasize common ground. However, there are liberals, communitarians, and difference theorists who all share some of the hopes of deliberative democrats that we can talk out our differences, or at least get to the point where shared understandings promote tolerance and recognition. As I note above, the central conclusion of my recent book on racial representation in Congress is that black majority districts promote a politics of commonality, rather than a politics of difference as was commonly assumed (Canon 1999a).

CAN MINORITIES RECEIVE SPECIAL CONSIDERATION?

The goal of enhancing racial representation through redistricting was challenged in the landmark decision *Shaw v. Reno* (1993) which held that bizarrely shaped black majority districts violated the rights of white voters if they were created solely on the basis of race and ignored traditional districting practices. Justice O'Connor, in the most widely quoted passage of the decision, argued that the challenged reapportionment plan "bears an uncomfortable resemblance to political apartheid. It reinforces the perception that members of the same racial group—regardless of their age, education, economic status, or the community in which they live—think alike, share the same political interests, and will prefer the same candidates at the polls. We have rejected such perceptions elsewhere as impermissible racial stereotypes" (Shaw v. Reno 1993, 2827).This decision created a new basis for challenging the constitutionality of a voting district. Prior to *Shaw*, only two bases existed on which to challenge a district: "one person one vote" and vote dilution. The

U.S. District Court noted in *Shaw v. Hunt* (the remand from *Shaw v. Reno*) that, "Until *Shaw*, no majority opinion of the Supreme Court had held that a state redistricting plan that did not cause concrete, material harm to the voting strength of an identifiable group of citizens in one of these two ways could nonetheless be challenged under the Equal Protection Clause on the grounds that it impermissibly took race into account in drawing district lines" (Lexis 11102, 10 1996). This new analysis emphasized "traditional districting practices" for the first time, citing the importance of compactness, contiguity, and respect for political subdivisions (respect for "communities defined by actual shared interests" was added in *Miller*). Or in O'Connor's words "we believe that reapportionment is one area in which appearances do matter" (Shaw v. Reno 1993, 2827). Richard Engstrom (1995) suggests that these criteria, which have no basis in the Constitution or federal statute, will create a confusing "conceptual thicket" to compound the difficulties posed by the "political thicket" of redistricting that for decades the court was loathe to enter (323–324).

Even those who see the landmark decision as a reasonable compromise recognized the problematic nature of the decision itself. Bernard Grofman (1995) argues that *Shaw* steers a course between "premature optimism that will lead to the elimination of safeguards vital to the continuing integration of minorities into American electoral politics, and an unrealistic pessimism that insists we will never get beyond judging people by the color of their skin" (34), yet notes the decision is "somewhat muddled" (29). The critics of *Shaw* are far less charitable. Morgan Kousser (1995) says, "It is true that the abstract, deeply ambiguous, and often unreflective opinion suggested only vague and unworkable standards that have led to much-heightened judicial intrusions in the political process, and that it encouraged a cruelly ironic interpretation of the 14th and 15th Amendments, an interpretation surely unintended by their framers, that aims to undermine the sharpest minority gains in politics since the First Reconstruction" (1).

Subsequent decisions expanded the scope of judicial scrutiny. *Miller v. Johnson* (1995) established that congressional districts were unconstitutional if race was the "predominant factor" in their creation while moving away from the importance of the appearance of the district. Bizarrely shaped districts were no longer a threshold requirement for an equal protection claim. As Justice Ginsberg pointed out in her *Miller* dissent, this was a dramatic shift from the relatively proscribed language of *Shaw*: "[In *Shaw*] the Court wrote cautiously, emphasizing that judicial intervention is exceptional: '[S]trict [judicial] scrutiny' is in order, the Court declared, if a district is 'so extremely irregular on its face that it rationally can be viewed only as an effort to segregate the races for purposes of voting' " (Miller v. Johnson 1995, slip op. 6). *Miller* also held that compliance with Section 5 pre-clearance was not an adequate reason for creating a black-majority district, even when the Justice Department insisted that additional black-majority districts be added. *Abrams v. Johnson* (1997) upheld the dismantling of two of Georgia's black-majority districts that followed the *Miller* decision, even though the state legislature had shown a clear preference for keeping one of those two districts during the redistricting process. This decision signaled increasing judicial activism in this area of litigation, rather than allowing the elected institutions to settle the issue. *Bush v. Vera* (1996) established that protecting incumbents was not a strong enough reason to dislodge race as the predominant factor when both motivations were present. The court recognized incumbency protection as a legitimate end of redistricting, and thus categorized *Vera* as "mixed mo- tive" case; however, race was seen as predominant and thus the district was subjected to strict scrutiny.

Many critics have argued that judicial activism is one of the greatest failings of the *Shaw* decisions. Christopher Eisgruber (1996) argues, "This judgment (*Shaw v. Reno*) is empirically contingent in a way that makes it appropriate for legislative, rather than judicial, resolution. That is why I think *Shaw* is a monster: not because I agree with the policy it declared unconstitutional (I don't), but because the Shaw Court wrongly interfered with legislative discretion to treat America's most severe and most intractable problem, the problem of racial inequality" (525). Ironically, liberals on the bench are the ones talking about self-restraint and states' rights.

Supporters of the districts predicted dire political implications of *Shaw* and the subsequent decisions. Just before her district was dismantled by a federal court, Rep. McKinney D–GA said *Shaw* and its progeny will "turn Black voters back into spare parts for the political machines of Dixiecrats. What Georgia does in redistricting will set the tone for the rest of the nation as majority–minority districts across America are sacrificed to feed the appetite of recently emboldened neo-Confederates" (McKinney 1996, 66). McKinney was able to survive several reelection attempts in the new district, but the new round of redistricting in 2002 and some extreme statements she made about the terrorist attacks of 9/11 led to her defeat in the 2002 Democratic primary by a surprisingly large margin of 58 percent to 42 percent (she was defeated by a more moderate African American woman and former state judge Denise Majette). McKinney's supporters argue that she was defeated by Republican crossover votes in the open primary.

The *Shaw*-type cases raise important questions concerning representation, but ironically the Court's majority opinions have almost completely ignored these issues (vigorous dissents from Ginsberg, Stevens, Souter, Blackman, White, or Breyer in nearly every decision have developed the importance of representation through the topic of standing). The argument I present in chapter 2 of my recent book, which is shared by most of the dissenters, is that white voters did not suffer any "cognizable harm like dilution of the abridgement of the right to participate in the electoral process" (Souter dissent in *Shaw* 1993, slip op. 5). Therefore, white plaintiffs should not have standing to sue unless they can demonstrate a particularized harm. There is no harm because white voters *are* adequately represented by blacks.

The legal questions surrounding racial redistricting are inextricably in- tertwined with policy and partisan politics. Ultimately, the solution to the legal quagmire may be judicial restraint. As Justice Souter points out in his *Bush* dissent, the Court has confused the issue without resolving anything and the political process had been making some progress with one of the nation's most persistent problems. Souter makes a plea to abandon *Shaw* as a "failed experiment": "While I take the commands of *stare decisis* very seriously, the problems with *Shaw* and its progeny are themselves very serious. The Court has been unable to provide workable standards, the chronic uncertainty has begotten no discernible reliance, and the costs of persisting doubt about the limits of state discretion and state responsibility are high." (*Bush v. Vera* 1996, slip op. 26). Souter goes on to note that redistricting that was built around ethnic neighborhoods played an important role in assimilating European immigrants into our political culture. "The result has been not a state regime of ethnic apartheid, but ethnic participation and even a moderation of ethnicity's divisive effect in political practice" (Souter dissent in *Bush*, 1996, slip op. 27).

This plea for restraint made it into a majority opinion for the first time in *Hunt v. Cromartie*, 2001, the last case from the 1990s' round of redistricting. This case was the Supreme Court's third crack at the North Carolina district centered in Charlotte. For the first time in a closely decided redistricting case, Justice O'Connor sided with the four liberals and the Court upheld the redrawn district, which had a 43 percent black voting age population. The majority of five held:

> Those attacking the district have the demanding burden of proof to show that a facially neutral law is unexplainable on grounds other than race. Because the underlying districting decision falls within a legislature's sphere of competence, courts must exercise extraordinary caution in adjudicating claims such as this one, especially where, as here, the State has articulated a legitimate political explanation for its districting decision and the voting population is one in which race and political affiliation are highly coordinated. (*Hunt v. Cromartie* 2001)[4]

While the Supreme Court upheld the use of race in that instance, it still was not clear when race would be considered the "predominant factor," or when it would fall below that threshold. This has produced a flood of litigation concerning redistricting based on the 2000 Census. States are getting sued from both sides: In some instances, they are sued by civil rights organizations on vote dilution grounds and in other instances they are sued because race was the predominant factor. Court challenges have been brought in California, Colorado, Florida, Minnesota, Mississippi, New Mexico, Oklahoma, Oregon, Texas, Virginia, and Wisconsin, among others. One of the most important cases comes from Mississippi where the Democrats sought relief in state court while the Republicans went to federal court. The Supreme Court has agreed to hear the case to determine which venue has priority.

Two other developments in the 2000 round of redistricting are worthy of note. The Justice Department has been accused of using its preclearance power under Section 5 of the Voting Rights Act for partisan gain. In Mississippi, the Justice Department delayed their decision until a state deadline passed, which meant that a federal panel's plan which was favorable to the Republican incumbent would go into effect for the 2002 election (Edsall

2002). On the other hand, when speedy action was required to help the Republicans in Florida, the Justice Department quickly complied (Rosenbaum 2002). Second, there has been an interesting reversal of the political coalitions on the issue in many states. In the 1990s' round of redistricting, Republicans and minority politicians were fighting for the minority–majority districts (obviously for different reasons). In the 2000 round, minority politicians in many states have sided with the Democratic Party's efforts to spread minority voters more evenly in "influence districts" rather than minority–majority districts to enhance their chances of regaining control of the U.S. House. In a potentially critical case on this topic, *Georgia v. Ashcroft* (2003), the Supreme Court overturned a district court decision that had ruled Georgia's state senate plan "retrogression" because it unpacked black majority districts and created five additional influence districts. The case was remanded to the district court and will be tried again under a broader "totality of circumstances" test for retrogression under Section 5 of the Voting Rights Act. One of the most fascinating aspects of this case is that race trumped party; that is, the conservative five justices voted with the Democratic Party's position (in favor of creating the influence districts) and the liberal four voted with the Republican Party's position (claiming that unpacking the districts was retrogression). It remains to be seen whether these same issues will be raised in the next round of congressional redistricting, but if the more comprehensive (and lenient) approach to retrogression sticks, Democrats will be able to shore up the districts of potentially vulnerable white Democrats while trying to preserve the gains made by African Americans in the 1990s.

OTHER REPRESENTATIONAL CONSEQUENCES OF RACIAL REDISTRICTING

Turnout

Redistricting can have an impact on turnout by generating interest in the electoral process among groups of voters who had previously felt alienated from the system. In addition to this "empowerment effect," which could help reduce the gap in turnout between white and minority voters, Brace et al. (1988) point out that higher turnout in redrawn districts could make it unnecessary to create "supermajority" districts to compensate for the lower participation of minority voters and create an opportunity to elect "candidates of choice (191; also see Donovan 1992; Duncan 1993).[5] Brace et al. analyze homogenous precincts in Florida (defined as at least 90 percent black or Hispanic) before and after the creation of a minority–majority district to see whether turnout changed. They find that turnout increased in the new congressional districts by 8 percent, compared to 4.5 percent in districts that did not change between 1988 and 1992. The same analysis for state House seats was less clear because of a more limited number of precincts. They also use cross-sectional data in the 1992 Florida legislative elections and find that turnout was higher in new black-majority congressional and state house indistricts but not in state senate seats. Ronald Weber's (1995) analysis of turnout in the 1994 elections, however, shows that some of these gains may have been short-lived, as black turnout in the new black districts did not remain as high as turnout in the older districts.

Latino-Majority Districts

The representation of Latino constituents is more complex than African American representation because their interests are much more diverse. Rudolfo O. de la Garza notes that 36 percent of the Mexican American respondents identified themselves as "conservative or very conservative," compared to 47 percent of Puerto Ricans, and 55 percent of Cubans (and 37 percent of Anglos; data are from the 1989–1990 Latino National Political Survey; cited in DiLorenzo 1997, 1733). However, Latinos are more support-ive of government spending for social programs than are Anglos. The early work on Latino representation in Congress assumed that Latinos would be more liberal than their Anglo counterparts and did not take into account dif-ferences among the Latino communities. Welch and Hibbing (1984) find that Hispanic representatives had Conservative Coalition support scores that were about 13 points more liberal than non-Hispanic representatives from 1973–1980 (328). However, Hero and Tolbert (1995) find that higher scores for Latino representatives on issues identified by the Southwest Voter Research Institute were not significantly different than non-Latino representatives and that House members are not responsive to the proportion of Latino voters in their district (644). Hero and Tolbert find a degree of *collective* representation, even if the dyadic representation is not evident for the institution as a whole. That is, "The roll-call votes deemed to be most important to Latinos were all decided consistent with Latino preferences. . . . This study is the first to find evidence of indirect substantive representation regarding Latinos" (648–49). Lublin's (1997b) findings are somewhat different; he controls for the propor-tion of Latino population, but also interacts Latino population with the party of the member. He finds that Republican members are significantly more conservative in response to higher Latino populations, while Democrats are significantly more liberal (82). Lublin attributes this to the differences in the Latino populations noted above (Republicans represent Cubans, Democrats tend to represent Mexicans and Puerto Ricans), however he does not control for these constituency differences within the Latino community.

Alternative Electoral Institutions

Some critics of racial redistricting argue that alternative electoral institu-tions, such as proportional representation or cumulative voting, may provide a more efficient voice for minority interests in a majority-rule political system than do majority—minority districts (or single-member geographic represen-tation more generally). Richard Morrill (1996) says, "With single-member districts, it is manifestly impossible to satisfy any but one dimension of these interests—that of the majority" (4). Lani Guinier's advocacy of alternative electoral institutions, in addition to her even more controversial views on minority veto powers, supermajorities, and cumulative voting on legislation of interest to the minority community in Congress (1991a, 1991b, 1994,

4–7, 94, 107, 260, note 118), led to the demise of her nomination as Assistant Attorney General for Civil Rights in the spring of 1993. These views constitute a subtle but important shift from voting rules that favored black candidates to rules that would favor black interests. Guinier's (1994) position is based on the belief that the "right to fair representation" under the Voting Rights Act should be measured by "the extent protected minority groups are provided meaningful voice in government" (93). This is the view that got Guinier into trouble. One critic points out that Guinier maintains that "it should be considered a violation of minority rights to fair democratic process when the majority refuses to implement a specific agenda of legislation (on which) there is consensus in a 'minority' community. With all due respect, it is simply impossible to reconcile this idea with any theory of governance that is called 'democratic' in ordinary, common speech" (Polsby and Popper 1996, 19). While Guinier's proposals for procedural changes in the legislative process are extreme (and in my view, unworkable), her cumulative voting plan (which she calls *semi-proportional representation*) is a more plausible mechanism for enhancing the representation of racial interests in Congress (or other legislatures).

Cumulative voting works in the following fashion: Members of the legislature would be elected from multimember districts in which voters would have one vote per legislative seat. Voters could allocate their votes between the candidates in any proportion, including "plumping" their votes by casting them all for one candidate. Thus, minorities who comprised at least 1/nth of the district (where n is the number of legislative seats) should be able to elect at least one of their preferred candidates. This electoral arrangement has received some attention in the popular press and among empirical scholars and formal theorists.

Formal theorists have long been interested in the process of aggregating individual preferences into collective outcomes. When more than two options are presented, there is no voting system that produces consistently fair and just results (see Riker 1982, chapter 4, for a summary of the various voting methods). While cumulative voting cannot satisfy all the conditions of a fair voting system, formal work suggests that it can serve as a mechanism for increasing minority representation. Most formal work has focused on the optimal voter strategies to elect candidates of their choice under various voting systems. Gary Cox (1990) finds that in two-member districts under straight voting, it is optimal to "plump" votes for a single candidate. In multi-member districts, cumulative voting promotes a dispersion of ideological positions among the candidates (927). Gerber, Morton, and Reitz (1998) find that under straight voting, the majority candidates in a three-candidate two-seat election (with two majority candidates and one minority candidate) constitutes one equilibrium. However, they also find that there are equilibriums that predict either a close three-way race, or even the minority candidate winning. Under cumulative voting in the same context, minority candidates win when minority voters have no preference between the majority candidates and cumulate their votes for their first choice. However, if the minority voters split their votes, the majority candidates can win (141–42). Burt Monroe (1995) proposes a "fully

proportional representation system" in which voters could express preferences over a full slate of candidates rather than being allowed to only express
their first preferences, as in all existing electoral systems. While this system
has no empirical referent in the political world, it raises intriguing possibilities
for providing richer and deeper representation of political views.

The empirical literature is relatively thin on the topic of cumulative voting in the United States because there are only a few offices for which the
practice is used. The most commonly cited examples in the literature are
Chilton County, AL; Peoria, IL (which only held one election under cumulative voting); Alamogordo, NM (which ended its experiment in 1994); and the
Illinois General Assembly from 1870–1982 (Sawyer and MacRae 1962; Cole,
Taebel, and Engstrom 1990; Cole and Taebel 1992; Van Biema 1994; Adams
1996, Issacharoff and Pildes 1996). Adams (1996) provides strong empirical
evidence that the cumulative voting system in Illinois produced more ideologically extreme members of the state assembly than those who were elected
by the single-member district system employed in 1982. Chilton County, AL,
which is 12 percent black, used cumulative voting to elect its first black com-
missioner since Reconstruction—Bobby Agee. There was some confusion
among voters. Bobby Martin, the probate judge that oversaw the elections
said that dozens of voters wrote in more than seven candidates: "There were so
many mistakes, we almost ran out of ballots" (Van Biema 1994, 43). Agee received votes from only 1.5 percent of the white voters (Issacharoff and Pildes
1996, 10), yet managed to win the most votes overall because nearly every
black voter in the county cast all seven of his or her votes for the only black
candidate (Van Biema 1994, 43). Peoria also used cumulative voting to elect
a black councilman and Alamogordo elected the first Hispanic councilperson
in decades. Furthermore, in the second election under cumulative voting in
Chilton County, Issacharoff and Pildes (1996) report that white candidates
were courting black voters and Agee was able to attract a few more white
votes. In addition to providing descriptive representation, cumulative voting
may help break down racial barriers (10). Brockington et al. (1998) find that
African American politicians under cumulative voting or limited voting win
at rates that are similar to large, non-Southern single-member districts (and
at higher rates than smaller Southern single-member districts), whereas the
results for Latino politicians are more mixed.

However, there are several potential problems with cumulative voting: (1)
it is relatively complex and will produce voter confusion, at least in the short-
term; (2) it will give even more power to groups of voters with higher turnout
rates (elderly, wealthy, highly educated, whites) because they would be able to
influence elections in a broader geographic area; (3) it would most likely benefit minorities of the right; (4) multi-member districts in which the cumulative
voting would occur would be so large as to virtually do away with the concept
of geographic representation that is so central to American politics (Morrill
1996, 4–5); and (5) it could produce a less stable, more fractured political
system (Forest 1996, 10). One other unintended effect often not mentioned by
proponents of the system: Republicans are likely to benefit from cumulative

voting even more than they did from the creation of black-majority districts. If Republicans "plump" their votes, they should be able to elect candidates roughly in proportion to their population, just like minorities would. For example, in Chilton County, an area where Republicans rarely won local office, three of the seven commission seats went to Republicans. Furthermore, minorities would need to construct powerful slating organizations to limit the supply of candidates or risk splitting their limited voting power. In Centre, AL, another community that tried cumulative voting, a black city councilman was elected when the plan was implemented in 1988. But in 1992, he had competition from other African American candidates and the city council reverted to all-white (Van Biema 1994, 43). The practice is clearly not a panacea for minority representation.

FUTURE DIRECTIONS FOR RESEARCH

How Has Democratic Inclusion Been Affected by Electoral Institutions over Time?

There has been tremendous variation in electoral institutions in our nation's history. Some U.S. Representatives were elected from multi-member districts until 1842, a uniform date for federal elections was not set until 1845, some states elected House members in odd-numbered years until 1880, the secret ballot was not widely used until the 1890s, district size varied dramatically until the 1960s, and so forth (Jacobson 1997, 7–12). Stephen Calabrese (2000) finds that there is greater partisan diversity in a state's delegation when they switch from a general-ticket to single-member elections, and the reverse happens with moves in the opposite direction. State legislature provides even more variation with multi-member districts, single-member districts, and the instance of cumulative voting in Illinois mentioned above. Scholars have only begun to uncover the representational consequences of these changes in electoral institutions and the cross-sectional variation at the state level. While these changes would not have had much of an effect on descriptive representation, it is possible that different electoral institutions, such as districting practices that produced an overrepresentation of rural areas in the South, could have had an impact on support for slavery.

What Is the Impact of Campaign Finance and Term Limits on Democratic Inclusion?

Campaign finance reform and term limits were two of the most significant changes in electoral institutions to emerge in the 1990s. Term limits for Congress were struck down by the Supreme Court, but it recently upheld the major provisions in the new campaign finance that went into effect for the 2003–2004 electoral cycle. These McCain/Feingold reforms will generate a fresh round of analysis at the national level, and states continue to serve as laboratories of experimentation in both areas. However, state-level variation in the versions of campaign finance and term limits allows some additional leverage on representational questions; research on these topics should help inform the debates at the national level. What impact does public financing have on candidate recruitment, competition in state legislative elections (Mayer and Wood 1995), or on broader representational questions including the representation of racial interests? Does public financing help control the influence of special interests, or do they simply find other outlets for their money? What are the implications of limited or lengthened terms for representation (Keech 1986)? Are term-limited members more responsive to the public? Is there a transfer of power to special interests and the "permanent" bureaucracy, as some critics maintain? Have minority members of state legislatures been adversely affected by term limits? Many members of the CBC opposed campaign finance reform because it is more difficult for members from relatively poor districts to raise hard-money contributions, thus they may be more dependent on the soft-money contributions that were recently banned. How will the recent reforms affect the relative fundraising efforts of minority members of Congress?

What Are the Policy Consequences of Democratic Inclusion in Legislatures?

Davidson and Grofman (1994) identify a "fourth generation" of work on voting research that examines the political process' "output so far as minority citizens at the grassroots are concerned" (14). That is, what difference does it make *for minority citizens* that minority politicians are in office? What policies are implemented that otherwise would not have been, and what impact do they have? Policy evaluation is always a tricky business, but especially when involving counterfactual scenarios. Perhaps because of this complexity, this is an area in which very little work has been done (for one good example of this type of research, see Button 1988). However, the ultimate significance of electoral institutions for representation lies in this generation of research.

Another set of "big-picture" questions that require additional research are presented by Jennifer Hochschild's important book *Facing Up to the American Dream* (1995). Her findings about the complex interplay between race and class and belief in the American dream—that one can get ahead through hard work and "playing by the rules"—raise important questions about the impact of specific policies and descriptive representation on those beliefs. To what extent does electing minority politicians help reinforce the belief in the American dream among poor African Americans? Which types of policies that are aimed at bridging the racial divide or reducing racial inequality can help restore confidence in the American dream among middle class blacks?

What Is the Impact of Institutions of Democratic Inclusion on Political Elites?

We also know very little about the impact of electoral institutions on political elites and their second-stage effects at the individual level. Armand Derfner (1972) outlines eight "candidate diminution" tactics used by southern states to discourage black candidates from running (555–556). Even more benign practices, such as redistricting that was intended to promote black representation, can create uncertainty and influence the nature of the candidate pool that emerges. Candidate slating groups, initially used in the south to dilute black voting power, may become essential to maintain black voting power in a system of cumulative voting. Even in black-majority districts with sizable white populations, black candidate-slating organizations may be necessary to prevent a split black vote from allowing a white candidate to win; but, there are few accounts of these groups beyond the anecdotal level (Canon, Schousen, and Sellers 1994). What impact do the various electoral institutions mentioned here and elsewhere in this essay have on the type of candidate who runs for office, and ultimately, how does this influence the nature of representation? Are practices such as slating groups consistent with participatory democracy?

One second-stage effect of electoral institutions is the impact of black candidacies on black voting turnout and participation. This "empowerment" hypothesis has received some support from the urban politics literature. Bobo and Gilliam (1990) find that black participation and turnout increases when there is a black mayor. Lublin and Tate (1992) find that black turnout in mayoral races increases when there is a black candidate and Vanderleeuw and Utter (1993) find slightly less drop-off from mayoral voting to city council voting in New Orleans when there is a black city council candidate. These findings have not been as consistent when applied to congressional districting (see the section above on turnout). Further research is needed to examine the impact of black candidacies on black turnout, especially in U.S. House races.

We also know very little about how white and black constituents' perceptions of representation and racial politics change when a black politician is elected, another second-stage effect. A well-established literature examines racial attitudes and other political activities (such as party-switching) of white constituents affected by the number of blacks that live in their district. Two competing hypotheses have received some support. The *racial threat* hypothesis (or *group conflict theory*) states that whites who live in areas with high concentrations of black population will be more prejudiced and less supportive of the civil rights agenda. This hypothesis dates back to V.O. Key's (1949) classic work, *Southern Politics*, in which he observed that the most strident segregationists and least tolerant whites lived in the "black belt" areas of the South (5–6, 8–10). Giles and Hertz (1994) conclude that the percentage of blacks in a district has a significant impact on partisan identification; that is, whites are less likely to be Democrats in areas of high black population and more likely to be Republicans (321). Research on resistance to school desegregation (Giles, Cataldo, and Gatlin 1975), attitudinal support for racial integration and other racial-political attitudes (Fossett and Kiecolt 1989; Glaser 1994), white support for policies to assist blacks (Reider 1985), and support for racist candidates (Black 1973; Wright 1977) provides some support for the threat hypothesis. Kinder and Sanders (1996) employ subjective indicators of perceived racial threat and find that they have a significant impact on racial attitudes, but are weakly connected to actual conditions, such as the racial composition of the respondent's workplace and neighborhood (60–68). Thus, racial attitudes are driven more by racial resentment than "actual condition of conflict and competition" (90).

The *contact* hypothesis suggests that contact between blacks and whites will lessen racial resentment, undermine inaccurate racial perceptions, and help create a healthier racial climate. Tests of this hypothesis have produced mixed results; Kinder and Mendelberg (1995) note, "Contact sometimes leads to greater racial tolerance, sometimes to heightened racial tensions, and some-times it makes no difference" (405, note 1, citing Amir, Jackman et al). Taking a slightly different tack, Kinder and Mendelberg find that whites who are iso-lated from blacks are more likely to have their opinions affected by prejudice (416–421).

While support for the contact hypothesis suggests that Sandra Day O'Connor's fears that black districts would create "political apartheid" may be unfounded, we do not know the extent to which political elites can help break down racial barriers. Anecdotal evidence suggests they can. Racial mod-erates such as Mike Espy, Sanford Bishop, Robert Scott, and Jim Clyburn increase their percentage of support from white voters with each successive reelection. However, systematic evidence to support these claims is not yet available. Longoria (1996) provides some support for the elite-driven contact hypothesis with evidence that white constituents who are represented by a black state legislator are 11 percent more likely to support the creation of black-majority districts than are whites who are represented by white legisla-tors (holding everything else in his multivariate logit model constant at their means levels; 884–885). Zoltan Hajnal (2001) finds that black leadership can have a "profound effect" on whites' racial sentiments and support for black candidates (603). Claudine Gay's (1997, 2001) evidence is less encouraging (she shows that whites who are represented by blacks report less contact and less confidence in their representative than whites who are represented by whites). However, her analysis does not make distinctions between styles of racial representation among blacks. Those who practice a politics of com-monality should provide evidence in support of the contact hypothesis, while "difference" black representatives may support the threat hypothesis. Sys-tematic analysis of these questions is not possible with current survey data. Available surveys, such as the National Election Study, do not have enough respondents in the relevant districts to conduct the necessary analysis. Thus, definitive answers to these questions await further research.

This survey should leave little doubt that race remains a significant vari-able in the representation equation and political scientists will continue to analyze the contours of this relationship. The productiveness and quality of the latter enterprise will substantially improve if scholars venture across sub-disciplinary boundaries. Empirical, normative, legal, and formal scholars all have something to contribute to our understanding of the nature of racial representation in legislatures. The obstacles to cross-fertilization are high: Jargon may be frustrating, and quantitative work and formal theory may be intimidating to the uninitiated. This review essay has attempted to show that a complete understanding of this topic must cut across disciplinary boundaries; subfields that ignore each other's work are mutually impoverished.

NOTES

Acknowledgments. This paper is a revised and updated version of "Electoral Systems and the Representation of Minority Interests in Legislatures," *Legislative Studies Quarterly* 24 (August, 1999): 331–385, which was reprinted in *Legislatures: Comparative Perspectives on Representative Assemblies*, edited by Gerhard Loewenberg, D. Roderick Kiewiet, and Peverill Squire (Ann Arbor: University of Michigan Press, 2002), 149–177. I would like to thank Rudy Espino for his assistance in the bibliographic search for this essay.

1. Of course, pluralist theorists have been guilty of equating parts of Madisonian theory with their own. Most important is the divergent starting point: Madison was concerned with controlling the effects of evil factions, while pluralists embrace factions as the essential embodiment of political action and expression of political interests.

2. These findings on the Republicans run counter to most other research that shows that Republicans are not responsive to black voters. Part of the differences may be explained by the time period of Lublin's analysis, which ends in 1992, before the impact of the new black-majority districts. As Bullock (1995) and others have shown, as the new districts were "bleached," Republican representatives were less responsive to black voters. Cameron, Epstein, and O'Halloran (1996) actually find that non-Northeastern Republicans and non-black Southern Democrats support Key's threat hypothesis, but the coefficients for percent black are not significant.

3. Greg Streich's excellent dissertation (1997) spends more than three hundred pages analyzing and critiquing this literature. Even his thorough presentation is not exhaustive.

4. Syllabus, internal citations omitted; see Guy and Fuentes-Rohwer 2001, for an excellent discussion of the difficulty of sorting out racial and partisan motivations in the redistricting process.

5. Of course, recent court decisions make this an academic point. Given that race can no longer be the "predominant factor" in redrawing district lines, creating supermajority–minority districts is clearly a thing of the past.

REFERENCES

Abrams, Kathryn. 1988. "'Raising Politics Up': Minority Political Participation and Section 2 of the Voting Rights Act." *New York University Law Review* 63:449–531.

Adams, Greg D. 1996. "Legislative Effects of Single-Member vs. Multi-Member Districts." *American Journal of Political Science* 40: 129–144.

Arnold, R. Douglas. 1990. *The Logical of Congressional Action.* New Haven: Yale University Press.

Barber, Benjamin R. 1984. *Strong Democracy: Participatory Politics for a New Age.* Berkeley: University of California Press.

Beitz, C. R. 1989. *Political Equality: An Essay in Democratic Theory.* Princeton: Princeton University Press.

Bianco, William T. 1994. *Trust: Representatives and Constituents.* Ann Arbor: University of Michigan Press.

———. 1997. "Evaluating Descriptive Representation: When Will Constituents Do Better with 'Someone Like Them?' " Working paper, Department of Political Science, Penn State University.

Black, Earl. 1973. "The Militant Segregationist Vote in the Post-*Brown* South: A Comparative Study." *Social Science Quarterly* 54:66–84.

Black, Merle. 1978. "Racial Composition of Congressional Districts and Support for Federal Voting Rights in the American South." *Social Science Quarterly* 59:435–450.

Bobo, Lawrence, and Franklin D. Gilliam. 1990. "Race, Sociopolitical Participation, and Black Empowerment." *American Political Science Review* 84(2): 377–393.

Brace, Kimball, Bernard Groffman, Lisa Handley, and Richard Niemi. 1988. "Minority Voting Equality: The 65 Percent Rule in Theory and Practice." *Law and Policy* 10(1): 43–62.

Bratton, Kathleen A., and Kerry L. Haynie. 1998. "Agenda Setting and Legislative Success in State Legislatures." *The Journal of Politics* 61(3): 658–679.

Brockington, David, Todd Donovan, Shaun Bowler, and Robert Brischetto. 1998. "Minority Representation under Cumulative and Limited Voting." *The Journal of Politics* 60(4): 1108–1125.

Bullock, Charles S. III. 1981. "Congressional Voting and the Mobilization of Black Electorate In the South." *Journal of Politics* 43:662–682.

———. 1985. "Congressional Roll Voting in the Two-Party South." *Social Science Quarterly* 76:789–804.

———. 1995. "The Impact of Changing the Racial Composition of Congressional Districts on Legislators' Roll Call Behavior." *American Politics Quarterly* 23:141–158.

Bullock, Charles S. III, and MacManus, Susan A. 1981. "Policy Responsiveness to the Black Electorate: Programmatic Versus Symbolic Representation." *American Politics Quarterly* 9 (July): 357–368.

Bush v. Vera. 517 U.S. 952 (1996).

Button, James W. 1988. *Blacks and Social Change: The Impact of the Civil Rights Movement in Southern Communities*. Princeton: Princeton University Press.

Calabrese, Stephen. 2000. "Multimember District Congressional Elections." *Legislative Studies Quarterly* 25(4): 611–644.

Cameron, Charles, David Epstein, and Sharon O'Halloran. 1996. "Do Majority-Minority Districts Maximize Substantive Black Representation in Congress? *American Political Science Review* 90:794–812.

Canon, David T. 1995. "Redistricting and the Congressional Black Caucus." *American Politics Quarterly* 23:159–189.

———. 1999a. *Race, Redistricting, and Representation: The Unintended Consequences of Black Majority Districts*. Chicago: University of Chicago Press.

———. 1999b. "Electoral Systems and the Representation of Minority Interests in Legislatures." *Legislative Studies Quarterly* 24(3): 331–386.

Canon, David T., Matthew M. Schousen, and Patrick J. Sellers. 1994. "A Formula for Uncertainty: Creating a Black-Majority District in North Carolina." In *Who Runs for Congress: Ambition, Context, and Candidate Emergence*, edited by Thomas A. Kazee, 23–44. Washington, DC: CQ Press.

———. 1996. "The Supply-Side of Congressional Redistricting: Race and Strategic Politicians, 1972–1992." *Journal of Politics* 58:837–853.

Carmichael, Stokley, and Charles V. Hamilton. 1967. *Black Power: The Politics of Liberation in America*. New York: Vintage Books.

Clausen, Aage R. 1973. *How Congressmen Decide: A Policy Focus*. New York: St. Martin's Press.

Clay, William. 1993. *Just Permanent Interests: Black Americans in Congress, 1870–1992*. New York: Amistad Press.

Cobb, Michael D., and Jeffrey A. Jenkins. 1996. "Who Represents Black Interests in Congress? Sponsoring and Voting for Legislation Beneficial to Black Constituents."

Paper Presented at the Annual Meeting of the Midwest Political Science Association, Chicago, Illinois, April 18–20.

Cole, Richard, and Delbert Taebel. 1992. "Cumulative Voting in Local Elections: Lessons from the Alamagordo Experience." *Social Science Quarterly* 73:194–201.

Cole, Richard, Delbert Taebel, and Richard Engstrom. 1990. "Cumulative Voting in a Municipal Election: A Note on Voter Reactions and Electoral Consequences." *Western Political Quarterly* 43(4): 191–199.

Combs, Michael W., John R. Hibbing, and Susan Welch. 1984. "Black Constituents and Congressional Roll Call Votes." *Western Political Quarterly* 37(3): 424–434.

Connoly, William. 1991. *Identity/Difference: Democratic Negotiations of Political Paradox*. Ithaca, NY: Cornell University Press.

Cox, Gary W. 1990. "Centripetal and Centrifugal Incentives in Electoral Systems." *American Journal of Political Science* 34:903–35.

Dahl, Robert A. 1956. *A Preface to Democratic Theory*. Chicago: University of Chicago Press.

Davidson, Chandler, and Bernard Grofman, eds. 1994. *Quiet Revolution in the South: The Impact of the Voting Rights Act, 1965–1990*. Princeton: Princeton University Press.

Derfner, Armand. 1972. "Racial Discrimination and the Right to Vote." *Vanderbilt Law Review* 26:523–584.

DiLorenzo, Vincent. 1997. "Legislative Heart and Phase Transitions: An Exploratory Study of Congress and Minority Interests." *William and Mary Law Review* 38:1729–1815.

Donovan, Beth. 1992. "New Majority–Minority Districts May Mean Lower Black Turnout." *Congressional Quarterly Weekly Report* 50(10): 563–564.

Downing, Lyle, and Robert Thigpen. 1986. "Beyond Shared Understandings." *Political Theory* 14:451–472.

Drysek, John S. 1990. *Discursive Democracy: Politics, Policy, and Political Science*. New York: Cambridge University Press.

Duncan, Phil. 1993. "Minority Districts May Fail to Enhance Turnout." *Congressional Quarterly Weekly Report* 51(13): 798.

Dworkin, Ronald. 1989. "Liberal Community." *California Law Review* 77:479–504.

Edsall, Thomas B. 2002. "Democrats Challenge Justice's Redistricting Review in Mississippi." *Washington Post,* February 16, A6.

Eisenstein, Zillah. 1988. *The Female Body and the Law*. Berkeley: University of California Press.

Eisgruber, Christopher L. 1996. "Ethnic Segregation by Religion and Race: Reflections on *Kiryas Joel* and *Shaw v. Reno*." *Cumberland Law Review* 26:515–526

Engstrom, Richard L. 1995. "Voting Rights Districts: Debunking the Myths." *Campaigns and Elections* (April): 24–46.

Fenno, Richard F. 1978. *Home Style: House Members in Their Districts*. Boston: Little, Brown.

Fiorina, Morris P. 1974. *Representatives, Roll Calls, and Constituencies*. Lexington, MA: Lexington Books.

Forest, Benjamin. 1996. "Where Should Democratic Compromise Take Place?" *Social Science Quarterly* 77:6–13.

Fossett, Mark A., and K. Jill Kiecolt. 1989. "The Relative Size of Minority Populations and White Racial Attitudes." *Social Science Quarterly* 70:820–835.

Gates, Henry Louis, Jr. 1992. *Loose Canons: Notes on the Culture Wars*. New York: Oxford University Press.

Gay, Claudine. 1997. *Taking Charge: Black Electoral Success and the Redefinition of American Politics*. PhD diss., Harvard University Department of Government.

————. 2001. "The Effect of Black Congressional Representation on Political Participation." *American Political Science Review* 95(3): 589–602.

Gerber, Elisabeth R., Rebecca B. Morton, and Thomas A. Rietz. 1998. "Minority Representation in Multimember Districts." *American Political Science Review* 92: 127–144.

Giles, Michael W., and Kaenan Hertz. 1994. "Racial Threat and Partisan Identification." *American Political Science Review* 88:317–326.

Giles, Michael W., Everett F. Cataldo, and Douglas S. Gatlin. 1975. "White Flight and Percent Black: The Tipping Point Re-examined." *Social Science Quarterly* 56:85–92.

Gilligan, Carol. 1982. *In a Different Voice: Psychological Theory and Women's Development*. Cambridge: Harvard University Press.

Glaser, James M. 1994. "Back to the Black Belt: Racial Environment and White Racial Attitudes in the South." *Journal of Politics* 56:21–41.

Grofman, Bernard. 1995. "*Shaw v. Reno* and the Future of Voting Rights." *PS: Political Science and Politics* 28:27–36.

Grofman, Bernard, Robert Griffin, and Amihai Glazer. 1992. "The Effect of Black Population on Electing Democrats and Liberals to the House of Representatives." *Legislative Studies Quarterly* 17:365–379.

Grofman, Bernard, and Lisa Handley. 1989. "Minority Population Proportion and the Black and Hispanic Congressional Success in the 1970s and 1980s." *American Politics Quarterly* 17:436–445.

Guinier, Lani. 1991a. "The Triumph of Tokenism: The Voting Rights Act and the Theory of Black Electoral Success." *Michigan Law Review* 89:1077–1154.

————. 1991b. "No 2 Seats: The Elusive Quest for Political Equality." *Virginia Law Review* 77:1413–1514.

————. 1994. *The Tyranny of the Majority: Fundamental Fairness in Representative Democracy*. New York: Free Press.

Gutmann, Amy, and Dennis Thompson. 1996. *Democracy and Disagreement: Why Moral Conflict Cannot be Avoided in Politics and What To Do About It*. Cambridge, MA: Harvard University Press (Belknap).

Guy, Charles, and Luis Fuentes-Rohwer. 2001. "Challenges to Racial Redistricting in the New Millenium: Hunt v. Cromartie as a Case Study," Washington and Lee Law Review v. 58.

Hajnal, Zoltan L. 2001. "White Residents, Black Incumbents, and a Declining Racial Divide." *American Political Science Review* 95(3): 603–617.

Hall, Richard L. 1996. *Participation in Congress*. New Haven: Yale University Press.

Hall, Richard L., and Frank W. Wayman. 1990. "Buying Time: Moneyed Interests and the Mobilization of Bias in Congressional Committees." *American Political Science Review* 84:797–820.

Handley, Lisa, and Bernard Grofman. 1994. "The Impact of the Voting Rights Act on Minority Representation: Black Officeholding in Southern State Legislatures and Congressional Delegations." In *Quiet Revolution in the South: The Impact of the Voting Rights Act: 1965–1990,* edited by Chandler Davidson and Bernard Grofman, 336–350. Princeton: Princeton University Press.

Haynie, Kerry L. 2001. *African American Legislators in the American States*. New York: Columbia University Press.

Hero, Rodney E. 2000. *The Face of Inequality: Social Diversity in American Politics*. New York: Oxford University Press.

Hero, Rodney E., and Caroline J. Tolbert. 1995. "Latinos and Substantive Representation in the U.S. House of Representatives: Direct, Indirect, or Non-Existent?" *American Journal of Political Science* 39:640–652.

Hill, Heather. 1996. "Creative Cartography: Some Effects of the 1992 Redistricting on Race and Roll Call Voting." Paper Presented at the Annual Meeting of the Midwest Political Science Association, Chicago, April 18–20.

Hill, Kevin. 1995. "Does the Creation of Majority Black Districts Aid Republicans? An Analysis of the 1992 Congressional Elections in Eight Southern States." *Journal of Politics* 57:384–401.

Hochschild, Jennifer L. 1995. *Facing Up to the American Dream: Race, Class, and the Soul of the Nation*. Princeton: Princeton University Press.

Hunt v. Cromartie. 532 US 234 (2001).

Issacharoff, Samuel, and Richard H. Pildes. 1996. "All for One: Can Cumulative Voting Ease Racial Tensions?" *The New Republic*, November 18, 10.

Jacobson, Gary C. 1997. *The Politics of Congressional Elections*. 4th ed. New York: Longman. Jewell, Malcolm E. 1967. *Legislative Representation in the Contemporary South*. Durham, NC: Duke University Press.

Johnson, James B., and Philip E. Secret. 1996. "Focus and Style Representational Roles of Congressional Black and Hispanic Caucus Members." *Journal of Black Studies* 26:3 (January): 245–273.

Jones, Mack H. 1985. "The Voting Rights Act as an Intervention Strategy for Social Change: Symbolism or Substance?" In *The Voting Rights Act: Consequences and Implications*, edited by Lorn S. Foster, 63–84. Westport, CT: Praeger.

Keech, William R. 1986. "Thinking about the Length and Renewability of Electoral Terms." In *Electoral Laws and Their Political Consequences*, edited by Bernard Grofman and Arend Lijphart, 104–110. New York: Agathon Press.

Key, V. O., Jr. 1949. *Southern Politics*. New York: Vintage.

Kinder, Donald R., and Tali Mendenberg. 1995. "Cracks in American Apartheid: The Political Impact of Prejudice among Desegregated Whites." *Journal of Politics* 57:402–424.

Kinder, Donald R., and Lynn M Sanders. 1996. *Divided by Color: Racial Politics and Democratic Ideals*. Chicago: University of Chicago Press.

King, Gary. 1989. *Unifying Political Methodology: The Likelihood Theory of Statistical Inference*. Cambridge: Cambridge University Press.

Kingdon, John L. 1989. *Congressmen's Voting Decisions*. 3rd ed. Ann Arbor: University of Michigan Press.

Kousser, J. Morgan. 1995. "*Shaw v. Reno* and the Real World of Redistricting and Representation." Working Paper 915, California Institute of Technology.

Kymlicka, Will. 1995. *Multicultural Citizenship: A Liberal Theory of Minority Rights*. New York Oxford University Press.

Levy, Arthur B. and Susan Stoudinger. 1976. "Sources of Voting Cues for the Congressional Black Caucus." *Journal of Black Studies* 7:29–45.

———. 1978. "The Black Caucus in the 92nd Congress: Gauging Its Success." *Phylon* 38: 322–332.

Longoria, Thomas Jr. 1996. "White Attitudes toward Minority Electoral Districts: Minority Population Size, National Politics, and Local Policy." *Social Science Quarterly* 77:4 (December): 877–87.

Loomis, Burdett A. 1981. "Congressional Caucuses and the Politics of Representation." In *Congress Reconsidered*, edited by Lawrence C. Dodd and Bruce I. Oppenheimer, 204–220. Washington, DC: CQ Press.

Lublin, David. 1997a. "The Election of African Americans and Latinos to the U.S. House of Representatives." *American Politics Quarterly* 25(3): 269–286.

———. 1997b. *The Paradox of Representation: Racial Gerrymander and Minority Interests in Congress*. Princeton: Princeton University Press.

Lublin, David Ian, and Katherine Tate. 1992. "Black Officeseeking and Voter Turnout in Mayoral Elections." Paper Presented at the Annual Meeting of the American Political Science Association, Chicago, IL.

Mansbridge, Jane. 1996. "In Defense of Descriptive Representation." Paper Presented at the Annual Meeting of the American Political Science Association. San Francisco, CA.

Mayer, Kenneth R., and John M. Wood. 1995. "The Impact of Public Financing on Electoral Competitiveness: Evidence from Wisconsin, 1964–1990." *Legislative Studies Quarterly* 20:69–88.

McClain, Paula D., and John A. Garcia. 1993. "Expanding Disciplinary Boundaries: Black, Latino, and Racial Minority Groups in Political Science." In *Political Science: The State of the Discipline II,* edited by Ada W. Finifter, 247–279. Washington, DC: American Political Science Association.

McKinney Cynthia. 1996. "The Politics of Geography," *Emerge* December/January 62–66.

Menifield, Charles E. 1996. "Caucuses as Sources of Cues: A Look at the Black, Women's, and Hispanic Caucuses." Paper Presented at the Annual Meeting of the Midwest Political Science Association, Chicago, IL, April 18–20.

Miller v. Johnson 515 U.S 900 (1995).

Miller, Warren E., and Stokes, Donald E. 1963. "Constituency Influence in Congress. *American Political Science Review* 57:45–56.

Monroe, Burt L. 1995. "Fully Proportional Representation." *American Political Science Review* 89: 925–40.

Morrill, Richard L. 1996. "Territory, Community, and Collective Representation." *Social Science Quarterly* 77:3–5.

NAACP. 1994. "Report of the NAACP Legal Defense and Educational Fund: The Effect of Section 2 of the Voting Rights Act on the 1994 Congressional Elections." Mimeo, November 30.

Nye, Mary Alice, and Charles S. Bullock III. 1992. "Civil Rights Support: A Comparison of Southern and Border State Representatives." *Legislative Studies Quarterly* 27:81–94.

Overby, L. Marvin, and Kenneth M. Cosgrove. 1996. "Unintended Consequences? Racial Redistricting and the Representation of Minority Interests." *Journal of Politics* 58:540–550.

Phillips, Anne. 1995. *The Politics of Presence*. New York: Clarendon Press/Oxford University Press.

Pinderhughes, Diane M. 1987. *Race and Ethnicity in Chicago Politics*. Urbana: University of Illinois Press.

Pinney, Neil, and George Serra. 2002. "A Voice for Black Interests: Congressional Black Caucus Cohesion and Bill Sponsorship." *Congress and the Presidency* 29(1): 69–86.

Pitkin, Hanna F. 1967. *The Concept of Representation*. Berkeley: University of California Press.

Polsby, Daniel, and Robert Popper. 1996. "Guinier's Theory of Political Market Failure." *Social Science Quarterly* 77:14–22.

Rawls, John. 1971. *A Theory of Justice*. Cambridge, MA: Belknap/Harvard University Press, 1971.

Reider, Jonathan. 1985. *Canarsie: The Jews and Italians of Brooklyn against Liberalism*. Cambridge: Harvard University Press.

Riker, William H. 1982. *Liberalism against Populism: A Confrontation between the Theory of Democracy and the Theory of Social Choice*. San Francisco: W. H. Freeman.

Rohde, David W. 1991. *Parties and Leaders in the Postreform House*. Chicago: University of Chicago Press.

Rosenbaum, David. 2002. "Justice Department Accused of Politics in Redistricting." *New York Times*, May 30, A14.

Sandel, Michael. 1982. *Liberalism and the Limits of Justice*. Cambridge: Cambridge University Press.

Sawyer, Jack, and Duncan MacRae, Jr. 1962. "Game Theory and Cumulative Voting in Illinois: 1902–1954." *American Political Science Review* 56: 936–946.

Shaw v. Hunt. 517 U.S. 899 (1996).

Shaw v. Reno. 509 U.S. 630 (1993).

Singh, Robert. 1998. *The Congressional Black Caucus: Racial Politics in the U.S. Congress*. Thousand Oaks, CA: Sage Publications.

Smith, Robert C. 1981. "The Black Congressional Delegation." *Western Political Quarterly* 34:203–21.

———. 1990. "Recent Elections and Black Politics: The Maturation or Death of Black Politics?" *PS: Political Science and Politics* 23:160–62.

Streich, Gregory W. 1997. *After the Celebration: Theories of Community and Practices of Interracial Dialogue*. PhD diss., University of Wisconsin-Madison.

Sunstein, Cass R. 1993. "Democracy and Shifting Preferences." In *The Idea of Democracy*, edited by David Copp, Jean Hampton, and John E. Roemer, 196–230. New York: Cambridge University Press.

Swain, Carol M. 1993. *Black Faces, Black Interests: The Representation of African Americans in Congress*. Cambridge: Harvard University Press.

———. 1995. "The Future of Black Representation." *American Prospect* 19 (Fall): 78–83.

Taylor, Charles. 1992. *Multiculturalism and the "Politics of Recognition."* Princeton: Princeton University Press.

Thernstrom, Abigail. 1987. *Whose Votes Count? Affirmative Action and Minority Voting Rights*. Cambridge: Harvard University Press.

Thernstrom, Stephan, and Abigail Thernstrom. 1997. *America in Black and White One Nation, Indivisible: Race in Modern America*. New York: Simon and Schuster.

Walton, F. Carl. 1995. "The Congressional Black Caucus and Its Liberal Ideology: A Search for Explanation." Paper Presented at the Annual Meeting of the American Political Science Association, Chicago, August 31–September 2.

Weber, Ronald E. 1995. "The Unanticipated Consequences of Race-Based Districting: The Impact on Electoral Competition and Voter Participation." Paper Presented at the Annual Meeting of the Midwest Political Science Association, Chicago, April 6–8.

Welch, Susan, and John R. Hibbing. 1984. "Hispanic Representation in the U.S. Congress." *Social Science Quarterly* 65:328–35.

Whitby, Kenny J. 1985. "Effects of the Interaction between Race and Urbanization on Votes of Southern Congressmen." *Legislative Studies Quarterly* 10:505–19.

———. 1987. "Measuring Congressional Responsiveness to the Policy Interests of Black Constituents." *Social Science Quarterly* 68:367–77.

Whitby, Kenny J., and Franklin D. Gilliam, Jr. 1991. "A Longitudinal Analysis of Competing Explanations for the Transformation of Southern Congressional Politics." *Journal of Politics* 53:504–18.

Wright, Gerald C. 1977. "Contextual Models of Electoral Behavior: The Southern Wallace Vote." *American Political Science Review* 71:497–508.

Van Biema, David. 1994. "One Person, Seven Votes." *Time* 143 (April 25): 42–43.

Vanderleeuw, James M., and Glenn U. Utter. 1993. "Voter Roll-Off and the Electoral Context: A Test of Two Theses." *Social Science Quarterly* 74:664–73.

Young, Iris M. 1990. *Justice and the Politics of Difference*. Princeton: Princeton University Press.

———. 1994. "Justice and Communicative Democracy." In *Radical Philosophy: Tradition, Counter-Tradition, Politics*, edited by Roger S. Gotlieb, 123–43 Philadelphia: Temple University Press.

14 The American Presidency and the Politics of Democratic Inclusion

No ACCOUNT OF THE EXTENSION OF THE RIGHTS and privileges of citizenship would be complete without reference to the actions of our nation's chief executive. Presidents are central players in the politics of democratic inclusion, and we expect them to be so. Our expectations for presidential action have grown along with the institution. In the past century, presidents have reinforced their identification with the people, expanded executive branch responsibilities and bureaucracy, and played a more active part in all stages of policy formation and implementation. It is hard to believe how significant progress could be made without their support or cooperation.

In popular mythology, presidents are great initiators and supporters of democratic inclusion. We dwell on the accomplishments of presidents such as Abraham Lincoln, Harry Truman, and Lyndon Johnson. But presidential power is a double-edged sword. Though presidents have the power to promote democratic inclusion, they also have the power to block it. Since the time of the founding, the majority of presidents have been indifferent or unfriendly to marginalized groups and hesitant to be at the forefront of social change. Some have actively stifled inclusion for the sake of their party's elites or electoral coalition. Only a small number have served at historical moments when their support dramatically altered the political landscape.

The president's role in the process of political incorporation has been severely neglected by scholars of the American presidency. There is little or no dialogue about democratic inclusion as a research agenda—no systematic discussion of how to measure responsiveness to marginal groups or form general explanations for presidential activism. We have hardly begun to understand the role that presidents have played, much less compare the president's responses with those of other national institutions.

In this chapter, I argue that we need to think seriously about how to measure presidential responsiveness to marginalized groups, incorporating the notion that presidents may encourage *or* discourage democratic inclusion. Presidents can advocate social policies aimed at helping members of marginalized groups become more fully incorporated into civil society and political life. But they can also advocate social policies that slow political incorporation. Presidents can actively mobilize voters and partisans for the cause of marginalized groups, or they can actively mobilize majorities to suppress marginalized groups. Presidents may actively encourage or discourage the formation of group consciousness. They can ignore groups or give them voice.

I also argue that the constitutional role of the chief executive provides the president with contradictory incentives so that the growth in presidential power has not always led to the promotion of democratic inclusion. For instance, the instruction to "preserve, protect, and defend" the Constitution of the United States and see that the laws are faithfully executed has led some presidents (like Lincoln) to further democratic inclusion when this reduces social turmoil or restores national unity. But this imperative has more frequently meant upholding a status quo based upon the exclusion of certain classes of citizens. Similarly, the singularity of the office and the fact that the President's geographic constituency is the entire nation has encouraged presidents to use populist rhetoric and promote themselves as the guardian of *all* of the people. However, these features also give the president incentives to ignore divisive and controversial issues. Presidential populism may lead the president to pander to a majority at the expense of minority groups.

Since the constitution does not dictate that the president promote the interests of marginal groups, the president's actions are best explained by considering his historical and political context. The president is embedded in his own sort of "political opportunity structure," where particular historical forces converge to provide incentives or disincentives for action—where the president interacts with and reacts to his environment (McAdam 1996). He is not an isolated and independent force for social change. Over time, presidential activism will be a function of changes in norms concerning the appropriate role of the executive, the development of the executive branch bureaucracy, and the changing dynamics of the political party system. In the short run, presidential responsiveness to marginalized groups will be a function of factors such as partisan support in Congress, pressure from activists and social movements, and re-election concerns. If the political climate is favorable, those presidents with leadership skills and ideological commitment will take action.

I begin the chapter with a working definition of presidential responsiveness to marginalized groups. Next, I examine various explanations for the president's behavior: his constitutional role, the historical growth of the executive branch, Congressional support or opposition, re-election concerns, pressure from interest groups and public opinion, and presidential character. In the final section, I offer suggestions for future research. I argue that we should abandon the "person vs. environment" framework that currently structures academic debate about the sources of presidential behavior. I also argue that we must study more than a handful of great presidents, so that our theories are more generalizeable and true to the historical record.

I should note two limitations at the outset. Though my empirical examples focus almost exclusively on African American civil rights, my theoretical discussion is meant to generalize to a wider spectrum of groups. Second, though the executive branch includes the cabinet, staff, and bureaucracy, I limit my discussion to the president and his closest advisors. The role of bureaucracy and the politics of democratic inclusion, particularly at the level of policy implementation, are beyond the scope of this chapter.

WHAT COUNTS AS PRESIDENTIAL RESPONSIVENESS?

A logical starting point for the study of a political institution and political incorporation is an examination of descriptive representation. This is a sobering exercise with respect to the chief executive: All forty-three occupants of the office have been white and male, all but one from a Protestant religious background. When we look at presidential candidates, cabinet members and staff, and presidential appointments, the picture is only marginally better. Nearly all disadvantaged or minority groups had no representation in the executive branch until the mid-to-late 1960s. Descriptive representation in the executive branch is a relatively recent and slow-growing phenomenon.

A few examples and statistics illustrate the historical lack of diversity in presidential electoral politics and executive administration. Geraldine Ferraro is the only woman to have been part of a major party presidential ticket; no person of color has ever been part of a major party presidential ticket. Lenora Fulani of the National Alliance Party is the only African American to have been listed on the presidential ballot in all fifty states. Margaret Chase Smith (1964) and Shirley Chisolm (1972) are the only women to have their names placed in nomination for President at a major party convention. The Reverend Channing Phillips (1968), Shirley Chisolm (1972), and the Rev. Jesse Jackson (1984, 1988), are the only people of color to win delegates at a major party convention. Only a handful of women and minorities beyond those already named have entered any state presidential primaries for either major party.

The diversity of executive branch cabinet and staff is not much better (See Borrelli and J. Martin 1997; M. Martin 1999; Miles et al. 2001). In the last two hundred years, only twenty-two of more than six hundred cabinet appointments have gone to women (J. Martin 1997, 60). Only fourteen cabinet appointments have gone to African Americans, with only five of these appointments occurring *before* the Clinton and Bush, Jr. administrations. Only five Latinos have been cabinet secretaries, with the first appointed in 1988. Norman Mineta, secretary of commerce under Bill Clinton and secretary of transportation under George W. Bush, is the first Asian American man to serve in the cabinet. Elaine Chao, George W. Bush's secretary of labor, is the first Asian American woman to serve in the cabinet. No Native Americans have ever served.

Presidential appointments to U.S. district and appeals court judgeships reflect a similar pattern, though Democratic presidents appoint a more diverse group of judges than do Republican presidents (Sourcebook of Criminal Justice Statistics 2000). Around 20 percent of George H. W. Bush's appointees and 30 percent of Bill Clinton's appointees to the courts were women. Roughly 7 percent of Bush's appointees to district court judgeships were African American as opposed to 17 percent of Bill Clinton's appointees to the district court. On average, only about 5 percent of appointees to district court judgeships are Hispanic. Asian and Native American appointees are still virtually nonexistent. The majority of appointees of all races hold undergraduate degrees from private or Ivy League institutions.

On the other hand, the trend is definitely toward more diversity. Prior to the 1960s, there were only a handful of judgeships awarded to women and minorities. Two percent of President Kennedy's appointments to positions of cabinet secretary, undersecretaries, regulatory commissions, and other posts were women; by the Clinton administration, women constituted 30 percent of all such appointments (J. Martin 1997, 58). In the time of Franklin Roosevelt, women constituted 10 percent of all White House staff. During the Clinton administration, women constituted nearly 40 percent of all White House staff, though these women were disproportionately concentrated in low-level positions (Tenpas 1997, 93).

When we turn to the general question of whether or not American presidents have advanced the struggle to extend the recognition, rights, and privileges of citizenship to disadvantaged groups, we see a decidedly mixed picture. On the one hand, some of the greatest advances in American political history involve moments where American presidents very publicly and courageously promoted the rights of disadvantaged groups. Abraham Lincoln is the most dramatic example. Teddy Roosevelt spoke publicly against the lynching of African Americans in the South. Franklin Roosevelt's New Deal programs addressed economic and social welfare issues relevant to poor and disadvantaged citizens. Harry Truman issued an executive order to desegregate the military and supported the civil rights plank in the 1948 Democratic platform that caused Southern delegations to defect from the party. Dwight Eisenhower ordered federal troops to Little Rock, AR, to enforce school desegregation. The efforts of John Kennedy and Lyndon Johnson were crucial for the passage of the 1964 Civil Rights Act and the 1965 Voting Rights Act. Ronald Reagan appointed the first woman to the U.S. Supreme Court. Bill Clinton was the first major party president to speak openly about gay rights.

On the other hand, these presidents and others have ignored or purposefully obstructed political incorporation (O'Reilly 1995; Riley 1999). With the exception of Lincoln, nineteenth-century presidents had an abysmal record in the politics of democratic inclusion (Riley 1999). In the twentieth century, Woodrow Wilson explicitly endorsed segregation in federal employment (Klinkner, with Smith 1999, 110). Herbert Hoover refused to speak publicly against the lynching of African Americans in the South (Brown 1995, 35). During his twelve years in office, Franklin Roosevelt made only one brief reference to voting rights (Shull 1989, 47). The Nixon and Ford administrations sought to curtail the enforcement of civil rights policy, particularly in the area of school desegregation (Shull 1989). Ronald Reagan opposed the Equal Rights Amendment and slashed budget expenditures for civil rights agencies such as the Equal Employment Opportunity Commission (EEOC) and the U.S. Commission on Civil Rights (Shull 1989, 146–151). In 1988, the Bush campaign ran the infamous "Willie Horton" ad as President George Bush repeatedly opposed civil rights legislation, referring to the legislation as "quota bills."

These examples highlight the challenge of measuring presidential responsiveness. How would we rank presidents? How would we describe variation within and across administrations? Presidential actions (and non-actions) may be located on a continuum from responsiveness to indifference to opposition. For the purposes of this chapter, I consider *responsive* behavior to be the appointment of disadvantaged group members in the executive branch and agencies; the provision of formal channels by which marginalized groups have voice in the White House; advocacy of legislation or executive orders aimed at ending discrimination and extending basic rights of citizenship (legal, civil, economic); and public rhetoric emphasizing equality and political incorporation. Presidents who are *indifferent* ignore issues of democratic inclusion altogether. Active *opposition* includes discrimination in appointments and access to the White House; advocacy of legislation or executive orders that perpetuate discrimination and deny basic rights of citizenship; and public rhetoric that promotes racism and the continued oppression of marginalized groups.

EXPLANATIONS FOR PRESIDENTIAL RESPONSIVENESS

Constitutional Role

According to Article II of the U.S. Constitution, the president's job is to "take care that the laws be faithfully executed" and "preserve, protect, and defend the constitution of the United States." The president is the only official with the entire nation as his geographical constituency. He represents our country in our interactions with other nation states and international actors. The president is a natural focal point for citizen expectations about public policy; he is a symbol of the nation.

The quest to preserve national unity is generally a conservative impulse with respect to social change. "The presidency has routinely served as a *nation-maintaining* institution on the issue of racial inequality ... one of the enduring roles each president is required to execute is that of nation-keeper, a protector of the inherited political and social order and a preserver of domestic tranquility" (Riley 1999, 10). The president's job is to defend the government structures and processes outlined in the Constitution as well as "the social and cultural institutions upon which the superstructure of that Constitution rests" (Riley 1999, 18). Civil Rights activist James Farmer, opposing Lyndon Johnson's attempt to halt civil rights demonstrations in 1964, observed "This wasn't just Johnson. Every administration, 'just try [*sic*] to keep it cool.' And one could understand it. If we were the administration, we'd want to keep it cool" (Miroff 1981, 22). As keeper of law and order, the president tries to discourage signs of internal division and protest.

At the same time, the president's nation-maintaining role may force him to take the lead in times of social crisis to heal the nation and bring peace. Civil rights have been advanced during times of domestic instability, when activists successfully mobilized mass movements behind change. "When demographic and political conditions ripened so as to make extensive mobilization possible, the disruptive force of mass movements created powerful incentives for presidents to revisit the logic of the nation-maintaining role. To have done otherwise under these new conditions would have cultivated a continuing threat to the strained fabric of the American polity" (Riley 1999, 19). Lincoln's goal, for instance, was preservation of the Union. "My paramount object in this struggle is to save the Union, and is not either to save or to destroy slavery. If I could save the Union without freeing any slave I would do it, and if I could save it by freeing all the slaves I would do it; and if I could save it by freeing some and leaving others alone I would also do that" (Riley 1999, 77). In the 1960s, members of the Kennedy and Johnson administrations felt that domestic peace and stability could only be restored through the passage of civil rights legislation.

The president's roles as our commander in chief and primary foreign diplomat also provide contradictory incentives. Presidents concerned about the international consequences of domestic disarray could suppress minorities or social movements rather than promote democratic inclusion. War could lead to the oppression of minority groups associated with the perceived foreign threat (for example, the internment of Japanese Americans in World War II). On the other hand, international pressures could force presidents to further democratic inclusion. Lincoln's preservation of the Union was related to fears about European intervention and alliance with the South (H. Jones 1999). Major advances in African American civil rights have occurred when government leaders had to reconcile wartime rhetoric promoting inclusiveness, democracy, and equality throughout the world with the reality of the political and social disenfranchisement of African Americans within the United States (Klinkner, with Smith 1999).

Though the executive branch is by no means a single unitary actor—if one includes the cabinet, executive departments, bureaucracy, and so forth—the president can move quickly and unilaterally relative to other national institutions. Unlike a legislature, the president suffers from no collective action problem (Moe 1985). Further, though he operates in a system of shared powers, the president has the capacity for unilateral action in the form of veto power and executive orders. Like other structural features of the executive branch, however, these traits reinforce the presidency as a place for action and responsibility, but do not guarantee that any individual president will work toward democratic inclusion.

The Evolution of the Presidency: Populism and Growth

Several scholars have compared the limited executive envisioned at the founding with the development of the "rhetorical" or "public" presidency of the modern era (Edwards 1983; Kernell 1986; Tulis 1987; Ellis 1998; Miroff 2000). In contrast to the executives of the early Republic, modern presidents publicly campaign for office, promote a policy agenda, and cultivate a close relationship with the public. They promote themselves as representatives and interpreters of the popular will. The presidential tendency to appeal directly to voters is reinforced by the political primary system and a nomination process no longer controlled by party elites (Polsby 1978). Furthermore, in the fragmented political system of the post-Watergate era, it is often more efficient for presidents to use public opinion to pressure Congress than to engage in more traditional forms of bargaining (Kernell 1986).

The rise of the rhetorical presidency has important implications for the politics of democratic inclusion. First, the claim to be a representative of the entire nation puts the president at the center of debates about the definition of "the People." A study of speeches from Truman to Reagan reveals that the primary subject or actor is not "I" or "this administration," but "We" (Hinckley 1990, 40). Presidents often cultivate their relationship with voters by promising that, unlike Congress, they will be "above" party and faction. Second, the rise of the rhetorical presidency means that the president is a natural agenda setter on the American political scene—he focuses collective attention on issues that he believes salient, he establishes policy goals, and he formally proposes policy initiatives. "No other single actor in the political system has quite the capability of the president to set agendas in given policy areas for all who deal with those policies" (Kingdon 1995, 23).

The chief executive is therefore a natural focal point for the politics of democratic inclusion and he seems well positioned to change the political agenda. But the rise of the rhetorical presidency does not necessarily mean that presidents will work to further the interests of the disadvantaged, particularly numerical minorities. Presidents are quite capable of wrapping antiminority initiatives or appeals in populist rhetoric. Presidents may justify their opposition to inclusive policies by claiming to speak for a "silent" majority. And whether or not the president seeks to further democratic inclusion, a president's public promises often far exceed his real capacity for effecting change (Cronin 1980; Lowi 1985). Going public may substitute emotional and symbolic appeals for real debate and serve as a substitute for careful policy formation (Hart 1987; Tulis 1987; Bessette 1994).

The growth of bureaucracy and policy responsibility from the time of the founding has also given presidents an increasingly larger role in policy making (Burke 1993; Arnold 1998; Pfiffner 1999). Presidents today have many more resources to use to promote or discourage the integration of diverse groups into American political life. The executive branch in the modern era includes cabinet level departments of education, housing and urban development, and health and human services in addition to the civil rights division of the Justice Department. The president works closely with independent agencies like the Commission on Civil Rights, the Federal Election Commission, and the EEOC. Implementation of inclusive public policies is centered in the executive branch bureaucracy. Like the rise of the rhetorical presidency, this is a mixed blessing. It is unclear how well the president can control executive departments and agencies and the president need not use his resources to promote inclusion (Pfiffner 1999).

Constitutional responsibilities and power and resources within the political system provide the general boundaries within which any individual president operates. The historical transformation of the office explains variation in level of activism over broad stretches of American history. Twentieth-century presidents, particularly post–New Deal presidents, have taken a much more active role in policy making, so we would expect them to be more active in the politics of democratic inclusion. Characteristics of the office are also crucial for understanding differences in responsiveness across national governmental institutions. Yet in order to know whether any individual president will act, and whether he will support or oppose democratic inclusion, we must turn our attention to explanatory factors that make more fine-grained distinctions between presidents: support in Congress, public pressure, and presidential character.

Politics inside the Beltway

The system of shared powers is one of the defining characteristics of American government; conflict between Congress and the president is inevitable (Neustadt 1990; Fisher 1991; C. Jones 1994; Bond and Fleisher 2000). As Charles Jones (1994) writes "The plain fact is that the United States does not have a presidential system. It has a separated system" (335). Thus one prominent explanation for variation in presidential responsiveness is the degree of congressional responsiveness and congressional support or opposition for the president's point of view. The most sympathetic and skilled president may not seek to promote democratic inclusion if he faces a hostile Congress. A president who would rather not act may be forced to take a stand when Congress passes legislation requiring his signature or veto.

The best predictors of the success of the president's policy agenda are the numerical strength of the president's party and party control of Congress. Using roll call votes from 1953–1984 on policies on which the president has taken a position, Bond and Fleisher (1990) find that the most important determinant of presidential success is whether or not the president's party controls both chambers of Congress and whether party leaders share his point of view. In a multivariate analysis, the authors find that congress-centered variables such as the size of the president's party base and opposition base, and the positions of congressional party and committee leaders have the strongest effects. The effect of presidential leadership skill and popularity are small and insignificant. Additional quantitative studies of presidential success in Congress confirm these findings (Edwards 1980; Peterson 1990). The primacy of Congress is reinforced by historical case studies. The most prominent recent examples are post- New Deal Democratic presidents faced with Southern Democrats in Congress who repeatedly attempt to block executive action in the area of African American civil rights.

If a president wants to pass legislation that promotes democratic inclusion, he must have support in Congress. Without strong support, he can still encourage or discourage progressive legislation by using veto power. Since presidential vetoes are rare, however, one might think that this is not a regular or viable way for a president to promote democratic inclusion. Charles Cameron (2000) makes a persuasive case that even though vetoes are numerically rare, presidential veto power significantly shapes bargaining between the president and Congress. Members of Congress anticipate presidential vetoes and modify the content of bills accordingly. Alternatively, presidents may exercise their veto power, and congress may alter and re-pass the bill, a process that Cameron labels *sequential veto bargaining.* (9) He offers the example of President Clinton and welfare reform. Through a sequence of vetoes, Clinton forced Republicans to offer him a bill that preserved billions of dollars in welfare expenditures and abandoned plans to give states almost total control over programs like Medicaid and food stamps (20–22).

Recent work on executive orders also suggests that the president has more of a capacity for unilateral action than is commonly understood (Mayer 2001; Howell, 2003). The civil rights arena is one area in which presidents have used executive orders to sidestep an intransigent Congress (Morgan 1970; Mayer 2001). Eleven percent of the executive orders issued by Democratic presidents and 7 percent of the executive orders issued by Republican presidents from Truman to Clinton pertained to social welfare or civil rights (Ragsdale 1996, 344–347). Democratic presidents are more likely to issue executive orders that affect labor and minority groups while Republican presidents are more likely to issue orders that affect business and industry (297–298). Through executive orders, presidents since Franklin Roosevelt have firmly established the chief executive as a prominent actor in areas such as affirmative action, equal employment opportunity, and housing discrimination (Morgan 1970; Shull 1989; Mayer 2001).

Politics beyond the Beltway

The interaction between the president and Congress takes place within a larger social and political context. Politics outside the beltway makes issues salient inside the beltway. Over time, the president's capacity for leadership in the politics of democratic inclusion is shaped by the rise and fall of party regimes and the number and variety of actors on the American political scene. At any particular moment, presidential responsiveness depends upon his election or re-election strategy, public opinion, and pressure from activists and interest group organizations. The president both responds to social forces and tries to shape them.

Stephen Skowronek (1997) argues that presidential leadership is best understood by taking into account two major aspects of the political context: the president's opposition or affiliation with the dominant political party regime and the extent to which this regime is vulnerable or resilient. Presidents with the greatest opportunity to build parties, expand the office of the presidency, and enact major policy changes come to power during realigning elections, opposed to a declining and no longer dominant party regime. Presidents affiliated with a strong dominant party can also expect to be fairly successful. On the other hand, those presidents (like Buchanan or Hoover) affiliated with a party in severe state of decline or minority party presidents (like Eisenhower or Nixon) who win elections despite being at odds with the current and strong party regime, have little warrant for making major policy changes. Skowronek has a more subtle argument about the ways these presidents practice different types of politics. But what is crucial here is that all of the presidents most recognized for their support or opposition to political incorporation fall into the first two categories above. Thus wider political context eliminates some presidents from activism because they do not have as much political capital as others.

The historical context of presidential action is also addressed in literature on changes in the political environment since Vietnam and Watergate. Reforms in the nominating process, campaign finance, and congressional reorganization in the 1960s and early 1970s fundamentally changed the way politics is played. The decline of political parties, the proliferation of interest groups, and the rise of mass media politics limit the president's ability to control and achieve policy change (Cronin 1980; Lowi 1985; Peterson 1990; Milkis 1993). Presidents before the Vietnam and Watergate era have higher average levels of popularity and success in Congress than presidents afterward. The literature suggests that expectations for success in any policy realm must be tempered by this structural break.

Within a particular historical context, variation in responsiveness is further explained by immediate political constraints such as the maintenance of party coalitions, electoral majorities, and public approval. Presidents, like other politicians, work to maintain the strength of their political party's base and widen their base of support without alienating blocs of voters who have been critical to electoral victory in the past. The Roosevelt administration, for instance, worked to keep immigration issues, including the issue of German Jewish refugees, off the policy agenda so as not to alienate Southern Democrats (Tichenor 2002). Harry Truman's advisors urged him to take stands on civil rights to keep the support of African Americans in key northern and Midwestern states who might otherwise be persuaded to vote for a third-party progressive candidate (Berman 1970; James 2000). In 1996, the Clinton administration did not conduct a vigorous campaign against state anti–affirmative action propositions for fear of losing the votes of moderate and conservative Democrats (Kahlenberg 2001).

The two-party system and the structure of presidential elections give politicians little incentive to work for the votes of minority groups. Since both major parties want the vote of the white majority, the interests of minorities are seldom put at the forefront of electoral politics. Minority groups are thereby held captive by the two-party system (Walters 1988; Frymer 1999). Presidents and parties pay attention to groups that have the numbers and ideological location to make a difference in swing states in the Electoral College. If a group is too small to make a difference, presidential candidates will not go out of their way to court them, particularly if doing so will alienate other voters. After the election, the president will not place a high priority on democratic inclusion unless it was prominent in his campaign and helped him achieve victory (Conley 2001).

Presidential attention to public opinion polls reflects this same concern with maintaining the support of a majority of voters. Potentially divisive issues that are not viewed as a high priority by a majority of the electorate are likely to be avoided. From the late 1950s through the late 1960s for instance, civil rights ranked as one of the top two "most important problems" in public opinion polls (Shull 1989, 10–11) and figured heavily in political campaigns. In other years, public concern has been centered on the cold war or the economy. To the extent that other issues are more salient to voters, the politics of democratic inclusion is set aside.

Beyond polls, presidents pay attention to the public represented by activists and interest groups working outside the organizational structure of the major political parties. Activists may encourage their followers to abandon the party or abstain from voting; they may threaten to lead mass demonstrations. Presidents are most attentive to this pressure when a social movement's constituency forms an important part of the president's electoral base, when he has similar objectives but wants to avoid solutions that would alienate other parts of his base constituency, and when the issue is central to the president's public image (Miroff 1981, 7). Presidents will work to maintain the financial and organization support of interest groups and the votes of their members.

Case studies of presidents and civil rights policy frequently attribute presidential responses to pressure from interest groups and social movements. Franklin Roosevelt issued an executive order for the establishment of the Fair Employment Practices Committee in 1941 so that black leaders would cancel a planned march on Washington (McCoy and Ruetten 1973; Riley 1999). Harry Truman issued an executive order to establish nondiscrimination in the military right before the 1948 election when black leaders threatened to urge blacks to refuse to serve in the military and his advisors believed that loss of the African American vote would cause him to lose key swing states (Berman 1970; McCoy and Ruetten 1973). The civil rights legislation of the 1960s followed years of sustained activism and pressure. Members of the Reagan administration wanted to reform (and abolish) affirmative action programs that stemmed from executive orders issued by Kennedy and Johnson, but they were stopped by opposition within the executive branch (EEOC, Department of Labor), civil rights organizations, and members of Congress (Mayer 2001, 206–208).

Presidents react to social pressures, but they also try to control their environment and shape politics in the future. Individual presidents change the parameters of the office and set standards for future presidents (Skowronek 1997). They may seek to transform their political party and social movements (Riley 1999, 240–242). In a study of the Johnson administration, Bruce Miroff (1981) argues that "The White House may try to modify the character of a social movement; it may seek to influence its leadership, to delimit its objectives, or to slow the tempo of its actions. It may attempt to forestall movement projects that conflict with its own projects, thereby averting the explosion into public notice of embarrassing clashes. It may hope, ultimately, to transform social movements from political liabilities into political advantages" (2). Like other politicians, presidents want to shape and define issues to their advantage. They want to maximize their support and solidify their electoral and partisan coalitions.

Presidential Character

Presidential behavior cannot be explained without reference to the person who occupies the office. In *Presidential Power*, Richard Neustadt (1990) focuses on the president's reputation, prestige, and skill at the bargaining table.

Political psychologists such as James David Barber (1972) explain success and failure according to the president's attitude toward the job (positive or negative) and his activity level (active or passive). More recent work focuses on traits such as ambition, self-esteem, and interpersonal relations (Renshon 1996); management and advisory style (Burke and Greenstein 1989; George and George 1998); and emotional intelligence (Greenstein 2000).

No typology of presidential character predicts who will be more likely to further democratic inclusion. Yet any explanation for presidential activism and policy success must consider variation in leadership skill. Individual level characteristics are important because the ability to lead depends on choices regarding information gathering, appointments, advisors, and managerial style. A maladaptive and ineffectual president is not likely to get much done, including promoting democratic inclusion.

The president's own attitude toward racial equality is important, but difficult to discern. Scholars have debated whether presidential rhetoric for the advancement of inclusion is sincere or politically strategic (Berman 1970 versus McCoy & Reutten 1973 on Truman) and whether the president is sincere but too constrained by other political forces to act (Brauer 1977 on Kennedy; Riley 2001 on Clinton). In many cases scholars have genuine disagreements about the president's personal beliefs (Lunardini and Knock 1980 versus Graham 1983 on Woodrow Wilson). More easily discernible is the president's ideological propensity to support greater inclusiveness. Liberal and conservative presidents have very different records (Shull 1989). The most vigorous recent efforts to promote inclusion have come from Democratic presidents, who are more liberal than their Republican counterparts. The president's views on race, gender, and social class are relevant, but so is his general ideology regarding the priority of these issues and the proper role of government in advancing political incorporation.

POSSIBILITIES FOR FUTURE RESEARCH

My discussion of explanations for presidential responsiveness is intended to be more than a laundry list of variables. I hope to convey that a comprehensive theory of presidential responsiveness involves multiple layers of explanation. The Constitution sets both a floor and a ceiling for presidential action. The development of the scope and resources of the office over time further delimits the president's options for activism. At any historical moment, larger social and political developments put democratic inclusion on or off the national political agenda. When these issues are prominent, immediate political circumstances such as support among congressional and electoral coalitions shape presidential responses. Political ideology will dictate whether the president responds in a manner that encourages or discourages political incorporation.

Future research should acknowledge that the relative importance of explanatory variables changes depending upon a particular president's location in historical time. Theories that seek to explain differences across multiple presidents must consider structural changes in national politics and in the executive branch. Within historical time periods, a look at more than a handful of presidents is necessary to understand how responsiveness varies with factors such as congressional support, public opinion, and re-election concerns. Explanations will vary according to the type of action we seek to explain (e.g., rhetoric, legislation, or appointments) and the substance of the policies being promoted (e.g., voting rights, school desegregation, and immigration law). Presidential responses are a function of the marginalized groups themselves, from their place in the president's electoral coalition to the intensity of their organized activism.

The Person or the Environment?

The debate over the primacy of the person or the political context in explanations for presidential behavior animates intellectual exchange in the presidency field (see Edwards, Kessel, and Rockman 1993; Shapiro, Kumar, and Jacobs 2000). This controversy is reinforced by arguments about methodology—qualitative researchers tend to focus on the individual while quantitative and formal researchers focus on aspects of the wider political environment. The examples of Abraham Lincoln and Bill Clinton illustrate why we should avoid framing our discussion of the president and democratic inclusion in the context of this debate.

In our political culture, Lincoln is the president most associated with political incorporation and equal justice for all (C-Span 1999; Schwartz 2000). Though Lincoln argued that slavery was immoral, he also argued that it should not be abolished in those states where it existed. His belief was that containment would eventually lead to extinction. From the start of his first inaugural address, he said, "I have no purpose directly or indirectly to interfere with the institution of slavery in the States where it exists. I believe I have no lawful right to do so and I have no inclination to do so" (Inaugural Addresses of the Presidents 1989). Yet the secession of southern states and the pressures of northern radicals pushed Lincoln to act. With the goal of preserving the union, Lincoln offered a series of plans such as colonization and compensation for emancipation that he thought would keep the allegiance of border states. He met with free African Americans to persuade them to leave the country as he felt that blacks and whites should be separated. As these proposals were rejected and foreign interference loomed on the horizon, Lincoln decided that emancipation "had become a necessity indispensable to the maintenance of government." (Riley 1999, 107) By the fall of 1862, he made his first public declaration that slaves in states not allegiant to the Union would be free. He then worked for passage of what would become the Thirteenth Amendment.

Why did Lincoln work toward democratic inclusion? Anyone in Lincoln's position would have been forced to take some kind of action. His presidency followed years of conflict over the issue of slavery, and states were seceding from the Union. Lincoln advocated several different plans before political pressure from fellow Republicans in Congress, war, and activists pushed him toward emancipation. As he said, "I claim not to have controlled events, but confess plainly that events have controlled me" (Riley 1999, 115). Social forces demanded that Lincoln act; the interaction between his own values and skills and immediate political pressures dictated the path of his decision making.

Contrast Lincoln with one of our most recent presidents. By many accounts, Bill Clinton personally values democratic inclusion (Maraniss 1995; Renshon 1996). His record of cabinet and judicial appointments was more diverse than any president before him. In 1992, Democrats controlled Congress and voters looked to an end of "gridlock." The circumstances of Clinton's election, however, were not conducive to putting democratic inclusion at the top of his policy agenda. Clinton received only 43 percent of the popular vote due to the strong showing by Ross Perot. He had promised to be a "New Democrat" who would govern from the center. Economic issues dominated his campaign, and they dominated his initial policy agenda. In 1994, the Republicans regained control of Congress, claiming a mandate for their "Contract with America" that included term limits, middle-class tax cuts, and deficit reduction. As much as Clinton may have personally valued inclusion, other issues topped the national agenda and his electoral coalition was fragile.

These issues did surface, however, when the Republican-led Congress heightened the salience of affirmative action issues and anti-affirmative action propositions were on the ballot in states such as California in 1996. Late in his first term, Clinton spoke of basing affirmative action policies on economic need rather than race. But Clinton strategists worried about how angering the party base would affect his chances for re-election; Jesse Jackson said he would challenge Clinton for the nomination if he didn't stand firm on affirmative action (Kahlenberg 2001, 95). Clinton ended up giving a major speech on "mending" not "ending" affirmative action that seemed to please his supporters. He avoided taking a stand on California's anti-affirmative action proposition 209, so that "race played no role in the 1996 presidential election even though anti-immigrant and anti-affirmative action ballot propositions threatened to make it the most racial of recent contests" (Dick Morris, quoted by Kahlenberg 2001, 98).

Why didn't Clinton do more? Electoral strategy seems to explain a great deal. The failing economy was viewed as the most important problem in public opinion polls in 1992. The economy was an issue that could build a large coalition for Clinton and possibly gain the votes of moderate Republicans and Perot voters without alienating his party base. When others eventually made race salient, his advisors recognized that this posed problems for Clinton's electoral coalition. If he took a strong stand against race-based affirmative action, he would alienate African Americans and the liberal wing of the Democratic Party. If he promoted affirmative action he would lose the support of moderate and potential swing voters, particularly in the Southern states. This was not the only issue of political incorporation where Clinton evidenced concern about his electoral coalition. He delayed his intended order to lift the ban on gays in the military when he was accused of pandering to interest groups and possibly alienating the Perot voters whose support he desperately needed (Frymer 1999). Clinton was not so much concerned with mending or unifying a nation as keeping together an electoral coalition.

Is it possible to comprehend the differences between these two presidents without attention to their place in American political history? Lincoln served at an extraordinary political moment (Burnham 1970; Ackerman 1998); Clinton did not. Is it possible to understand their responsiveness without taking into account their electoral concerns, congressional pressure, or the intensity of social activism? Can we understand their differences without attention to the substance of the policies at hand (slavery vs. affirmative action)? Do we expect that any other person would have given exactly the same attention to political incorporation, with the same kinds of actions, if put in their position?

An intellectual debate that forces us to choose a favorite set of variables is static and potentially misleading. No set of variables is totally irrelevant. Nor do they work in isolation from one another. No single variable or set of variables is most important all of the time for all presidents. Explanations differ depending on the substance and type of responsive behavior that serves as our dependent variable. When reinforced by preferences for particular research methods, the person versus environment debate limits the possibilities for theory building.

Multiple Cases and Multiple Methods

Research on presidents and the politics of democratic inclusion is oriented around a handful of supportive and activist presidents such as Abraham Lincoln and Lyndon Johnson. Unfortunately, the focus on a small number of positive cases diverts attention from the rest of the historical record. The absence of great moments in the politics of democratic inclusion means that these issues are either being ignored, opposed, or moving along at a slower pace. Our theories should not be built around a truncated dependent variable. Moreover, the focus on presidential heroes easily degenerates into a "soul mate" theory of the presidency, in which good things depend upon finding one good man. This ignores the role of social and institutional forces in providing the opportunity for policy change. Future research should incorporate more cases; more variation in presidential responsiveness will provide a better sense of the relative weight of explanatory factors.

A wider variety of marginalized groups should be studied to determine whether variation in presidential responsiveness is a function of the nature of the groups themselves (size, ideological cohesion, voting patterns, level of activism, strategy, etc). Variation in responsiveness across groups may depend on the ways in which members of the executive branch define groups and their interests. Presidential responses may depend on the interaction between the president's goals and the strategies of activists and interest groups (Tichenor 2003). Presidential responses may vary depending upon who mediates the relationship between the executive branch and marginalized groups-interest groups, policy networks, members of congress or congressional caucuses, party leaders, or local politicians.

In addition to increasing the number of presidents and groups, we should be open to multiple methodological approaches. Qualitative research dominates the study of presidents and the advancement of minority groups, offering detailed accounts of presidential psychology, incentives, and historical events. Unfortunately, few historical case studies explicitly formulate hypotheses about when and why presidents will promote democratic inclusion. Russell Riley's book *The President and the Politics of Racial Inequality* (1999) is an important exception.

Quantitative research on democratic inclusion is scarce, because of a "small n" problem: There are only forty-three presidents from George Washington to George W. Bush, and a mere twelve presidents if we restrict our attention to the modern presidency of the post–New Deal era. But we need not use the president as the unit of analysis and come up with a summary measure of responsiveness for each president. We can increase the number of cases by disaggregating responsiveness into specific behaviors that vary within and across administrations. Steven Shull (1989) ranks presidential promotion of civil rights according to measures like the volume of legislation, number of staff, budget outlays, and numbers of references in state of the union and public papers. Other measures could include the number and range of groups with access to the executive branch (Peterson 1992) or the priority of democratic inclusion relative to other domestic policy programs (Light 1991).

More and better measures will allow us to gauge variation within and across administrations and identify historical trends. Quantitative measures of presidential responsiveness can be related to variables like the state of the economy, presidential popularity, support in Congress, support from electoral coalitions, and public opinion. This will bring us closer to general explanations of the politics of democratic inclusion and provide tests of theories developed using historical methods. We may find that the patterns in the data are not consistent with impressions garnered from a handful of case studies.

CONCLUSION

Long ago, James MacGregor Burns criticized Richard Neustadt for accepting that the role of the president is to bargain, negotiate, and persuade. "Divorced from ethics, leadership is reduced to management and politics to mere technique" (Burns 1978, 389). Burns contrasted Neustadt's bargaining president with "transforming leadership," where leaders and followers engage one another for the sake of values such as liberty and equality. Can the American president be a transforming leader? Burns' answer was yes, so long as there exists a strong social and political mass movement headed in the same direction.

The historical evidence suggests that Burns is right. The chapters in this volume attest to the overall inertia of the political system and the convergence of forces required to produce real social and political change. All of the actors in the political system—members of marginalized groups, activists, and politicians—have interdependent political opportunity structures. Windows of opportunity do not emerge out of thin air; they emerge from a cumulative process where various actors push and shape political culture, institutions, and each other until the time is right for change. The president is embedded in this system. He does not initiate or produce social and political change all by himself.

Though the president is not the primary mover or initiator of social change, his behavior is not trivial or irrelevant for the politics of democratic inclusion. His support makes a difference. That part of the popular mythology is true. But the story of the American presidency and democratic inclusion must acknowledge that the president, like other political actors, can obstruct as well as accelerate change. His official job description does not require him to promote inclusion. If presidents are used as symbols of democratic inclusiveness, we should continue to assess whether they are worthy of such admiration.

NOTE

Acknowledgments. I would like to thank conference participants, particularly Peri Arnold, for insightful comments and suggestions. I am grateful to Catherine Paden for research assistance.

REFERENCES

Ackerman, Bruce. 1998. *We the People: Transformations*. Cambridge: Harvard University Press.

Arnold, Peri E. 1998. *Making the Managerial Presidency*, 2nd ed. Lawrence: University Press of Kansas.

Barber, James David. 1972. *The Presidential Character*. New York: Prentice-Hall.

Berman, William C. 1970. *The Politics of Civil Rights in the Truman Administration*. Ohio State University Press.

Bessette, Joseph M. 1994. *The Mild Voice of Reason*. Chicago: University of Chicago Press.

Bond, Jon, and Richard Fleisher. 1990. *The President in the Legislative Arena*. Chicago: University of Chicago Press.

———, eds. 2000. *Polarized Politics: Congress and the President in a Partisan Era*. Washington, DC: Congressional Quarterly Press.

Borrelli, MaryAnne, and Janet M. Martin, eds. 1997. *The Other Elites: Women, Politics, and Power in the Executive Branch*. Boulder, CO: Lynne Rienner Publishers.

Brauer, Carl M. 1977. *John F. Kennedy and the Second Reconstruction*. New York: Columbia University Press.

Brown, Ronald E. 1995. "Moving with the Grain of History: An Examination of Presidential Action in the Civil Rights Domain 1892–1968." In *Presidential Leadership and Civil Rights Policy*, edited by James Riddlesperger and Donald Jackson, 29–42. Westport, CT: Greenwood Press.

Burke, John, and Fred Greenstein. 1989. *How Presidents Test Reality*. New York: Russell Sage Foundation.

Burke, John P. 1993. *The Institutional Presidency*. Baltimore: Johns Hopkins University Press.

Burnham, Walter D. 1970. *Critical Elections and the Mainsprings of American Politics*. New York: W. W. Norton.

Burns, James MacGregor. 1978. *Leadership*. New York: Harper and Row.

Cameron, Charles M. 2000. *Veto Bargaining: Presidents and the Politics of Negative Power*. Cambridge: Cambridge University Press.

Conley, Patricia. 2001. *Presidential Mandates: How Elections Shape the National Agenda*. Chicago: University of Chicago Press.

Cronin, Thomas E. 1980. *The State of the Presidency*. Boston: Little, Brown.

C-Span Survey of Presidential Leadership. 1999. www.americanpresidents.org/survey/historians/justice.asp

Edwards, George C. III. 1980. *Presidential Influence in Congress*. San Francisco: WW Freeman.

———. 1983. *The Public Presidency: The Pursuit of Popular Support*. New York: St. Martin's Press.

Edwards, George C. III, John H. Kessel, and Bert A. Rockman eds. (1993) *Researching the Presidency*. Pittsburgh: University of Pittsburgh Press.

Ellis, Richard J., ed. 1998. *Speaking to the People: The Rhetorical Presidency in Historical Perspective*. Amherst: University of Massachusetts Press.

Fisher, Louis. 1991. *Constitutional Conflicts between the President and Congress*, 3rd ed. Lawrence: Kansas University Press.

Frymer, Paul. 1999. *Uneasy Alliances: Race and Party Competition in America*. Princeton: Princeton University Press.

George, Alexander, and Juliette George. 1998. *Presidential Personality and Performance*. Boulder, CO: Westview Press.

Graham, Sally Hunter. 1983. "Woodrow Wilson, Alice Paul, and the Woman Suffrage Movement." *Political Science Quarterly* 98(4): 665–679.

Greenstein, Fred I. 2000. *The Presidential Difference: Leadership Style from FDR to Clinton*. New York: Free Press.

Hart, Roderick P. 1987. *The Sound of Leadership: Presidential Communication in the Modern Age*. Chicago: University of Chicago Press.

Hinckley, Barbara. 1990. *The Symbolic Presidency*. New York: Routledge.

Howell, William G. 2003. *Power without Persuasion*. Princeton: Princeton University Press.

Inaugural Addresses of the Presidents of the United States 1789–1989. 1989. Washington, DC: U.S. Government Printing Office.

James, Scott C. 2000. *Presidents, Parties and the State*. Cambridge: Cambridge University Press.

Jones, Charles O. 1994. *The Presidency in a Separated System*. Washington, DC: Brookings Institution.

Jones, Howard. 1999. *Abraham Lincoln and a New Birth of Freedom*. Lincoln: University of Nebraska Press.

Kahlenberg, Richard. 2001. "President Clinton's Race Initiative." In *One America?* edited by Stanley Renshon, 91–110. Washington, DC: Georgetown University Press.

Kernell, Samuel. 1986. *Going Public*. Washington: Congressional Quarterly Press.

Kingdon, John. 1995. *Agendas, Alternatives, and Public Policies*, 2nd ed. New York: Harper Collins.

Klinkner, Philip, with Rogers Smith. 1999. *The Unsteady March: The Rise and Decline of Racial Equality in America*. Chicago: University of Chicago Press.

Light, Paul. 1991. *The President's Agenda*. Baltimore: Johns Hopkins University Press.

Lowi, Theodore J. 1985. *The Personal President*. Ithaca, NY: Cornell University Press.

Lunardini, Christine, and Thomas Knock. 1980. "Woodrow Wilson and Woman Suffrage: A New Look." *Political Science Quarterly* 95(4): 655–671.

Maraniss, David. 1995. *First in His Class: The Biography of Bill Clinton*. New York: Simon and Schuster.

Martin, Janet M. 1997. "Women Who Govern: The President's Appointments." In *The Other Elites: Women, Politics, and Power in the Executive Branch*, edited by M. Borrelli and J. M. Martin, 51–72. Boulder, CO: Lynne Rienner Publishers.

Martin, Mart. 1999. *The Almanac of Women and Minorities in American Politics* Boulder, CO: Westview Press.

Mayer, Kenneth R. 2001. *With the Stroke of a Pen: Executive Orders and Presidential Power.* Princeton: Princeton University Press.

McAdam, Doug. 1996. "Conceptual Origins, Current Problems, Future Directions." In *Comparative Perspectives on Social Movements: Political Opportunities, Mobilizing Structures, and Cultural Framings*, edited by Doug McAdam, John McCarthy, and Mayer Zald, 23–40. Cambridge: Cambridge University Press.

McCoy, Donald R., and Richard T. Ruetten. 1973. *Quest and Response: Minority Rights and the Truman Administration*. Lawrence: University of Kansas Press.

Miles, Johnnie H., Juanita Davis, Sharon Ferguson-Robert's, and Rita Giles 2001. *Almanac of African American Heritage*. Paramus, NJ: Prentice Hall Press.

Milkis, Sidney M. 1993. *The President and the Parties*. New York: Oxford University Press.

Miroff, Bruce. 1981. "Presidential Leverage over Social Movements: The Johnson White House and Civil Rights." *Journal of Politics* 43:2–23.

———. 2000. "The President and the Public: Leadership as Spectacle." In *The Presidency and the Political System*, edited by Michael Nelson, 301–324. Washington, DC: Congressional Quarterly Press.

Moe, Terry. 1985. "The Politicized Presidency." In *The New Direction in American Politics*, edited by J. Chubb and P. Peterson, 235–271. Washington, DC: Brookings Institution.

Morgan, Ruth P. 1970. *The President and Civil Rights: Policy-Making by Executive Order*. New York: St. Martin's Press.

Neustadt, Richard. 1990. *Presidential Power.* New York: Free Press.

O'Reilly, Kenneth. 1995. *Nixon's Piano*. New York: The Free Press.

Peterson, Mark. 1990. *Legislating Together.* Cambridge: Harvard University Press.

———. 1992. "The Presidency and Organized Interests: White House Patterns of Interest Group Liaison." *American Political Science Review* 86(3): 612–625.

Pfiffner, James P., ed. 1999. *The Managerial Presidency.* College Station: Texas A&M University Press.

Polsby, Nelson. 1978. "Interest Groups and the Presidency: Trends in Political Intermediation in America." In *American Politics and Public Policy*, edited by W. D. Burnham and M. W. Weinberg, 41–52. Cambridge: MIT Press.

Ragsdale, Lyn. 1996. *Vital Statistics on the Presidency: Washington to Clinton*. Washington, DC: Congressional Quarterly Press.

Renshon, Stanley. 1996. *High Hopes: The Clinton Presidency and the Politics of Ambition*. New York: New York University Press.

Riley, Russell L. 1999. *The Presidency and the Politics of Racial Inequality: Nation-Keeping from 1831–1965*. New York: Columbia University Press.

———. 2001. "The Presidency, Leadership, and Race." In *One America?* edited by Stanley Renshon, 69–90. Washington, DC: Georgetown University Press.

Schwartz, Barry. 2000. *Abraham Lincoln and the Forge of National Memory*. Chicago: University of Chicago Press.

Shapiro, Robert Y., Martha J. Kumar, and Lawrence R. Jacobs eds. 2000. *Presidential Power*. New York: Columbia University Press.

Shull, Steven A. 1989. *The President and Civil Rights Policy*. New York: Greenwood Press.

Skowronek, Stephen. 1997. *The Politics Presidents Make*. Cambridge: Harvard University Press.

Sourcebook of Criminal Justice Statistics, 2000. 2001. Washington, DC: U.S. Department of Justice, Bureau of Justice Statistics.

Tenpas, Kathryn Dunn. 1997. "Women on the White House Staff: A Longitudinal Analysis, 1939–1994." In *The Other Elites: Women, Politics, and Power in the Executive Branch*, edited by M. Borrelli and J. M. Martin, 91–106. Boulder, CO: Lynne Rienner Publishers.

Tichenor, Daniel J. 2002. *Dividing Lines: The Politics of Immigration Control in America.* Princeton: Princeton University Press.

———. 2003. "The Presidency and Interest Groups: Programmatic Ambition and Contentious Elites." In *The Presidency and the Political System*, edited by Michael Nelson, 329–354. Washington, DC: Congressional Quarterly Press.

———. 1987. *The Rhetorical Presidency.* Princeton: Princeton University Press.

Walters, Ronald. 1988. *Black Presidential Politics in America: A Strategic Approach.* Albany: State University of New York Press.

About the Contributors

KRISTI ANDERSEN is the Laura J. and L. Douglas Meredith Professor of Teaching Excellence in the Department of Political Science of the Maxwell School, Syracuse University. Her research focuses on women and politics, political parties, and American political history. Her works include *After Suffrage: Women in Partisan and Electoral Politics before the New Deal* and *The Creation of a Democratic Majority, 1928–1936*. She has published articles on such topics as the gender gap, voting for male and female candidates, the effects of entering the work force on women's political participation, the prospects for electing more women to Congress, and the changing meanings of U.S. elections.

PERI E. ARNOLD is Professor of Political Science at the University of Notre Dame. He studies the American presidency from the perspective of political development. Arnold is the author of *Making the Managerial Presidency* and numerous articles and book chapters. His current work focuses on the presidency of the Progressive Era.

DAVID T. CANON is a Professor of Political Science at the University of Wisconsin–Madison. He has previously taught at Duke University. His teaching and research interests are in American political institutions, especially Congress. He is author of *Race, Redistricting, and Representation* (winner of the Richard F. Fenno award for best book on legislative politics), *The Dysfunctional Congress? The Individual Roots of an Institutional Dilemma* (with Ken Mayer), *Actors, Athletes, and Astronauts: Political Amateurs in the U.S. Congress*, several edited books, and various articles and book chapters.

DENNIS CHONG is the John D. and Catherine T. MacArthur Professor of Political Science and a Fellow of the Institute for Policy Research at Northwestern University. He specializes in the study of public opinion, political psychology, and collective action. His most recent book, *Rational Lives: Norms and Values in Politics and Society*, examines value formation and change and conflict over social norms and lifestyles. He is also the author of *Collective Action and the Civil Rights Movement*, a study of the dynamics of social movements. He is the co-editor of the Cambridge University Press book series *Studies in Political Psychology and Public Opinion*.

SUSAN E. CLARKE is Professor of Political Science at the University of Colorado–Boulder. Her research centers on local economic development, cross-border regionalism, the politics of workforce development, and democratic inclusion processes in American and European cities. In addition to numerous articles, her publications include *The Work of Cities* (with Gary Gaile). At CU, she is Director of the Center to Advance Research and Teaching in the Social Sciences (CARTSS), a campus-wide interdisciplinary program. She is currently editor of *Urban Affairs Review*, with Gary L. Gaile and Michael Pagano.

ELIZABETH F. COHEN is Assistant Professor of Political Science at The Maxwell School of Syracuse University. Her research interests include modern political theory, citizenship studies, and the politics of immigration. Currently she is at work on a book-length manuscript entitled *The Myth of Full Citizenship: A Comparative Study of Semi-Citizenship in Democratic Polities*, which analyzes divisions in types of formal citizenship and the ways both citizens and states exploit these divisions.

PATRICIA CONLEY is a visiting Assistant Professor at the University of Chicago. She received the American Political Science Association's E. E. Schattschneider Award for best dissertation in American politics. In her book, *Presidential Mandates: How Elections Shape the National Agenda*, she examines the relationship between election outcomes and presidential policy making. She has published articles and book chapters on the American presidency, distributive justice, and the role of self-interest in public opinion formation.

ANNE N. COSTAIN currently serves as Associate Vice President for Human Relations and Risk Management for the University of Colorado System. She is Professor of Political Science at the University of Colorado–Boulder. Costain is author of *Inviting Women's Rebellion: A Political Process Interpretation of the Women's Movement*, coeditor, with Andrew McFarland, of *Social Movements and American Political Institutions*, and coeditor, with Simone Chambers, of *Deliberation, Democracy, and the Media*.

PAUL FRYMER is Associate Professor and Director of Legal Studies at the University of California–Santa Cruz. He is the author of *Uneasy Alliances: Race and Party Competition in America*.

RODNEY E. HERO is Packey J. Dee III Professor of American Democracy at the University of Notre Dame. His research and teaching interests are in the areas of American democracy and politics, especially as viewed through the analytical lenses of Latino and ethnic/minority politics, state/urban politics, and federalism. He is the author of *Latinos and the U.S. Political System: Two-Tiered Pluralism* and *Faces of Inequality: Social Diversity in American Politics*, as well as numerous journal articles.

JENNIFER L. HOCHSCHILD is the Henry LaBarre Jayne Professor of Government at Harvard University, with a joint appointment in the Department of African and African American Studies. Hochschild studies the intersection of American politics and political philosophy, particularly in the areas of racial and ethnic politics and policy, educational and social policy, and public opinion or political culture. Hochschild is, most recently, the coauthor (with Nathan Scovronick) of *The American Dream and the Public Schools*, and she is the author of *Facing Up to the American Dream: Race, Class, and the Soul of the Nation.* She is the founding editor of *Perspectives on Politics,* sponsored by the American Political Science Association.

MICHAEL JONES-CORREA is Associate Professor of Government at Cornell University. His research interests include immigrant politics and immigration policy, minority politics and inter-ethnic relations in the United States, and urban and suburban politics. He is the author of *Between Two Nations: The Political Predicament of Latinos in New York City* and the editor of *Governing American Cities: Inter-Ethnic Coalitions, Competition and Conflict.* He is currently completing a book looking at the renegotiation of ethnic relations in the aftermath of civil disturbances in New York, Los Angeles, Miami, and Washington, DC and is engaged in two additional projects: one on the increasing ethnic diversity of suburbs and its implication for local and national politics, and the other a joint project designing a new national survey of Latinos in the United States.

MIKI CAUL KITTILSON is Assistant Professor of Political Science at Arizona State University. Her research is rooted in a theoretical interest in the expansion of political participation—both in the inclusion of previously under-represented groups and in the adoption of more direct forms of participation. She compares participation, parties, and women and politics across established industrial democracies, with a focus on Western Europe. Her current project examines changing patterns of both political participation and group mobilization. She has published in the *Journal of Politics, Comparative Political Studies,* the *American Review of Politics,* and *Party Politics.*

JAN E. LEIGHLEY is Professor of Political Science at the University of Arizona. Her research focuses on political participation, social context, and democracy, with a special interest in how social and political processes structure individuals' participation in politics and the consequences of such processes for democratic representation. She has published in leading political science journals and is the author of *Strength in Numbers? The Political Mobilization of Racial and Ethnic Minorities.*

GEORGE LOVELL is Assistant Professor of Political Science at University of Washington. His research examines interaction among branches of government and the effect of courts and other political institutions on social movements. His book, *Legislative Deferrals,* challenges conventional understandings of American labor history and judicial power by showing how legislators deliberately empower judges to resolve policy controversies.

MICHAEL MCCANN is Gordon Hirabayashi Professor for the Advancement of Citizenship at the University of Washington. A former chair of the Political Science Department, he is the founding director of the Comparative Law and Society Studies (CLASS) Center as well as of the undergraduate Law, Societies, and Justice Program. McCann is the author of *Taking Reform Seriously: Perspectives on Public*

Interest Liberalism, the multi-award-winning *Rights at Work: Pay Equity Reform and the Politics of Legal Mobilization*, and (with William Haltom) *Distorting the Law: Politics, Media, and the Litigation Crisis*, as well as a host of essays in social science journals, law reviews, and edited books.

KENNETH J. MEIER is the Charles Puryear Professor of Liberal Arts and Professor of Political Science at Texas A&M University. A former editor of the *American Journal of Political Science*, Meier has eclectic research interests that cover a wide range of subfields in political science. His essay in this volume reflects his long-standing research interest in questions of race, equity, and democratic inclusion. He is currently directing a study of the politics of educational equity using the 1,800 largest school districts in the United States.

REUEL ROGERS is Assistant Professor of Political Science at Northwestern University. His primary research and teaching interests are race, ethnicity, urban politics, immigration, and African American politics, all within the field of American government. He is currently working on a book manuscript that explores how racial minority status and discrimination affect the process of political integration for Caribbean- and native-born blacks in New York City. Rogers has published essays on political incorporation patterns among recent non-white immigrants, the political significance of racial and ethnic group identities among minorities, and multi-racial political coalitions in American cities.

KATHERINE TATE is Professor and Chair of Political Science at the University of California–Irvine. Her research has focused on the electoral behavior of African Americans as well as the politics of race, women, and minority groups. She is the author of *Black Faces in the Mirror: African Americans and Their Representatives in the U.S. Congress* and *From Protest to Politics: The New Black Voters in American Elections*. She is also the coauthor of *African Americans and the American Political System*, 4th edition.

ALVIN B. TILLERY is Assistant Professor of Political Science at the University of Notre Dame. His research interests are in the fields of racial and ethnic politics and American political development. He is currently working on a project that examines the role black Americans have played in the shaping of U.S. foreign policy toward Africa.

CHRISTINA WOLBRECHT is Packey J. Dee III Associate Professor of Political Science at the University of Notre Dame. She specializes in political parties, interest groups, and gender politics. Her book, *The Politics of Women's Rights: Parties, Positions, and Change*, received the 2001 Leon D. Epstein Outstanding Book Award from the Political Organizations and Parties Section of the American Political Science Association. She is currently engaged in a collaborative project using new ecological inference techniques to examine women's voting behavior and its impact on the American political system in the period immediately following the granting of women's suffrage in 1920.

Index

Entries followed by *f* and *t* refer to figures and tables.